Indians and Leftists

in the Making of Ecuador's

Modern Indigenous Movements

A book in the series

LATIN AMERICAN OTHERWISE: LANGUAGES, EMPIRES, NATIONS

Series editors:

Walter D. Mignolo, Duke University

Irene Silverblatt, Duke University

Sonia Saldivar-Hull, University of Texas, San Antonio

Indians and Leftists
in the Making of Ecuador's
Modern Indigenous Movements

MARC BECKER

——◆——

Duke University Press

Durham & London

2008

© 2008 Duke University Press
All rights reserved
Printed in the United States of
America on acid-free paper ∞
Designed by Katy Clove
Typeset in Dante
by Keystone Typesetting, Inc.
Library of Congress Cataloging-in-
Publication Data appear on the
last printed page of this book.

For an electronic appendix, please see
http://www.yachana.org/indmovs/

About the Series

Latin America Otherwise: Languages, Empires, Nations is a critical series. It aims to explore the emergence and consequences of concepts used to define "Latin America" while at the same time exploring the broad interplay of political, economic, and cultural practices that have shaped Latin American worlds. Latin America, at the crossroads of competing imperial designs and local responses, has been construed as a geocultural and geopolitical entity since the nineteenth century. This series provides a starting point to redefine Latin America as a configuration of political, linguistic, cultural, and economic intersections that demands a continuous reappraisal of the role of the Americas in history, and of the ongoing process of globalization and the relocation of people and cultures that have characterized Latin America's experience. *Latin America Otherwise: Languages, Empires, Nations* is a forum that confronts established geocultural constructions, rethinks area studies and disciplinary boundaries, assesses convictions of the academy and of public policy, and correspondingly demands that the practices through which we produce knowledge and understanding about and from Latin America be subject to rigorous and critical scrutiny.

In his new work, Marc Becker provides a full and detailed account of contemporary Indigenous movements in Ecuador and their complex relationship with the Marxist left. Becker offers historical as well as cultural substantiation for the reader to understand that we are facing, in Ecuador and elsewhere in the Andes, the unfolding of a new phenomenon of "Indigenous Movements." This new phenomenon represents a break with the past, because activists insist that more than a "movement," they are and should be thought of as a "nation." The entire debate and conceptualization of a "plurinational state" in both Ecuador and Bolivia today is grounded in this historical, political, and intellectual shift.

Becker's well-informed account blends history with analyses of gender, class, and ethnic struggles. In the final section of the book he shows that we are no longer witnessing a romantic return to the past, an idealistic rehearsal of the image of the Indians. Instead he demonstrates that now we are witnessing the emergence of "Indianism" (rather than "Indigenism") as a new articulation of the politial through the insertion of a distinctive Indian actor that blurs the lines between "friend" and "enemy." Indians were neither; they were outcast by the internal struggles among blanco-mestizos who totalized the political sphere, and have been forced to find new avenues for political action. With the rise of these new Indigenous movements, the "colonial revolution" of the sixteenth century has reached a point of crisis and decay—a radical shift, a "pachakutik," that is reorienting five hundred years of imperial, colonial, and national history.

Solo los obreros y campesinos irán hasta el fin
—AUGUSTO CÉSAR SANDINO

Nayawa jiwtxa nayjarusti waranga waranqanakawa kutanipxa
—TÚPAC KATARI

Ñuca tierra es Cayambe,
y no me jodan carajú
Porque somos libres como el viento
libres fuimos, libres seremos
Todo manos, todos oídos,
todo ojos, toda voz
—DOLORES CACUANGO

Die Proletarier haben nichts in ihr zu verlieren als ihre Ketten
Sie haben eine Welt zu gewinnen
Proletarier aller Länder, vereinigt euch!
—KARL MARX AND FRIEDRICH ENGELS

Contents

Acknowledgments

I arrived in Ecuador for the first time in June 1990, a week after a massive Indigenous uprising had shaken the consciousness of the country's elite classes. I was interested in leftist revolutionary movements and searching for new research material, and I had come to the country's capital city Quito as a participant in a study abroad program with Oregon State University. Earlier that spring, the Sandinistas had lost the elections in Nicaragua, an act that seemed to have stopped the possibilities of further popular uprisings in Latin America. Still, here in the South American Andes a historically marginalized group had risen up to challenge their exclusion from power, and this act stimulated the imagination of young idealists and political activists such as myself. Rather than using guerrilla warfare, the Indians in Ecuador used *armas de razón*; it was a battle of reason—a political and largely nonviolent struggle. The protests I witnessed in the streets together with material I studied in anthropology classes under Marleen Haboud's direction at the Universidad Católica challenged my understandings of revolutionary movements and cast them in a new light. In emphasizing ethnic identities rather than a class consciousness, Indigenous peoples placed themselves at the center of a political struggle for control over their own destinies and identities. My intellectual interests were caught up in the euphoria of the potential of rural, Indigenous sectors in society redressing five hundred years of oppression and exploitation.

When I returned three years later to continue my research, John and Ligia Simmons, friends from Kansas, put me in contact with Ligia's brother

Cristóbal Galarza, who in turn introduced me to Marco Maldonado. Marco and Nancy Pinos welcomed me into their family in the canton of San Pedro de Cayambe, a rich agricultural area that straddles the equator about seventy kilometers northeast of Quito. Tourists and scholars often bypass Cayambe, which becomes lost between the capital city of Quito to the south and the attractive tourist markets of Otavalo to the north. Nevertheless, it has played a critical role in the history of twentieth-century popular movements in Ecuador. Leaders such as Jesús Gualavisí and Dolores Cacuango, who still figure prominently in the pantheon of Indigenous heroes, organized some of the country's first rural *sindicatos* (peasant unions) in Cayambe in the 1920s. Their political innovations deeply influenced the subsequent evolution of Indigenous and popular movements in Ecuador.

In many ways, Cayambe was a familiar place for me to learn about class, ethnicity, and the politicization of Indigenous rights movements. I grew up on a farm in Turner County, South Dakota, with an agricultural economy not unlike that of Cayambe. Hard-working farmers in both areas raised a broad array of crops, dairy herds, and other livestock. Over time, economic production became concentrated in the hands of fewer and fewer people. Today, multinational agribusiness corporations such as Archer Daniels Midland, Cargill, and Monsanto increasingly make small family farms economically unfeasible. As such, the struggles in South Dakota and in Cayambe become the same and are depressingly similar to the difficulties that people faced in the early part of the twentieth century: A small elite controls an emerging global capitalist economy to the detriment of the rest of us. Our struggle continues to be to gain control over the society in which we live and to implement a more just social order. Both Cayambe and my home community in South Dakota possess strong ethnic heritages, and those traditions give us strength to face difficulties and to challenge injustices. Strong-willed women provided leadership as well as a historical memory, preserving language and cultural patterns longer than did the men. In both cases, the dominant society has slowly eroded ethnic traditions, food, dress, and language. But ethnicity is deeper than these external manifestations, and even though I do not speak Plautdietsch or eat zwieback, it does not mean that my heritage does not inform my values and ideology. Similar things could be said for the Kayambis.

In addition to John, Ligia, Cristóbal, Marco, and Nancy, I relied on the support and assistance of many people in writing this book. Mercedes Prieto graciously provided me with invaluable material and assistance from her own research collection. Antonio Crespo and the late Eduardo Estrella cordially provided me access to the Junta Central de Asistencia Pública archival collections. Likewise, Ramiro Avila capably assisted with materials in the Fondo Bonifaz at the Archivo Histórico del Banco Central del Ecuador. Sandra Fernández Muñoz and Jorge Canizares kindly granted me access to the Private Collection of Leonardo J. Muñoz in Quito. The staff at the Biblioteca Ecuatoriana Aurelio Espinosa Pólit in Cotocollao provided professional research assistance with their collection. FLACSO-Ecuador granted me an institutional affiliation during numerous research trips to the country. Betsy Kuznesof, Charley Stansifer, Tony Rosenthal, Gail Bossenga, Kate Berry, Ronn Pineo, Cheryl Musch, Gina Castillo, Maarten van den Berg, Cynthia Radding, Karen Powers, Tony Lucero, Chad Black, David Cole, Jean Johnson, and others have read and commented on this manuscript as it evolved through various stages. Bob Schwartz efficiently and capably provided the index for the book.

Over the years, I have received funding from numerous sources that supported my research. These included a University of Kansas Summer Graduate School Fellowship, a Pearson Fellowship, a University of Kansas Dissertation Fellowship, five (three summer and two year-long) Foreign Language and Area Studies (FLAS) graduate fellowships, an American Historical Association Albert J. Beveridge Grant, support from Gettysburg College, and a Fulbright fellowship. Most significantly, I received a two-year award from the Social Science Research Council of an SSRC-MacArthur Foundation Fellowship on Peace and Security in a Changing World. This award allowed me to expand and deepen this project, including spending a year as a visiting scholar at the Center for Latin American Studies at the University of California, Berkeley, and as an intern at the South and Meso American Indian Rights Center (SAIIC) in Oakland, California. My experience at SAIIC profoundly deepened my understanding of Indigenous cosmology, and I would like to thank Nilo Cayuqueo, who made that experience exceptionally valuable. Without this support, I could not have completed this project.

Chronology

1578 Jumandi leads an uprising against Spanish colonists in the Ecuadorian Amazon

1599 Legendary Shuar revolt in the Ecuadorian Amazon

November 1777 A revolt against a census spreads throughout the northern Audiencia of Quito

1791 Indigenous rebellion against a public works mita labor draft at Lita

1803 Indigenous uprising at Guamote, Chimborazo, against diezmos

May 24, 1822 Antonio José de Sucre defeats Spanish forces at the battle of Pichincha, leading to Ecuador's independence as part of the country of Gran Colombia

1830 Ecuador separates from Gran Colombia

1852 Ecuador eliminates slavery

1857 Ecuador eliminates forced tribute payments

December 1871 Fernando Daquilema leads a revolt in the central highland province of Chimborazo

September 5, 1884 Alejo Saez leads an uprising against the payment of diezmos in his home community of Licto, Chimborazo

1892 Foundation of the Sociedad Artística e Industrial de Pichincha (Artistic and Industrial Society of Pichincha), which subsequently provides logical support to Indigenous movements

June 5, 1895 Eloy Alfaro leads the Liberal Revolution to victory

August 10, 1895 Eloy Alfaro stops in Guamote, Chimborazo, where he elevates Alejo Saez to the grade of general in his liberal army

1896 Junta de Beneficencia (Social Welfare Junta) formed in Quito

January 12, 1897 Promulgation of Ecuador's eleventh constitution

April 12, 1899 "Patronage Law" regulates but does not abolish the system of concertaje

October 12, 1904 Ley de Cultos expropriates church-owned land

December 23, 1906 Promulgation of Ecuador's twelfth constitution

November 6, 1908 Ley de Beneficencia (better known as "manos muertas") passes control of church land to the Junta Central de Asistencia Pública

January 28, 1912 Mob kills Eloy Alfaro in Quito

October 25, 1918 The Reformas de la Ley de Jornaleros (Reform of the Laborer Law) theoretically abolishes the concertaje system

March 1920 New agricultural taxes lead to uprisings in Cuenca

May 1920 Revolts against taxes in Chimborazo leave fifty Indigenous people dead

August 24, 1920 Uprising in Ricaurte, Azuay, against taxes

May 1921 Uprising at Guano, Chimborazo

November 15, 1922 Police massacre striking workers in Guayaquil

September 13, 1923 The army kills thirty-seven Indigenous workers on Leito hacienda in Tungurahua

November 16, 1924 Socialists in Quito form La Antorcha, which publishes a newspaper that supports Indigenous struggles

1924 Matilde Hidalgo de Procel is the first woman to vote in Ecuador

July 9, 1925 A military coup leads to the Revolución Juliana (July Revolution)

September 22, 1925 The Mexican diplomat Rafael Ramos Pedrueza organizes the Sección Comunista de Propaganda y Acción Lenin (Communist Section for Propaganda and Action Lenin), which later becomes the Ecuadorian Communist Party (PCE)

January 1926 Jesús Gualavisí forms the Sindicato de Trabajadores Campesinos de Juan Montalvo (Peasant Workers Syndicate of Juan Montalvo), the first peasant-Indigenous organization in Ecuador; Gualavisí subsequently leads uprisings at the Changalá hacienda in Cayambe over land issues

May 16–23, 1926 Leftists hold the founding congress of the Ecuadorian Socialist Party (PSE) in Quito

October 1926–March 1927 The Kemmerer Mission visits Ecuador, which leads to the founding of the Banco Central

1927–1928 Ricardo Paredes visits the Soviet Union for the tenth anniversary of the October Revolution and the Sixth Congress of the Communist International

February 1928 The army massacres fourteen Indigenous workers at Tisaleo, Tungurahua

January 10, 1929 The military and police allegedly massacre hundreds of Indigenous workers at Colta, Chimborazo

January 12, 1929 Ricardo Paredes gains control of the PSE at a meeting of the Central Committee and brings it closer in line with the Communist International

March 26, 1929 Promulgation of Ecuador's thirteenth constitution grants the right to vote to women and provides for functional representation for Indigenous peoples

September 29, 1929 Ten workers petitioning for an end to abuses and for lower work demands are massacred on the Tigua hacienda

1930 Formation of El Inca, Tierra Libre, and Pan y Tierra peasant syndicates at the Pesillo, Moyurco, and La Chimba haciendas in Cayambe

August 21, 1930 The Socialist Party creates Socorro Obrero y Campesino (Worker and Peasant Help) to defend Indigenous and peasant struggles

December 1930–January 1931 Indigenous workers strike on the Pesillo and Moyurco haciendas in Cayambe

February 1, 1931 Military repression prevents the Primer Congreso de Organizaciones Campesinos (First Congress of Peasant Organizations) from taking place in Juan Montalvo, Cayambe

October 6–15, 1931 At its second congress, the PSE formally changes its name to the Partido Comunista Ecuatoriano (PCE, Ecuadorian Communist Party)

October 20–21, 1931 Neptalí Bonifaz Ascásubi, owner of the Guachalá hacienda, wins the presidential election

August 28–31, 1932 Bonifaz is prevented from assuming the presidency of Ecuador in a four-day war called the Guerra de los Cuatro Días

January 1, 1933 Socialists reestablish the PSE

December 14–15, 1933 José María Velasco Ibarra is elected president for the first of five times; Ricardo Paredes runs unsuccessfully as a candidate for the PCE

1934 Jorge Icaza publishes *Huasipungo*, Ecuador's most famous indigenista novel

September 1, 1934 Velasco Ibarra takes office for the first of five times

February 1935 Indigenous uprisings on the Licto, Galte, and Pull haciendas in Chimborazo for better salaries and an end to abuses

July 25–August 25, 1935 Seventh congress of the Communist International

November 5–7, 1935 Conferencia de Cabecillas Indígenas (Conference of Indigenous Leaders) is held in Quito

December 25–29, 1935 I Conferencia Nacional del Partido Comunista Ecuatoriana (First National Conference of the Ecuadorian Communist Party) is held in Milagro

1936 Founding of the Comité Central de Defensa Indígena (Indigenous Defense Committee)

November 28, 1936 Páez suppresses the Communist Party as a legal organization after accusing it of participating in a coup against his government

August 6, 1937 Promulgation of the Ley de Comunas (Law of Communities)

August 5, 1938 Promulgation of the Código del Trabajo (Labor Code)

September 28, 1938 Formation of the Confederación Ecuatoriana de Obreros Católicos (CEDOC, Ecuadorian Confederation of Catholic Workers)

1941 Border war with Peru leads to the loss of half of Ecuador's territory

January 29, 1942 Signing of Río de Janeiro Protocol

September 14, 1943 Urban intellectuals establish the Instituto Indigenista Ecuatoriano (IIE, Ecuadorian Indigenist Institute) in Quito

May 28, 1944 Victory of the Glorious May Revolution; Velasco Ibarra takes power for the second time

July 4–9, 1944 Labor leaders found the Confederación de Trabajadores del Ecuador (CTE, Confederation of Ecuadorian Workers) in Quito

August 6–8, 1944 Indigenous leaders found the Federación Ecuatoriana de Indios (FEI, Ecuadorian Federation of Indians) in Quito

1945 Ministry of Labor and Social Welfare creates the Departmento de Asuntos Indígenas (Department of Indian Affairs) and Junta de Cuestiones Indígenas (Council of Indian Matters) in order to supervise compliance with laws and prevent abuse in regard to land, water, and other issues

March 6, 1945 Promulgation of Ecuador's fourteenth constitution

1946 Indigenous leaders found bilingual schools at Yanahuaico, San Pablourco, Pesillo, and La Chimba in Cayambe

February 8–12, 1946 Second FEI congress is held in Quito

November 16–22, 1946 Third PCE congress is held in Quito

December 31, 1946 Promulgation of Ecuador's fifteenth constitution

1947 Establishment of the Junta de Cuestiones Indígenas y Campesinas (Council of Indian and Rural Affairs)

April 19, 1947 The FEI organizes a Conferencia de Dirigentes Indígenas (Conference of Indigenous Leaders) at Quito's Central University

April 19–23, 1948 Third FEI congress is held in Quito

May 1948 Uprisings in Cayambe end payment of diezmos and primicias

September 1, 1948 Hacendado Galo Plaza Lasso inaugurated president, introducing the beginning of a twelve-year period of stability and economic growth

August 1–7, 1949 Fourth PCE congress is held in Guayaquil

September 1949 The FEI defends workers on Razuyacu hacienda

November 18–20, 1950 Extraordinary FEI congress discusses responses to Ecuador's first national census

July 24–28, 1952 Fifth PCE congress is held in Ambato

August 1952 Fourth FEI congress is held in Quito

September 1, 1952 Velasco Ibarra becomes president for the third of five terms in office, the only one he manages to complete

July 22, 1953 An eight-month strike at Galte hacienda in Chimborazo ends with gains for Indigenous workers

August 6, 1953 Massacre at La Merced hacienda in Pintag

January 10, 1954 Police attack workers at Pitaná on the Guachalá hacienda, killing four people and injuring others

September 1954 Formation of the Federación de Trabajadores Agrícolas del Litoral (FTAL, Federation of Coastal Agricultural Workers)

1954 First agrarian census

September 1, 1956 The conservative Camilo Ponce Enríquez becomes president

April 27–28, 1957 Conference of Campesinos from Pichincha, Imbabura, and Cotopaxi is held in Quito

May 24–28, 1957 Sixth PCE congress is held in Quito

January 1, 1959 Triumph of the Cuban Revolution

1959 Indians march on Quito and hold a ninety-day strike at Pesillo

August 20, 1960 Uprising at Milagro

September 1, 1960 Velasco Ibarra takes power as president for the fourth time

October 15–17, 1960 The CTE organizes the Primera Conferencia Nacional Campesina (First National Peasant Conference) in Quito

December 18, 1960 Uprising on the Carrera hacienda in Cayambe

February 5, 1961 Uprising on the Columbe hacienda in Chimborazo

September 13–17, 1961 The Local Association of Jívaro Centers is organized in the southern Amazon with the assistance of Salesian missionaries

November 7, 1961 Fall of Velasco Ibarra; Vice-President Carlos Julio Arosemena Monroy takes power

December 16, 1961 Twelve thousand Indigenous people from the FEI march on Quito for agrarian reform

December 16–18, 1961 Third FEI congress is held in Quito

March 9–13, 1962 Seventh PCE congress is held in Guayaquil

March 1962 Workers take over the United Fruit Company's Tenguel hacienda on Ecuador's southern coast

May 1962 Protests are held in Cotopaxi, Tungurahua, Chimborazo, and Azuay against the agricultural census; Indigenous workers strike at Pesillo for higher wages and for land for landless workers

August 15, 1962 Salasaca Indians in Tungurahua demanding access to water are massacred

July 11, 1963 Military coup overthrows the civilian government of Carlos Julio Arosemena Monroy

July 11, 1964 Military government promulgates agrarian reform law

August 3, 1964 Approximately 150 Indigenous workers revolt on El Chaupi hacienda, Cayambe

October 22, 1964 The Ministry of Social Welfare approves the statutes that formally establish the Federación de Centros Shuar (Shuar Federation)

March 9, 1965 CEDOC founds the Federación Ecuatoriana de Trabajadores Agropecuarios (FETEP, Ecuadorian Federation of Agricultural Workers), which then becomes FENOC in 1968

March 29, 1966 Military turns government back over to civilian control

October 21–22, 1966 The FEI holds its fourth congress in Quito

October 28, 1966 Indigenous workers take over the Pisambilla, Muyurco, El Chaupi, San Pablourco, and Pesillo haciendas

May 25, 1967 Promulgation of Ecuador's sixteenth constitution

1968 Strike begins at Pull hacienda in Chimborzo and spreads to neighboring haciendas, paralyzing production in the canton

July 2, 1968 Land occupation at the Santa Ana hacienda in Canton Calvas in Loja leads to a massacre of eight arrimados and injury of twenty-two more

August 4, 1968 Eighth PCE congress is held in Guayaquil

September 1, 1968 Velasco Ibarra assumes presidency for the fifth and final time

November 26–28, 1968 Catholics found the Federación Nacional de Organizaciones Campesinos (FENOC, National Federation of Peasant Organizations)

1969 Formation of the Federación Provincial de Organizaciones Campesinas de Napo (FEPOCAN, Provincial Federation of Peasant Organizations of Napo), which in 1973 changes its name to the Federación de Organizaciones Indígenas del Napo (FOIN, Federation of Indigenous Organizations of Napo)

February 15, 1972 Military coup led by Guillermo Rodríguez Lara removes Velasco Ibarra from office for the fifth and final time

June 2, 1972 Activists organize Ecuarunari (Ecuador Runacunapac Ricchari-mui, a Kichwa phrase that means "awakening of the Ecuadorian Indians")

June 17, 1972 Fifth congress of the FEI is held in Quito

1972 The FEI, FENOC, and Ecuarunari together with coastal groups organize the Frente Unido de Reforma Agraria (FURA, United Front for Agrarian Reform)

May 17, 1973 Landlords kill Cristóbal Pajuña in Tungurahua, giving Ecuarunari its first martyr

August 18–20, 1973 FURA organizes the I Encuentro Nacional Campesino por la Reforma Agraria (First Peasant Encounter for Agrarian Reform) in Quito

October 9, 1973 Government implements the second agrarian reform law

November 15–18, 1973 Ninth PCE congress is held in Guayaquil

September 26, 1974 Police kill the Ecuarunari leader Lázaro Condo in Chimborazo

January 11, 1976 Military triumvirate replaces Rodríguez Lara in power

October 18, 1977 Massacre of hundreds of striking workers at Aztra sugar mill

November 2, 1977 Police torture and kill Rafael Perugachi, a local Indigenous leader in Cotacachi

April 8, 1978 The FEI, FENOC, and Ecuarunari meet in Columbe, Chimborazo, to form the Frente Unico de Lucha Campesina (FULC, United Front for Peasant Struggle)

1978 Kichwa, Achuar, Shuar, and Zápara peoples form the Organización de Pueblos Indígenas de Pastaza (OPIP, Organization of Indigenous Peoples of Pastaza)

August 10, 1979 Promulgation of seventeenth constitution gives illiterates the right to vote, thus extending citizenship rights to many Indigenous peoples for the first time

August 10, 1979 Election of Jaime Roldós Aguilera as president transfers control of the government from military to civilian control

1980 Sixth FEI congress is held in Quito

August 22–24, 1980 The Confederación de Nacionalidades Indígenas de la Amazonía Ecuatoriana (CONFENIAE, Confederation of Indigenous Nationalities of the Ecuadorian Amazon) is formed at the First Regional Conference of Indigenous Nationalities of the Ecuadorian Amazon in Puyo

October 16, 1980 Ecuarunari, FENOC, and FEI organize the National Peasant Indigenous March "Martyrs of Aztra" in Quito

October 20–25, 1980 Meeting of CONFENIAE and Ecuarunari in Sucúa at the First Encounter of the Indigenous Nationalities of Ecuador forms the Consejo Nacional de Coordinación de las Nacionalidades Indígenas del Ecuador (CONACNIE, National Coordinating Council of Indigenous Nationalities of Ecuador)

April 16–17, 1982 FENOC and Ecuarunari organize the First Peasant and Indigenous National Encounter in Quito

December 2–3, 1983 First FEI provincial congress is held in Riobamba

April 11–14, 1984 CONACNIE holds the Second Encounter of Indigenous Nationalities

July 15, 1984 FENOC and FEI hold the Second Peasant and Indigenous National Convention in Quito

July 27–28, 1984 Second FEI provincial congress is held in Riobamba

July 27–28, 1985 Third Peasant and Indigenous National Convention is held in Chordelég

November 13–16, 1986 Indians organize the Confederación de Nacionalidades Indígenas del Ecuador (CONAIE, Confederation of Indigenous Nationalities of Ecuador)

August 10, 1988 Rodrigo Borja inaugurated president

November 10–13, 1988 Second CONAIE congress is held in Cañar

July 27–28, 1989 Seventh FEI congress is held in Quito

May 28, 1990 Indigenous activists occupy Santo Domingo church in Quito demanding resolution of land disputes

June 4, 1990 Nine-day CONAIE-led Indigenous uprising begins

July 17–23, 1990 First Continental Conference on Five Hundred Years of Indigenous Resistance is held in Quito

April 11–23, 1992 OPIP leads a march from Puyo in the Ecuadorian Amazon to Quito demanding land titles and the declaration of Ecuador as a plurinational state

October 12, 1992 Quincentennial of Columbus's voyage to the Americas

1993 Amazonian Indians in Ecuador file a lawsuit in New York against Texaco for environmental damages to their lands

June 1994 Peasant and Indigenous groups unify in an uprising called "La Movilización Por la Vida" (Mobilization for Life) in protest of a new agrarian law

December 15–16, 1995 Eighth FEI congress is held in Riobamba

May 19, 1996 Luis Macas, president of CONAIE, wins a post as a national deputy in the National Assembly on the Movimiento Unidad Plurinacional Pachakutik Nuevo País (MUPP-NP, Pachakutic Movement for Plurinational Unity-New Country) ticket

February 5, 1997 Uprising evicts president Abdalá Bucaram from power

June 5, 1998 Promulgation of Ecuador's eighteenth constitution declares the country to be a pluricultural and multiethnic state

January 21, 2000 Indigenous-military coup removes president Jamil Mahuad from power

March 21–23, 2002 Tenth FEI congress is held in Quito

April 20, 2005 Popular uprising forces President Lucio Gutiérrez from power

Acronyms

AFE Alianza Femenina Ecuatoriana
Ecuadorian Feminine Alliance (founded in Quito in 1939)

CEDOC Confederación Ecuatoriana de Obreros Católicos, Central Ecuatoriana de Organizaciones Clasistas
Ecuadorian Confederation of Catholic Workers, Ecuadorian Central of Classist Organizations (founded in 1938 by the Catholic Church and Conservative Party; changed name in 1957 and 1965 before adopting current name in 1972)

COICE Coordinadora de Organizaciones Indígenas de la Costa Ecuatoriana
Coordinating Body of Indigenous Organizations of the Ecuadorian Coast (coastal affiliate of CONAIE)

CONACNIE Consejo Nacional de Coordinación de las Nacionalidades Indígenas del Ecuador
National Coordinating Council of Indigenous Nationalites of Ecuador (forerunner of CONAIE founded in 1980)

CONAIE Confederación de Nacionalidades Indígenas del Ecuador
Confederation of Indigenous Nationalities of Ecuador (umbrella group for Ecuadorian Indigenous organizations, founded in 1986)

CONFENIAE Confederación de Nacionalidades Indígenas de la Amazonía Ecuatoriana

Confederation of Indigenous Nationalities of the Ecuadorian Amazon (umbrella group for Amazonian Indigenous organizations founded in 1980)

CTAL Confederación de Trabajadores de América Latina
Confederation of Latin American Workers (founded by the Mexican labor leader Vicente Lombardo Toledano in the 1940s)

CTE Confederación de Trabajadores del Ecuador
Confederation of Ecuadorian Workers (founded in 1944; helped found FEI)

FADI Frente Amplio de Izquierda
Broad Leftist Front (political party founded in 1977 to unify various leftist groups

FEI Federación Ecuatoriana de Indios
Ecuadorian Federation of Indians (founded in 1944)

FEINE Federación Ecuatoriana de Indígenas Evangélicos
Ecuadorian Federation of Evangelical Indians (Evangelical Christian Indigenous organization founded in 1980)

FENOC Federación Nacional de Organizaciones Campesinos
National Federation of Peasant Organizations (Ecuadorian peasant organization founded in 1968; name subsequently changed to FENOCIN, Confederación Nacional de Organizaciones Campesinas, Indígenas y Negras, or National Confederation of Peasant, Indigenous, and Negro Organizations)

FEPOCAN Federación Provincial de Organizaciones Campesinas de Napo
Provincial Federation of Peasant Organizations of Napo (forerunner of FOIN founded in 1969 under the influence of Josefina missionaries)

FETEP Federación Ecuatoriana de Trabajadores Agropecuarios
Ecuadorian Federation of Agricultural Workers (founded in 1965 by CEDOC; becomes FENOCin 1968)

FOIN Federación de Organizaciones Indígenas del Napo
Federation of Indigenous Organizations of Napo (founded 1973)

FTAL Federación de Trabajadores Agrícolas del Litoral
Federation of Coastal Agricultural Workers (founded in 1954 by PCEand CTE)

FTP Federación de Trabajadores de Pichincha
Pichincha Workers Federation

FULC Frente Unico de Lucha Campesina
United Front for Peasant Struggle (founded 1978)

FULCI Frente Unico de Lucha Campesina e Indígena
United Front for Peasant and Indigenous Struggle

FURA Frente Unido de Reforma Agraria
United Front for Agrarian Reform (founded 1972)

IERAC Instituto Ecuatoriano de Reforma Agraria y Colonización
Ecuadorian Institute of Agrarian Reform and Colonization (agrarian reform institute formed in 1964)

IIE Instituto Indigenista Ecuatoriano
Ecuadorian Indigenist Institute (Ecuadorian affiliate of the Instituto Indigenista Interamericano [Inter-American Indigenist Institute, III] founded in 1943)

JCAP Junta Central de Asistencia Pública
Public Assistance Coordinating Body (administered state-owned haciendas, later changed to Junta Central de Asistencia Social)

OPIP Organización de Pueblos Indígenas de Pastaza
Organization of Indigenous Peoples of Pastaza (founded 1978)

PCE Partido Comunista Ecuatoriano
Ecuadorian Communist Party (split-off from PSE; founded in 1931)

PCMLE Partido Comunista Marxista-Leninista del Ecuador
Marxist-Leninist Communist Party of Ecuador

PSE Partido Socialista Ecuatoriano
Ecuadorian Socialist Party (founded in 1926; one of three "traditional" Ecuadorian political parties)

PSR Partido Socialista Revolucionario
Revolutionary Socialist Party (radical leftist party in the 1960s)

URJE Unión Revolucionaria de Juventudes Ecuatorianas
Ecuadorian Youth Revolutionary Union

URME Unión Revolutionaria de Mujeres del Ecuador
Revolutionary Union of Ecuadorian Women

ONE

What Is an Indian?

In June 1990, Indigenous peoples shocked the dominant *blanco-mestizo* (white) population of Ecuador with a powerful uprising that paralyzed the country for a week.[1] Thousands of protestors blocked highways with boulders, rocks, and trees and then converged on the streets of the capital city of Quito. Militants presented President Rodrigo Borja with a list of sixteen demands for cultural, economic, and political rights, insisting that the government address long-standing and unresolved issues of land ownership, education, economic development, and the Indigenous relationship with state structures. This Indigenous *levantamiento* (uprising) became one of the most significant events in the history of Ecuador's popular movements. The Confederación de Nacionalidades Indígenas del Ecuador (CONAIE, Confederation of Indigenous Nationalities of Ecuador), a pan-Indigenous organization formed only four years earlier, used the uprising to force an ideological realignment within Ecuador's social movements. The Indigenous occupation of the public stage represented a tectonic shift with important consequences for the nature of popular organizing efforts across Latin America.

In a manner rarely seen in Latin America, Indigenous activism in Ecuador spawned an academic "Generation of 1990" with numerous articles, books, and doctoral dissertations on the subject of Indigenous politics.[2] Anthropologists, political scientists, and sociologists analyzed the uprising and the ideological shifts engendered within the Indigenous world. Academics came to see the uprising, the organizational process leading to it, and the political

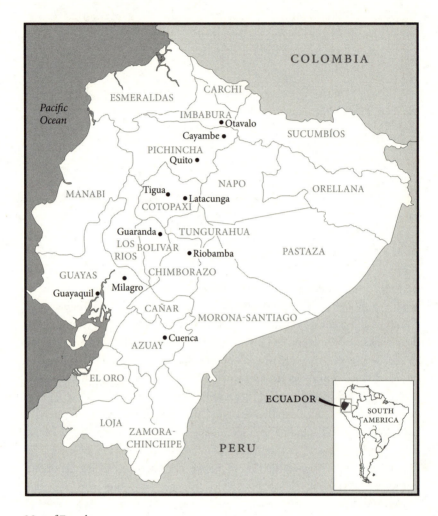

Map of Ecuador

negotiations following it as representing the birth of a new Indigenous ideology and organizational structure.

In contrast, as CONAIE's history of Indigenous movements in Ecuador observed, "Popular, community, syndicate, associate organizations, peasant and Indigenous movements do not appear overnight, nor are they the fruit of one or two people who meet and decide to create them. A movement does not appear because a group of leaders decides to call it by this or that name. A movement, a mass organization is the fruit of a long process of organization, of consciousness-raising, of decision making, of uniting many ideas. More than anything, it is the fruit of problems and contradictions that are produced between oppressors and the oppressed at a specific time and place."[3] The 1990 uprising was not the birth but the culmination of years of organizing efforts that introduced innovative strategies and discourses to advance Indigenous rights and preserve ethnic identities. A longer perspective reveals continual cross-fertilization between urban left-wing intelligentsia and rural Indigenous activists, and a fluidity in activist thinking that has consistently foregrounded economic needs as well as identity issues. This book examines how over the course of the twentieth century these factors influenced Indians and leftists who worked together to build the strongest Indigenous movements in the Americas.

Long Histories

Although Ecuador has been studied less by historians than the rest of the Andes, it has a long history of Indigenous revolts. The Inkas incorporated Ecuador into Tawantinsuyu (their "Land of Four Quarters") only a few years before the arrival of the Spanish in 1534. For local inhabitants, both the Inkas and Spanish were outside invaders. As a result, the northern Andes endured from 1450 to 1550 a one-hundred-year Age of Conquests. This period of conquest was not a peaceful one: historians have documented seventy uprisings against Spanish colonial control of this region.[4] Most sixteenth-century revolts sought to expel the European invaders. In the seventeenth century, colonial abuses triggered complaints against the confiscation of lands as well as against tribute payments, labor drafts, and censuses. *Diezmos* (a compulsory tithe on agricultural products that functioned as an ecclesiastical tax) and *primicias* (the Catholic Church's claims to the first fruits of harvest) were particularly burdensome. Protests commonly targeted abusive individuals rather than the structures of Spanish domination, and often involved tactics such as working slowly, breaking tools, or even committing suicide.[5]

In contrast to the largely individual acts of resistance in the seventeenth century, more than one hundred open revolts rocked the Andes during the eighteenth. This Age of Andean Insurrection culminated in the powerful 1780 Túpac Amaru II uprising. In a second, more radical phase, Túpac Katari articulated a vision of emancipation and self-determination. His last words, "I will return and I will be millions," were a prophetic statement that activists interpret as being fulfilled in subsequent Indigenous mobilizations. These calls to recover Tawantinsuyu did not resonate in Ecuador, and this fact has contributed to a myth of the passive Indian. Nevertheless, unrest also increased dramatically in the northern Andes. A 1777 census triggered one of most significant revolts, with Indians attacking estates and killing several whites.[6] Rather than accepting Spanish rule, active Indigenous resistance forced the elimination of abusive labor systems. Even after independence in 1822, Indians remained subjugated to an exclusionary regime. Protest continued; Hérnan Ibarra records forty-six "rural collective actions" against taxes, labor drafts, land, and water rights in the province of Tungurahua between 1815 and 1933.[7]

In the 1920s, Indigenous peoples began to form rural syndicates that fostered a mature political consciousness. In the 1930s and 1940s, activists made two failed and then a successful attempt to form a national-level organization to present their unified concerns to the government. Observers commonly characterize CONAIE as "Ecuador's first truly national indigenous organization."[8] Although CONAIE was a significant milestone in the development of Ecuador's Indigenous movements, this depiction is problematic. In the absence of a longer history, Indigenous peoples appear to move quickly from being subjects of governmental administration to actors who shaped those policies. This simplistic interpretation of complex relationships reflects Keith Jenkins's distinction between "past" and "history," with the past being what happened and history being how humans construct and remember those events.[9] Indians, as subalterns everywhere, have long been present in distinct ways in political debates. They did not exist passively outside broader processes of national development, but rather fundamentally altered the nature of state formation.[10] Recognizing this history, heedful scholars now note that "the Indigenous movement has its own deep roots."[11] Throughout the twentieth century, activists drew on this history as they searched for new ways to make their presence felt on the public stage.

Gendered Histories

Manuela León played a leading role in a December 18, 1871, revolt in her community of Yaruquíes, Chimborazo. Protestors captured and killed two government officials in charge of a road *minga* (labor draft) and another official who collected primicias and diezmos. This uprising, the most significant in the nineteenth century, is best known for the leadership of León's husband Fernando Daquilema, whom community members proclaimed to be king of Cacha.[12] As with Túpac Amaru a century earlier, the revolt spread quickly before the government cracked down on and executed the leaders. The traditional telling of these stories focuses on male leadership to the exclusion of key contributions by women. In Peru, Túpac Amaru's wife Micaela Bastidas was a shrewd commander and the revolt's chief propagandist. Like Bastidas, León chastised her male followers for their timidity. Both women were executed with their husbands as leaders of the revolts.

Luis Miguel Glave depicts female leadership as not unusual, and he claims that "women frequently egged men on to increasingly daring violence."[13] Rosalind Gow notes that "women often appeared to understand what was going on better than their husbands and also to be more radical."[14] In the 1777 protests, women prevented priests from announcing the census, threatened to burn a tax collector alive, and were executed together with men for their leadership. In 1803, Lorenza Avemañay mobilized women at Guamote, Chimborazo, in a revolt against diezmos, and was similarly executed along with three other leaders.[15] In 1899 at Pesillo in northern Ecuador, Juana Calcán led an uprising with her infant daughter Lucía Lechón on her back. Government soldiers shot her, and blood commingled with milk as young Lucía remained suckling at her breast.[16] As William Taylor notes for Mexico, "the entire community turned out for local rebellions." Women often led attacks and frequently were more aggressive than men.[17]

When activist women emerge in historical accounts, they are often cast in a more negative light than are their male counterparts. Mestizos have remembered both Avemañay and León as "a devil of an Indian."[18] Alfredo Costales described León as a crazy, dirty woman with a macabre presence who was "stupidly cruel" and burned villages with a "savage joyfulness." He

Woman wearing a rainbow scarf representing diversity at the 2004 Continental Summit of Indigenous Nations and Peoples of the Americas in Quito. Photo by Marc Becker.

Kayambi woman in the 2004 Inti Raymi (Sun Festival). Photo by Marc Becker.

contrasted her militancy with "Pacífico Daquilema" who was more reserved and rational.[19] Erin O'Connor notes that Costales wished to depict the uprising as just, and therefore he assigned any abuses to the irrational behavior of women. O'Connor argues that depictions of Indigenous women as alternatively submissive and savage are erroneous, and that their roles in rebellions grew out of their normal community functions. Willing to suffer and die for their beliefs, women directly confronted patriarchy.[20]

The gendered nature of Indigenous movements contrasts significantly with what typified relations in the dominant culture. Elite white women could exploit gendered stereotypes to their advantage. For example, perceptions of "women as innocents, incapable of deception and inappropriate behavior" allowed women during the wars of independence to work as spies and couriers.[21] Indigenous women, however, were not permitted the same privileges. Given that Indigenous women faced repression, imprisonment, and even executions, it is hard to envision strategic advantages in placing themselves in positions of leadership. Louisa Stark argues that rebellions are less frequent when strong relations exist between subalterns and the dominant class. Most of elite society's interactions were with Indigenous men, which resulted in a weaker and less stable domination of women. While the government could regulate female activities in other realms, their active presence in "illegal" protests could not so easily be repressed. Furthermore, the fact that women enjoyed relative autonomy and equality within their communities led to recognition and respect for their leadership.[22] Nevertheless, as Muriel Crespi notes, "it was convenience and not a desire for equality that permitted women to occupy leadership positions."[23] Women's leadership thus often became a pragmatic issue rather than an ideological one.

Gender complementarity had long been part of Andean societies, with both male and female labor critical to survival strategies.[24] Although Andean cosmology assigned gender-specific duties, it did not privilege one gender over the other in the manner of Spanish-imposed patriarchy. Further, dominant society saw Indigenous men as children undeserving of the rights and responsibilities accorded to white men. As a result, O'Connor notes, "Indian peasants (unlike the state) more readily recognized these women's productive and public . . . capacities and importance." This "sometimes gave Indian women greater powers within their communities than state laws condoned." Building on these social dynamics, Indigenous women placed themselves at the center of conflicts between Indigenous communities, landed estates, and the government.[25]

As Lilya Rodríguez observes, history does not have a gender. Men and women participate equally in historical actions, but it is in the *writing* of history that women disappear into the shadows of male heroes. The result is an ideologically oriented history that serves the interests of the dominant culture.[26] Elizabeth Dore contends that incorporating gender into historical analysis "does not simply add missing pieces to the historical puzzle; it fundamentally changes our understanding of the past."[27] Recognizing the central role of women as not exceptional but rather characteristic of Indigenous movements is key to understanding the development of popular movements in Ecuador.

Class Struggles

In the nineteenth century, much of the subordination of Indigenous peoples took place in the economic realm on large landed estates (called haciendas or *latifundios*),[28] with estate owners (the *hacendado* or *latifundista*) using legal maneuvers, natural disasters, and other tactics to take their land. Emilio Bonifaz noted that "the epidemics, mitas, plagues, and hunger helped the owners of Guachalá extend the size of pastures toward zones that Indigenous peoples occupied; every time a piece of land was unoccupied because the family was extinguished, the hacienda would take it for itself."[29] Without land, Indigenous peoples worked on haciendas in exchange for a salary and access to its resources to feed their families. This contracted labor system known as *concertaje* led to workers (called *conciertos*) falling deeply into debt. Landowners expected conciertos to mobilize their entire family's resources to complete assigned tasks on the estates. When a landowner sold a hacienda, the indebted Indians were included as part of the value of the property.[30] Landowners worked hand in hand with civil authorities and parish priests to control Indigenous labor. According to Friedrich Hassaurek, Abraham Lincoln's minister to Ecuador, the priests "are said to be the worst of all."[31] Priests charged for baptisms, marriages, and burials, and threatened with eternal damnation those unable to pay. They collected diezmos and primicias and taught Indians the *doctrina* (religious instruction) that often provided a pretext to extract free labor from the Indians.

Eloy Alfaro, leader of the 1895 Liberal Revolution, regulated but did not abolish concertaje. He required work contracts to be signed in the presence of a civil-military authority (the *jefe político* or "political boss"), established a minimum wage, outlawed unpaid labor requirements for a concierto's fam-

ily, and eliminated the doctrina.[32] Rather than benefiting Indigenous workers, these reforms subjugated them to an emerging central state power
under elite control. The jefe político in a canton and the *teniente político*
(political lieutenant) in a *parroquia* (civil parish) were often local hacendados
who extended the government's judicial and administrative reach to a local
level.[33] Local elites commonly ignored inconvenient reforms. For example,
the doctrina remained a common mechanism of coercive control well into
the twentieth century.[34]

Many liberal reforms had a strong anti-clerical bend, such as the 1904 *Ley
de Cultos* (Law of Worship) that provided for freedom of religion and also
confiscated Church lands.[35] The 1908 *Ley de Beneficencia* (Law of Charity)
created *Juntas de Beneficencia* (Welfare Boards) in Quito, Cuenca, and Guayaquil to administer the state-owned haciendas. Known as the law of *manos
muertas,* this legislation took control over properties expropriated from the
Church's "dead hands" for the benefit of the public through the funding of
hospitals, clinics, orphanages, and asylums.[36] The government later consoli-
dated the regional Juntas into one *Junta Central de Asistencia Pública* (JCAP,
Central Committee for Public Welfare, later known as *Asistencia Social* or
Social Welfare). Rather than terminating historically abusive land tenure
patterns, the government rented the haciendas to individuals who came
from the same agrarian bourgeois class (and often were the very same
people) who owned neighboring private haciendas. State power increasingly
was a daily presence in Indigenous lives, but it did not act in their interests.
In 1922, Alfredo Pérez Guerrero reflected that "in one hundred years of
republican life we have made little to no progress in solving" Indigenous
problems of poverty and abuse.[37]

The 1918 *Reformas de la Ley de Jornaleros* (Reform of the Day Laborer Law)
outlawed imprisonment for debts and abolished the inheritance of a parent's
debts, thereby effectively bringing a legal end to the concertaje system.
Nevertheless, the labor relations underlying concertaje continued with the
name simply changed to *huasipungo*—a system that sometimes left Indians
in a worse situation than before.[38] Decades later, Aníbal Buitrón rhetorically
observed, "[L]et the reader decide whether or not concertaje has actually
been abolished," and Xavier Albó dismissed these changes as "a rhetorical
modernization of Indian exploitation."[39] Systems of coerced labor and government control of Indian labor on state-owned haciendas persisted until
the 1964 agrarian reform.

The political scientist Amalia Pallares states that "the contemporary

Ecuadorian Indian political movement is distinctive not because the indigenous have never engaged in struggles, but because today indigenous people have been politicized as Indians rather than peasants."[40] Such attitudes have led to assumptions that "Indigenous people who became involved in politics usually did so under the banner of the traditional left, which considered the indigenous struggle to be subordinate—or even inimical—to the larger class struggle."[41] Both contemporary opponents as well as subsequent academics have often depicted the left as a paternalistic force or, worse, as another example of politicians opportunistically exploiting the poverty of Indigenous communities for their own personal gain. An assumption is that the left is an ideological heir of nineteenth-century liberalism whose adherents Andrés Guerrero depicts as projecting a "ventriloquist image" that exploited Indigenous concerns as tools to fight their own enemies rather than defending the vindications of the Indians.[42] The left allegedly operated within an integrationist and assimilationist paradigm that perceived Indigenous peoples and their social organizations as remnants of an earlier society that logically would evolve to a higher stage and disappear into a homogenous proletariat.[43]

This is a faulty reading of history. Historical sources disclose that Indigenous activists in Ecuador in the 1920s and 1930s relied heavily on urban leftists to form organizations to address ethnic and structural issues. Although early agricultural syndicates are seldom recognized, they fostered a mature political consciousness and contributed much to subsequent Indigenous movements. This was not a paternalistic relationship. Rural workers and urban leftist intellectuals labored together as comrades in a common struggle for social justice.[44] Together they tried to figure out what it meant in the twentieth century to be Indian with an ethnic identity and marxist with a class-based interpretation of the world. Socialists made significant contributions to Indigenous movements and were often the first to defend Indigenous languages, cultures, and social organizations. Among the contradictions and complications of these encounters, labor unions and political parties introduced rural activists to new tools and tactics such as demonstrations and petitions that they had developed in urban popular struggles for social justice. Most importantly, as the marxist historian Osvaldo Albornoz Peralta mentions and the Indigenous educator and activist Neptalí Ulcuango concurs, contact with leftist groups introduced the concept of the strike as "one of the best weapons in the struggle" for Indigenous demands.[45] A well-planned strike that paralyzed work on haciendas at a critical moment such as at harvest could lead to dramatic results. Through this method, agricultural workers gained land titles in the 1960s. Even commentators critical of leftist involvement with Indigenous organizations concede the left's influence on Indigenous tactics.[46]

Often those critical of the left applaud the Shuar Federation, founded in the Ecuadorian Amazon in 1964, as the first truly "authentic" (if one were to essentialize the concept) Indigenous ethnic organization. Scholars commonly call it "the first modern indigenous organization in Latin America."[47] Although the federation represents an important development, its history is more complex than might appear on the surface. International volunteers, local nongovernmental organizations, governmental officials, and in particular foreign Catholic Salesian missionaries attended assemblies and played a significant role in its formation.[48] Although both the Shuar and the Salesians wish to appear independent of each other so that the first receives credit for founding the federation and the second is not accused of controlling the organization, in reality their histories are tightly woven together.[49] The Shuar Federation would not have achieved its success were it not for outsiders who provided critical technical assistance so that its members could successfully interface with the outside world. Given the Church's historical alliances with conservative landowners, as well as the Salesian missionaries' role as political agents to carry out a government mandate to assimilate the Shuar into a Western nation-state, leftist peasant syndicates might be seen as more "authentic" Indigenous organizations than the Shuar Federation.

Does this history undermine the Shuar Federation as a legitimate articulation of the views and concerns of Shuar people and communities? Or does it simply demonstrate that political organizing never occurs in a vacuum and astute leaders are ready to cooperate with sympathetic outsiders to achieve shared goals? While it is important to recognize and emphasize the agency of Indigenous peoples, failing to acknowledge the presence of alliances leads, in Bob Boughton's words, "to a de-historicised and sometimes over compensating liberalism which under-rates the continuing importance of non-indigenous working class activism in achieving any lasting social change."[50] The historian Howard Zinn dismisses criticism of the role of "outside agitators" in the civil rights movement in the southern United States in the 1960s with the rhetorical question, "What great social movement ever did without such people?"[51] Social movements do not develop in isolation. Developing alliances with non-Indians does not negate an ethnic identity but rather demonstrates a confidence in, and maturation of, that identity.

In 1989 José Sánchez Parga asked, "To what does the marxist left owe this sudden and no less quick conversion to the Indigenous cause?"[52] Far from being latecomers, Ecuador's Indigenous movements have deep roots in leftist organizational efforts, and their character must be understood as an integral part of that history. A leftist-oriented strand of Indigenous activism led to the founding in 1944 of what this book argues was the first national federation for and by Indigenous peoples in Ecuador—the Federación Ecuatoriana de Indios (FEI, Ecuadorian Federation of Indians). This is not to say that the founding of the Shuar Federation twenty years later was not a significant event. Rather, it is to argue that Indigenous struggles have a longer, richer, and more diverse history than many observers recognize. Fernando Guerrero and Pablo Ospina point to the "triple origin" of Indigenous movements, first growing out of the political left (particularly the Communist Party), then progressive factions in the Catholic Church, and finally from development projects (especially the Misión Andina).[53] Indigenous peoples, as with any historical actors, have always identified with a wide array of ideological perspectives. As a result, it is a mistake to speak of a singular united Indigenous movement; instead, it is important to recognize the multi-vocality that led to a plurality of movements with different tendencies. These currents often intersected as well as diverged, and it is perhaps this diversity that led to such vibrant Indigenous activism in Ecuador.

Similar to the diverse ideological trends within Indigenous movements, there were also many leftist strands with varying degrees of consciousness. One of these strands was surprisingly open and dynamic in its understanding of the workings of gender, class, and ethnicity. Together, urban leftists and rural activists engaged these issues in ways that influenced and strengthened each other's ideologies, struggles, and social organizations. This leftist tendency became dominant in Indigenous organizing for much of the twentieth century, and it is out of these alliances that a strong Indigenous movement emerged in Ecuador.

Leftist influences helped trigger a shift in Indigenous strategies from reacting to local and immediate forms of exploitation to addressing larger structural issues. A rapid expansion of international capital throughout the Ecuadorian countryside in the 1920s forced popular organizations to develop new forms of resistance, dramatically influencing subsequent Indigenous organizing efforts. Activists found that the changes that a modernizing

Kayambis celebrate the 2003 Inti Raymi (Sun Festival) in the town of Ascazubi.
Photo by Marc Becker.

capitalist elite favored ran counter to their economic and ethnic interests, and so began to articulate their own counterdiscourse. This pushed protest from the private sphere of negotiated relations with individual landholders and church officials into the public sphere of engaging and ultimately influencing the nature of state formation. Rather than a stereotype of clinging to a quickly disappearing past, activists embraced a forward-looking agenda. Moving from a local to a macro organizational strategy represented a profound ideological shift that marked the birth of Ecuador's modern Indigenous movements.

Ethnic Identities

Indigenous peoples have played unique roles in Ecuadorian society. Historically, a lack of adequate clothing and nutrition led to very high infant mortality rates, often from respiratory illnesses and diarrhea. Few people attended school, and illiteracy rates remained very high. In socioeconomic

terms, Indians remained at the very bottom of the ladder.[54] "Whole genera-
tions of peasant laborers in Ecuador," the historian Brooke Larson reminds
readers, "lived grim lives of grinding poverty and harsh labor routines,
punctuated perhaps by occasional acts of petty resistance, without ever
experiencing the opportunity to participate in collective mobilization or
insurgent action."[55] The anthropologist Mary Weismantel shows that although race was not always openly discussed in polite company and often
was coded in other language such as that of class or ethnicity, it remained a
very real and powerful force in the Andes.[56] As Stuart Hall observes, "power
uses difference as a way of marking off who does and who does not belong."[57] In Ecuador, poor rural farmers did not belong and would not have
belonged to elite conceptualizations of citizenship regardless of their race,
class, or gender, though these factors reinforced each other and helped
consolidate their exclusion.

The anthropologist Xavier Albó summarizes academic studies of Indigenous movements in Ecuador as a long, contentious, and seemingly irrecon-
cilable debate between class-based and ethnic-based strategies for organization.[58] In recent years, scholars have commonly discarded class analyses in
favor of an emphasis on ethnic identities. The anthropologist Guillermo
Delgado-P. notes that "indigenous peoples' histories remain colonial when
reduced to class."[59] Pointing to factors such as ideologies and linguistic
diversity, the anthropologist Alcida Rita Ramos maintains that "to subsume
the logic of ethnicity under the logic of class is to miss its most significant
attributes as a social, cultural, and political phenomenon."[60] The geogra-
pher Roberto Santana has been the most aggressive to argue in favor of an
ethnic interpretation of Ecuador's Indigenous movement by contending
that class politics are essentially integrationalist in nature. He strongly criticizes leftist unions and political parties that treated "Indians as poor peasants
whose salvation would only come through access to ownership of land."[61]
Galo Ramón also advocates for an ethnic interpretation of Ecuador's peasant movements: "Although externally it has taken a classist form, it has a
profound ethnic dimension" that although not always explicitly articulated
as a political program is still present in "the growth of comunas, the persistence of symbols such as the Quichua language, dress, Andean behavior
patterns, challenges to modernity, and even in the emergence of a more
explicit ethnic discourse among Indian intellectuals."[62]

A careful analysis of organizational strategies and demands reveals that
both class and ethnicity have been critical to the success of an Indigenous

movement; the two cannot be easily separated. As more scholars come to this conclusion, Albó observes that the two positions have "been converging toward a more synthetic common vision."[63] Ileana Almeida notes that while class structures do not necessarily coincide with ethnic divisions, Indians comprise the most oppressed social group. She argues that the Indigenous problem was one of class in the sense that it was a result of the agricultural exploitation of rural populations that were overwhelmingly ethnically Indian. It was this double exploitation that placed them at a particular disadvantage.[64] The sociologist Alicia Ibarra asserts that ethnicity is neither incompatible with nor independent of class but rather is a socioeconomic manifestation of class relations.[65] To invert Ramos, it is equally a mistake to subsume the logic of class under the logic of ethnicity. These categories blur to the point where, as Nancy Postero and Leon Zamosc note, they "appear as two faces of the same coin" or as "two aspects of a lived identity."[66]

Pallares proposes that instead of interpreting "indigenous struggle as either a class or an ethnic struggle, or . . . as both a class and an ethnic struggle," we should examine how "class, race, and ethnicity are remade by the activists in the process of political struggle."[67] As Peter Wade concludes, deliberation between the primacy of class or ethnicity is "a rather fruitless exercise."[68] Furthermore, Elizabeth Kuznesof observes, "gender and race as social categories are embedded in one another."[69] Instead, it is more important to examine how race, ethnicity, class, and gender interact and reinforce each other in what bell hooks terms systems of domination.[70] This leads Anne McClintock to note that a "triangulated theme" of "race, gender and class are not distinct realms of experience, existing in splendid isolation from each other." Rather, she continues, "they come into existence *in and through* relation to each other—if in contradictory and conflictual ways."[71]

Class, ethnicity, and gender are constructed—often for very specific purposes. In a study of activism in Chiapas, Mexico, Shannan Mattiace observes that leaders would engage ethnicity in significantly distinct manners depending on the context, audience, and goals.[72] As Frans Schryer notes, "The point is not whether people have a class identity or an ethnic identity—this is an erroneous question because people can have multiple identities—but rather how people abandon, maintain or change their ethnic identity depending on their position in the class structure."[73] One example of this comes from Juchitán in Oaxaca, Mexico, where Zapotec Indians organized themselves into a powerful leftist force that became the first successful challenge to the entrenched ruling Institutional Revolutionary Party (PRI) government. Their gains in cultural autonomy and social justice provided, as Jeffrey Rubin notes, "a rare affirmation of an indigenous culture's ability to sustain and reinvent itself and to appropriate the outside from a position of equality and power."[74] Indigenous movements in Ecuador illustrate that while such successes may be perceived as rare, the Juchitán experience is by no means unique. Political gains do not emerge out of a vacuum but are the result of years of organizing radical political movements that negotiated political rule and relations of economic production.

Ecuador has a longer and more diverse history of Indigenous movements engaging issues of gender, class, and ethnicity than most scholars and activists realize. Indigenous rights activists in Ecuador came to rely not on staged military battles but rather on nonviolent tactics such as civic strikes borrowed from the labor movement in what they came to conceptualize as a *lucha de razón*—a struggle of reason, not weapons. This book traces these histories of Indigenous resistance from the creation of the first rural syndicates in the 1920s, the strike activity in the 1930s, the failed and then successful attempts to establish the FEI in 1944, the constant agitation that led to the passage of an agrarian reform law in 1964, and finally the pressing of an ethno-nationalist agenda at the end of the century. Current Indigenous movements could not exist without the FEI and earlier mobilizations in the 1920s and 1930s, and to argue otherwise is to deny the historical roots of Indigenous movements. Examining the flow of this history elucidates the evolution of Indigenous organizations and leads to a deeper and more thorough understanding of, and appreciation for, current Indigenous ethnic rights movements in Latin America.

TWO

Socialism

On May 16, 1926, at the inaugural session of the founding congress of the Partido Socialista Ecuatoriano (PSE, Ecuadorian Socialist Party), an Indigenous leader named Jesús Gualavisí took the floor to propose a salute to "all peasants [*campesinos*] in the Republic, indicating to them that the Party would work intensely" on their behalf. His proposal passed unanimously.[1] Gualavisí was the first Indian to participate in a political party congress in Ecuador, and he helped set the stage for subsequent relations between rural communities and urban leftist activists. Unlike the traditional liberal and conservative parties, the PSE welcomed the dispossessed into its ranks.[2] The party welcomed Gualavisí as a representative of "the humble Indian that for five centuries has been bound to the vilest servitude." Gualavisí actively participated in discussions, particularly those related to issues of land and Indigenous peoples. He proposed that the party create an office to defend the interests of peasants and workers; the delegates accepted the proposal.[3]

During a period in which many elites maintained deeply held racist sentiments toward Indigenous peoples, socialists comprised a rare group willing to defend their interests. Pointing specifically to the situation of land concentrated in the hands of a few wealthy elites while a large Indigenous population worked like slaves, the new party declared that "Ecuador has a social problem that needs to be resolved as soon as possible."[4] The paternalism that the left allegedly displayed toward Indigenous peoples was largely absent at the socialist congress, as was a sense of dependency of rural

Indians upon urban intellectuals. Rather, the congress provided an arena for Indians and leftists to develop a peer relationship as they struggled together to achieve common goals.

Nor did socialists remain in Quito removed from local struggles, manipulating events at a distance. Rather, they worked hand in hand with laborers on haciendas to develop organizational structures. Often they suffered the same threats of police action and imprisonment as Indigenous activists. Socialists later proudly proclaimed that they had been the first and only ones to come to the defense of the Indians. Intercultural alliances had long been part of successful social movements and would characterize leftist agitation for decades to come. For example, George Reid Andrews points to such collaboration as having helped to end slavery in Brazil in 1888.[5] A century later, Subcomandante Marcos and old Antonio were similarly critical in bridging dialogue between urban revolutionaries and Indigenous communities.[6] As the historian Anton Rosenthal notes, such alliances that develop in socially fluid environments tend to influence the ideology of social movements.[7] These linkages were critical to the success of Indigenous movements in Ecuador.

Revolución Juliana

The PSE formed in the aftermath of the Revolución Juliana (July Revolution). Led by a cadre of young military officers disillusioned with what they saw as a corrupt and opportunistic coastal liberal oligarchy that was unable to bring about any real change, their July 9, 1925, coup "declared that the Liberals had not been liberal enough."[8] Two months earlier, the coup plotters drafted a twelve-point program that promised "to implement laws that seek to dignify the Indigenous race."[9] The new government launched a series of social reforms including labor legislation that set a minimum wage, an eight-hour day, one day of rest per week, and a federal retirement fund. They created a Ministry of Social Welfare that provided a legal avenue for Indigenous workers to agitate for their rights on haciendas.[10] "For the first time in Ecuador's history," the PSE founder Ricardo Paredes observed, "the large financiers and superior officials were overthrown." This triumph "gave a great impulse to the socialist movement."[11] Nevertheless, rather than emerging out of a subaltern movement the July Revolution reflected the frustrated aspirations of a growing middle class. Although the young army officers called themselves socialists, their main concern was to modernize the state bureaucracy and engage in public works projects based on national rather than regional objectives. Influenced by the Mexican Revolution, the military leaders sought to assimilate Indigenous peoples into their concept of a national state. The result was not a radical alteration of social relations but an attempt to stabilize a potentially explosive situation.[12]

The July Revolution materialized out of a crisis resulting from the classic contradictions of a monoculture export economy. Raw materials such as cacao and coffee comprised 90 percent of Ecuador's exports, whereas 80 percent of imports were processed or manufactured goods, with the country becoming increasingly dependent on the United States for foreign trade.[13] Post–World War I inflation caused consumer prices to almost double from 1920 to 1926, resulting in unemployment and food shortages. Furthermore, by the mid-1920s disease decimated cacao production, international competition rose, and world prices dropped—thus throwing the economy into a depression. The 1920s witnessed growing protest, leading to some of the worst violence in the history of Ecuador's popular movements. One of the first indicators of serious problems was a large general strike that culminated in a massacre of perhaps one thousand workers in Guayaquil on November 15, 1922. Rather than ending protest, the massacre became, in the words of Richard Milk, "a rallying cry for labor and thus served as a milestone in the growth of Ecuador's labor movement."[14] Rosenthal notes that "the strike marked the transformation of Ecuador from a sleepy Latin American republic run by caudillos and ravaged by violent regional politics into a 20th century nation-state fostering industrialization and responsible for the attendant social conflicts."[15]

On September 13, 1923, the army killed over thirty Indians, including women and children, on the Leito hacienda in Patate, Tungurahua. An observer characterized the treatment of workers on the hacienda as "the most cruel and inhumane exploitation."[16] The owner assigned workers *tareas* (tasks traditionally defined as the amount of work one man could complete in one day) that took three days and required the participation of the entire family. Rather than addressing the underlying causes of the problem, Carlos Loza, the *jefe político* of Pelileo canton, asked the governor for the assistance of seventy soldiers. In the early morning fog, workers presented Loza with a petition requesting land. Treating them like criminals, Loza shot the workers Leonidas and Belisario Muñoz at point-blank range. Seeing her relatives laying dead on the ground, Olimpia Muñoz clubbed Loza and pinned him to the ground. Loza yelled "fire! fire!" to the soldiers, who shot blindly into the fog until the screaming ended. Thirty-nine people, including Loza, lost their lives and twenty were injured. Even the conservative daily newspaper *El Comercio* editorialized that "never have we seen a crime more horrible."[17] The Leito massacre was not, unfortunately, an uncommon event, and it did not halt Indigenous protest.

Ecuador could follow one of two paths. The first was that of modernizing capitalist forces that benefited a small wealthy elite allied with foreign capital. The second favored the workers, including the rural Indigenous majority who sought to defend their land and gain control over local affairs. Indigenous activism surged in the context of these dramatic social and political changes. Allan Kulikoff notes that in the United States capitalism "began in the countryside" and engendered conflict between those who welcomed changes and those who resisted threats to their economic independence. Capitalism, he notes, "both made agrarian America and was instrumental in its demise."[18] Similar changes were at play throughout Latin America and shaped subaltern responses to economic forces that, as Jeffery Paige observes, created "unprecedented wealth for the few at the expense of the general impoverishment of the many."[19] Rural communities were not withdrawing themselves from the global economy, but rather sought to influence the nature and direction of those changes with an eye toward preserving what was good and positive in their local cultures.

In April 1926 a second more moderate junta took control of the government and named Isidro Ayora as civilian provisional president. Ayora proceeded to implement policies that were less beneficial to subaltern interests, including inviting Edwin Kemmerer to head a group of economic advisors from the United States to modernize and centralize Ecuador's financial system. Like the later International Monetary Fund (IMF) measures, Kemmerer's economic policies ensured maintenance of an inequitable distribution of wealth. He favored a dictatorial government that would be able to implement policies quickly without any discussion or dissent. Based on his recommendations, the government set up a national bank (the Banco Central) with Neptalí Bonifaz, the owner of the important Guachalá hacienda, as president. This office soon gained power equal to that of the president of the republic.[20]

Two decades of economic crisis leading to chaotic and frequent extra-legal transfers of political power followed the July 1925 coup. It was also during this time that much of the agrarian legislation that dealt with the "Indigenous question" (or "Indian problem") originated. In elite discourses,

Cayambe volcano. Photo by Marc Becker.

Indigenous peoples were viewed as obstacles to their goal of nation building and thus rarely were consulted in drafting political projects. For example, the 1929 constitution provided for fifteen "functional" senators to represent education, media, agriculture, commerce, labor, and the military. Whereas these groups had the right to select their own representation, the Council of State elected a senator "for the guidance and defense of the Indian race."[21] Indigenous peoples, by far the single largest group of those named in the law, together with their sympathetic supporters, fought for years without success to gain control over this position.[22] Rather than supporting Indigenous struggles, the politicians who filled this post were antagonistic toward the very people they were supposed to guide and defend. Pedro Leopoldo Núñez who subsequently assumed this position opposed its creation, considering it to be "an inadequate fantasy" and a "joke" because Indians lacked the civic credentials and formation necessary for representation in congress.[23] Fidel López Arteta was equally ineffective in using the position to press demands with the government.[24]

The constitution also extended to literate women the right to vote,

Central square in the city of Cayambe. Photo by Marc Becker.

making Ecuador the first country in Latin America to do so. This was not, however, intended to be a progressive move. Many male liberals who otherwise supported progressive social legislation opposed female suffrage because they viewed women as a conservative force in society that would create barriers to the successful implementation of progressive social legislation. In contrast, conservatives favored female suffrage as a bulwark *against* a growing socialist threat.[25] The roles of Indigenous peoples, women, and other subalterns became central to debates over the type of political economy that was being crafted in Ecuador.

Juan Montalvo

At the same time that the leftists were organizing in urban areas, Indigenous peasants formed Ecuador's first syndicates in rural communities. One of the most important of these appeared in 1926 in the *parroquia* (civil parish) of Juan Montalvo just south of the city of Cayambe in northern Ecuador.[26] The Sindicato de Trabajadores Campesinos de Juan Montalvo (Peasant Workers

Syndicate of Juan Montalvo), with a membership of about a thousand, fought to defend peasant lands, protect huasipungo plots, raise salaries, lower the required number of tasks and the number of work hours, gain better treatment, and suppress abuses from hacienda owners and their over-lords. A final and persistent demand was to end nonpaid work requirements that in particular weighed heavily on Indigenous women who accompanied their fathers and husbands on landed estates. These tasks included milking cows, *huasicama* (domestic service in the property owner's house), *chagracama* (protecting crops), and *pongas* (the rights of priests and clergy to require Indians to work for them on a rotational basis).[27] This was the first of a new type of organizational strategy that moved from defensive positions of protecting traditions to pushing more aggressive demands. These in-cluded better salaries and working conditions (including demands that ha-cienda owners provide tools and work clothes), housing, an end to abusive treatment from hacienda overseers, and respect for their organizing efforts. Rather than the stereotype of peasants as isolated and conservative, these new syndicates began to engage broad social issues.

The immediate context of the formation of the Juan Montalvo syndicate was a February 1926 land conflict on the Changalá hacienda. Community members presented claims that the hacienda had taken over lands for which the Indians held historic title. When Changalá's owner Gabriel García Al-cázar ignored these petitions, the Indians occupied the disputed land. García Alcázar called on the government to protect what he asserted was his per-sonal property from communist and Bolshevik attacks.[28] Revealing their political alliances, the military junta that had come to power the previous July sent the Pichincha and Carchi battalions from Quito and Ibarra to evict the protesters. The image of seventy soldiers with machine guns facing a large group of unarmed peasants led one editorialist to caution against the threat of bloodshed comparable to the November 15, 1922, massacre of workers in Guayaquil.[29] The repression did not end the Indians' willingness to fight, and the following November the newspaper reported that a group attacked the police at Changalá shouting, "Long live socialism."[30] In con-trast to earlier actions, this protest did not appear spontaneously as a defen-sive posture but rather emerged out of an organized movement with a specific ideological agenda.

Jesús Gualavisí, who was born in 1867 on the Changalá hacienda, emerged as the primary leader of these protests. He was what Steven Feierman justifiably termed a peasant intellectual because he was "best able to shape

23

Statue of the historic Kayambi
leader Jesús Gualavisí (1867–1962).
Photo by Marc Becker.

Statue of Dolores Cacuango (1881–1971),
founder of Ecuador's Indigenous movement, in Cayambe.
Photo by Marc Becker.

discourse," define political language, and construct a peasant class consciousness.[31] Gualavisí launched a new generation of Indigenous leaders who were not necessarily elders in the community or from traditional leadership families but instead "were elected according to their activities, fighting spirit, and thoughts."[32] Gualavisí "was known for his activities of being a social agitator among the Indian class," and, according to the government, local leaders followed Gualavisí's orders.[33] He drew on the community's experiences to develop a political ideology and agenda. Gualavisí served as the secretary-general of the Juan Montalvo syndicate from its founding until his death in 1962. He dedicated his entire life to the struggle for Indigenous rights, becoming known as a *caudillo* (leader) of the Kayambis.[34] In addition to being one of the earliest and most important Indigenous leaders in Ecuador, Gualavisí was also a communist organizer, beginning with representing the syndicate at the PSE's founding congress. Although he was deeply involved in leftist politics and class struggles, he retained his ethnic identity and mannerisms. Gualavisí can be compared to Manuel Quintín Lame Chantre, a contemporary Indigenous leader from the Cauca region of Colombia who possessed a "double consciousness" in which he embraced a strong ethnic identity as well as espousing the moral values of Western civilization. This facilitated alliances with non-Indians for the common goals of ending oppression and fighting for social justice.[35] Gualavisí believed that the communists could give organizational expression on a national level to the Indigenous peoples' local demands. The marxist historian Osvaldo Albornoz Peralta argues that Gualavisí understood the exploitation of Indigenous masses because of his communist orientation, which he saw as a way to combat those injustices. Similarly, an ethnic consciousness can also emerge out of a situation of racial discrimination that highlights differences and privileges in society.

Gualavisí was the first Indigenous person to become deeply involved in leftist politics in Ecuador, but he was not the only one to do so. Two women from Cayambe played similarly important roles. Dolores Cacuango, who was born on the San Pablourco hacienda in 1881, is particularly renowned for her leadership skills. As partial payment of her parents' debt to the hacienda, at fifteen years old she was sent to Quito to work as a huasicama in the landowner's house. Although the huasicama system was designed as a method of exploitation, it strengthened nascent rural organizations. Cacuango observed the dramatic contrasts between the miserable lives of Indians on the hacienda and the wealthy and privileged landholding class.

These contradictions sparked her class consciousness and led her to commit her life to a struggle for the liberation of her people. In the city, rural workers became aware of urban organizations and were able to bring new insights and contacts back to their communities. Although Cacuango never attended school or learned to read or write, she fought tirelessly for Indigenous education and was instrumental in setting up the first bilingual schools in Cayambe. She impressed urban leftists with her "uprightness, firmness, and intelligence," which led to a position on the Central Committee of the Ecuadorian Communist Party alongside Ricardo Paredes, Pedro Saad, Luisa Gómez de la Torre, and Nela Martínez.[36] Cacuango's life was an embodiment of Rosa Luxemburg's observation that "socialism gives to every people the right of independence and the freedom of independent control of its own destinies."[37] When Cacuango died in 1971, people came from as far away as Guayaquil on the southern coast to commemorate the passing of a national treasure.[38] Her reputation subsequently attained mythological proportions, as the anthropologist José Yánez del Pozo notes, "not only for peasants from the zone, but also for many other peasants and popular organizations throughout the country."[39] Her image increasingly appeared in Indigenous movements, including in the name of an Indigenous women's training school.[40]

Tránsito Amaguaña, who was born in 1909 at La Chimba, was another important leader. Her mother, Mercedes Alba, had also led political struggles. Amaguaña married at the age of fourteen, and at fifteen, with a baby on her back, she joined clandestine meetings on the hacienda. She met Cacuango, and together they organized strikes, unions, and schools for Indigenous children. In 1990 Indigenous immigrants to Quito launched a bilingual school named in her honor. Amaguaña has been called "a tireless fighter" who "represents the female memory of the history of past struggles." Together with Cacuango, she represents the key role of women in bridging Indian rebellions with Western politics to advance the work of popular movements in Ecuador.[41]

The leftist activist and novelist Joaquín Gallegos Lara cast the Chimborazo Indigenous leader Ambrosio Lasso in a similar light.[42] Born to huasipungueros on the Pull hacienda in Palmira, Chimborazo, in 1905, Lasso noted: "I was not born a leader. Life and the bosses, their exploitation, made me one." In 1928, Lasso was evicted from the Pull hacienda because of his complaints against the owner.[43] On a rainy May 1, 1934, he joined hundreds of workers and students in an International Workers Day commemoration at the Casa del Obrero in Quito.[44] After leading a 1935 strike on the Pull hacienda, Lasso continued to provide militant leadership. He joined the Communist Party in 1946 and became "very well known and respected by the Indigenous peoples due to his audacity and firmness in confronting land-lord power." He founded the Sindicato de Trabajadores Agrícolas (Rural Workers Union) in the neighboring community of Galte in 1958, and won labor lawsuits against the government in 1958 and 1963. Enrique Bazantes, a later peasant leader, remembered that under Lasso's organizing skills and strict discipline he grouped "all of the haciendas together with only one goal in mind, that of revindicating the peasant class in Chimborazo." He made the Indigenous masses conscious of their rights and mobilized them in a battle against the hacienda system. Even while landowners feared Lasso, they respected his ability to mobilize people.[45]

Agustín Vega was another important early Indigenous leader. From a young age, Vega had been forced to pasture animals in the high *páramo* grasslands above the Tigua hacienda in Cotopaxi. When he reached eighteen, he demanded a huasipungo plot, but the *mayordomo* (overseer) refused and the disagreement came to blows. Vega escaped to the neighboring town of Quevedo where he met labor activists. Through them, he met Paredes who was already working with Gualavisí, Cacaungo, Amaguaña, and Lasso. With their support and encouragement, Vega returned to Tigua. Hidden in canyons under cover of night away from the watchful eyes of hacendados, Vega began to organize the community to fight for an end to abuses, termination of endless debts, and ownership of land. In September 1929, Tigua workers pressed Governor Gustavo Iturralde to force the hacienda owner to address these issues. When the hacendado refused, three hundred Indians paralyzed work on the hacienda. To restore order the governor sent the police, who fired into the peacefully assembled crowd. Ten protestors, including a pregnant woman, were left dead, although Vega himself escaped into the páramo. From exile, he wrote to the National Congress denouncing attempts to silence the workers, demanding justice, and requesting a return of their possessions.[46]

The anthropologist Alfredo Costales compared the importance and significance of these activists to that of the nineteenth-century Indigenous leader Fernando Daquilema.[47] In addition to organizing local communities, they joined the Communist Party's Central Committee and brought their concerns to the broader popular movement. Albornoz Peralta states that "only in a revolutionary and authentically popular party" could Indians rise to such positions of leadership. "Other parties never took Indians into account for anything, much less made them leaders, because they were considered to be inferior beings."[48]

Although what occurred in Ecuador is little studied and often unknown, it was part of a much broader historical phenomenon. In the southern Andes new revolutionary tactics including "the strike, the union organization, the regional congress, the sit-in and land-invasion" gave Indigenous organizations strength and an effective means to combat abuses on haciendas. These strategies surfaced in part as a result of emerging alliances with radical socialist and anarchist organizations in the cities. They gave militants the "versatility and ability to adapt to new political and economic conditions" and a "faith in the justice and eventual victory of the Indian cause."[49] It transformed the rural environment. "This new form of organization, until then unknown by the Indians," Albornoz Peralta claims, "gave strength and cohesion to their struggles."[50]

In addition to being one of the first organized land protest actions to use modern strategies, the events at Changalá were also significant for the support that the Indians received from urban leftists. One of the most significant of the nascent leftist groups was La Antorcha (The Torch), which attacked capitalist tyranny and called for people to protest for their rights. "We will not slack in the fight against inept, corrupt, and rotten rulers," the urban militants wrote in their newspaper, "nor against the exploiters who cause hunger." This group saw a strong potential for socialism emerging out of "subaltern public employees, the worker of the land (the Indian), the apprentice worker, the common soldier, the school teacher."[51] Their initial statements, reminiscent of José Vasconcelos's thinking in *The Cosmic Race*, called "to unify the race: fuse the enslaved race, the Indigenous, ancient owner of the land, with the dominant race. In this way," the statement continued, "ethnic differences and caste prejudice will disappear," replaced by a robust people.[52] Rather than embracing ethnic diversity, mestizaje contended that Indigenous identity must be suppressed and society must be whitened in order for the country to progress forward.[53] Nevertheless, as urban socialists came in greater contact with rural activists and became more conscious of their realities, calls to assimilate Indigenous peoples into a homogenous mestizo population quickly disappeared, pointing to how Indigenous activists altered socialist ideology and discourse. In the 1920s, black radicals in the United States faced similar dynamics when they began to work with white communists. As Harry Haywood recounts in *Black*

Bolshevik, African Americans "resented the paternalistic attitude displayed toward them by some of the white comrades, who treated Blacks like children and seemed to think that the whites had all the answers." Haywood continues to note that "membership in the Party did not automatically free whites from white supremacist ideas" nor "Blacks from their distrust of whites." Instead, "interracial solidarity—even in the Communist Party—required a continuous ideological struggle." This led to a transformation to the point where the most committed and motivated party leaders "exhibited not a trace of race prejudice."[54] Instead, ideologically driven activists closed ranks in a class-based struggle for social justice.

As Indigenous organizations grew beyond a "peon-patron" relationship with the left, they engaged in increasingly equal and reciprocal alliances in which urban marxists and rural Indians joined forces to address common concerns and build relationships that were mutually beneficial. Ricardo Paredes, Luis Felipe Chávez, and other socialists from La Antorcha came to the defense of Indigenous struggles against hacienda owners and helped present their demands to the national government. They introduced "the strike as a powerful battle arm which will never be abandoned and from the beginning demonstrated its great effectiveness." In combining "the peasant movement with the working class, it forged their alliance and gave a greater guarantee of victory."[55] Socialists pointed to the 1926 uprising at Juan Montalvo as the type of struggle against large landlords that peasants and workers should support.[56] As a measure of the potency of these alliances, Mercedes Prieto notes that "leftist attempts to organize the Indians exacerbated the fears of landowners," and as a result "the strike lost its initial meaning as a legitimate expression of discontent and came to be seen as a weapon of subversion."[57] Leftist propaganda led "hundreds of community members to revolt against private property in Cayambe," the conservative *El Comercio* newspaper editorialized, "and they will not bow their heads except under the threat of force."[58] Conflicts increasingly appeared to be inevitable as rural leaders built alliances with urban militants in order to press for fundamental structural changes in society. Their effectiveness frightened conservative elites.

Elsewhere in the Andes, scholars have painted different pictures, which caution against drawing a singular universalized reduction of the nature of these Indigenous-left interactions. In Peru, the Comité Pro-Derecho Indígena Tawantinsuyu (Tawantinsuyu Committee for Indigenous Rights) developed a heavily millenarian tone that ultimately defended Indigenous concerns in a paternalistic fashion. Their racial assumptions "kept them from seeing Indians as political leaders."[59] In Bolivia, Erick Langer describes socialists attempting but failing to subordinate peasants to the labor movement. Rather than relying on urban indigenistas as in Peru, communal authorities in what is known as the "cacique movement" used ethnicity as a tool to fight for political and economic demands. The movement included a tendency toward political autonomy, including the positioning of Nina Qhispi as the president of the Republic of Collasuyo, the southern section of the Inka empire.[60] Whether because of the personalities involved or because variations in the land tenure system engendered variations in class consciousness, urban leftists and Indigenous workers in Ecuador together envisioned a different world and engaged in mutually beneficial relationships that prevailed for decades. Nevertheless, a shared experience, as Xavier Albó notes, was that rural "movements were frequently connected with urban movements that supported them."[61] And these influences did not flow in only one direction.

The socialist newspaper *La Vanguardia* argued that Ecuador should join "the Indigenous revolution already raising its red flag in Cuzco, Puno, and the Bolivian sierra." Indigenous peoples should make common cause with other workers and "defend with guns their rights against exploiters and landowners who until now have been supported by the government, reflecting the centrality of Indigenous issues to the struggle."[62] The Communist Party newspaper *Frente Obrero* printed the classic marxist slogan "Workers of the world unite!" in both Spanish and Kichwa on its masthead.[63]

Indigenous leaders who acquired a class analysis of society did not necessarily lose their ethnic identities. Collaborating with urban leftists appeared to heighten and deepen a sense of ethnic difference.[64] Moreover, their actions reflect significant changes in the nature of Indigenous activism during the first decades of the twentieth century. Beginning with Gualavisí's involvement in leftist politics, Indigenous peasants looked beyond local solutions to global structural problems. Economic and social relations on the haciendas were integrally tied to the broader capitalist world system. Rural activists gained a deep understanding and critique of the nature of Ecuadorian society and the changes necessary to improve their situation. Increasingly, they discovered that the best way to realize gains as Indigenous peoples in a struggle for social justice was through fostering and embracing alliances with the urban left.

In his study of coastal peasant movements in Ecuador, John Uggen notes that scholars seem to be in "unanimous agreement that peasant movements cannot succeed without the support of urban political allies."[65] A tradition of semiprofessional or petty lawyers known as *tinterillos* who mediated legal or cultural conflicts can be traced back to the colonial period and even to Spain. Tinterillos exploited their privileged position to their own benefit, and socialists denounced them for dragging peasants through "costly and interminable lawsuits."[66] Socialist discourse, however, was significantly more radical than much of the previous urban discourse on the Indigenous "problem." Brooke Larson points to "critical Marxist research on the 'agrarian question' [that] interrogated the political possibility of peasants to transcend their presumed political naïveté and parochial concerns to forge an alliance with progressive sectors of the working class and intelligentsia."[67] Thomas Olesen adds that "groups and organizations without a skilled communicator run the risk that their message will fail to reach beyond their locale."[68] Outside intermediaries can be critical in breaking through information blockades. To assume without presenting evidence that such interactions automatically degenerate into ventriloquism is to disempower the people involved and, further, leads to misunderstandings of social struggles.[69]

Indigenous activists in particular remembered Ricardo Paredes—a medical doctor from Loja who founded both the socialist and communist parties—as one of their most important allies. In a 1977 interview, Luis Catucuamba remembered him as a "man who had been most just and loyal with the peasant." Neptalí Ulcuango noted that it was Paredes who "began to mobilize people in the city to help organize in the countryside." Paredes "was a good person" who "was the first and best comrade" to defend Indigenous interests and to awaken an Indigenous consciousness.[70] Paredes employed a variety of tools to advance the struggle, including publishing press reports and petitioning the government. Even before the uprising at Changalá, his newspaper *La Antorcha* denounced abuses of Indians. *La Antorcha* dismissed racist assumptions that Indians were incapable of participating in the political process, and he called on the "Indigenous race" to claim their rightful place in Ecuador and to demand social justice.[71] In a front-page editorial in the socialist newspaper *Germinal,* Paredes, as secretary of the Núcleo Central Socialista (Central Socialist Nucleus) in Quito, called for the nationalization of the lands at Changalá so that they could be returned to their rightful owners. In a report to the Communist International on the status of the worker movement in Ecuador, Paredes pointed to Changalá as the first and most important example of rural communist organizing efforts. "The movement in Cayambe," Paredes wrote, "demonstrated the important revolutionary role of the Indians in Ecuador against the capitalist yoke." For his vocal opposition to governmental policies, the military junta warned him to stay off the Changalá hacienda.[72]

Literacy, knowledge of governmental apparatuses, and access to public officials seemingly gave urban leftists an upper hand in this relationship that many scholars have derided as unequal, paternalistic, and manipulative. In actuality, leftists entered into types of reciprocal relations to which Indigenous communities were long accustomed. With leftist involvement, they created new potential for social change. Urban intellectuals had access to skills and tools that Indigenous peoples typically did not enjoy, but far from being a hindrance this provided an advantage in advancing Indigenous struggles. Indians who lacked formal educational training had the lived experiences of global capital that led to a penetrating analysis of exploitation. Similar to contemporary developments in El Salvador, "regional mass movements continued to push the national leadership into increasingly militant positions."[73] Rather than needing urban activists to awaken a revolutionary consciousness in a pre-political peasant population, Indigenous peoples gained their own political consciousness and then helped awaken that of their urban allies while intellectuals helped frame the issues.

Partido Socialista Ecuatoriano

Despite leftist support, rural organizations were not direct outgrowths of the Socialist Party but developed simultaneously as organic reactions to the same economic realities. In an article published in the party newspaper *El Pueblo* twenty-five years later, the Communist Party appears fully cognizant that Indian organizing efforts in Cayambe predated the founding of the PSE, and formed part of the impetus for its birth.[74] Raquel Rodas also notes that the uprising at Changalá grabbed the urban left's attention, inspiring socialists from the Antorcha group to come to Cayambe to fight on the behalf of the disposed.[75] At the socialists' founding assembly several months later, Paredes noted that the peasant syndicate in Juan Montalvo was the first rural organization in the highlands. "Given that one of the fundamental demands of Ecuadorian socialism is the redemption of the Indian," Paredes proposed that the delegates congratulate and support the struggle in Cayambe against landlord abuses.[76] This helped set the stage for what would be a long and congenial relationship between urban leftists and rural Indians united in pursuit of common goals.

The PSE was also significant for incorporating women into its ranks. Three years before the constitution gave women the right to vote, Luisa María Gómez de la Torre, the first woman to teach at the prestigious all-male Colegio Mejía school in Quito, helped found the Socialist Party. Paredes noted Gómez de la Torre's presence as a "representative of the great social victim: the woman," who "remains enslaved by political and civic limitations and social prejudices that leave her defenseless in the arms of exploiters." Gómez de la Torre joined Gualavisí and Paredes in a commission to report on the PSE's initiatives to the country's presidency.[77] She subsequently became an important leader in socialist and Indigenous struggles, particularly in her support of Indigenous education projects. Activists remembered her "as a fighter for democratic agrarian reform, education, and the rights of the exploited and oppressed Indigenous masses."[78] The Socialist Party was a shared space, and this collaboration elucidates Indigenous and leftist attitudes toward gender, class consciousness, and ethnic identity.

Gualavisí and other Indigenous leaders understood that in order to end oppression they would need to effect radical changes in society. Indians experienced racism and discrimination in their daily realities. Socialist leaders appreciated the role that race played in the structure of class societies. "The working class is subject to a double burden," Paredes noted. They face "racial oppression (prejudice for being an 'inferior race') and economic oppression." This double oppression led to a growing "consciousness of their distinct class interests." Paredes recognized the nature of ethnic and economic structures in the Andes, and he argued that they led to a high degree of class consciousness among Indians who "formed a potent revolutionary factor."[79]

Paredes traveled to Moscow for the tenth anniversary of the Russian Revolution in 1927 and the Sixth Congress of the Communist International (or Comintern) the following year. Paredes actively participated in this congress, particularly in regard to issues concerning the role of the rural masses in a communist revolution. He brought to the attention of the assembly the importance of Indigenous revolts in Ecuador, which provided evidence of the "widening and deepening of the revolutionary process" in Latin America.[80] He disagreed with a proposal to expropriate land from large estates and distribute it to the poor in small private parcels. First, this approach

Luisa Gómez and Dolores Cacuango, 1968. Photo by Rolf
Blomberg. Courtesy of the Archivo Blomberg, Quito, Ecuador.

would not address fundamental problems with the land tenure system. As
E. Bradford Burns notes, what was needed "was total change, the restructuring of all inherited institutions to the benefit of the majority."[81] Second,
building on existing community structures would prove rewarding in developing a socialist system. Indigenous society naturally tended toward
socialism, Paredes argued, and Spanish colonization had disrupted this process. "The American Indians are imbued with a remarkable collectivist
spirit," Paredes stated. "These elements must be utilised in the proletarian
State for the construction of socialism." As evidence of the potential for this
strategy, he pointed to four recent Indigenous insurrections, including the
one Gualavisí had led.[82] His arguments swayed the congress, and the Comintern's final resolution advocated that land expropriated from large estates
be handed over for "the collective cultivation of the agricultural workers."[83]

The 1928 Sixth Congress launched what has come to be known as an
"ultraleft" phase with a "class against class" organizing strategy replacing

that of building alliances with other leftist forces. The Comintern urged local parties to work in rural areas, organizing worker-peasant coalitions to demand higher salaries, the return of lands to peasants, and the cancellation of debts.[84] Even before the Comintern dictated this line, Latin American communists (with Mexico taking the lead) had developed strong connections with peasant movements.[85] In Ecuador, even though the PSE had incorporated Indigenous peoples and issues into the founding of the party, the Sixth Congress triggered an intensification of rural activism. The political scientist Alison Brysk somewhat famously notes that "the Indian rights movement was 'born transnational,'" dating this assertion to the 1971 Barbados Conference.[86] From its beginnings in the 1920s, however, Indigenous activism must be understood and contextualized within international trends.

At a January 1929 Central Committee meeting of the PSE, Paredes announced that the previous year the party had joined the Comintern and now its program had to be brought in line with the international organization.[87] At its second congress in October 1931, the PSE formally changed its name to the Partido Comunista Ecuatoriano (PCE, Ecuadorian Communist Party). Its base was to be purely proletarian and "incorporate elements of other classes: peasant and intellectuals."[88] The party vowed to support the demands of hacienda workers, comuna (Indigenous community) members, and Indian "tribes." Communists advocated for Indigenous interests in the national press, accompanied Indians when they presented petitions to authorities, helped Indians with their organizations, defended workers against hacienda abuses, and assisted in the formation of schools and literacy campaigns.[89] The first national communist congress in Milagro in December 1935 included in its honorary directorate Ambrosio Lasso, who at the time was in prison as a result of an uprising on the Pull hacienda earlier that year. Following the Comintern's lead, party activists called for a worker-peasant alliance to unify the left and continue the struggle against imperialism.[90]

On several occasions, Paredes ran as a PCE candidate for president and congressional deputy. In the 1933 presidential election, Paredes campaigned as the "candidate of the workers, peasants, Indians, and soldiers" and promised bread, work, land, and liberty for the people.[91] He sought to build a "worker-peasant bloc," calling on the urban proletariat to "ally itself intimately with peasants in a common struggle against feudal capitalism." Indicating dedication to the rights of subalterns excluded from political discourse, communists announced that they would fight through their elected representatives in congress and the revolutionary action of the masses on the streets for universal suffrage, minimum wage legislation, the return of land and water to rural communities, and the cancellation of agricultural worker debts on haciendas. Parts of the platform came from theses that the Communist International had adopted. Both included a call to expropriate hacienda land, suppress debts, arm a popular militia, and defend "Indians and Blacks, not only as exploited and oppressed classes, but also as oppressed nationalities."[92] Significantly, agrarian reform headed the campaign platform and continued to be a principal demand that the left pushed during much of the remainder of the twentieth century.

With his rural base of support excluded from voting, Paredes garnered only about five hundred votes in the 1933 election and thus ran a distant fourth. Nevertheless, as the PCE platform and Indigenous organizational demands converged, the two forces became natural allies in a unified struggle against the Ecuadorian oligarchy. Paredes's campaign literature noted that Indians knew and appreciated him because of his involvement with their movements, and that he remained a symbol in the struggle against large landowners and exploitation. Leftists commonly incorporated Indigenous peoples into broader alliances, as in 1933 when they called on "workers, intellectuals, peasants, Indians, *montuvios,* and soldiers" to join together to overthrow the dictatorship of Juan de Dios Martínez Mera.[93]

Paredes did not represent the only ideological trend within the Ecuadorian left. Other activists did not find Moscow's vision of a proletarian struggle applicable to their local reality, which led to a split between socialists and communists.[94] Although communists were most closely associated with Indigenous concerns, they were not alone. A dissident group reconstituted a Socialist Party in 1933 and included in its platform the "liquidation of the Indian problem, through their economic, social, political, and cultural exaltation."[95] Three years later the party declared that it would fight "on behalf of the Indian and montuvio, subjected to the inhumane exploitation of the semi-feudal regime that exists in the countryside."[96] Reflecting a certain growth in its thinking, in 1938 the socialist congress expanded this statement to note that "the Indigenous race, knocked down by the exploitation that has victimized it since the conquest, will not only enjoy rights equal to that of other ethnic groups that inhabit the country, but will also receive economic support and cultural attention from the state, for its complete social liberation."[97] While this language tends toward paternalism, and while often there is a gap between rhetoric and implementation, it is noteworthy that only leftist parties engaged Indigenous issues. Liberals and conservatives conceptualized political activity, including the rights of members of a society to shape the world around them, to be the exclusive domain of wealthy, white, propertied males. Urban leftists played an important role in creating spaces for their rural counterparts to participate in these discussions.

Pesillo

Many of Ecuador's most radical rural organizing efforts in the twentieth century took place on state-owned haciendas, with Indigenous workers and wealthy white renters fighting for control of land that neither of them owned. Paredes notes that it was easier to organize on these haciendas because the oversight of political activities was less than what would be found on private estates.[98] The Pesillo hacienda, located one hundred kilometers north of Quito in the canton of Cayambe, became a particularly strong focus of Indigenous organizing efforts. The hacienda originated in 1560 with a small land grant from the Spanish crown to the Merced order. Over time, the Mercedarians expanded the size of the hacienda until it became one of the largest in Ecuador—as such, it controlled a wide and ecologically diverse area.[99] After the government expropriated church-owned haciendas in 1904, it advertised Pesillo for an annual rent of 30,000 sucres with a 150,000 sucre deposit.[100] Only the wealthiest could afford these high rents. For example, in 1913 Aquiles Jarrín Espinosa, one of Cayambe's "city fathers" who played a central role in municipal policy decisions that affected the haciendas, rented the estate. The anthropologist Muriel Crespi noted that although "in some respects expropriation implied little more than the transfer from one managerial patron to another . . . the disruptions it precipitated made expropriation a springboard to unionization."[101] Because of its unwieldy size and difficulties in finding renters, the government divided Pesillo into five separate haciendas or "departments" named La Chimba, Pesillo, Pucará, Moyurco, and San Pablourco. These were then administered separately as part of the *Junta Central de Asistencia Pública* (JCAP) program.

By the end of the 1940s, 52 percent of the land in Cayambe was in the hands of various state agencies, as well as 12 percent in the neighboring canton of Pedro Moncayo.[102] Many analysts considered the JCAP program to be a resounding failure. One study observed that before expropriation these haciendas held some of the country's best land and were recognized for their high levels of production. Eight-year leases were not long enough for renters to realize a return on investments, and thus improvements designed to modernize agricultural production predictably were discouraged. Renters exploited the land for short-term profit, and by the mid-twentieth century the level of production had fallen. Critics also condemned the abuse and exploitation of human capital, the true value of the haciendas.[103] Even the JCAP director criticized the renters for using the Indians "as a form of replaceable animal traction."[104] To complicate matters, fiscal mismanagement meant that the program was chronically short of funds.

State ownership of haciendas dramatically influenced the nature of rural organizing efforts. The anthropologist Paul Cliche contrasts the militant syndicates on state-owned estates in Cayambe with the more hidden forms of ethnic differentiation and protest on privately owned haciendas in the neighboring canton of Pedro Moncayo. State ownership thrust conflict overtly into the public realm in Cayambe, whereas in Pedro Moncayo it only emerged under cover of events such as the annual public San Pedro festival.[105] Significantly, one of Ecuador's first rural syndicates emerged not on a hacienda but in the free community at Juan Montalvo. In Mexico, Barry Carr observes that "agricultural workers, in fact, embraced several strategies to improve their conditions—forming agricultural unions (*sindicatos*), occupying state lands on occasion, and, where they were entitled, soliciting land grants under the agrarian legislation of the day." Carr notes that various factors influenced the selection of a particular strategy, including the class status of the peasantry and the responses of the government and property owners.[106] Similarly in Ecuador, rural activists were not exclusively wed to one approach and were likely to adapt and shift organizing strategies to meet the needs and demands of a particular context.

Hiding in caves, creek beds, and under cover of night to avoid authorities, Indigenous workers formed some of Ecuador's first peasant unions in northern Cayambe: El Inca (The Inka) in Pesillo, followed by Tierra Libre (Free Land) in Moyurco and by Pan y Tierra (Bread and Land) in La Chimba.[107] While working in the fields, activists communicated with each other in code to avoid detection and persecution. "Are you going to so-and-so's house for the wedding tonight?" they asked in order to let each other know when and where to meet. Ignacio Alba organized the first meetings. He brought people together and asked them, "Why do we continue to put up with these abuses? We need to stand up and put an end to these customs." He convinced fellow workers to "demand their rights, to defend themselves against abuses, to demand their salaries." In this way, CONAIE later observed, "the first peasant syndicates comprised primarily of Indigenous peoples began to form." The syndicates were largely the efforts of huasipungueros and their family members, and included all men and women older than fifteen years old. Members elected a secretary-general who was valiant, articulate, and not afraid to speak out in defense of Indigenous rights. The most important issues they tackled were land rights, access to water and pasture, better salaries, education, and an end to abuses.[108] Through agrarian reform in the 1960s, these syndicates led much of the rural organizing efforts.

By all appearances, activists founded El Inca and Tierra Libre in mid-1930, and their first action was to protest a hacienda employee's beating of Rosa Lechón. In May 1930, the urban socialists Ricardo Paredes, Luis Fernando Chávez (also called *chiquito*, or the younger, to distinguish him from his father who was a founder of the PSE and supported the Indians at Changalá several years earlier), and Rubén Rodríguez met furtively with Indigenous activists to help them organize and present their demands. Neptalí Ulcuango related that an organizing trigger was the abusive actions of a hacienda employee named Toribio Valladares who "beat, kicked, and punched" the workers. When Ulcuango's father could not take it anymore he fought back, which led Valladares to press criminal charges. Paredes came to the elder Ulcuango's defense. "Or rather," Ulcuango remembered, "it was my father who practically began things." Together with Juan Albamocho, he led the meeting that brought in Paredes to help defend their interests.[109]

Rather than taking action to stop abuses, the JCAP director Augusto Egas blamed socialists for stirring up trouble with the seditious intent of organizing a revolt. Elites seemingly were never able to accept the fact that subalterns were able to organize themselves, and therefore they always looked for external subversive forces that allegedly manipulated them for nefarious ends.[110] In August 1930, Carlos Torres and Gustavo Araujo, two socialist activists, were helping organize agricultural syndicates on the Pesillo and La Chimba haciendas. According to the renter José Rafael Delgado, agrarian workers on the Pesillo hacienda formed El Inca at a meeting on the afternoon of August 16, 1930. In September, Delgado noted that "the same socialists" (three in total) were once again on the hacienda. Delgado wanted to remove them by force, but it was impossible without a strong military presence because the socialists were "well protected by the Indians who are armed in their entirety with sticks and knives." Fortunately, the harvest had been completed ("the Indians are working, because those socialists ordered them to do so"), and he reported rumors of night-time meetings of all the people at Moyurco, San Pablourco, Pesillo, and La Chimba "to sign I do not know what document."[111]

These organizational efforts posed a serious threat to the hacienda, to JCAP, and to the elite power structure. Indians were preparing a general strike at La Chimba in response to the imprisonment of two syndicate members for their organizing activities, and the insurrection threatened to spread to Pesillo. Egas asked the police to send in troops to protect Delgado's interests. Throughout the second half of 1930, reports indicate an escalation of organizing efforts. Egas felt threatened by these "Bolshevik" efforts to resist hacienda administration and disrupt the country's social order. Although he was aware that workers had a constitutional right to form syndicates, he resolved not to allow them to utilize this as a basis for a social revolution.[112]

In the face of increasingly violent attacks from "landowners, authorities, and priests who carry to an extreme their actions to rob and crush rural workers," socialist activists stepped up their support for rural organizational efforts. On August 21, the Socialist Party announced the formation of Socorro Obrero y Campesino (Worker and Peasant Aid) "to help with the demands of workers and peasants in their conflicts with capitalists, landlords, and authorities."[113] The organization's first action was to free the imprisoned members of the El Inca syndicate, as well as members of the Juventud Comunista (Communist Youth) who had come to their assistance. In addition, the socialist senator Luis Maldonado spoke in the National Congress on behalf of the Kayambis, and the Socialist Party collected money that it then sent to Cayambe along with another compañero to continue organizing efforts. *La Hoz,* the "central organ of the Ecuadorian Socialist Party, Section of the Communist International," defiantly proclaimed that workers would continue to resist the terror of the property owners and the government. Such repression "would only serve to accelerate the revolution that these miserable agents of capitalism try in vain to stop." The party claimed success for its new support organization, as the rapid and efficient mobilization of resources led to the release of the imprisoned activists.[114]

While earlier leftist newspapers such as *La Antorcha* had given passing, almost token, attention to Indigenous issues, Paredes and Chávez prominently featured agrarian struggles in the pages of the new socialist newspaper *La Hoz.* A front-page article noted that united rural syndicates "will reject the ferocious repression of their enemies." It championed the efforts of El Inca and Tierra Libre to bring their concerns to the government. Their struggles for an eight-hour work day and other demands infuriated landowners who realized that a "growing class consciousness among the Indigenous peoples would decrease their iniquitous exploitation." Paredes and Chávez called on their urban allies to defend these Indigenous struggles.[115] In November 1930, the El Inca syndicate wrote to compañero Paredes to outline the abuses suffered by the "comrades" on the Pesillo hacienda, including overwork, treatment as beasts of burden, exploitation of women, and payment of very low wages. Signed *"rebeldía y trabajo"* (rebelliousness and work), the letter struck a tone of informing their urban counterparts of their daily realities without engaging in a submissive discourse that would indicate a perceived inferiority or a paternalistic relationship.[116] "The syndicates and the party were closely tied together," Paredes later remembered. "There was a convergence between the needs of the Indian peasants and the positions of the party."[117] Common concerns and good relations translated into a strong organizational structure.

Indians and Communists

Peasant syndicates emerged in the context of the Great Depression, which highlighted flaws in the existing world capitalist system. Exports fell, commercial activities paralyzed, businesses went bankrupt, and financial resources were depleted. The crisis weakened both the liberal coastal Guayaquil commercial bourgeois and their traditional opponents, the conservative sierra landowners. In 1931, Isidro Ayora's government fell, ushering in a chaotic decade with frequent changes in government. "The deepening economic depression," Barry Carr notes in a history of the Mexican Communist Party, "appeared to support the Comintern's argument that capitalism was in crisis and therefore creating the conditions for a revolutionary breakthrough."[118] In the United States, the onset of the depression "restored Communist dreams of revolution, and the party gained widespread publicity by leading a series of dramatic strikes and demonstrations."[119] Similar forces were at work in Latin America. "It was not simply economic exploitation," Robert Wasserstrom notes in Mexico, "but the relentless ideological repression" that drove Indigenous peoples to insurrection.[120] While the encroachment of capitalism on an agricultural economy led to a deterioration of peasant livelihoods, it also brought formerly isolated peasants into contact with outsiders searching for allies in a struggle against traditional elites.[121] As Indigenous peasants gained a growing political consciousness, they unified diverse rural organizing efforts.

Protest activity in rural communities was part of a larger popular movement in the turbulent decade of the 1930s. Urban workers fought against capitalist forces that were undermining workers' social and economic interests. At the same time, Indigenous peasants maintained that large landowners were leading Ecuador down a path of dependent capitalist development that would only benefit the wealthy and result in further economic impoverishment for the masses. They engaged in new forms of organizational strategies that were not "traditional" in nature but very modern. The conceptualization of this activity as "strikes" rather than "uprisings" (as Indigenous protests had often been termed in the nineteenth century) reveals the growing influence of urban labor movements in rural communities. Increasingly, Indigenous peoples believed that a socialist revolution was the only logical solution to their underdeveloped economic situation.

Previous unrest was often the result of localized reactions to specific injustices with a limited goal of removing a particularly abusive hacienda employee. Now, protests increasingly played out in the public arena with Indigenous activists forming organizations to press for policy reforms. They became progressively more aware of the larger national dimensions of their struggle and inserted themselves into these discussions. In addition, urban leftists assisted with organizational structures to facilitate their political engagement. Muriel Crespi notes that in the aftermath of the July 1925 coup, "the government was evidently too disorganized or preoccupied to protect its haciendas from leftist interlopers."[122] In exploiting this power vacuum, leftists created their own spaces within haciendas to provide a bridge between Indigenous societies and the elite power structures they sought to change.

Contact with the urban left became a defining characteristic of Indigenous organizations, especially in areas such as Cayambe that were located a convenient day's trip from Quito. At the same time, mestizo peasants were also actively organizing in Milagro on the coast, similarly located about a day's travel from the principal coastal city of Guayaquil. Communist leaders such as Joaquín Gallegos Lara and Enrique Gil Gilbert provided active support. In both Cayambe and Milagro, rural leaders fostered important organizational connections with urban activists. A statement in 1928 from the first peasant organization in Milagro, the General Assembly of Peasants, proclaimed that "with a spontaneous flower of rebelliousness, the class consciousness of peasants in Ecuador has been born." They presented a long list of demands to the National Assembly, including a request to limit the size of landed estates, create agrarian colonies and cooperatives, allow for peasant selection of local authorities, expand rural work inspections, create rural schools, support rural medical services, and expand the rural road infrastructure. "The problems of the peasant proletariat are many and deep," the statement concluded, "on the coast as well as in the highlands."[123] As Uggen notes, such rural-urban coalitions emerged out of a situation of "an aspiring urban political group . . . challenging traditional elites for political power" and therefore seeing "the peasantry as a possible ally."[124] Both Cayambe and Milagro emerged as significant centers for rural protest that subsequently spread throughout the country.

Indigenous uprisings and strikes appeared to be spontaneous and unplanned affairs, even while communists attempted to position themselves as providing vanguard leadership. Neither perspective fully captures the dynamics underlying the protests. In the midst of the Great Depression, the policies of the Communist International during its "third period" sought to take advantage of the global crisis to launch a new agrarian and anti-imperialist revolutionary offensive. For this purpose, the Comintern's South American Bureau urged the building of "worker-peasant" alliances. Urban marxist militants had little previous contact in rural areas, and they realized their best successes where local activists had already been organizing their communities. The presence of new urban allies strengthened and encouraged ensuing protests.[125]

In the 1940s, the anthropologist Aníbal Buitrón noted that rather than interacting directly with civil or religious authorities, Indigenous peoples would search out white intermediaries to intercede with political power brokers on their behalf.[126] Years later anthropologists noted the continued legacy of these relationships, with former huasipungueros kneeling and kissing white people's hands through their ponchos as a sign of deference.[127] These were not the types of relationships that Indigenous activists developed with urban socialists. Indigenous leaders claim that they requested that urban marxists come work with them to help defend Indigenous rights. Outsiders did not show up uninvited to cause trouble, as elites maintained. The Indians called them compañeros, a term that roughly translates "companions" and has connotations of being joined together in a common political struggle. Activists at La Chimba published a note in the communist-affiliated Indigenous newspaper Ñucanchic Allpa (Kichwa for "Our Land")

Kayambis celebrate the 2003 Inti Raymi (Sun Festival) in the town of Ascazubi.
Photo by Marc Becker.

addressed to "compañero Doctorcito Ricardo Paredes and all of the other compañeros in Quito," informing them of abuses they were suffering. "We have begun the struggle," they stated, "but to continue it we need help from Quito and elsewhere."[128]

Urban activists took advantage of weddings, baptisms, and other festivals to meet with community members. Neptalí Ulcuango recalled that during a San Juan festival, Paredes and Chávez arrived together with Indigenous leaders at the patio of his family's house singing and playing traditional music on the guitar, flute, and pan pipes. "Long live the El Inca Agricultural Syndicate!" the people shouted. "Long live organized peasants! Down with the landlords! Long live the struggles of agricultural workers!" After singing, dancing, and presenting demands for better treatment and salaries, the group moved off in the night to another house. Tránsito Amaguaña later told stories of dressing up Chávez as a Kayambi in a red poncho, white shirt, *alpargata* sandals, and hat in order to hide him from the authorities while he helped organize the new syndicates. When authorities came, he put on a

Kayambis take over the city of Cayambe in the 2004 Inti Raymi (Sun Festival).
Photo by Marc Becker.

poncho, pulled a hat down over his eyes, and played a flute to escape
detection.[129]

The entrance of the marxists into Indigenous communities under the
cover of San Juan or Inti Raymi, the June solstice or "Sun Festival"—one of
the most important celebrations in the Andes—challenges commonly repeated assumptions of a marxist "disdain for explicitly ethnic or cultural
issues."[130] Rather, socialist actions reflected what José Carlos Mariátegui
argued for neighboring Peru: "The problem is not racial, but social and
economic; but race has a role in it and in the methods of confronting it."[131]
In joining the most hallowed event of the Indigenous calendar, the urban
leftists embraced rather than rejected ethnic rituals.

Ethnic observances lent strength to, rather than detracted energy from, a
class struggle. Embracing and organizing on the basis of an ethnic identity is
a far cry from common elite attitudes that maintained that if Indians "want
to be something and rise in society, they have to deny their origins, carefully
concealing them so as not to be recognized as Indian."[132] Alcida Rita Ramos

contends that "ethnic logic and class logic do not merge easily into one another."[133] Nevertheless, activists in Ecuador in the 1920s managed to navigate this difficult terrain of identity politics. There is little recorded evidence of communists decrying race as a "false consciousness" that needed to be replaced with class rhetoric, as seemingly was the case in Peru and has often been assumed to be the case in Ecuador as well.[134] While undoubtedly some marxist theorists did, as the anthropologist Mary Weismantel maintains, "turn away from race as an analytical category" within the different strands of Ecuador's popular movements, there is a significant trend that recognized and denounced the persistence of racial subjugation.[135] These marxists interpreted the Indigenous peasantry as facing the "double dimension" of class exploitation and racial discrimination and therefore their realities needed to be theorized and addressed on both fronts.[136]

Ecuadorian leftists understood that, as Mariátegui noted in Peru, "Indian peasants will only truly understand people from their midst, who speak their own language." Mariátegui proposed training Indian leaders who would then return to work for "the emancipation of their race." Leftist outsiders would not indoctrinate the Indians as to the nature of the demands they would make, but rather their role would be to help give an organizational cohesion to those demands. Pointing to a long history of insurrections, Mariátegui rejected the notion that Indians were incapable of a revolutionary struggle. The Indians already had "demonstrated a quite astounding level of resistance and persistence" in pursuit of their demands. Reflecting Mariátegui's constructions, the Ecuadorian communist leader Nela Martínez pointed to how the PCE "had awoken a messianic and religious faith . . . in that immense deprived and insulted mass that for the first time feels a road growing under their feet." Both Mariátegui and Martínez believed that once Indigenous peoples were introduced to a revolutionary consciousness they would be unequaled in their struggle for socialism.[137]

It was not so much that urban elites, socialists, and indigenistas were taking an increased interest in rural subalterns, but that Indians forced a broader awareness of their concerns and outsiders could no longer ignore them.[138] Aníbal Quijano refers to this development as the politicization of the peasant movement.[139] Throughout Latin America in the 1930s, new movements challenged the economic, social, and political power structures that underlay agrarian societies. Rural movements engaged in new forms of political organization, including utilizing labor union styles of organization and strikes to achieve their goals. Although the support of sympathetic outsiders was critical to Indigenous success, the leaders and issues were authentic and homegrown. Communist Party activists might present themselves as founding rural syndicates, but they were simply building on pre-existing efforts. Their success and rapid growth of Indigenous organizations was due to their roots in existing community structures. "Internally, they continued to function as traditional organizations," Xavier Albó observed in a similar situation in Bolivia, "while externally they would be called syndicates."[140] The dual aspect ultimately contributed to their strong success.

Liberals and communists represented two fundamentally different interpretations of the role that Indigenous peoples should play in Ecuadorian society. Liberal policies led to paternalistic domination, with leftists representing empowerment and liberation. Mercedes Prieto notes that elite liberals feared rural protests as irrational mob actions, and that they had wanted to "modernize" the peons into workers who would embrace progress and accept mestizo constructions of citizenship. Leftist intervention in organizing Indigenous syndicates, however, disrupted these plans. As a result, "[I]ndigenous protests came to be seen as more intricate weapons that, according to elite spokesmen, enhanced their unruliness."[141]

The U.S. State Department also feared the spread of communist propaganda into rural areas. Socialist agitation, the U.S. ambassador William Dawson fretted, had "resulted in an awakening of the consciousness of the Indians."[142] The U.S. consul Harold Clum added: "The great mass of the population in the interior consists of illiterate indians, who probably have communistic traditions from the time of the Incas. As few of them can read, this mimeographed and printed propaganda can not reach them directly, but they can be reached in other ways, and their uprisings which occur from time to time at different places in the interior, and their seizure of lands belonging to neighboring estate owners, indicate that they are being reached by communistic agitators. If they ever become thoroughly imbued with communism and realize their power, the comparatively small number of white people of Spanish descent who, with those of mixed race, form the land owning and ruling element will not be able to withstand them." The U.S. consul urged Quito to take control of the situation to prevent an Indigenous-communist alliance from shifting power balances in the country, even if it meant violating constitutional guarantees.[143]

Minister of Government Miguel A. Albornoz concurred with Clum's analysis. He reported "that propaganda is being translated into Indian dialects and read to the Indians at nocturnal gatherings," which contributed to growing leftist strength in the country.[144] These simple peasants were easily and "shamefully deceived and exploited by false defenders of the destitute." Communists, he complained, were inflaming rebellion "in all forms and all the time" through the broad distribution in rural communities of newspapers and fly sheets with "imprudent and exaggerated language." Nevertheless, Albornoz claimed that "the government has been able to maintain the public order despite the serious difficulties that communist agitations have caused and are still causing by some individuals and erroneously misty groupings in transplanting to the bosom of our healthy, peaceful, and moral people, certain violent procedures that lead to disruptive and dangerous doctrines."[145] Privately, Albornoz declared that he had assumed control of the Interior Ministry in order "to combat communism in Ecuador."[146] This also meant combating the growing strength of Indigenous syndicates.

Charles A. Page argued in a confidential report for the U.S. Foreign Service that in previous assessments rhetoric and paranoia had led to overestimations of the threat of communist strength in Ecuador. He declared that gaining accurate information on the extent of communist penetration into rural Indigenous communities was difficult to obtain. "Communist agitators are devoting a great deal of attention to the Indians" and making it the chief focus of their efforts, Page reported, but it was unclear if they had made alarming progress as some contended or whether they had made no progress due to "the indolence and century-old sense of subjugation of the race." In support of this latter position, Page noted that literature could not reach the illiterate Indians. Paredes and Chávez "are practically the only agitators who have been willing to go out among them to stir up trouble. It would take a force of hundreds of agitators throughout the Sierra to bring about a dangerous situation." Because of Catholicism's continued strong hold on the region and the fact that uprisings often resulted from specific abuses rather than a new political consciousness, the communists would need a permanent presence in rural areas to achieve an ideological shift. On the other hand, Page argued that the communist threat must be real because "the Government is frankly worried, and the Government must know" and because "communism is inherent in the Inca tradition."[147] Neither of these arguments is particularly sophisticated or compelling, and they do not reveal an extensive knowledge or understanding of Indigenous communities. Nevertheless, the government did fear the willingness of leftist activists to organize in rural areas and believed that it was in those areas where it faced the greatest threat to its hegemonic control over the country.

The JCAP director Augusto Egas consistently placed leftist activities in the most negative light: communists were deceiving and misleading the Indians and were taking advantage of their ignorance and simplicity. He informed hacienda renters that they should not permit anyone to enter the estates without his written permission. The threat, according to Egas, was from those who sought to subvert order on the hacienda. If the Indians had a complaint to make, they should do it directly to the JCAP program without the intervention of lawyers or other mediators. Not only did Egas want the outside agitators expelled from the haciendas, he wanted them arrested and imprisoned on charges of inciting rebellion.[148] A test of Indigenous organizational strength came with a December 1930 strike that marked the first time that rural syndicates mounted a direct and sustained challenge to state power. The ramifications of this strike were felt across the country. The strike showcased the sophisticated political nature of Indigenous demands and highlighted the importance of strategic alliances with urban leftists.

THREE

Strike!

Jorge Icaza's *Huasipungo,* Ecuador's best-known novel, largely defined popular perceptions of the Indians living in that country. Published in 1934, the novel denounced elite abuses against Indians and sounded a clarion call for social justice and better treatment for the most miserable people in Ecuador. Painting a dreary picture of Indigenous life, Icaza depicted native workers on haciendas reacting as an irrational force against the inevitable process of modernization. Rather than being capable of confronting the future, they clung desperately to the past and feared change. Icaza's Indians were lazy, dirty, smelly, stupid, brutal, and lacked any sort of ethnic pride, class consciousness, or political ideology. They were victims—unable to defend their communal interests and powerless in the face of the imposition of state power. Instead, they relied on outsiders to defend their interests. Readers did not identify with the Indians, nor did they recognize any positive contributions that they might make to society. Icaza's portrayal of passive and powerless Indians is ironic because as he penned *Huasipungo,* Indigenous peoples were staging a sustained systematic critique of Ecuador's political economy by engaging in massive acts of social protest designed to end their marginalization and demanding expanded citizenship rights.

Social historians such as Barrington Moore, E. P. Thompson, and James Scott point to "the importance of the moral outrage created by unequal economic and social conditions" in triggering protest. Yet as the Russian revolutionary Leon Trotsky famously observed, "the mere existence of privations is not enough to cause an insurrection; if it were, the masses would always be in revolt."[1] This leads the anthropologist Suzana Sawyer to note that "there was nothing inevitable about an indigenous politics of opposition; it had to be produced."[2] Activists organized actions and presented demands that led to a clearly defined political agenda. Although an Indigenous movement's ethnic component was undeniable, it was its class components that lent strength and cohesion to the struggle. As Joe Foweraker observes in Mexico, "class and class struggle continue to be far more important than many want to admit."[3] In addition, successful social movements emerge out of strong organizations, the mobilization of resources, the development of solidarity networks, political opportunities, and the consolidation of an identity that provides for internal logical cohesion. Finally, Nancy Postero and Leon Zamosc point to a useful "distinction between indigenous rights as an *issue* to be fought for, and indigenous movements as *actors* in the struggle."[4] Subalterns framed these issues, and it was people who made this history.

The Pesillo Strike of 1930–1931

On December 30, 1930, Cayambe's jefe político sent a telegram to the minister of government in Quito reporting that the Indians of Pesillo had revolted. No one was working; some had fled to the high páramo grasslands, while others had gone to Quito. The jefe político noted that the leaders had not been found, but he urged the government to take immediate action to contain the situation. The Indians attacked the main hacienda house, the hacienda's employees fled, and, according to the JCAP director Augusto Egas, even the teniente político had to hide. Responding to requests from Egas, the haciendas' renters, and local officials, the government sent 150 soldiers (fifty each for the Moyurco, Pesillo, and La Chimba haciendas) along with bloodhounds to protect the hacendado's interests and to arrest, torture, and destroy the houses of the revolt's leaders. Officials arrested five leaders and sent them by train to Quito to face charges of rebellion. The uprising at Pesillo shocked the white population and set the tone for Indigenous protest in Ecuador for the next several decades.[5]

The workers who had gone on strike presented a petition to the government with a list of seventeen demands for higher salaries, a forty-hour work week, return of huasipungo plots, an end to the Church's abusive practice of charging diezmos and primicias, compensation for women's labor, and an end to the huasicama practice of demanding personal service in a hacendado's house. All of these issues concerned economic conditions and Indigenous workers' relations to social structures on the haciendas.[6] The anthropologist Mercedes Prieto characterizes these demands as "ambiguous" because while they advanced an ambitious agenda, they were largely reformist rather than challenging to the fundamental nature of the hacienda system.[7]

As illuminating as what the Pesillo militants included in their laundry list of demands is what they left out. There was no call for agrarian reform; the issue of land is absent except for a demand to return huasipungo plots. It seemed outside the realm of possibility for the workers that they could own the means of production on the haciendas. Indians only later raised this issue due to the influence of the Communist Party. Six years earlier, urban socialists had already been pressing the land issue in the pages of *La Antorcha*. They noted that a few elite families owned most of the land, while the majority of Indians lived in miserable and impoverished conditions. A socialist platform included land as its second point, noting that "land belongs to everyone and it is only due to the abusive monopolistic practices of the wealthy that they have lost it."[8] According to Egas, the socialists offered land titles to the Indians and filled their heads with the idea that the land was rightfully their property.[9] Demands for the "division of large haciendas and giving the land to those who work it" became common among working-class organizations, even those with little contact with rural struggles.[10]

When Indigenous militants began to embrace demands for agrarian reform, their desire was not to have individual plots but instead to administer the hacienda as a cooperative based on communal arrangements. This reflected Mariátegui's analysis in Peru that an agrarian reform that merely liquidated feudalism would only benefit the capitalist class. Replacing the old aristocracy with a new and more powerful bourgeoisie would further subjugate Indigenous peasants. What was needed instead was a profound change that altered the very structures on which society was based.[11] Interactions with leftist intellectuals brought about a significant conceptual shift, and by the 1980s Indigenous activists argued that the haciendas were rightfully theirs because the land had originally belonged to their ancestors.[12]

Notably, none of the seventeen demands at Pesillo explicitly addressed ethnic issues. There is no call to end racial discrimination, to have Ecuador's ethnic diversity affirmed, or to extend the franchise to Indigenous peoples. Nevertheless, although it is not explicitly spelled out, an ethnic ideology underlies the entire petition. The petition indicates the underlying racialized nature of class structures on haciendas. The *patrones* were white, absentee landowners who lived in Quito. The hacienda workers were impoverished Indigenous peoples. In the process of analyzing their realities, land and ethnic consciousness became deeply intertwined. For Indigenous peoples, Luis Fernando Botero notes, "land is the privileged space where they carry out a symbolic interaction that allows an ideological reproduction that permits the maintenance of an identity."[13] Indigenous organizing efforts fostered a hybrid or perhaps synthesized form of identity. Analyzing similar communist attempts to build a worker-peasant alliance in the Laguna region of Mexico, Barry Carr casts doubt "on the extent to which the status, demands, and actions of the Laguna agricultural workers can be neatly classified as peasant / *agrarista* or proletarian / *sindicalista*." In fact, an analysis of pronouncements illustrates "that 'proletarian' and 'agrarista' demands could go side by side."[14] The same could be said for rural activists in Ecuador as they conceptualized their struggles.

On January 7, José Rafael Delgado and Julio Miguel Páez, the renters of the Pesillo and Moyurco haciendas, reached an agreement with their workers for an eight-hour day, one day of rest per week, payment for the work of women and children, abolishment of huasicama customs, and the dismissal of workers only for bad conduct or insubordination. After signing the agreement, the agricultural workers returned to work.[15] On January 12, the labor inspector Alberto Batallas visited the haciendas with local jefe político Alfonso Jarrín and reported that everything appeared to be normal. His report, however, indicates that he spoke only to white administrators. Given the presence of racial and class tensions, entering rural communities with the jefe político who was a member of a powerful local landholding family would skew his findings against the Indigenous workers.[16]

Away from the eyes of outsiders and government officials, however, a reign of terror descended on the hacienda. Local activists reported that "in order to punish us for having complained, between eight and ten well-armed hacienda employees attacked our houses at night and whipped the Indians." The hacienda engaged with impunity in these repressive actions, "knowing that there would be no defense because the houses were so distant from each other." Leaders could not travel alone because the hacienda was sending out henchmen to attack them. Indigenous workers reported that the renters were "bandidos," crooks. The repression, they claimed, was done with the blessing of both Egas and the Isidro Ayora, the president of the country.[17]

Delgado and Páez refused to adhere to the agreement they had signed.

The Indians stopped working, and it appeared that another uprising was imminent. Delgado feared that he was losing money because the fields were not planted. He asked the government for help, and he contended that the only way to solve the situation was to remove and punish the leaders and others who refused to work. He asked for troops to protect the hacienda from the fury of the Indians. Egas also feared that this crisis would negatively affect the work of the JCAP program. The Indian workers attacked an institution working for communal interests, and their actions threatened the program's work with the "truly needy" who were in hospitals and orphanages in the cities. Not once did he indicate a concern for the social welfare of the workers on the state's haciendas.[18]

The Kayambis continued to receive significant support from urban leftists. At the beginning of the strike, Dr. Juan Genaro Jaramillo, a lawyer known for his work among agricultural workers, accompanied Indians from Moyurco and Pesillo to the JCAP offices in Quito to protest the arrest of their companions and to present demands for higher salaries and better work conditions. Urban leftists published Indigenous demands in newspapers, and Ricardo Paredes assisted with negotiations to settle the strike.[19] A support committee proudly proclaimed that "the strike lasted two weeks thanks to the unconditional and effective support of the Communist Party . . . that helped the syndicates triumph."[20] Urban leftists had become key players in rural protests.

This strike had significant repercussions among Quito elites who feared a social realignment that would threaten their privileged position in society. José María Velasco Ibarra, the future president who penned a popular column in El Comercio, noted that hacienda owners needed to respond to worker unhappiness, but he also feared a "Bolshevik" threat from the Indigenous uprising.[21] This was a common attitude among elite conservatives who criticized the workers' rebellious spirit. They did not understand the economic exploitation and racial oppression that led to the strike. Indians, in their view, were passive and ignorant people, incapable of organizing protest actions. Elites searched for outsiders to explain the strikes and laid blame on socialist agitators. Egas blamed an Indian evolutionary inferiority that left them susceptible to the communists' simplistic solutions.[22] The conservative newspaper El Comercio also editorialized that socialists "hoodwinked" the Indians, using them as "raw material almost barbarically predisposed to everything bad just like the semi-savage multitudes of the lower class and the peasants in Russia."[23] The liberal El Día noted that whereas Indigenous demands were just, they lacked the basic moral structures or work habits necessary to make their implementation a success.[24]

In response to these attacks, strike supporters denounced "the bourgeois press at service to the large landholders" that either maintained complete silence about the strike or published "distorted facts" even though the syndicates had sent statements and delegations to the newspapers. El Día had taken a lead in the "anti-union and anti-communist campaign," allies claimed, because the paper's director was a brother of the police chief and the paper received "favors" from the government and money from the large landholders. The government acted as if it were "a crime for Indigenous peoples to organize and demand their rights." In the face of these challenges, the support committee called on urban laborers to aid Indigenous workers who had demonstrated such a "combative spirit and class solidarity."[25] Assistance from outside allies was critical to communicate Indigenous demands to the broader public.

Primer Congreso de Organizaciones Campesinas

Immediately on the heels of the strike at Pesillo and before all the issues in this conflict could be settled, Indigenous activists converged at the Primer Congreso de Organizaciones Campesinas (First Congress of Peasant Organizations). The congress was planned for the beginning of February 1931 in the parroquia of Juan Montalvo where Jesús Gualavisí had organized the Peasant Workers Syndicate five years earlier. Socialist organizers noted that the increasingly arduous life of rural workers made this congress necessary. Drawing on a memory of abuse and exploitation, a call for the congress recounted how "the Indians who were despoiled of their land by the Spanish conquerors and those who succeeded them have lived in the hardest servitude for four centuries." Suffering low wages and miserable working conditions, "laborers are treated as of an inferior race in the most despotic manner." Most rural communities did not have access to schools, and surrounding haciendas increasingly encroached on their land and water resources. The congress was explicitly meeting "for the purpose of unifying laborers and seeking the means of saving them from slavery."[26]

Despite the timing, the congress was not an immediate outgrowth of the Pesillo strike. Although it had been planned months in advance of the January protests, it is significant that it was to be held in Cayambe, an area with exceptionally militant organizations. Kayambis provided vanguard leadership and an example for nascent rural protest movements. Every syndicate, comuna, peasant league, land rights committee, and water committee had the right to send to the congress one delegate for every fifty members. Delegates were responsible for their own travel costs, but the local organizing committee in Cayambe would provide housing and cover other expenses. In addition to planning strategies and tactics, the congress would draft statutes and elect an executive committee for a Federation of Agricultural Laborers and Peasants of Ecuador to "defend the interests of rural laborers."[27]

As the news of the gathering spread, even more people planned to attend. Members of agrarian syndicates from throughout Ecuador mobilized to come to the congress. The socialist newspaper *La Hoz* had predicted that "the Congress will have a good number of delegates from a variety of provinces."[28] Quiteño newspapers carried reports of thousands of Indians and peasants flooding to Cayambe from all over the country, including from as far away as the southern highlands and the coast. Many people traveled on foot or on horseback for days or weeks to attend.[29] Organizers had expected one to two thousand delegates representing about one hundred thousand peasants and Indians, but already a week before the congress two thousand people had gathered and many more delegates were on the way.[30] Organizers announced that the congress would begin with an enormous procession of thousands of Indigenous and montuvio peasants in native dress carrying banners from their local organizations, and that it would end with an Indigenous festival. Expectations for a successful meeting ran high.[31]

Although the delegates were behaving themselves and abstaining from all alcoholic beverages, and the jefe político reported that arriving participants were not causing any problems, the massive mobilization made the government very nervous. They feared attacks on haciendas (particularly given Gualavisí's history of organizing peasants at Changalá) and accused communists from Quito of instigating a revolution in Cayambe. On January 31, the government closed roads to prevent more delegates from arriving. When several hundred assembled activists attempted to proceed with the congress, troops shut the meeting down entirely. Cayambe once again became a police state. The military stopped all movement in the canton and detained the leaders of the congress. The government defended its actions with claims that it needed to maintain public order and defend the country from a communist threat. Minister of Government Miguel A. Albornoz declared that had he not acted, "bloodshed could not have been avoided."[32] Even so, a largely unarmed peasant movement without a previous history of engaging in armed tactics did not present a threat of violence. Only one side in the conflict had guns.

On February 1, the government arrested several socialists who had come from Quito to help with the meeting, and charged them with disturbing the public order and committing acts of violence.[33] They were to be held until they signed a statement promising not to meddle in affairs against the public order. Telegrams of support for the imprisoned activists arrived from organizations as far away as Milagro on the coast, requesting respect for constitutional guarantees and asking that the congress be allowed to proceed as planned. Rather than demanding action, the liberal party's functional senator for the Indigenous Race, Pedro Leopoldo Núñez, called for the situation to be "studied." On February 3, all but two of the detained socialists signed the statement and were released. Ricardo Paredes took a more principled stance and refused to agree to the government's conditions. Authorities considered Luis Chávez a key instigator and continued to hold him at the army base in Cayambe. Juan Bustamante, a Chilean, was deported from the country for his involvement.[34] Both Chávez and Paredes were eventually released on February 19 after giving statements but without having to sign the agreement pledging not to engage in further subversive activities.

Two important issues emerge from these events. First, without logistical support from urban socialists, many people would not have heard of the meeting or planned to attend. About three to four months earlier, a group of activists in Quito discussed the congress, named Chávez as secretary general of the organizing committee, and sent him to Cayambe to begin preparations. They sent circulars to peasant groups throughout the country. The government intercepted some of these, including one that Paredes had written to activists in Latacunga to urge their attendance.[35] Socialists also advertised the congress in its newspaper *La Hoz*. Without this logistical support, far-flung organizations may not have heard of the gathering. Rather than the image that Andrés Guerrero paints of socialists inheriting a nineteenth-century liberal "ventriloquist's voice," indications are that the Indians and urban socialists worked together as equals for a successful meeting.[36] Indians would not have flooded to a meeting in which they had no ownership or vested interest.

The second issue is more striking. During this month of heightened militancy, the mainstream media had treated Indigenous peoples as nameless (and mindless) objects whom outside agitators had manipulated. On February 3, *El Comercio* and *El Día* mentioned by name for the first time the rural activists whom the police had arrested. Virgilio Lechón, Marcelo Tarabata, Juan de Dios Quishpe, and Benjamin Campos, all "peons" from the Moyurco hacienda, were being held until they could be sent by train to Quito where a judge would decide what to do with them. A large group of Indians congregated at the military barracks in Cayambe to demand the release of their comrades and threatened a general strike if they were not released. The following day the police freed Virgilio Lechón, whom the authorities had identified (along with Ignacio Alba) as the primary troublemaker at Moyurco. They were still looking for "Gualambisí," who was in hiding. Egas complained that these agitators did not work on the hacienda but remained on it taking advantage of the benefits of friends' and family's huasipungos and were engaged in no activity other than leading Indigenous uprisings.[37]

It is not surprising that the police captured Indigenous leaders; testimonies make it clear that such repression was a common occurrence. During the Pesillo strike a month earlier, the government also arrested and sent Indigenous leaders to Quito, but the newspapers never mentioned their names and barely noted the event in passing. This was the first indication in the mainstream press that Kayambis had been actors and that the government considered them a serious threat to its hegemonic control. It is particularly surprising that no previous mention had been made of Jesús Gualavisí, who had played a leading role in the organization of the congress in his home community of Juan Montalvo. When the newspapers finally mentioned his name, unlike the others they omitted his first name and misspelled his last name. Racial stereotypes led the press to stress the actions of urban leftists, while making the actions of the Indigenous activists invisible. A lasting legacy of the press reports is a warped understanding of the role of communists in Ecuador's modern Indigenous movements.

Improvements in infrastructure also made rural communities more susceptible to repressive instruments of state power. During the nineteenth century, there was little communication or trade between different regions. For example, when Eloy Alfaro gained control of the presidency in 1895, he had never previously set foot in the capital city of Quito. In 1911, traveler Harry Franck met people who had never visited neighboring population centers, who had no reason to make the journey, and who were surprised that it was actually possible to do so.[38] Until the 1920s, only an old, dangerous mule trail linked Cayambe with the capital city of Quito, and it took three days to deliver agricultural produce to market. The only telegraph office in the canton was located in the city of Cayambe, and the national network of post offices did not extend throughout the entire canton.[39] This isolation encouraged a degree of self-sufficiency and autonomy in political negotiations between haciendas and Indigenous communities. The central state apparatus was a distant and almost irrelevant structure, and protest was far removed from the public eye.

By the late 1920s under the July Revolution's newly centralized governmental control, the communication infrastructure extended into Ecuador's remotest corners. On July 9, 1928, the government inaugurated a 110-kilometer stretch of railroad that linked Cayambe with Quito, and a year later the railroad reached the northern city of Ibarra.[40] Unlike elsewhere in Latin America, the purpose of the railroad was not to provide for an extractive export economy, but rather it was designed "to boost national integration and governmental authority as well as economic growth."[41] For elites, new infrastructure developments like railroads were symbols of progress and modernity; for subalterns, they often represented little more than the imposition of foreign capital and the undermining of local autonomy. Since the colonial period, Indians had revolted against labor drafts for such projects, while elites feared these threats to their modernizing projects.[42]

Roads improvements, particularly in what later became the Pan-American highway, facilitated access to Quito by automobile, which made Cayambe less of an isolated provincial city.[43] Thus Cayambe began to lose "its primitive aspect," and what had been a grueling two-day trek on foot to Quito had slowly evolved into a simple eighty-kilometer bus ride that by the 1950s took only three hours and cost seven sucres (about fifty cents).[44] With these improvements, it was easier for the government to send in troops to quell revolts and to extract leaders to Quito where they would stand trial for sedition.

Infrastructure developments had another unforeseen consequence. Writing in a similar situation in Peru in 1929, Mariátegui noted that the closed nature of the traditional hacienda made it very difficult for union organizers to reach agricultural workers. The increase in automobile traffic opened "a breach in the barriers that keep the haciendas closed to political propaganda." Improvements in transportation played directly into Mariátegui's organizational strategy. "When the peones on the hacienda know that they can count on the fraternal solidarity of the unions," Mariátegui stated, "the will to struggle that is missing today will easily be awakened."[45] Rosenthal notes that transport workers carried a revolutionary spirit into sleepy rural towns and helped awaken political protests.[46] Similarly in Ecuador, contact with urban leftists helped lend strength and public exposure to previously isolated Indigenous struggles on haciendas.[47] Perhaps the most threatening aspect of communist involvement in Indigenous communities was not that they would instigate revolts, but that their support gave protests visibility and sustainability that exceeded the capability of the government to contain.

Marches to Quito

Indigenous activists realized that altering Ecuador's land tenure system would require more than localized individual actions. It necessitated taking demands directly to the seat of power. So, they began to walk, often barefoot with women carrying babies on their backs, to Quito for meetings and protests. Similar to what Seth Garfield observed with the Xavante in Brazil, bringing struggles for land and rights to the seat of governmental power inverted the process of the insertion of state power into rural communities. These actions irrevocably changed the government's notions of nation-state formation, as well as Indigenous political economies and ethnic identities.[48] The first recorded march to Quito occurred on March 10, 1931, barely a month after the government shut down the peasant congress in Juan Montalvo, when 141 Indians left Pesillo for Quito. They first walked to the town of Cayambe to sleep and left from there at 3 AM. At noon they rested at Guayllabamba, reaching Calderón by nightfall. The activists arrived in Quito the following morning, where they faced various obstacles including logistical problems of where to stay and what to eat. Many Kayambis were unschooled, monolingual Kichwa speakers. Petitions to the government were to be written in Spanish and presented in a specific legal format. The issue was not a question of intelligence, the conceptualization of issues, or the mapping out of political strategies; rather, it was a pragmatic concern of how to overcome cultural and language barriers to present demands to the government.

Previously the tinterillos had provided this mediation with the government, but they were not necessarily sympathetic to Indigenous demands. Now, subalterns turned to urban leftists for assistance in pressing a more explicitly political project. Urban labor organizations had constructed a Casa del Obrero ("Worker's House") on the Plaza del Teatro in central Quito as a meeting place and training center for those interested in social justice.[49] Indigenous activists commonly used it as a gathering place, and they would stay there anywhere from a few days to a month when they came to the capital to participate in protests or to petition the government. Osvaldo Albornoz Peralta views this support from urban labor unions as "one more step in the creation of a worker-peasant alliance."[50] In Quito, as in the countryside, leftist logistical support proved important in advancing an Indigenous agenda.

Urban leftists assisted in drafting petitions and presenting demands to the government. The lawyer Luis Felipe Chávez—founder of the PSE and the father of Luis Fernando Chávez who had helped organize the congress in Cayambe—not only provided the marchers with housing in Quito but also pressed for their rights with government officials. He convinced the JCAP director Egas to arrange a meeting between the Kayambis and the president of the republic, and to force the renters of the government's haciendas to raise their salaries five centavos. Unfortunately, success was not guaranteed. Rather than consenting to this agreement, Egas sent the Indians to the police who arrested them and forcibly returned them to Cayambe. In the process, the police injured several Indians including Virgilio Lechón, Rosa Catujuamba, and a boy named José Amaguaña.[51]

In addition to alliances with urban leftists, the marches to Quito also highlight the gendered nature of Indigenous protest movements. Of the 141 Kayambis who participated in the 1931 march, 57 were women and they brought along about 12 children. Tránsito Amaguaña made twenty-six such trips.[52] Women's active involvement at the forefront of these movements was not unusual, with women commonly pressing their husbands to become more involved.[53] Unlike the stereotypical male guerrilla fighters, these women were not young, unattached single militants who could act with little thought as to the consequences of their actions. They were mothers and grandmothers with deep roots in their communities, which became a significant factor in pushing them to action. For centuries they and their ancestors had suffered abuses from hacendados, and now they—along with their male relatives—faced eviction and imprisonment at the hands of the central government. Rather than condemning their descendants to the same fate, they (as Subcomandante Marcos of the Zapatista rebels in southern Mexico would say at the end of the twentieth century) "bet the present to have a future."[54] Indigenous women fought for their rights not because they had nothing to lose but because they had everything to gain.

Despite public claims of calm in Cayambe, persistent unrest compelled the military to retain control. In the face of ongoing repression, committed activists were determined to continue their protests as long as economic exploitation and racial discrimination persisted. Egas noted that Indigenous demands were becoming more radical, and perhaps as a result of the peasant congress they would now be happy with nothing less than a full-fledged program of agrarian reform.[55] Indigenous peoples questioned global structural inequalities, and the military perceived a need to implement a permanent "solution" to the problem.

On March 19, 1931, Egas and Major Ernesto Robalino, the head of the military garrison in Quito, traveled to Cayambe to study the situation. Egas called the workers "insolent and lazy," and he blamed problems on "communist agents who had ingrained in the Indians the idea that the haciendas are theirs." In a later private report to the anti-communist minister of government Albornoz, Egas claimed that the Indians were at "a very low level of human inferiority." No renter, he continued "could meet the capricious desires of the Indians, or rather those of the communists." Egas described the "Pesillo Indians as very rich with no need to work for someone else because their huasipungos and animals provide all their necessities." In fact, "the Indians should pay the hacienda" for the resources they used. Even the soldiers who occupied the hacienda were jealous of the Indians' wealth, and their situation "would be desirable for any proletariat who earns two to five sucres in the city." Egas reported that the Indians begged to stay on the hacienda, "alleging that they had been born there and did not have anywhere else to take their cattle." Pesillo's problems were due to a few communist lawyers stirring up trouble. Within the tiny communist group, Egas concluded, "there is only one, maybe two, men who are truly idealist and sincere and the rest are violent and impulsive people without knowledge of our social reality."[56]

Egas criticized the press for overstating the importance of the conflict. "The situation in Cayambe is calm," he proclaimed, "and only here in Quito is it exaggerated with national dimensions being assigned to a merely local affair." At the same time, playing on elite fears, Egas declared that without swift action Cayambe faced a serious threat of a *revolución comunista indígena*, "Indigenous communist revolution."[57] Local activists rejected these attempts at red-baiting. The uprising was "not instigated by communists," a group of more than one hundred Kayambis finally responded in a letter to the daily newspaper *El Día*; rather, it was "the cry of hunger, of misery; the clamor against inhumane and merciless treatment." The Kayambis reiterated a litany of ongoing abuses that Egas had disregarded as insignificant, while at the same time scorning the director's depiction of them as wealthy. It was not necessary to be a communist to protest this injustice, but Egas had made these charges "only to disadvantage our cause."[58]

Across Ecuador, elites repeatedly blamed communists for inciting Indigenous uprisings, as Alfredo Cordovez Bustamante did when the community of Simiatug protested on his Tanlahua hacienda in Bolívar. Albornoz Peralta retorted that this "ghost of communism" that landowners employed to pull in government forces to defend their class interests merely indicated that "the communists were tied to the defense of the rights of exploited peasants."[59] And this appeared to be ever increasingly the case. In Otavalo, the teniente político of the González Suárez parroquia arrested the socialist leaders Ricardo Paredes, Luis Maldonado, Luis Chavéz, and César Endara and expelled them to Quito for attempting to establish contacts with local Indigenous communities.[60]

Evictions

In the face of growing protest, Egas remained determined to crush Indigenous resistance. He had long advocated eviction of Indigenous leaders as a solution to problems on haciendas. In September 1930 and again in January 1931, Egas recommended that a police detachment be sent to Pesillo to expel Virgilio Lechón and other troublesome leaders. Egas declared that the rights of agricultural workers were not protected under existing labor laws, so the Indians could be evicted without any legal formalities.[61]

Finally, Egas got his wish. Arguing that only those Indians who worked had the right to remain on the hacienda and that those who did not wish to work were free to leave, Egas convinced Minister of Government Albornoz to have the police forcibly evict the leaders.[62] Pesillo's renter Delgado responded that expelling the leaders had "magnificent results," with quiet finally returning to the hacienda. He profusely thanked the government for coming to his defense.[63] Egas reported that the troublemakers willingly left, with the hacendados graciously allowing them to keep their possessions. The Indigenous activists, however, described an entirely different scene. While Egas told El Comercio that "there had been a need to dismiss nine leaders," activists counted about twenty-six affected by the order.[64] As a small boy, Neptalí Ulcuango watched the soldiers come and destroy the

Indians' dwellings. They ripped the thatched roofs off huts, dumped stored grain on the ground, and burned everything. Rather than showing fear, Ulcuango's grandmother Rosa Alba grabbed a stick and called on the others to chase the soldiers away. The soldiers overpowered her and demanded Ulcuango's father to reveal where he had stored the guns. When he responded that he didn't have any weapons, they swore at him, tied him up by his thumbs, and beat him with their rifles.[65] The soldiers drove the leaders, together with their wives and children, off the hacienda, although they allowed the radicals to keep their cattle and personal belongings.

The military also evicted another young boy, Luis Catucuamba, the son of Dolores Cacuango. The soldiers targeted his house because they wanted to capture Cacuango in order to imprison or even kill her. Cacuango, however, escaped and went into hiding. She became "nomadic, wondering, restless." Catucuamba remembered his family crying as the soldiers tore their house apart, destroying their possessions, wondering if they would ever see their mother again. The Yaguachi army squadron destroyed about twenty-six houses in Moyurco, San Pablourco, and Pesillo, and the impact extended far beyond individual leaders.[66]

Evicting the primary leadership represented a strategic setback both for the Indigenous communities as well as their urban colleagues, and an entrenchment of elite landholder power. Some of the expelled activists moved to the town of Olmedo. Many settled as landless *apegados* ("stuck-on") alongside the road between Cayambe and Olmedo at Yanahuaico (later called Santa Rosa). Several years later Cacuango joined the radicals there, and together they continued their organizing efforts in exile.[67] Tránsito Amaguaña also went into exile in Yanahuaico, and it was twelve years before her family again set foot on their native soil. During this time, she never gave up the struggle.[68] Prieto notes that the strike allowed rural activists "to identify more clearly their allies and enemies." Despite the alleged neutrality of local political leaders and government institutions, both acted on the behest of the landholding classes. On the other hand, the socialists emerged as strong allies of rural Indigenous workers.[69] Furthermore, expulsions spread the radicals' influences and fostered the emergence of new leadership in their former communities. The urban communist militant Nela Martínez later noted how watching her house burn with her three children converted the thirty-eight-year-old Cacuango from a mother of a small family to "the mother of her people," a "hunter of the future" who awoke a consciousness and demanded action to strengthen and advance the

Dolores Cacuango's house, 1968. Photo by Rolf Blomberg.
Courtesy of the Archivo Blomberg, Quito, Ecuador.

work of the Indigenous syndicates.[70] "Close to the haciendas but outside of their direct control," Prieto observes, "Yanahuaico became the center of the Communist Party operations." Clandestinely entering the haciendas at night, Cacuango and others met with Indigenous workers, formed a party apparatus, and trained new leaders.[71]

Why were activists so distressed over losing their huasipungo plots, which, in reality, represented the fundamental exploitative nature of labor relations on haciendas? Why did Indians subsequently fight to recover their positions on haciendas? As Icaza vividly portrayed in *Huasipungo,* workers became very attached to their small plots and revolted if landowners took them away. Icaza's novel ends on a very emotional note, with the Indians chanting in Kichwa "¡Ñucanchic huasipungo! ¡Ñucanchic huasipungo!"[72] Indians treasured their plots for both cultural and economic reasons, and they were willing to work for lower wages in order to have access to land.[73] According to Aníbal Buitron, this was due to a great love for the land that flowed in their blood. It was a central part of Indigenous culture and ethnic heritage.[74]

A development study in Chimborazo revealed that 95 percent of the Indigenous workers were unwilling to move to another area where more land was available, no matter how much land they might receive there. "We cannot go to another part," one person stated. "The women would die from sorrow."[75] The historian Arnold Bauer notes that "the ultimate threat against unsatisfactory tenants was often dismissal from the hacienda."[76]

The historian Charles Gibson discovered that during the colonial period Indians sometimes remained on haciendas because they could enjoy a better lifestyle there than they would in *obrajes* (textile sweatshops), mines, or independently working their own land. "The hacienda, for all its rigors," Gibson concluded, "offered positive advantages to Indian workers."[77] Others have concurred with Gibson that haciendas provided their workers with a degree of economic security. Bauer, in particular, pushed historians to move beyond interpreting labor relations on haciendas as oppressive and counter to the interests of an Indigenous peasantry. Noting that debt and bondage are independent and separate concepts, Bauer contends that peasants could manipulate credit arrangements to their own benefit. While it was rare for urban workers to be paid in advance, hacienda workers received a significant amount of their salary up front. Although workers left haciendas for a variety of reasons (interpersonal conflicts, poor working conditions, or to search for better opportunities elsewhere), they would be hesitant to do so voluntarily because it would mean losing their line of credit with the hacendado.[78]

It is little wonder that Indians clung so desperately to their places on haciendas. Losing a huasipungo meant eviction from their home community and a loss of support networks, survival strategies, and land that was the core of their being. Friedrich Hassaurek observed that when there was a large demand for labor, a worker would make "an arrangement with his new master before he left the old one," and "some Indians are shrewd enough to do this to their advantage."[79] Landowners understood this, and used the small plots to tie workers to the hacienda and prevent them from migrating out of the region (with the threat of never returning) during the slow season. Increasingly elites leveraged more control over their workers. "Peasants, in truth," as Peloso notes, "always were at a disadvantage in the contract and they undoubtedly knew it." Furthermore, he points to these contracts as "the key to legitimacy and power on the plantations."[80] During the nineteenth century as expanding haciendas eroded the land base of surrounding Indigenous communities, the peasants' range of options became more limited than had been the case in the colonial period and the degree of coercion increased.

After the evictions from Pesillo, Delgado promised Egas that "the rest of the Indians will be content, will cease revolting, and more than anything will stop being deceived by people who only try to exploit their ignorance."[81] The expulsions, however, triggered another protest march to Quito. Representing a virtual "who's who" of Indigenous protest in Cayambe in the 1930s, a total of 127 Kayambis including such well-known activists as Virgilio Lechón and Dolores Cacuango made the trek. In Quito, Chávez again helped draft a legal appeal to the government citing physical beatings, Delgado's failure to allow the evicted leaders to keep their cattle and personal possessions, and a failure to respect the length of the work week. At the end of May, out of frustration but somewhat prophetically, Egas stated that "we will never be done with these little incidents."[82]

With the failure of repressive policies to destroy the incipient Indigenous movement, the government engaged in alternative strategies. The Ministry of Government and Social Welfare proposed to create local Committees for the Defense of the Indigenous Race to investigate and resolve land conflicts between Indians and landlords. The committee would be comprised of the local jefe político, a hacendado, and an Indian designated by the government. This committee would review the situation of the Indians, including schooling, land, salaries, and unpaid work obligations. The committees were charged with reporting monthly on these affairs to the Ministry.[83] Despite the apparently positive nature of this development, the Indians interpreted it as an attempt to spy on their organizational efforts. Under government control, this committee would act against the interests of the Indians. Naturally, the Indians rejected such attempts to subvert their organizational efforts. Without their support, the committees were a failure. Over the following decades, Indigenous communities consistently rejected government initiatives as conflicting with their own interests.

Even after the first three months of 1931 when rural protest actions in Cayambe repeatedly made front-page headline news, Indigenous unrest continued. In August, Paredes and Maldonado once again were in Cayambe helping to organize an uprising of about five hundred Indians.[84] The following March, Julio Miguel Páez, the renter of the Moyurco hacienda, informed the Ministry of Government that Antonio Lechón, one of the workers who had left the hacienda more than a year earlier, had returned and attempted to claim a piece of land as his personal huasipungo. Páez's employees on the hacienda refused to let Lechón work, and as a result "the rest of the peons have abandoned their work and are in insurrection." Páez asked the government to send a military squadron to reestablish order on the hacienda.[85] The government quickly sent in troops to suppress the strike and accused four Indians (Marcelo Tarabata, Carlos Churuchumbi, Antonio Lechón, and José Quishpe) of leading the revolt. The soldiers and hacienda employees rounded up the four workers' animals and placed them in a corral. They then entered their houses, confiscated all of their belongings (grain, clothes, and the few utensils that they owned), and dumped everything into a pile on the patio of the hacienda. They padlocked the houses to prevent the families from returning, and took the four protestors to jail in Quito. By this time the four had reputations as troublemakers. The government had identified Tarabata as a leader of the strike the previous year and had taken him to face criminal charges in Quito. The government accused these activists of not working on the hacienda and of engaging in no other activity than leading uprisings.[86]

In June 1935, landowners in Cayambe again reported that communist leaders were planing a massive strike. Heriberto Maldonado, the renter of the Pisambilla and Carrera haciendas, denounced these acts as the work of the "five known instigators" Rubén Rodríguez, Manuel Canizares, Max Alvares, Alejandro Torres, and Jesús Gualavisí. Of the five, only the last one (Gualavisí) was Indigenous. Rodríguez, a well-known and respected white leftist leader in Cayambe, became one of the Indians' most important allies.[87] Torres had previously been arrested in January 1931 when he came to Cayambe from Quito to help organize the peasant congress.[88] Although local leaders were acquiring the skills necessary to press forward with their struggles, urban marxists remained dedicated to supporting them. These socialists were the only ones willing to bring Indigenous concerns to the halls of power. They saw Indigenous demands as integral and even critical to the success of the larger class struggle.

Unrest in Cayambe set the stage for protests throughout Ecuador. *El Comercio* described an uprising for land in April 1931 at the Quinuacorral hacienda in Guaranda as "almost equal to Cayambe" with the threat of a "true communist movement." As in Cayambe, the government sent in troops to suppress the uprising and to prevent it from spreading to other haciendas.[89] Arcesio Paz, owner of the Quilolumba hacienda in Latacunga, sent a panicked telegram to Minister of Government Albornoz that agitators were stirring up ten thousand Indians to attack his property.[90] The following year at Palmira, Indians protested against the expropriation of community lands for railroad construction. Again, the government sent in the police to squash the uprising.[91] And yet the tidal wave of rural protest continued. The community of Pastocalle in Cotopaxi protested against soldiers conducting a topographical survey in their community. In 1933, members of the Agricultural Association of Sanancajas in Tungurahua revolted against the owners of the Mochapata hacienda in defense of their lands. At Rumipamba in Imbabura in 1934, Indigenous activists demanded lands that the owners of the La Magdalena hacienda had confiscated from them. At Cusubamba in Cotopaxi, Indigenous peoples protested against abuses by the employees on the La Compañía and Atocha haciendas. At Salinas in Bolívar, community members revolted against the Matiavi hacienda for access to land.[92] It was as if the Pesillo strike had opened the floodgates for workers on other haciendas to express their discontent.

Ambrosio Lasso

Many of the details of these 1930s uprisings are lost to history, but several stand out for their lasting influence on Indigenous movements in Ecuador. One of these was a 1935 strike at the Licto hacienda in Chimborazo that pushed Ambrosio Lasso into the limelight as an important Indigenous leader. The Licto, Galte, and Pull hacienda owners had increased the number of days that each huasipunguero worked from four to six, thus reducing the available time for Indians to tend to their own small plots. These increased work requirements undermined survival strategies and threatened the workers with starvation. Rather than listening to Indigenous demands, the landowners imprisoned the workers—including men, women, children, and the elderly. Lasso reported that the landowners burned his hut along with those of others, and he had received death threats for his work with the Pull peasant syndicate. Lasso came to Quito to report these abuses, and he even met with President José María Velasco Ibarra, but nothing came of promises to solve these problems. Upon returning to Pull, authorities imprisoned and tortured Lasso.

With the situation deteriorating, and without any apparent legal redress, workers on the Licto hacienda revolted in February 1935. Armed with sticks and machetes, they took over hacienda buildings and kidnapped the employees. A newspaper report claimed that "the uprising was secretly organized by certain agitators surely from the city of Riobamba." Playing off racial and gendered fears, the report emphasized that Indian men had kid-napped the wives and children of white employees on the hacienda. Police repression was swift and fierce, with authorities killing three Indigenous workers and imprisoning others. The hacienda owner Nicolás Vélez Merino claimed not to know what triggered the uprising but assumed that it was the result of the actions of "ignorant agitators." Albornoz Peralta points out, however, that Vélez Merino had kept his workers in feudalistic conditions, and despite legal petitions to the hacendado, authorities, and even President Velasco Ibarra, the Indians had not been able to find justice. After waiting fruitlessly for months, the workers finally went on strike only to be "re-pressed in the most bloody and savage way possible by the police placed in the unconditional service of the landholders."[93]

In response to the massacre, Rosendo Naula and Ricardo Paredes led a Communist Party delegation to meet with Velasco Ibarra. They brought a statement that denounced abuses and called for a right to assemble peace-fully and to strike; an end to feudal conditions including the practices of huasicamas, diezmos, and primicias; an increase in salaries; access to pasture land; and freedom for those detained during the protests. The leftist author Joaquín Gallegos Lara published a front-page article in *Ñucanchic Allpa* de-nouncing actions "against the movement of Indian liberation," and he called on writers, artists, intellectuals, women, workers, and others to launch a campaign to defend Lasso and his fellow activists. Gallegos Lara blamed Velasco Ibarra's policies for being indirectly responsible for this repression.[94] The PCE energetically protested when Velasco Ibarra subsequently named Vélez governor of Chimborazo.[95] As Albornoz Peralta observes, the bour-geois did not grant concessions freely but did so only as a result of intense organization and continued agitation.[96]

Although Lasso survived the 1935 massacre, the president imprisoned him on the Galapagos Islands. There, he learned to read and write. Recognizing his valor, the PCE included him as an honorary member in their congress in December. With his improved literacy skills and increased determination, Lasso returned to Chimborazo where he became a community organizer, traveling door to door talking with Indigenous workers about their experi-ences of abuse and exploitation. As a badge of success, the following year he was named one of the main leaders in an alleged communist uprising against the government. In 1938, Indigenous workers at Pull once again revolted against the monopolization of land and abuses at the hands of the local landowners and governmental authorities. Lasso continued working for decades in neighboring communities for an end to abuses on the haciendas, better pay and working conditions, and a right to land. Through his leadership Lasso became known as the "Colonel," and his organizing skills put fear into elites. The government worried that unless abuses stopped on the neighboring hacienda of San Martín, the Indigenous workers "would do the same as what they did in Pull." Gallegos Lara called Lasso a "grandchild of Rumiñahui," who represented "the rebirth of the Quichua spirit."[97] Lasso represents a leftist activist who bridged urban and rural struggles, and his work points to a recognition that marxists had for the important role of ethnicity in popular movements.

Legislative Reforms

Although elites excluded Indians from a direct and active role in political deliberations and popular pressure, and the growing strength of leftist parties provided a major mobilizing force behind 1930s legislative reforms. Initially representing a swing to the left, Federico Páez took power in the aftermath of a 1935 military coup that deposed the perennial populist president José María Velasco Ibarra for the first of five times. Páez appointed socialists to the Ministries of Social Welfare and Education as well as to lesser posts, and he indicated that he would quickly implement extensive social reforms.[98] He also promulgated legislation to address persistent problems of economic underdevelopment and social inequality.

Páez drafted a 1936 labor law that created a special office for the "tutelage and defense of the Indigenous worker" to administer legal petitions related to work, salaries, and relations with employers.[99] The 1936 Ley de Tierras Baldias y Colonización (Empty Land and Colonization Law) attempted to solve land tenure problems, but rather than breaking up haciendas and giving the estates to landless agricultural workers, it opened up unused territory for settlement. Although Páez advocated resettling landless peasants on public lands, he did not want to use JCAP haciendas for this purpose. "To break up the estates," he argued, "would produce a disruption and agricultural crisis with fateful results for the country's economy." Reforms had to be done slowly. "Social evolution: yes; social revolution: no," he emphasized.[100] From the left, his socialist allies pressed for deeper reforms. At its third congress in 1936, the PSE advocated expropriating hacienda lands to form agricultural cooperatives and to reestablish Indigenous communities. Reflecting a certain amount of paternalism and assimilationist tendencies, the party demanded legislation to govern rural communities that would "respect the Indian and montuvio problem, elevating their economic, social, and political condition until they are effectively incorporated into the national life."[101] In the end, Páez's legislation failed to address underlying structural conditions and ultimately did little to improve the lives of Indigenous peasants.

While at first Páez had implemented moderately progressive legislation, when leftists pressed for deeper reforms he refused and became more dictatorial—finally outlawing the Communist Party in November 1936. One of the primary examples of his move to collapse independent leftist organizing efforts was the 1937 Ley de Organización y Regimen de Comunas (commonly called the Ley de Comunas or Law of Communes). This legislation provided a new level of organization to govern rural communities in order to improve their social, moral, intellectual, and material development. The paternalistic intent of this law is apparent: the government claimed the right and obligation to protect and tutor rural communities, and the authority to modify or reject leadership and organizational structures that were not to its liking.[102] A goal was to control peasant organizations in order to shield them from the influence of more radical social movements, and to undercut the strength of existing rural organizing efforts. Even before the law was approved, the press reported that the legislative intent was to terminate litigation and protests that hacienda owners faced from Indigenous communities.[103] This strategy was largely successful as subsequent Indigenous movements emerged primarily on haciendas not subject to this legislation. Indigenous communities that formed comunas tended not to be centers of militant activism. Activists criticized attempts to divide and control Indigenous organizing efforts. Nevertheless, as is often the case, subalterns were able to subvert the intent of the legislation and eventually used it to gain more rights including access to land.[104]

Shortly after promulgation of the comuna law, General Alberto Enríquez Gallo overthrew Páez. Enríquez proceeded to abolish the most repressive aspects of Páez's legislation, including implementing new statutes designed to salvage positive aspects of the comuna law.[105] Labor unions used this political opening to win passage of a progressive 1938 Labor Code that established a minimum wage, an eight-hour workday, and the right to organize and strike. An entire section of the law was dedicated to agricultural labor, but often it did little more than codify what was already custom or common practice within labor relations between landowners and agricultural workers. In rural areas with an isolated and largely nonliterate work-force, hacendados could conveniently ignore many of its more progressive aspects. Nevertheless, activists sought to take advantage of elements of the code governing labor conflicts and collective agreements.[106]

Indigenous organizations did not hesitate to utilize provisions of the Labor Code to win concessions from hacienda owners. For example, pro-mulgation of the code quickly and dramatically changed the nature of the discourse and demands of agricultural workers on the Zumbahua hacienda. Caught in seemingly endless conflict, the socialist lawyer Gonzales Oleas chastised the hacendado General Francisco Gómez de la Torre for firing the Indigenous workers Mariano Pallo and Francisco Ante "for having re-quested the elimination of the free huasicamia service and using animals to fertilize fields, demands which Article 263 of the Labor Code forbids." They also "demanded the elimination of the forced purchase of crops, animals, and other belongings of the peons, traditions which Article 263 of the Labor Code also outlaws."[107] In 1940, sixty-seven workers (both male and female) on the Pesillo hacienda protested Labor Code violations to the Ministry of Labor. The protest was not in vain. The ministry acknowledged that Article 253 of the Labor Code gave agricultural workers the right to cut firewood and pasture animals on the hacienda. Furthermore, the ministry informed local officials of these laws so that they would respect the rights of the Indigenous peoples.[108]

Indigenous activists also used provisions of the Labor Code to force modifications in traditional labor relations on haciendas. On January 5, 1944, the Ministry of Labor notified the Guachalá hacienda of four violations of the Labor Code—underpayment of wages, length of the workday, nonpay-ment for the labor of a huasipunguero's wife and family, and mistreatment in word and deed. The labor inspector stated that "only huasipungueros are obliged to work on the hacienda, because it is they who have contracted their services and therefore they are the ones who must comply with their personal obligations with the owner. In no case can huasipungueros' fami-lies be required to work." If these family members worked, the inspector concluded, they must be paid their legally due and just salary.[109] This re-quirement was not only a change from tradition, but it also struck at the very root of the large profits that the hacienda could hope to gain from its Indigenous workforce. In contracting a huasipunguero, the hacienda owner fully expected to be able to access the free labor of the worker's wife and children. A worker without such a family was worth only half as much to a hacienda. Women could not inherit huasipungo plots, which ensured that they remained attached to a male and could be called on to provide free labor on the hacienda, including personal huasicama service. If the hacienda owner could not utilize what essentially amounted to slave labor, there was less motivation to provide huasipungueros with plots of land, access to water, firewood, and pasture land as stipulated in a standard contract. Rather than holding to tradition, activists aggressively used this legislation to shape and determine the nature of their world.

Subaltern demands revealed an intimate knowledge of the details of this law, representing a success of urban labor activists in educating their rural counterparts. Leftist activists translated relevant sections of the law into Kichwa and published them in *Ñucanchic Allpa*.[110] Dolores Cacuango reportedly memorized and could quote extensive passages from the legislation. With the assistance of urban sympathizers and under the threat of revolt, rural workers utilized the code to force concessions from their employers. As Indigenous activists gained awareness of the new legislation that "defended the peasants, the Indian workers," hacienda owners had to be more cautious.[111] No longer could elites claim, like Egas had in 1931, that landowners could do whatever they wished to workers on the haciendas because the Labor Code did not apply to them.[112] Over the next several decades, rural activists would increasingly use this legislation to their advantage.

New Politics

The anthropologist Neil Harvey, in his study of peasant movements in Chiapas, Mexico, asks, "How do oppressed groups create spaces for not only contesting their material conditions but also the political and cultural discourses that reproduce their subordination?"[113] Indigenous movements provide an example of how subaltern groups break out of subordination. It is one thing to organize locally to resolve a land dispute with a hacienda owner or to gain better working conditions and wages; it is a different matter altogether if an organization's goals include effecting changes on a national level. This is the fundamental difference between colonial and nineteenth-century Indigenous revolts, and the organizations that rural actors began to form in the 1930s. The goals these organizations embraced required interacting with a state apparatus, and this necessitated the accumulation of new skills.

Although urban leftists had provided Indians with inspiration, encouragement, and advice on how to pursue their struggles with the government, in

Statue of Rubén Rodríguez, a long-time leftist leader in Cayambe. Photo by Marc Becker.

the end it was the Indians themselves who were responsible for articulating their demands and concerns. While deeply influenced by marxism, the struggle remained overwhelmingly *Indigenous*. Despite entrenched racism in Ecuador, it did not become a racial struggle. Rather, it was a popular struggle against agrarian capitalism that had concentrated the wealth of the country in the hands of a small elite. Indigenous activists and urban marxists together imagined a more just social order, and one that reenvisioned social and ethnic divisions in the country.

The Kayambi leader Virgilio Lechón maintained that strikes were ultimately responsible for ending forced labor on the haciendas.[114] In the process of these struggles, the Indians began to lose their fear. "We quit hiding when the army showed up," Neptalí Ulcuango remembered. "We did not act violently toward them, but rather presented ourselves as an organized and disciplined force." With this presence of mind, the Indians began to achieve some of their objectives.[115] The historian Galo Ramón observes that these rural actions "profoundly broke the hacendado system." Peasant actions permitted the leftist leader Rubén Rodríguez to be elected to Cayambe's municipal council, thus "tearing from the landlords' hands the absolute control which until that point they had maintained over regional power structures."[116] Rodríguez used this position to defend the rights of Indigenous peoples, helping to establish bilingual schools and advocating that Kichwa be made an official language. Indigenous actions had initiated a process of social change that could no longer be stopped.

Strike actions in the 1930s marked an important turning point in the history of Indigenous organizing efforts. For the first time, broad-based actions sought to shift political balances. Indigenous activists unified isolated local struggles and brought people into contact with their counterparts across Ecuador. Rural workers allied with urban leftists to press for political, economic, and social demands, which strengthened the presence of socialist and communist parties in rural areas. Increasingly during protest actions, as the anthropologist Kim Clark observed in Chimborazo, Indigenous workers claimed citizenship rights and demanded equal treatment from the central government.[117] These changes represented a significant step forward for Indigenous movements and set the stage for the creation of the first national Indigenous federation in Ecuador.

FOUR

Federación Ecuatoriana de Indios

On May 28, 1944, an uprising of workers, students, peasants, Indians, women, and lower-ranking military personnel overthrew the increasingly unpopular presidency of Carlos Arroyo del Río, bringing an end to the political hegemony that liberals had enjoyed since the 1895 liberal revolution. Masses of people flooded the streets in Guayaquil, Quito, Cuenca, and Riobamba to demand deep-seated reforms. Riding this wave of discontent, the populist caudillo José María Velasco Ibarra returned from exile to take office for the second of five times. The "Glorious May Revolution" was a time of euphoric optimism that seemed to signal the emergence of new social relations and the end of exclusionary state structures. Ecuador, one author observed, finally "was in the hands of its legitimate owners."[1]

This was a period of high expectations for deep changes. Leftists saw May 28 as the beginning of a marxist revolution. The next several months witnessed an explosion of organizing efforts as groups that had been prevented from gathering under Arroyo del Río's repressive government capitalized on this opening to forward their political agendas. Students, workers, women, peasants, Indians, and agriculturalists all held organizational meetings during the months of June to August. Most notably, labor leaders took advantage of this opportunity to organize the Confederación de Trabajadores del Ecuador (CTE, Confederation of Ecuadorian Workers) whose founding the previous government had obstructed. This powerful leftist trade union helped shape Ecuadorian politics over the next several decades.[2]

Among all of the other political organizing, Indigenous leaders met with labor leaders and leftist activists to form the Federación Ecuatoriana de Indios (FEI, Ecuadorian Federation of Indians). Although subsequently surpassed by other organizations, the FEI was the first successful attempt in Ecuador to establish a national federation for and by Indigenous peoples.[3] The federation stands out as a milestone in the history of Ecuador's popular movements. From the 1940s through the 1960s, it flourished as the main national organizational expression of highland Indigenous and peasant groups.

Conferencia de Cabecillas Indígenas

The 1944 FEI congress was the third attempt to organize Ecuador's rural population into a mass movement for social change. As recounted in the previous chapter, the military foiled the first attempt in 1931, but this did not stymie efforts to create such an organization. Several years later the Communist Party once again began to organize an Indigenous congress, contending that "in view of the actions of peasant and Indigenous struggles" such a meeting "could not be more timely or necessary." The congress would have the goal of assisting in the ideological formation of the Indigenous masses, which at the time the party found to be inadequate. Building a unified organization "should not only be reflected in a greater influence of the party over the Indian masses, but also in a better understanding of the necessary factors to accelerate the march of an agrarian anti-imperialist revolution."[4]

From an international perspective, the evolution of Indigenous organizing tactics might be seen as an outgrowth of Comintern policies. The 1935 Seventh Congress represented a turn away from an "ultraleft" and "sectarian" strategy of organizing class against class and toward a popular front strategy to fight the growing fascist threat in Europe. In pursuing political alliances with centrist forces, local parties moved away from insurrectionary and worker-peasant strategies that had previously helped fuel Indigenous uprisings. In studying a 1934 Mapuche uprising, the historian Olga Ulianova notes that this shift on an international level represented an end to the "first (and only) time in the history of Chilean communism that the possibilities of a revolution would be linked with the idea of an insurrectionary movement coming from the countryside."[5] In Mexico, changes in Comintern policies similarly led to a decline in worker-peasant alliances.[6] Ecuadorian communists, however, do not appear to have undergone such noted or dramatic shifts in strategies. A 1935 statement called for a popular front, but it addressed in much more detail Indigenous demands for land, higher salaries, and freedom of organization. "Your interests are our interests," the party declared. "Your blood is ours."[7] Many activists continued to collaborate along the lines that had led to their original alliances in the late 1920s. Even though no longer part of a grand international strategy, these years had a powerful influence on the growth and strength of rural radical movements in Ecuador. On the margins of Comintern control, Ecuadorians enjoyed relative freedom to design and chart a path to social revolution appropriate to their local realities. Over the next decades, rural and urban activists maintained these alliances to their mutual benefits.

In November 1935, Indigenous leaders gathered at the Casa del Obrero in Quito for the second attempt to create a regional or national organization. A flyer announcing the closing session of the Conferencia de Cabecillas Indígenas (Conference of Indigenous Leaders) stated that the activists had discussed their common problems and had compiled a list of demands to present to the government. Indicating that the nascent Indian movement was not isolated from broader protests, the flyer identified the conference as a "key moment in the movement for the emancipation of the working, peasant, and Indigenous masses of the country." Indians, the statement declared, "have demonstrated yet again that when organized they are perfectly conscious of their rights and are not criminals as they are sometimes described." The meeting frightened the elite, with the liberal newspaper *El Día* denouncing their "sensational accusations against abuses made by large landholders."[8]

On an ideological level and in terms of logistical support, the conference underscored the importance of the coalitions between urban leftists and rural Indians that first emerged with peasant syndicates in the 1920s. In the flyer announcing the meeting the use of the third-person form seems to indicate that it was written by non-Indians. "All of their petitions are just," it states, "because Indians only want bread, land, work, and freedom." The unnamed authors also point to the meeting's ideological affinity with the Communist Party. The conference celebrated the eighteenth anniversary of the triumph of the Russian Revolution, with two speakers discussing the gains that ethnic minorities and peasants had made under Soviet rule. At the closing session, the noted communist leader Ricardo Paredes discussed the creation of training schools for Indigenous leaders. The party leaders Primitivo Barreto and Joaquín Gallegos Lara also participated, with Alejandro Narváez explaining why workers should support the Indians.

Despite the impetus for a meeting of Indigenous leaders coming from the urban left, rural activists shared in the agenda. The Indigenous leader General Juan Sáenz led the meeting, and Jesús Gualavisí presented a resolution from the Comité de Defensa Indígena (Indigenous Defense Committee). Gualavisí emerged from the conference as the secretary-general of the Consejo General de Cabecillas Indios (General Council of Indian Leaders). Osvaldo Albornoz Peralta declared the conference to be a "success," providing the basis for realizing the objectives of the Indigenous movement and building future organizations.[9] In a note in the Indigenous newspaper *Ñucanchic Allpa* several months later, Gualavisí requested that syndicates, comunas, and Indigenous leaders contact him to receive information about, and help from, the new organization.[10] While not as well-organized as later federations, the Consejo supported local syndicates, organized several strikes on haciendas (efforts that largely met with failure), and occasionally published the *Ñucanchic Allpa* newspaper that elites complained created openings for leftists in rural areas.[11] Although this organization ultimately had a minimal lasting impact, it created the basis for future national organizations of rural workers.

Even with its limited activity, the meeting triggered an increase in Indigenous activism. A month later, a labor inspector complained that Gualavisí was stirring up the workers on the Carrera and Pisambilla haciendas in Cayambe, encouraging them to present complaints to his office.[12] The *Ñucanchic Allpa* newspaper was full of denouncements of abuses against Indigenous peoples, many of these on the government-owned haciendas in Cayambe. So many reports had come in that there was not enough space to publish them all.[13] These constant complaints led Minister of Government A. Aguilar Vazquez to complain that "Indigenous 'uprisings' against landowners are not uncommon events." He dismissed those who advocated for social revolution as nothing other than common criminals. "Certain saboteurs of the social order under the context of organizing and protecting Indigenous peoples," he wrote, manipulated "crassly ignorant people" engaged in illegal strikes. Constant vigilance, Vazquez asserted, was necessary to maintain order.[14]

Recognizing the unique ethnic and economic situation of Indians, the organization published a list of instructions in *Ñucanchic Allpa* to "unify and organize Indians for the defense of their class interests and oppressed nationalities." The organization noted that "the Indian workers have something else that differentiates them from other white, mestizo, black and mulatto workers and peasants: the Indians have languages that only they speak (Kichwa, Cayapa, Cofan, etc.), they have their own clothes and customs, they belong to their own races and nationalities or peoples that have lived free for more than four hundred years without being subjected as today to whites and mestizos. It is for this reason that Indians have been for more than four centuries subjected to a great oppression of their people or nationality, rejected as if they were an inferior race."[15]

Although by the 1980s the construction of *nacionalidades indígenas* had become common within Indigenous movements, in the 1920s the Comintern pioneered the conceptualization of Indigenous peoples as nations with their own language, traditions, culture, and territory.[16] A 1933 Comintern document repeatedly referred to African and Indigenous "oppressed nationalities" and advocated increased organization among "Indian and Negro peasant masses" in order to bring about a revolutionary movement.[17] The flyer for the 1935 Indigenous conference pointedly indicated the "freedom and help" that the Soviet Union extended "to all of the nationalities that before had been oppressed (as are the Indigenous nationalities in our country)."[18] A 1937 party document observes that backwardness, underdevelopment, and isolation prevented the emergence of a unified national identity in Ecuador, with an Indigenous "oppressed nationality" existing alongside that of the dominant white and mestizo classes.[19]

Activists were adamant, however, that this was not to be a racial struggle. In addition to emphasizing an identity from nationalities, the communists pushed agricultural workers to develop a class consciousness and join in a unified struggle with an industrial working class. "Indian peon workers," they said, "should never consider as their enemies the white, mestizo, black or mulatto workers or peasants, because they are also exploited by hacendados, capitalists and oppressed by the authorities."[20] Indigenous leaders reflected this ideology in their activism. In July 1943, Dolores Cacuango and her son Luis Catucuamba gathered a group of fifty people in Yanahuaico to form the first rural anti-fascist committee. The following month, Jesús Gualavisí organized a similar committee in Juan Montalvo. Both served as delegates to the Pichincha Provincial Anti-Fascist Conference held in Quito in September 1943, where they were singled out as a stimulating model for the rest of the country. Nela Martínez observed that "in Kichwa Cacuango and Gualavisí condemned the fascism that they already had experienced."[21] Racism was a very real force but whites were not the issue; instead, the problem resided in capitalist exploitation.

Luis Catucuamba, son of Dolores Cacuango and a leader of Indigenous schools in Cayambe from the 1940s to the 1960s. Photo by Marc Becker.

An article in *Ñucanchic Allpa* argued that Indigenous agricultural laborers and mestizo textile workers should join in a common struggle. "Your needs are ours," the newspaper declared. "We are pursuing the same objectives."[22] Indians engaged class issues without setting aside their ethnic identity, and, in fact, they used that identity as a vehicle to advance a broader economic and political agenda. C. L. R. James in his landmark 1938 study of the Haitian slave revolt noted that "the race question is subsidiary to the class question in politics, and to think of imperialism in terms of race is disastrous." James continued, however, to argue that "to neglect the racial factor as merely incidental is an error only less grave than to make it fundamental."[23] A similar ideology drove Indigenous organizations in Ecuador. The May Revolution provided a political opening for rural workers to come together with their urban compatriots to form the Federación Ecuatoriana de Indios as a platform to advance this struggle.

Federación Ecuatoriana de Indios (1944)

In July 1944, delegates from peasant syndicates traveled to Quito to join urban workers in founding the CTE. Activists placed Indigenous issues front and center on the labor federation's agenda. At the inaugural session, the communist leader Pedro Saad noted the significance of the participation of these "eternal pariahs of Ecuador's history." In turn, Cacuango gave a long speech in support of Saad for the presidency of the congress. Delegates warmly received her call to include Indigenous communities in the work of the congress and her eloquent defense of Indigenous aspirations for land and freedom.[24] Saad presented Jesús Gualavisí and Ambrosio Lasso to the congress. Lasso, "a leader of a powerful Indigenous insurrection against a former dictator," called on the congress to denounce abuses on the Tigua hacienda. The socialist party leader Juan Isaac Lovato presented a report on the "Indigenous problem," blaming four centuries of bad governments and a feudal landholding system for their "hunger, misery, ignorance, vices, and lack of aspirations." Lovato declared that improving the conditions of Indigenous peoples was a "sacred and inevitable" mission of the CTE. Land should be returned to them, not as private property but as collective farms or agricultural cooperatives. In addition, agricultural salaries should be raised and huasipungueros should receive title to their plots. Finally, using rather paternalistic language Lovato advocated liberating Indigenous peoples from "the exploitation of the teniente político, the priest, the tinterillo, and the curandero [natural healer]" since their backwardness had left them susceptible to such abuses. The CTE passed his proposals unanimously.[25]

The CTE announced plans to group all agricultural syndicates, peasant leagues or committees, Indigenous communities, and agricultural cooperatives into a Federación Nacional Campesina e India (National Peasant and Indian Federation).[26] A month later, activists returned to Quito to found this peasant wing of the CTE. The tone of the discourse and the outcome of the Primer Congreso Ecuatoriano de Indígenas (First Ecuadorian Indigenous Congress), however, were notably different from what the CTE had originally proposed. As would happen repeatedly, rather than letting outsiders organize them, Indigenous peoples overtook these efforts and pressed their own agenda.

Delegates who attended the August 1944 Indigenous congress at the Casa del Obrero came primarily from the northern and central highland provinces of Imbabura, Pichincha, Cotopaxi, and Chimborazo. Over the course of several days, Indigenous activists met and discussed problems and then drew up plans to address their concerns. Cacuango, Gualavisí, Vega, and Lasso presented reports on their work with their local organizations in Pesillo, Juan Montalvo, Tigua, and Chimborazo.[27] The congress approved a list of thirty-three demands that encompassed a broad range of issues, starting with an insistence for complete freedom of organization in Indigenous communities. It called for humane treatment on haciendas, abolishment of forced labor, creation of a Ministry of Indigenous Affairs, provision of adult education and schooling for Indigenous children, compliance with the Labor Code, and free medical treatment. Most of the demands addressed political and economic needs. Although they were framed as Indigenous concerns, none of the demands addressed specifically ethnic issues such as a defense of Indigenous cultures or languages. The presence of a pervasive racism, however, can be seen as underlying the entire document—especially in the cries for an end to abusive treatment and for the payment of minimum salaries that white landowners often refused their Indigenous workers.[28]

Most of the leaders at the founding of the FEI and those who subsequently provided leadership were from the Communist Party. According to César Endara, one of the founders of the PCE, "the party never stopped considering for a moment that a fundamental task was to organize the Indian movement." The result "of this huge force was the construction of the Ecuadorian Federation of Indians (FEI) in 1944."[29] This has led to a common assumption that the FEI "was not led by indigenous people but rather by the [Communist] Party" or that "urban mestizo intellectuals and a few indigenous activists" led the federation.[30] This misreading of the history of the FEI partially grows out of an assumption that the Communist Party, like other political parties of that era, was uniquely a phenomenon of urban elites. Indians, however, had a small but significant presence in the party. The communist militant Nela Martínez later wrote that for Gualavisí, Cacuango, Lasso, and Vega, "Marx was their best companion" and their hardships and protests need to be understood within that context.[31] Surveying the participation of activists in the founding of the FEI reveals that far from white domination to the exclusion of Indigenous activists, it was a shared space where Indians and whites, men and women, worked together to struggle for Indigenous rights.

Activists from Cayambe, where government officials had foiled the attempt to found its precursor in 1931, dominated positions of leadership at the 1944 congress. Delegates elected Gualavisí as president of the congress, Rubén Rodríguez as vice president, and Cacuango as treasurer. Of the congress' leaders, only the secretary (Carlos Bravo Malo) was not from Cayambe. Francisco Andrango further underscored the importance of Cayambe in a talk on the role of Kayambis in the May Revolution. Delegates selected Gualavisí as the new federation's first president and Cacuango as its secretary-general. Despite a stipulation in the federation's statutes that the headquarters for the executive committee be located in Quito, delegates decided to place it temporarily in Cayambe where Gualavisí and Cacuango lived. For much of the next decade, Cacuango dominated the organization. She was not alone, as especially on a local level other Indigenous women led organizations comprised primarily of men.[32]

At the congress' closing session in Teatro Sucre in downtown Quito, Matías Llanqui spoke on the situation of Indians in Ecuador, Ricardo Paredes summarized the efforts of the congress, and finally Cacuango welcomed Velasco Ibarra as the honorary president of the congress to close the meeting. The children's theater of the Unión Sindical de Pichincha (Syndicate Union of Pichincha) presented a "Social Hour" in homage to the delegates. Activists labeled the congress an event of transcendent historical importance, a significant advance in the struggles for Indigenous rights.[33]

The composition and ideological orientation of the FEI was in marked contrast to the Instituto Indigenista Ecuatoriano (IIE, Ecuadorian Indigenist Institute) that a prominent group of urban physicians, economists, sociologists, and lawyers had formed in Quito a year earlier. When the Mexican president Lázaro Cárdenas organized the 1940 Patzcuaro Congress out of which the IIE emerged, Ñucanchic Allpa asked why the Ecuadorian government was not sending any Indigenous delegates when they were building their own organizations and could represent themselves. "If they want to situate Indians in their appropriate place," the newspaper editorialized, "listen to their voice, the authentic voice of their race."[34] Whereas Indigenous women were in positions of leadership in the FEI, the IIE was comprised exclusively of white urban males, with the sociologist Pío Jaramillo Alvarado serving as the institute's first director and Leopoldo N. Chávez, minister of social welfare, as subdirector.[35] The IIE sought to establish a governmental Department of Indigenous Affairs to study Indigenous life and customs with the goal of using state structures to reform their lifestyle.[36] The FEI, on the other hand, emerging from a nongovernmental and subaltern perspective, advocated a much more radical agenda. Unlike the IIE, the FEI was a collaborative project that cultivated the active participation of Indigenous militants.

Although the IIE and the FEI emerged at the same time and confronted similar issues, they occupied two entirely separate spheres. They did not refer to each other in their publications, and no one was involved in both organizations. This division contradicts Roberto Santana's assertion that leftist activism on Indigenous issues emerged out of indigenista ideologies.[37]

Ecuador is also notably different from Peru where "indigenismo competed with an insurgent leftist rhetoric of class."[38] The activist, Indigenous-led nature of the FEI was too radical for the paternalist impulses of the indigenistas who founded the IIE. Larson notes a similar irony in Peru where moderate indigenistas presented a "view of the hapless and helpless Indian" while at the same time rural protests rocked the countryside.[39] In the end, indigenista organizing strategies that inevitably co-opted incipient community organizations remained weak in Ecuador. This permitted more political space for Indigenous leaders to coordinate their efforts, gain critical organizing experience, and agitate for real and significant social, political, and economic changes. Rather than being based in millenarian movements that glorified the Indian past or in indigenista rhetoric that objectified the Indian as an "other," Indigenous / socialist movements emphasized a specific, concrete structural analysis of society. Out of a weak indigenista movement a strong Indigenous movement emerged in Ecuador.

On the surface, the rhetorical use of the Spanish word *indios* in the name of the Ecuadorian Federation of Indians appears to be discordant with prevailing trends in public discourse in Ecuador. Over the course of centuries, the term "indio" had assumed strong negative and discriminatory connotations of being dirty, stupid, and generally not worthy of holding citizenship rights. Delegates at the Second Labor Congress in Quito in 1920 "resolved that labor organizations desist from using the term 'indio,' for it was demeaning to the nation's original inhabitants." Rather, they were to use "indígena," which was considered more respectful and proper.[40] In the 1940s, elite white intellectual indigenistas denounced the use of the term as insulting and offensive.[41] Initially the FEI was to be called the Federación Indígena Ecuatoriana or the Federación Indígena del Ecuador (Ecuadorian Indigenous Federation). Why would leaders change the organization's name to include an obviously stereotypical and negative label? In the 1990s it became common for Indigenous leaders in Ecuador as well as throughout the Americas to reappropriate the term "indio." In part, the use of this word parallels the emergence of a pan-Indian identity, and the recognition that in societies where identities were overwhelmingly local only colonial terms were available to describe the creation of new and broader constructs. In a "queering" of the language, activists maintained that since they were colonized with the term "indio," they would utilize it to gain their liberation. Given a history of racist oppression, appropriating hegemonic discourse tapped into deep popular resentment, made it counterhegemonic, and mobilized militant activism. Similar dynamics may have been at work in the 1940s. Alternatively, already in the 1935 meeting of Indigenous leaders, the terms "indios" and "indígenas" were used interchangeably and seemingly without ideological intent. Mercedes Prieto notes that varying terms for native peoples reflected the contested terrain of language, and that these identities were constructed for different purposes.[42]

Significantly, Indigenous activists also intentionally rejected the ethnically neutral term "campesino" (peasant) to describe their new organization. Rather than following the CTE's plans to found a National Peasant and Indian Federation, those gathered in the Casa del Obrero in August deliberately formed an *Indian* organization. The Peruvian peasant leader Hugo Blanco similarly reclaimed the term "indio," contending that "the simple act of exalting something Indian is already revolutionary." Doing so demonstrated that Indians "are a people with a personality and that we have the intention of seeing that that personality is respected."[43] Stressing the ethnic component challenged both liberal discourse that sought to engender a color-blind society as well as marxist dogma that emphasized class-based interpretations. Their hybrid approach underscores Alcida Rita Ramos's observation that "ethnic awareness, like class awareness, emerges from specific historical processes which can, in fact, initially converge with class."[44] In seemingly marching out of step with the prevailing intellectual trends of the day, the FEI broke new ground and contributed to the evolution of identity politics that would not be broadly recognized for another fifty years. Their position challenges what has become a commonly accepted dogma among academics that the FEI was a "principally class-based, and not explicitly ethnic-based" organization.[45]

Delegates to the FEI's founding congress drafted statutes that defined a popular program of social reform for the new organization. The federation sought to:

1. Gain the economic emancipation of Ecuadorian Indians;
2. Raise the Indians' cultural and moral level while conserving whatever is good in their native customs;
3. Contribute to national unity;
4. Establish links of solidarity with all American Indians.[46]

These goals reveal the founders' dramatic forward-looking ideologies on ethnic and economic issues, and they touch on themes that would become significant half a century later. The first goal indicated that the FEI would engage economic issues in the context of a class struggle but with a focus on an ethnic population. Although the document mentioned "national unity," it did not advocate the replacement of an Indigenous ethnic identity with a homogenized mestizo national identity. Rather, it called for a preservation of the uniqueness of Indigenous cultural identity. Unlike liberal assimilationist indigenista ideologies that contended that Indigenous identities needed to be suppressed in order to raise their economic standing in society, the FEI believed that ethnicity did not exclude economic development. Although the FEI was organizing a class struggle, it did not ignore the presence of racism or the importance of ethnicity. For example, in embracing a deep interest "in developing in Ecuador the handicraft arts of the Indians," the FEI announced a competition of Indigenous art for April 19, 1946, as part of the Inter-American Indian Day.[47] The strong presence of ethnic language and demands disrupts the carefully constructed academic models that point to an evolution from class-based organizations before the 1960s to ethnic federations in the 1970s and finally to ethnic nationalities in the 1980s, and it challenges assumptions that the FEI "did not have ethnic demands."[48] Ideologies of class, ethnicity, and nationality were all present to varying degrees at the founding of the FEI, with activists emphasizing different aspects to meet current needs and demands.

Fredrick Barth, in his groundbreaking work *Ethnic Groups and Boundaries*, notes how ethnicity results from a combination of self-identity and external proscriptions. Building on this notion, the sociologist Joane Nagel argues that people construct ethnic identities "for both material and symbolic purposes."[49] The organizational use of this language indicates a belief that ethnic identities could be used as a tool for political mobilization. Although the FEI couched its agenda in terms of Ecuadorian "Indians" and not peasants or a rural proletariat, many of their subsequent demands engaged common working-class concerns of raising salaries, shortening the work week, and ending forced labor for women. Added to this, agrarian reform—the most "peasant" of demands—quickly became the FEI's principal objective. One of the most significant outcomes of the federation was not an ideological shift on class issues but rather the consolidation and institutionalization of the Indigenous struggle.[50]

Rather than calling for an international working-class movement, the FEI's fourth goal indicates a consciousness of a pan-American Indian identity. Pan-Indianism is uniquely a phenomenon of the twentieth century, and the germ of this ideology is similar to that which had previously emerged in the

United States. The anthropologist Nancy Oestreich Lurie succinctly defines pan-Indianism as the diffusion of traits from tribe to tribe to the extent that these traits come to characterize virtually all Indian groups to some degree.[51] The anthropologist James Howard identifies five factors (racial discrimination, economic changes, intermarriage, urbanization, and education) that facilitated the emergence of pan-ethnic identities.[52] In Ecuador, similar factors brought previously isolated Indigenous peoples into contact with one another, and they came to see their shared problems, concerns, and aspirations. Lurie notes that this could result either in the watering down of Indian identity to the point that it becomes simply "an adjustive way station to the long predicted assimilation of Indians into the general society," or alternatively, it could be that intertribal activities "are part of a complex whole making up articulatory adaptations" that would reinforce an ethnic identity.[53] Rather than representing a last gasp of aboriginal consciousness before completely vanishing, the anthropologist Robert Thomas argues that pan-Indianism was "the expression of a new identity and the institutions and symbols which are both an expression of that new identity and a fostering of it. It is the attempt to create a new ethnic group, the American Indian." This new identity expressed itself in the political realm: "It is also a vital social movement which is forever changing and growing." It would create "a new identity, a new ethnic group, if you will a new 'nationality' in America."[54] Federal policies in the United States were intended to assimilate Indians into the dominant culture, but instead they triggered a political consciousness and mobilization.[55]

As activists discovered in the United States, working in a pan-ethnic setting often heightens a sense of local identity. Stephen Cornell argues that where Native Americans increasingly accepted an "Indian" identity, "tribal identifications remain at least as strong and usually stronger."[56] Nagel observes how scholars expected "traditional" forms of ethnic identity to disappear with the onslaught of modernization, but instead there was a resurgence of ethnicity resulting in heightened political activism.[57] In his study of the 1969 occupation of Alcatraz Island, Steve Talbot notes that increased pan-Indian political militancy led to "an inclination to studying one's tribal language, especially on the part of those not speaking it fluently."[58] Significantly, Alcatraz demonstrated that pan-Indian and local tribal identities are not necessarily contradictory impulses, but rather unified pan-Indian protest actions triggered a deeper interest in and appreciation for individual tribal cultures, languages, histories, and religions.

A similar phenomenon occurred in Ecuador. Urbanization and intermarriage brought different groups together. Schooling provided Indigenous peoples with tools of political analysis to critique their socioeconomic conditions, leading to a new cadre of leaders. Whereas previously an "Indian" had simply been a person from one's home community, coming into contact with other ethnic groups led to the development of a dual identity as an "Indian," both in a local sense and in a broader sense of being an "Ecuadorian Indian."[59] Rather than displacing local identities, the FEI helped strengthen, deepen, and politicize Indigenous consciousness.

As with pan-Indian organizations in the United States, the FEI grouped many different Indigenous groups under its umbrella. Its statutes indicated that it would be comprised of syndicates, comunas, cooperatives, cultural and Indigenous defense institutions, and *tribus* or tribes, a term rarely utilized in the Ecuadorian highlands but rather more commonly applied in the Amazon. Previous organizing efforts, as evidenced with the flourishing of peasant syndicates in Cayambe in the 1920s, had focused primarily on haciendas. The FEI's statutes indicate an intent to reach far beyond that narrow base. Particularly significant was the desire to expand its focus out of the highlands to make the federation a truly national organization operating within the context of an international struggle. Improvements in infrastructure brought isolated groups into contact with each other and fostered the formation of a pan-ethnic "Indian" ideology.

Similar Indigenous organizations emerged around this same time in other Latin American countries. In 1945, the National Indigenous Congress in La Paz, Bolivia, took advantage of recent political openings to provide a platform for over a thousand Indians to discuss common concerns. The congress was a politicizing experience that helped foster a pan-Indian identity, while at the same time invoking fear among the white residents of La Paz and sparking opposition from landowners and other local elites in the countryside. Many participants returned to their communities empowered to carry on the struggle, resulting (much like in Ecuador) in a period of renewed agrarian activism that seriously challenged the hacienda system.[60] In 1953 a group of Mapuches formed the National Association of Chilean Indians with an explicitly leftist orientation based on strong alliances with the Chilean Communist Party. The association sought to unify all Mapuches in a struggle for their emancipation that included ending racial discrimination, preserving Indigenous culture, regaining access to land, and elevating the economic, political, social, and cultural level of Chilean Indians.[61] These meetings proved to be critical in fomenting Indigenous awakenings.

In Ecuador, the Ministry of Social Welfare and Labor accepted the FEI's statutes with two small but politically charged changes that dealt a serious blow to the federation's intent to establish itself as the primary and exclusionary representative of all Indigenous peoples. First, the ministry narrowed the base of the new organization through the exclusion of comunas and by limiting membership to those syndicates, cooperatives, cultural institutions, and tribes that were present at the FEI's First Ecuadorian Indigenous Congress. Apparently the government hoped that as Indigenous communities formed comunas, the FEI would wither away and disappear. The strategy of siphoning off this organizational strength was somewhat successful. The FEI had a much weaker presence in areas where free Indigenous communities formed comunas than among workers on haciendas. Roberto Santana criticizes the FEI for focusing on wage laborers on haciendas where they believed they could foster a proletarian consciousness to the exclusion of a much more numerous comunero population, but this ignores governmental attempts to limit the new organization's reach.[62] Recognizing this as a critical weakness of the FEI, later organizations pointed to its narrow base as a reason why the FEI lost strength in the 1960s and new ethnic-based federations replaced it.

The ministry's second change eliminated the FEI's ability to name functional representatives for the "Indigenous Race" in the National Congress. Since implementation in the 1929 constitution, the paternalistic white outsiders who filled this position were not accountable to Indigenous organizations and often betrayed the interests of the Indians they were charged with defending. In claiming the right to name this delegate, the FEI attempted to position itself as the single central representative of all of Ecuador's Indigenous peoples. At its founding congress in August 1944, the FEI gained presidential permission to name this person, and the organization subsequently designated Ricardo Paredes to be its representative to the 1944–1945 National Constituent Assembly. Ñucanchic Allpa noted that Paredes, who had dedicated himself "to the cause of the oppressed masses, and in particular the Indian," was "elected democratically" to the post "in a direct and spontaneous vote by the delegates to the Indigenous Congress." The long-time activists Luis F. Alvaro and Rubén Rodríguez served as alternates.[63]

While ideally an Indigenous person would have represented his or her concerns in Congress, literacy restrictions on citizenship eliminated most Indians from consideration. Strategically, it would be advantageous to have a person in this position who had garnered respect and could be forceful in pressing demands. In the National Assembly, Paredes made effective use of this post to advocate for the interests of Indigenous peoples, and he exerted a positive influence on petitions brought before the body. He worked for legal reforms to benefit Indigenous peoples, including proposing the formation of a Ministry of Indigenous Affairs and expanding citizenship rights for Indigenous peoples.[64] The FEI applauded Paredes's efforts, who "with the support of representatives of leftist parties, secured various special constitutional dispositions that favored Indians, including their right to use their mother tongues." Together the FEI and its functional representative "solved many lawsuits from Indigenous communities that had dragged on for many years, causing great unrest and injury to the Indians."[65] Naming a prominent and effective communist leader perhaps explains why when the government approved the FEI's statutes, it conceded that the federation could nominate the representative, even though it did not allow them to have exclusive authority over this position.[66]

Issues of representation have become critically important in understanding dynamics within Indigenous rights movements.[67] The anthropologist Kay Warren observes that "the politics of 'who speaks for whom' will always be important" because "it raises the issue of . . . who claims the authority to craft representation of ongoing social and political realities." She then proceeds to pose "an intersubjective question" with perhaps the deeper implications of "'who speaks with whom'; that is, how do individuals and groups selectively engage and influence each other, often across politicized cleavages"?[68] Both rural and urban activists came to understand that ideological influences did not flow in only one direction. The communist activist Celso Fiallo later noted that "Indigenous peoples' thoughts have influenced our reflections to the point where our perceptions are significantly different than that of orthodox Ecuadorian communist thought."[69] The politics of representation tend to be paternalistic, while those of conversations tend to be empowering.

Reflecting a dual consciousness, the FEI's statutes emphasized leftist influences on its ideology as much as it did the ethnic aspects. Its statutes codified an organizational affiliation with the CTE, and it would come to rely on its mother organization and the Communist Party for support, guidance, infrastructure, ideological oversight, and training in strategies. The new organization's ideology is also reflected in the selection of a hammer and sickle as its insignia.[70] The FEI's subsequent actions further underlined its close affinity for leftist (specifically communist) political organizations. In one of the organization's first statements made only weeks after its founding, Cacuango denounced an attack against Paredes in the city of Esmeraldas, referring to him as "our dignified functional representative."[71] Many Indigenous gains were accomplished "thanks to the advocacy of men from the left, in particular the Communist Party," the FEI leaders Gualavisí and Alvaro argued, glossing over the central role of women in the struggle. "With the support of these same organizations and men, the FEI is prepared to defend the rights of the Indians."[72]

The FEI supported leftist causes and viewed these alliances as critical to the advancement of the Indigenous movement. In February 1945, the FEI declared that "the Indian is not an enemy of the white urban worker," but rather the two are "brothers and equals in the suffering of exploitation" and united in a struggle for "humane treatment, better living conditions, education, and a legitimate pay for their work so that they can live like men and citizens."[73] In December 1946, when Velasco Ibarra imprisoned student and worker leaders for challenging his increasingly dictatorial policies, Alvaro published a circular in the name of the FEI's Executive Committee calling for their liberty because "the accused have defended and helped Ecuadorian Indians to gain many of their demands."[74]

Together, the FEI and PCE played a key role in defending Indigenous interests and assisting peasant syndicates with their organizing efforts. The FEI utilized a variety of tools to advocate for social changes. It resurrected the newspaper *Ñucanchic Allpa,* an "organ of syndicates, communities, and Indians in general," which underwent repeated deaths and rebirths during the course of its history. The communist leaders Nela Martínez and Ricardo Paredes played central roles in editing and publishing *Ñucanchic Allpa.* Martínez, born to an elite landholding family in southern Ecuador in 1912, had a commitment to solidarity "with her people, with humble people, with the workers, Indians, and women."[75] Illustrating the central role of literate intermediaries, she helped bridge the gap between the Kichwa-speaking, rural Indigenous world and the white dominant culture that held power in Quito. Without this type of assistance, the Indians' effectiveness would have been greatly diminished.[76] *Ñucanchic Allpa* requested that organizations send news of their struggles for publication, and it suggested that "the newspaper be read in sessions to Indigenous peoples who cannot read."[77] Reflecting a sense of ownership, the federation noted that the paper's costs must be covered by affiliated organizations if the publication were to continue to appear on a regular basis. In response, Cacuango's community of Yana-huaico raised money to fund the enterprise.[78] Echoing Mariátegui's writing on the "Indian problem," the newspaper contended that Indigenous oppression was a national problem and its solution would only be found in changes to the agrarian system. "Indigenous peoples are oppressed nationalities," the newspaper editorialized. "The true solution rests in the right of self-determination."[79] *Ñucanchic Allpa* sought to reflect Indigenous concerns while at the same time advancing their struggles and being a voice to the outside world.

The Communist Party also used its newspaper *El Pueblo* to publicize abuses on haciendas. On occasion, the paper would dedicate an entire section, entitled "Luchas campesinas" (Peasant struggles) or "Boletín de la Federación Ecuatoriana de Indios," to land conflicts and Indigenous struggles. The PCE maintained that agricultural workers would only realize improvements in living and working conditions through unity, organization, and solidarity with organized workers in the city. The party called on rural workers to organize syndicates as the best way to persuade landowners and government officials to attend to their demands.[80] *El Pueblo* demanded that Pisambilla return huasipungo plots to workers, pay salaries, provide tools, and fire employees who oppressed Indigenous workers. When the hacienda did not comply, the paper accused it of carrying out a campaign of terror and abuse against huasipungueros and day laborers. The Communist Party rallied government officials and the broader public to defend the rights of hacienda workers and to take steps to improve their working conditions.[81]

White leftists also used their international connections to advance Indigenous issues. Martínez demonstrated the important, and perhaps even critical, role that whites played in supporting Indigenous struggles. Making use of her skills, she served as a personal secretary to Dolores Cacuango, accompanying her to the Second Congress of the Confederación de Trabajadores de América Latina (CTAL, Confederation of Latin American Workers) in Cali, Colombia, in 1944. In 1949, Martínez traveled to Moscow for the International Women's Congress where she spoke about Ecuador's political and social situation including that of the Indigenous peoples.[82] In the 1950s, Paredes represented the FEI to the Central Council of the Latin American Syndicalist Confederation in Bucharest, and Modesto Rivera represented the federation at the Conference of Latin American Agricultural Workers in

Mexico.[83] Through these exchanges, a significant current within the Ecuadorian left became "indigenized," thereby influencing communist strategies and actions.

The FEI in Action

As had happened in the aftermath of previous Indigenous gatherings in 1931 and 1935, the formation of the FEI in August 1944 triggered an immediate increase in the level of agrarian activism.[84] On August 23, the Chimborazo work inspector telegraphed President Velasco Ibarra claiming not to know what had alarmed agricultural workers in Palmira, Guamote, Columbe, and Tixán, but their representatives were in his office demanding compliance with the 1938 Labor Code. Not finding a satisfactory resolution to their complaints on a local level, Indians from Chimborazo, Cotopaxi, and Pichincha descended on Quito to present their demands to the central government. The press reported a "real invasion" of protesters, leaving haciendas abandoned. Property owners feared that they would not be able to complete the harvest, and they asked the government to order the workers back to the haciendas. Finally, the governor of Chimborazo requested that leaders of the socialist and communist parties intervene so that Indigenous workers would return to their labors. Months later, the situation on various haciendas still had not normalized. In the first weeks of 1945, Indigenous uprisings swept through Sanguicel and Colta (in Chimborazo), Pangua (in Cotopaxi), and Cayambe (in Pichincha). Property owners in Chimborazo publicly denounced the "uneducated passionate attacks of the communist Paredes," whose irate actions lacked any justification. "The Indigenous agitation created by the communist Paredes and his henchmen," they denounced, "has revolutionary goals." The Minister of Social Welfare blamed the unrest on "the interference of people who claim to be defenders of the Indigenous race but are no more than exploitative tinterillos who continue to incite Indigenous leaders." Finally, Velasco Ibarra traveled to Cayambe where he denounced the work of "tinterillos who exploit Indigenous peoples." He argued, either naively or ingeniously, that all the Indians would have to do is request housing and schools from the patrón and everything would be improved. The conflict between communists and hacendados came to blows on the floor of the National Assembly, with one side denouncing abuses against Indigenous workers and the other defending the rights of private property.[85]

In Cayambe, Gualavisí and Cacuango continued to organize Indigenous workers. Hacienda administrators complained that they were telling workers that as descendants of the Inkas they were the rightful heirs to the land. When overseers told Gualavisí and Cacuango to leave, they refused by saying that renters were not the owners of the JCAP estates. One night in 1946 an administrator encountered Gualavisí at Pisambilla. Gualavisí had intended to sleep in the hut of one of the workers, but the administrator forced him to sleep outside and leave the next morning. Upon this eviction, Gualavisí solicited assistance from Paredes, and together they filed suit to defend Gualavisí's right to organize hacienda workers under the stipulations of the labor code. Rather than responding to the workers' demands, the hacienda considered firing one or two of the most dangerous Indigenous leaders in order to intimidate the others.[86] External support and pressure helped defend Indigenous rights and prevented elite abuses from continuing unchecked.

The FEI inspired rural protests both directly by forwarding an explicit agenda and indirectly by motivating subalterns through their example of challenging power. The federation embraced an increasingly broad range of demands that revolved around three general themes. First, it engaged daily economic struggles on haciendas including fighting for higher salaries, for a shorter work week, for pay for women's work, and for an end to huasicama service requirements. While the FEI focused much of its work on haciendas, they also demanded land, water, schools, housing, health care, and financial credit for Indigenous communities.

Second, the FEI desired to participate in the political life of the country on an equal footing with other sectors of society. Indigenous militants embraced what James MacGregor Burns and Stewart Burns term an activist citizenship that involved debates much deeper than mere electoral contests. This type of democratic citizenship not only concerned the " 'outer frame' of duties such as voting, paying taxes, and obeying laws," but also engaged the struggle for political, civil, economic, and social rights.[87]

Third, to advance these goals Indigenous teachers established four independent bilingual schools at Yanahuaico, San Pablourco, Pesillo, and La Chimba in Cayambe. With this training, graduates would "teach their brothers the path to liberation." The schools were a model that Indigenous communities should follow. "Our spirit has not died," the FEI argued, "and our race is the most productive in the country. We are men and we want conditions of life for men."[88] The government felt threatened by the schools and attempted to shut them down. Nevertheless, Neptalí Ulcuango and Luis Catucuamba kept the schools open and operating.[89] Economic, political, and educational struggles translated into claiming a larger role in civil society. Joe Foweraker and Todd Landman conclude that "the essentially *individual* rights of citizenship can only be achieved through different forms of *collective* struggle."[90] A redefinition of citizenship lay at the very heart of the demands that Indians were making.

In February 1946, the FEI held its Second Congress of Ecuadorian Indians at the Sucre Theater in Quito.[91] Three leftist leaders—Cacuango for the FEI, Paredes as the functional deputy for the Indians, and Alvaro as the secretary-general of the Indigenous Defense Committee—signed a letter written in Spanish and Kichwa calling on labor unions, Indigenous defense committees, cooperatives, tribes, comunas, and other Indian organizations and population centers to attend this meeting. Each organization was to name a delegate for every one hundred members and to cover the costs for its delegates. The principal objectives of the meeting were to discuss the activities of the federation; receive a report on the National Assembly from Paredes; gather reports from local communities; critique legislation, including the comunas law, the Labor Code, and minimum salary regulations for agricultural workers; publish *Ñucanchic Allpa;* support the Tigua cooperative; revise the federation's statutes; and develop training courses for the organization's members.[92]

At the congress, the FEI reelected Gualavisí as president and selected Alvaro to replace Cacuango as secretary-general. They reported that the "congress revealed the level of organization and consciousness of the Indians, and the development of their labors was truly admirable."[93] Reports in *El Día* also indicated that the congress was a success and that the FEI was functioning and engaging many of the issues critical to Indigenous peoples in Ecuador.[94] The leftist university newspaper *Surcos* noted that the congress "was but the beginning, an embryo of what should be." Emphasizing the significance of the meeting, *Surcos* pointed out that since "the Indian comprises the majority of the Ecuadorian population and most of its agriculture labor," the congress should really be that "of the Ecuadorian nationality." The article then concluded with the statement, "Indian brethren, we are always with you, dedicated to the task of helping with your complete liberation."[95] In addition to electing new leadership, the FEI passed resolutions advocating the creation of Indigenous schools, the establishment of training classes to improve agricultural production, and the instruction for Indigenous nurses and midwives. The congress also drafted a new mission statement that argued for "the necessity to group all Indigenous inhabitants of Ecuador" because together "in one bloc they can more effectively defend their rights." Even though the Social Welfare Ministry attempted to limit the scope of the federation, the FEI still presented itself as the unitary voice of the Indigenous movement. It continued to organize "the Indigenous masses into unions, comunas, and cooperatives" in order to provide an "ideological orientation" that included making communities aware of laws that favored Indigenous peoples, protecting autochthonous cultural values, and providing technical training particularly in the field of agriculture. A goal was to improve Indigenous peoples' living conditions and to elevate their standard of living, with a clear eye to defending Indigenous peoples and their cultures from racist attacks. Pointing to the importance of the printed word, the FEI called on organizations to support the publication of their newspaper Ñucanchic Allpa, noting that it played a central role in denouncing abuses and in advancing their agenda.[96] After the congress, activists returned to their communities to continue their work. The administrator of the Moyurco hacienda complained that "this pernicious woman" Cacuango was on the hacienda helping Indians build houses even though they did not have a formal contract for a huasipungo plot.[97]

On March 30, 1946, less than two months after the congress, Velasco Ibarra assumed dictatorial powers, imprisoned Indigenous leaders, and abolished the position of functional representative for the Indigenous race. "Indians have lost much of what they had gained," the FEI reported.[98] Authorities threatened to exile Cacuango to the Galápagos Islands, and a priest in Cayambe tried to bribe her to stop causing trouble and to leave the Communist Party.[99] As a further blow to the FEI, in a complete rout, socialists gained control of the CTE from the communists at the union's second congress in November 1946. When the communists protested their exclusion, the socialists proclaimed that it "did not matter who occupied leadership positions whether they are from one party or the other; what is important is to work for class interests."[100] The change in leadership, however, did alter the flavor and focus of the CTE's actions. This would be particularly noticeable in the CTE's relationship with the FEI, given a weaker tradition of rural organizing among socialist activists and the FEI's close affiliation with the communists. A month before the CTE's leadership change, the FEI had observed that its gains had been largely due to "leftists, and in particular the Communist Party." With their help, "the FEI was prepared to defend the rights of

High paramo grasslands at Tigua, the site of a communist-supported Indigenous cooperative in the 1940s. Photo by Marc Becker.

Indians."[101] Of the three named to the CTE's commission for Peasant and Indigenous Affairs, only the communist Luis F. Alvaro had a deep and long history supporting highland rural struggles.[102]

Another setback for leftist Indigenous organizing efforts involved the frustrated attempts to organize a cooperative on the Tigua hacienda in Cotopaxi. Taking advantage of the political openings of the Glorious May Revolution, Indigenous workers organized a cooperative, obtained a bank loan, and purchased part of the hacienda. In February 1945, the National Assembly formally recognized the cooperative and provided it with financial credit, technical assistance, schooling, and access to water. The FEI leaders converged with the PCE militants to work on this experiment, which for a time in the 1940s became a leftist cause célèbre. Outsiders applauded the Tigua activists for their initiatives and pointed to the cooperative as a model that others should follow.[103] The PCE sent Rubén Rodríguez from Cayambe to help organize and direct the cooperative. The party's proposal that the land be owned and worked collectively in a type of soviet council, however, clashed with a desire for individual plots of land. *Ñucanchic Allpa* denounced this development as the corrupting influence of the large landowners who were determined to see this experiment fail.[104] Others came to see it as an example of the incongruity between the left's class-oriented analysis and an Indigenous community's ethnic identity, as well as an example of the failure of a vertical and mechanical implementation of marxist ideology.[105] After this fiasco, the PCE was forced out of the zone.

Despite these setbacks, the FEI pressed forward with the goal of achieving a more just social order. On April 19, 1947, the "Day of the American Indian," the FEI organized a Conferencia de Dirigentes Indígenas (Conference of Indigenous Leaders) at Quito's Central University.[106] While Indigenous leaders discussed important political and economic issues, white elite indigenistas held their own cultural celebration that presented a folkloric image of an aboriginal population.[107] In contrast, the FEI pressed a political agenda that emerged out of Indigenous issues and concerns.

The FEI's third congress began on April 19, 1948, with an exposition of Indigenous art intended to represent the value and capabilities of the Indigenous masses. In order to advance the FEI's class struggle against the Indians' primary enemies, the large landholders, the congress urged "Indigenous compañeros on haciendas, comunas, and all members of the race," to "form a syndicate and affiliate with the Federation." The FEI was the "maximum organization that ties together all Indians in Ecuador." Together the struggle for liberation would gain force and achieve "its sacred mission."[108] The congress also addressed the issue of building Indigenous schools and expanding social legislation in order to end feudal exploitation. The socialist minister of social welfare, Alfredo Pérez Guerrero, in an address to the congress, indicated his willingness to collaborate with the FEI, and he championed efforts to create a "Junta de Cuestiones Indígenas" (Bureau of Indian Affairs) to address the "Indian problem."[109]

At this congress, Modesto Rivera replaced Alvaro as secretary-general, and he worked closely with Cacuango who was now president. The executive committee of the PCE applauded Rivera for this "valiant and honest" work on behalf of the "glorious" FEI. It pledged to "continue lending its support to the struggles of the FEI and all of Indigenous masses until they obtain their final liberation."[110] This pattern of an Indigenous president and a white or mestizo secretary-general persisted for decades. The distinction between the president and secretary-general was not that one was Indigenous and the other a communist, for both were always active members in the PCE and both were sincere and committed radicals who dedicated themselves to ending oppression and exploitation. Rather, they brought complementary skills such as legal training, an ability to mobilize people, and contacts in both rural communities and urban areas that proved to be useful in building the organization. Their actions challenge Roberto Santana's criticism of the federation for its close and congenial relationship with non-Indigenous leftists and dismissal of the FEI as the "peasant wing" of the PCE organized with the only purpose of incorporating Indigenous peasants into labor unions.[111]

After the congress, officials criticized the FEI leaders and the PCE activists Paredes, Cacaungo, Rodríguez, and Gualavisí for promising hacienda lands to Indigenous workers once the communists took power. Cayambe's jefe político complained that the workers were borrowing money from the hacienda to give to the agitators, and this entailed a fierce exploitation of Indigenous peoples.[112] The PCE, of course, cast their role in a positive light. "The peasant masses do not need saviors," the party noted. "They have already learned that the only path to their liberation is through their own struggle." Rather than hiding their involvement, the party proudly proclaimed that "the Communist Party heads the process of this struggle," providing a working-class orientation and organization to the peasant and Indigenous masses. The Indians "have obtained schools and other aspects of culture thanks to the patient, unselfish, heroic work of the communists" on behalf of the "most humble and long-suffering sector of our population."[113] Because of their high-profile work, both white activists such as Paredes and Rodríguez and Indigenous activists including Cacuango and Gualavisí became known as "prestigious leaders, unselfish fighters for the Indian Federation and the Ecuadorian left."[114] In the minds of these militants, Indigenous and socialist struggles were one and the same.

One echo of the congress was a refusal of Pesillo Indians to continue the diezmos and primicias payments. In response, the local priest initiated an intensive campaign against Indigenous and communist leaders that allied the church with conservative local politicians, police, and mayordomos—or, in the words of the leftist university newspaper *Surcos*, "the whole servile band of gamonalismo" that exploited Indigenous workers.[115] On a rumor that Indigenous workers were planning a general uprising to occupy the haciendas, the police arrested the leaders of the syndicate "El Inca" and took them to prison in Quito. Revealing the importance of outside allies, FEI's secretary-general Modesto Rivera wrote to the Ministry of Government to denounce these abuses. "Ecuador's history is constantly stained with Indian blood shed in massacres," Rivera proclaimed. He declared that the arrests were politically motivated and were designed to discredit "certain groups or parties." He urged the ministry to pursue "an active investigation" and to implement an "exemplary sanction." The FEI's intervention proved to be effective. The charges were dropped, the leaders released, and they returned to their homes where *El Comercio* reported that they were "dedicated to their agricultural labors."[116]

Rather than reacting as victims, Indigenous peoples emerged as important players in these political debates. "I risked my life," said Neptalí Ulcuango, whom hacienda employees had attacked during these protests. "But it was through the organized struggle of the peasantry that we uprooted these traditions in Pesillo and the following year on haciendas throughout the area." Fearing another uprising and possible threats to the hacendados, Archbishop Carlos María de la Torre agreed to meet with the Indians. The Indians worked out an agreement in which the diezmos and primicias would become voluntary payments. "Bit by bit by means of an organized struggle," Luis Catucuamba noted, "we were able to end these traditions."[117] In response, an urban leftist argued that "first popular democracy and then socialism are the only paths to the liberation of the Indian."[118] Elite efforts "to justify the bloody repression and destruction of syndicate organizations" had failed. *Surcos* pointed to the FEI as "the primary organizational expression of agricultural workers," indicating the federation's central importance in these struggles.[119]

In September 1949, FEI's secretary-general Modesto Rivera accompanied forty huasipungueros from the Razuyacu hacienda to the Social Welfare Ministry in Quito to complain about violations of the Labor Code, including low pay and long workdays. The Social Welfare minister agreed to discuss the issue with José Antonio Tapia Vargas, the renter of the JCAP hacienda. When Tapia Vargas refused to respond to the charges, the Ministry of Government ordered his arrest. Instead of turning himself in, Tapia Vargas published a letter in *El Comercio* denying the validity of the charges and accusing Rivera of being a tinterillo. Under orders of the communist party, Tapia Vargas claimed, Rivera was "infiltrating the Indigenous masses, exploiting them with copious collections," and stirring them to action. He claimed that neighboring property owners would corroborate his charges. Not only Tapia Vargas's interests but those of the entire country were at risk.[120]

Both the FEI and the CTE responded to these charges in *El Comercio's* competing newspaper *El Día*. In a forcefully worded letter, the FEI's Executive Committee pointed out that even the Ministry of Labor ordered Tapia Vargas to come to a "harmonious and legal arrangement" with his workers in order to settle the conflict. The FEI only become involved when these legal petitions appeared to come to a dead end. The compañero Rivera "is not a tinterillo; he has never been involved in lawsuits, nor has he charged any honorarium," his supporters declared. In fact, the FEI claimed, authorities knew Rivera as a serious person who facilitated solutions to problems. Rather, they charged Tapia Vargas of using an unscrupulous lawyer to dodge his legal responsibilities and to stir up problems. The president of CTE, Humberto Navarro, similarly defended Rivera from charges of being a "vulgar tinterillo and exploiter of Indians." Navarro accused Tapia Vargas of being a typical "new rich who ignoring his humble and Indian past, becomes a true executioner of his own race, permitting and sponsoring the greatest violations and ridiculing the labor code." Rather than resolving the situation, he was deflecting attention with his attacks on Rivera. The CTE defended their colleague's "high moral quality and unselfish spirit of sacrifice in favor of oppressed masses."[121]

Tapia Vargas quickly responded with another letter in *El Comercio*. The republic's president, he preened, knew him as an "hombre de bien" (good man), whereas "the comrade Rivera is only known as the opposite, and at the right hand of Dolores Cacuango, the one who has been discovered in her repugnant reality." He denounced the communist tactics of "throwing a stone and hiding the hand" and referred to the Italian thinker Domingo Guilioty's definition of communism as "a rotten mass kneaded by Jewish hands in enslaved minds." For this reason, he declared, he had made his accusations publicly known and would not "return to gather filth from a communist stream."[122]

This lengthy public exchange reflects the challenges and racism that the FEI and their collaborators faced in demanding the rights of Indigenous peoples. In employing standard red-baiting tactics, conservatives increasingly complained that communists incited revolts. The anthropologist Eileen Maynard notes that mestizos labeled as communist "any organization or individual whose purpose is to aid Indians." Communism became a gloss for "something bad," although local inhabitants had "no way of determining whether the accused is really a Communist" and whether it would be beneficial to cooperate with them.[123] Indian supporters countered these charges, and instead of a "communist ghost" they pointed to the "terrible exploitation" of abusive landowners, "whose libido seems to feel fully satisfied in the merciless lashing of the coppery Indigenous backs."[124] Meanwhile, Indigenous militants came to rely heavily on urban socialist supporters who drew rural activists deeply into leftist political activism and helped to consolidate their organizations.

These years after the founding of the FEI were some of the most radical in the history of rural organizing in Ecuador. "In the face of unbearable oppression," CONAIE's history of Indigenous movements states, "we began to rebel on each hacienda, in each community, demanding that they give us the lands on which we worked, that they pay us better salaries, that they better our living conditions."[125] As the FEI strengthened its institutional cohesion, it also advanced the political objectives of its sponsoring organizations—the PCE and CTE. Drawing on these inter-ethnic class-based alliances, the FEI engaged social and political causes that extended far beyond immediate local community concerns, and in so doing it became a key actor in bringing social justice to the Ecuadorian countryside.

⟪FIVE⟫

Guachalá

In 1954, Indigenous workers on the Guachalá hacienda rebelled, citing the fact that they had not been paid for over three months and had suffered other abuses at the hacendado's hands. In response, the local police force arrived armed with machine guns. Rather than attempting to resolve the situation peacefully, the police shot at the unarmed protestors, killing four people, injuring many others, and imprisoning a dozen Indigenous peasants.

Was this simply one more example of an all-too-common occurrence of rural workers presenting legitimate grievances only to have the landowners reject the petition and call in the police? This event was similar to the 1931 strike on the Pesillo hacienda, only this time the action did not occur on a government-run Asistencia Pública hacienda where such strikes had become common occurrences, but rather on a privately owned hacienda. The elite Ascásubi and Bonifaz families who owned Guachalá had mastered paternalistic administrative methods to avoid protest. Any dissent was hidden from public view and controlled within the confines of the hacienda's own judicial systems. Privately held estates had access to control mechanisms such as the fictive kinship *compadrazgo* (godparent) system to keep open dissent in check. Publicly, Guachalá projected an image of a modernizing and progressive administrative system. The lived realities, however, were often quite different. Rosalind Gow disputes that "hacienda populations were generally highly dependent and fearful of the hacendado and hence unlikely to make revolutionary demands." Instead, she paints a picture of the hacienda long being an arena of Indigenous resistance.[1] Whether public or private, by the 1950s Indigenous revolts on haciendas had become common events.

The 1950s and the "Democratic Parentheses"

The FEI matured and flourished during a remarkable (for Ecuador) twelve-year "democratic parentheses" from 1948 to 1960, during which three chief executives were able to finish their terms and hand power to an elected successor from an opposing party. Population and economic shifts strengthened a growing commercial and financial bourgeoisie rooted in a coastal export-oriented banana boom that led to the advance of capitalism as the dominant mode of production. In the highlands, the traditional landholding oligarchy increasingly assumed characteristics of a modernizing agricultural bourgeoisie. Reflecting these modernizing trends, Galo Plaza Lasso, a moderate politician and owner of the large Zuleta hacienda in northern Ecuador, won the 1948 presidential elections.[2]

In 1950, Plaza conducted Ecuador's first modern census. Indians feared that governmental attempts to enumerate rural communities primarily served to increase tax burdens and labor drafts. Illustrating the exclusionary nature of the Ecuadorian state, the government had not bothered to consider how the census would appear to rural communities. In response, the FEI called an extraordinary congress. With the FEI's encouragement, Plaza agreed to meet with three hundred Indigenous leaders to explain the benefits of the census. After the government addressed their fears, various Indian leaders including Dolores Cacuango promised, in Spanish and Kichwa, to cooperate with the impending census.[3]

Plaza's response to this conflict represented a noticeable shift from previous reactions to Indigenous organizational efforts. Rather than sending in military troops, the government relied on Indigenous leaders to implement their policy decisions. Turning to the FEI to mediate the concerns of rural communities indicates the level of prestige and legitimacy that the organization had achieved.[4] The rhetoric also points to a conceptual shift among political elites from repression to assimilation and co-optation. Pursuing a typical indigenista discourse, Luis López Muñoz, the director of the census, told the gathered FEI delegates that "we constitute a country that is of Indian origin," something of which all Ecuadorians should be proud. Unfortunately, according to López Muñoz, many Indians were uneducated and ignorant and needed government services to improve their lives. The purpose of the census, therefore, was to count the population in order "to incorporate the Indian into economic and social relations" of the country. Following López Muñoz's lead, Plaza reiterated that all Ecuadorians should be proud of their Indigenous heritage. He justified the census because it would help give land and more resources to rural communities. Despite these efforts, on November 29, the day of the national census, Indian uprisings halted the census in Chimborazo. Although constructed as antimodern and isolationist reactions, the protests challenged the government's strong modernizing and assimilationist ideology that discounted local economic concerns and ethnic identities.[5]

Building on the strength of its ongoing campaigns, in August 1952 four hundred delegates from six highland provinces gathered in Quito for the FEI's fourth congress. The communist newspaper El Pueblo reported that the congress demonstrated that the FEI was "a solid classist organization that struggles, effectively and efficiently, for the structuring and defense of Indigenous peoples in the entire country." Osvaldo Albornoz Peralta echoed this sentiment with the observation that the FEI had "attracted to its ranks the most combative and conscious sectors," providing the Indigenous masses with "a clear political consciousness" rooted in "the study of their problems and the development of a just program of demands." The organization's influence was spreading into new regions, as evidenced by the attendance of delegates from Cañar in the south of the country, who previously had not been involved in the organization. Nevertheless, without the participation of Indigenous peoples from the coast or the Amazon, the FEI still fell short of gaining a truly national dimension. The congress affirmed an agenda of continuing its work to raise salaries, eliminate abusive work demands, return land and water to communities, provide agricultural technical training, extend investment credit, expand social security programs, provide better housing, and establish Indigenous schools in the countryside. The FEI acknowledged that they had made little progress in achieving these goals but blamed its shortcomings on feudalism that was still deeply embedded in Ecuador, even in such organizations as the JCAP. Significantly, and in contrast to later criticisms that the FEI was exclusively a classist organization that ignored ethnic dimensions of the struggle, it demanded a "defense of Indigenous cultural traditions," although it remained vague on how it would achieve that objective. Finally, reflecting the FEI's broad perspective, it called for conserving and expanding Ecuadorian democracy, defending national sovereignty, and conserving world peace. The federation, *El Pueblo* noted, was critical to a national struggle for liberation.[6]

In August 1952, the conservative populist leader José María Velasco Ibarra returned to the presidency for his third of five terms. He presided over an increased Cold War paranoia of communist subversion, organizing, and uprisings. Hacendados, concerned with the continued force of rural organizing efforts, sought to intimidate Indigenous leaders and destroy rural syndicates. In the aftermath of a May Day rally at Pesillo, landlords engaged in a fierce persecution of Neptalí Ulcuango. Both hacienda workers and the educator Luisa María Gómez de la Torre, who assisted Ulcuango with his Indigenous schools, came to his defense. Their intervention gained his release, and the syndicate continued with its organizational efforts.[7]

In 1953, a new owner of the Galte hacienda in Chimborazo, long a site of Indigenous unrest, tried to expel thirty-nine huasipungueros in order to confiscate their land so as to modernize production. Workers launched a strike that lasted eight months. The National Guard descended on the hacienda in search of the leaders, destroying their houses and beating and arresting people, including Ambrosio Lasso. In response to the repression, the PCE rallied support for the Indians. "Our party, as always," they declared, "is irrefutably in the vanguard of the anti-feudal struggle."[8] The Galte workers finally reached a resolution with the hacienda to raise salaries, rebuild housing, respect the peasant union, and free strikers who had been imprisoned. *El Pueblo* emphasized that these gains were realized "thanks to the peasant union and strike." The victory demonstrated the benefits of remaining "unified on the hacienda, within the Ecuadorian Federation of Indians and within the great army of all Ecuadorian workers."[9]

In August 1953, a massacre on the La Merced hacienda near Quito left three Indigenous workers dead, fourteen hurt, and twenty-five imprisoned. Police arrested the FEI secretary-general Modesto Rivera, who had been helping hacienda workers press their demands with the labor inspector, as an accomplice in the uprising. The PCE and the Federación de Trabajadores de Pichincha (FTP, Pichincha Workers Federation) came to Rivera's defense, and called on other popular organizations "to lend their solidarity to the huasipungueros at La Merced, victims of the landlord's abuses." Indigenous organizations in Tigua, Cayambe, and elsewhere responded with petitions, demonstrating the nationwide solidarity that the FEI sought to build. Under pressure, the government released Rivera and the other imprisoned Indigenous workers, although they never prosecuted the perpetrators of the massacre. In December, the police returned to La Merced in another attempt to remove the troublesome workers. The *Hispanic American Report* noted that the repression formed part of the government's "all-out drive against the syndicalistic and communal organizations of the Indians."[10]

In 1954, Helge Vorbeck, the owner of the La Victoria brewery in Quito and Pesillo's current renter, announced plans to lower huasipunguero salaries and to shrink the size of huasipungo plots. Vorbeck gave approximately thirty day laborers minuscule plots he called "huasipungos" and correspondingly lowered their salaries to that of a huasipunguero. In addition, he imported higher-producing dairy cows, thereby doubling the work of the milkmaids, but he did not give the women a corresponding raise. This translated into increased labor without an increase in remuneration for the cuentayos who cared for the cattle. In addition, huasipungueros accused hacienda administrators of raping women. Workers informed the FEI of the situation, and the federation used their communist allies and *El Pueblo* to denounce the exploitation. With outside pressure, the workers extracted concessions from Vorbeck, including promises to raise salaries, end the abuse on the hacienda, and build a literacy center.[11]

Although the FEI originally emerged on traditional haciendas like Pesillo where huasipungo labor systems helped engender an agrarian working-class consciousness, the federation increasingly spread its influence to new regions where it previously had little presence. For example, when Juan Frías attacked Indigenous workers on his hacienda Quillocillín in Cotopaxi, the workers turned to the FEI for assistance in defending their rights.[12] The federation supported workers on the Tipin hacienda in Guamote, Chimborazo, with a petition to the labor inspector for better salaries, improved working conditions, and access to huasipungo plots.[13] The FEI took advantage of these opportunities to establish a foothold outside of its traditional base of support. In this way, the federation came to Guachalá. Because of private ownership, protest was not as visible as it was elsewhere and thus took longer to surface in the public arena as hacienda owners attempted to resolve issues without outside intervention. The social and political forces unleashed at Guachalá drew the FEI into new and important struggles.

Guachalá

Guachalá was one of the largest, oldest, and best-known haciendas in Ecuador. At the height of its operation, from about 1700 to 1947, the estate

Patio of the Guachalá hacienda, one of Ecuador's most wealthy haciendas and the site of a 1954 massacre. Photo by Marc Becker.

extended over twelve thousand hectares. The owners of Guachalá grew wealthy through raising sheep and producing textiles, and whereas the workers were marginalized and disenfranchised, the owners were some of Ecuador's most important and influential citizens. In the twentieth century, Guachalá belonged to the Bonifaz family, which represented traditional hacendado attitudes. The owners, however, also modernized the hacienda through the introduction of new products and technologies such as eucalyptus trees, Holstein dairy cows, automobiles, and photography.[14]

For years, Indigenous workers at Guachalá had complained to the government about Labor Code violations.[15] The 1954 massacre brought these simmering issues into public view for the first time. Indians described a situation of virtual slavery in which they were forced to work from 7 AM to 3 PM for one sucre a day. If the huasipungueros experienced a crop failure on their marginal garden plots, they would go hungry that year. Esteban Collago, one of the workers, declared that he did not have a huasipungo but was still forced to work on the hacienda without payment in order to protect his brother's daily wages.[16] According to the Indigenous workers, César Troya Salazar, the hacienda's administrator, was a "declared enemy of the Indians" and "one of the principal organizers of criminal acts." In September 1953, workers had denounced Troya's brutality in submitting Indians to "an intolerable regime" of abuses, beatings, and threats.[17] In response, the agricultural work inspector reached an agreement to pay women for their labor, to grant workers rights to pasture lands, and to treat workers better. An article in *El Pueblo* proclaimed that these advances were gained thanks to recent organizational efforts on the hacienda.[18]

Barely three months later, this apparently collegial agreement collapsed. On January 10, 1954, the government sent in seventy police to the Pitaná section of the hacienda to suppress an uprising of several hundred Indians against Troya and Rafael Mosquera, the hacienda's *escribiente* (scribe). The police fired on the assembled group, killing four huasipungueros, injuring eleven more, and detaining twelve people whom the government claimed to be leaders.

According to one organizer's testimony, on the eve of the massacre the FEI was busy distributing flyers urging the workers to press their demands with Troya.[19] The workers claimed that the hacienda had dropped their daily wages from one and a half sucres to one sucre. They also accused Mosquera of failing to credit them in the accounting books for the days they had worked, and they claimed that Troya owed three months of back wages to the men and eight months to the women.[20] Troya denied that the hacienda was behind in payments, asserting that it did not owe a centavo to anyone. Rather, he claimed that during the holiday festivals many people did not work. In fact, January 10 was the day that these accounts left in limbo were to be settled. Troya claimed that he worked hard to prevent the hacienda from being converted into *una granja colectiva comunista*, "a collective communist farm," even while conceding that perhaps he had been too zealous in protecting the hacienda from Indians who "believe that the hacienda is land of no one and belongs to all."[21]

The previous Friday morning, January 8, about eighty workers confronted Troya and Mosquera about the discrepancy between the days worked and the accounting records. The workers took the accounting book to verify its contents. When Troya and Mosquera came to Manuel Collago's house to reclaim the book, they found only two small children; Collago had left the hacienda. According to the employees, on their return to the hacienda house, they met a force of perhaps two to five hundred workers chanting "we want meat." It was only "with great fortune they were able to flee with their lives from the fury of the Indians."[22]

According to a female relative of one of the hacienda's employees, several workers arrived at the house carrying sticks, exhibiting an aggressive attitude, and demanding three months of back pay. She heard the Indians chanting "Where are they?" with others responding, "They went to Cangahua [the parroquia's capital], but they are in our hands."[23] The women telephoned the police in Cayambe, who immediately sent three officers to the scene. Fearing for their lives, the women retreated to the city of Cayambe where they notified local officials of the insurrection. Troya also called Pichincha's police chief to request assistance.

Early on Sunday morning, January 10, the police chief dispatched thirty officers to the hacienda. They found Troya hiding in the hacienda house with his wife and servants, but otherwise everything was quiet; the alleged protesters were peacefully sleeping in their homes. Four police officers made rounds of the hacienda to appraise the situation. Upon seeing the police, four or five hundred Indians (according to police reports) came out to meet them. The squad signaled for help and the other twenty-six officers came to their assistance. According to the police account, the Indians shot at the four officers, and the police had to shoot back to defend their lives. The workers resisted this attack, and so the police kept firing on the protesters. They tried to disperse the Indians with tear gas, but that had no effect. The Indians only responded, "That does not kill us, let's go on!"[24]

Different parties put different spins on these events in order to advance their own agendas. According to the Communist Party, the police chief sent the four officers not simply to review the situation on the hacienda but to arrest the leaders. Presenting what "should serve as an example of solidarity for peasant struggles," the huasipungueros resisted their fellow workers being carried off to prison. The police called in reinforcements with machine guns and attacked the Indians as if they were on a battlefield. The result was a massacre of Indians not only defending their comrades but now their own lives. *El Pueblo* called the claims that five hundred peasants were involved in the strike "fantastic" and an "absurd lie" since "in Guachalá, there are no more than one hundred Indian men." The PCE declared that all of Ecuador was in solidarity with the massacred Indians. The workers "directed in large part by the communists, reject the abuses that were committed at Guachalá," *El Pueblo* stated. "The peasant masses, workers, democratic parties, and all people have to mobilize to defend the peasants at

Guachalá." They called for the release of the imprisoned huasipungueros, condemned the country's landholding class, and issued a call to arms against fascism.[25]

The discrepancies in these competing reports are intriguing. Sympathetic accounts sometimes exaggerate the size of events in order to emphasize their importance. In this case, hacienda employees seemingly inflated the numbers to stress the seriousness of the situation they faced. Would not the PCE likewise desire to inflate numbers to underscore the level of popular discontent on the hacienda? Or are *both* figures correct? *El Pueblo* notes that "there are no more than one hundred Indian *men*" on the hacienda, but undoubtedly women and children also participated in the protest. Given the large size of peasant families, their presence easily could have raised the total number involved to five hundred. Newspaper reports (including those from *El Pueblo*) only mention men as among those revolting, but the list of injured in the massacre includes a woman (Rosa Collago). The reports do not indicate what role (if any) she had in the protests or how she was injured, but they do attest to the presence of women in the foray. In all probability, Indigenous women did play an active role in the protests, but due to dominant society's cultural biases their role was ignored. Does discounting women's involvement reveal a level of sexism within the Communist Party? Or does it indicate the party's tenuous connections with Guachalá's workers that would have prevented them from knowing the true size and characteristics of the protest?

The FEI presented a slightly different version. The Indians were not protesting, but rather were simply on their way to Sunday mass when the police attacked.[26] Another version stated that the police flanked the path the Indians took to mass, and when the Indians peacefully passed by, the police attacked, killing four people and injuring ten others.[27] In this scenario, the Indians became innocent victims of racist white power structures. Osvaldo Albornoz Peralta in *Las luchas indígenas en el Ecuador* presents yet another twist. In order to avoid having to settle the accounts with the workers, the hacienda administrator attempted to arrest one of their leaders to provoke a revolt that would justify bringing in the troops, who then would violently crush the Indigenous resistance and end their demands.[28] Rather than being passive, Albornoz Peralta depicts the Indians as political actors with a class consciousness. Pompeyo Andrade, a neighboring hacienda owner, speculated that Troya had embezzled the hacienda's payroll, and that he triggered these actions to cover his fiscal mismanagement.[29] These competing accounts, of course, are not necessarily contradictory but present different perspectives on these events.

Typical of indigenista responses, Pío Jaramillo Alvarado condemned the government's repression. In particular, he stressed that the police brought machine guns rather than simply rifles to put down the uprising, and that defenseless women and children were caught in the massacre. "In 1954 the Ecuadorian Indian continues to suffer as during the colonial period," Jaramillo Alvarado noted as he wondered what was happening on other haciendas removed from public scrutiny.[30] From his perspective, Indigenous peoples were victims who relied on outsiders to defend their interests. Rather than protecting them, the government had become the aggressor.

In all accounts, the hacienda called in the police force overnight and caught the workers by surprise. It also appears that the troops fired on what had started as a peaceful protest. The police killed two Indians (Abel Pacheco and Ramón Quishpe) and injured eleven others. According to a coroner's report, Pacheco died from two gunshot wounds, and Quishpe died from tear gas exposure. Elías Quishpe declared that he saw Troya shoot Pacheco as well as club him on the head.[31] The coroner reported marks on the bodies that indicated hand-to-hand struggles with the police. Two police officers (Alfonso Castro and Primero Ramírez) were also injured, with Indians allegedly beating Ramírez with clubs and destroying his machine gun. Two days later, Luis Quishpe, one of the injured, died in the Eugenio Espejo hospital in Quito. The following day, Emilio Quishpe, who was not previously listed among the injured, was found dead of a bullet wound—thus bringing the number of fatalities to four.

The PCE expressed its "profound solidarity with the Guachalá victims" and called on "workers, students, men of the party" to accompany Emilio Quishpe to his final resting place in the San Diego cemetery. "Free men of this country," the PCE declared, support the struggle of "Indians to reconquer the lands that the lords stole from them." The communists took advantage of his death to denounce the "assassins' bullets of Ponce Enríquez' police," and to call for an end to the current government's policies of "exploitation and slavery."[32] The previous September the party had blamed Velasco Ibarra's conservative minister of government Camilo Ponce Enríquez for being the intellectual author of a failed assassination attempt on the communist leader Pedro Saad.[33] The PCE seemed to be more interested in fighting its battles with the government than building a grassroots movement at Guachalá. Ponce responded in kind, and in his annual report he denounced the communists for their attempts to stir up revolutionary senti-ments in populations far removed from their daily lives. First at the Galte hacienda then at La Merced and finally at Guachalá, the communists had caused "serious disorders and regrettable acts." Communist agitation car-ried out through the FEI, Ponce declared, resulted in undesirable conse-quences that did not benefit anyone. To make things worse, Ponce claimed that "the press had twisted the truth in search of sensationalist news."[34] While these political battles were fought out on the public stage, the upris-ing at Guachalá had very real human costs. Emilio Quishpe left behind four orphaned children, driving home the point that reverberations echoed be-yond those immediately involved in political agitation.

After the confrontation, the Cayambe police chief sent in an additional forty officers. After putting down an uprising of eight hundred workers (according to the police's increasingly exaggerated numbers), they detained about one hundred protesters. The police sent twelve whom they consid-ered to be the leaders to Quito to stand trial on charges of rebellion. If they detained all of the Indians, they would have drained the hacienda of its workforce, which was not their intent. Several of those imprisoned claimed not to have participated in the action but rather were caught up in a police sweep after they left mass. The Indians complained that they could not hope to receive justice from the government, and that they faced hunger in Quito because they were removed from their families who could bring food. "We want to return to the land where we will die," the prisoners said. "Where else do we have to go?"[35] As a result of popular pressure, the judge in Quito released the detained workers. Fifteen police officers remained on the ha-cienda in order to prevent further disturbances.

Of note, but understated in reports, was the presence of non-Indians at these events. Specifically, Rubén Rodríguez was one of those arrested. Rodríguez, a long-time organizer who played an important role in the FEI, was no stranger to Indigenous organizations. Troya had the police detain Rodríguez because he was a known communist agitator and was believed to be the intellectual author of the uprising, even though he had not been present at the massacre. If Indians were incapable of organizing themselves, uprisings must have an external locus. Rodríguez later claimed that he was arrested at his house before that Sunday morning's events. This suggests a premeditated action, with the government opportunistically utilizing the unrest as a pretense to crack down on dissent.[36]

Even while the PCE denied organizing the Guachalá uprising, and probably did have a minimal role, they provided a crucial service in linking local events to a global movement. The same week as the massacre, the PCE criticized Velasco Ibarra for signing "a contract with the yanqui imperialists of the ILO [International Labor Organization] 'to undertake work to improve the living conditions of the Indian masses.'" For the government, the PCE declared, "improvement meant bullets instead of salaries" and "silencing with terror the just demands of the peasant masses who ask for land, better salaries, and humane treatment." The editorial closed with a call for "all workers, peasants, intellectuals, students, men and women of all political ideologies to unite to bring an end to the assassination of Indians and to resolve democratically the land problem in Ecuador."[37] Similarly, the CTE denounced repressive police actions that repeatedly led to bloodshed, and called on workers in an act of solidarity to join a mass movement in "defending the Indigenous compañeros at Guachalá."[38]

While the PCE maintained that they had not been responsible for the protest, the FEI claimed a leading role. "The FEI was the one which instigated the uprising," the FEI director Marieta Cárdenas later remembered. "Without us, I doubt that the peasants at Pitaná would have dared to do it." Several workers were members of the FEI and had participated in their congresses. From Quito, the FEI lent organizational and moral support to the struggle.[39] "The infamous feudal exploitation that rural workers suffer," the FEI stated, "can only be maintained through bloody repression." Because of this, landlords used repression to "silence the just and legitimate demands of the peasants." The FEI called on all "Indians and peasants to struggle in an organized manner for better salaries, the stability of their huasipungo plots, and for land." The federation criticized the government for placing police power at the disposition of landholders rather than using it to bring about social justice. It called on all Ecuadorians "without regard to political opinions and religious beliefs to struggle for the immediate liberty of the Indigenous peoples of Guachalá, for the satisfaction of their rights, and for the liberation of the Indigenous masses which form the majority of the Ecuadorian population." They concluded that although landowners and the government intended to paralyze the struggle for better working and living conditions, the FEI and Indians in general would continue their fight.[40] These demands did not fall entirely on deaf ears. As an editorialist in Guayaquil's *El Universo* stated: "We believe that the hour has arrived to correct these injustices, returning those lands [in Guachalá] to their former owners from whom they were snatched."[41] Rural protest in Guachalá, which previously had been carefully hidden in the private arena, had catapulted land reform and ethnic rights issues onto the national stage from which it would never disappear, and the FEI leveraged that visibility to its advantage.

The leftist university newspaper *Surcos* chimed in to note that "the case of Guachalá is nothing but a repetition of a tragic history that happens daily throughout the country." On one hand, the workers justly demand payment of their salaries, while on the other "landowners exploit the peasants and rob their salaries." The government was at fault for defending the hacendados' interests rather than those of the peasants and workers. As with the PCE and CTE, the students blamed Velasco Ibarra's government for these actions, and in particular his minister of government Ponce Enríquez. "The Indians of Guachalá have fallen heroically," the students declared. "Their blood has not been spilled in vain; it will become a red symbol behind which will emerge new Indigenous heroes who will have better luck defending their rights." While they predicted that this massacre would lead to more resistance, their focus was much broader than the specific complaints at Guachalá. Rather, the students declared that they were "ready to go to the aid of workers, peasants, and the people in general."[42] While urban leftists rushed to take political advantage of the massacre, their actions also revealed a class consciousness that sought to defend the interests of the subaltern masses.

Throughout this conflict, the Bonifaz family managed to remain above the fray. The Indians and their supporters in the PCE and FEI leveled accusations of misconduct against the hacienda's administrators, but never directly against the Bonifaz family. In fact, the FEI director Cárdenas claimed to be personal friends with the Bonifaz family and asserted that they did not openly oppose the FEI's organizing efforts.[43] "Any of the Bonifazes," Andrade claimed, "would have solved that problem in less than five minutes." He claimed that Guachalá was not a revolutionary zone. The workers only wanted peace and were loyal to the hacienda's owners. Furthermore, Neptalí Bonifaz was one of the most generous of Ecuador's hacendados.[44]

This uprising was the first time that protest on a privately held modernizing hacienda was carried out so openly in the public arena. Due to the lack of a history of contact with workers on private haciendas, initial statements from the PCE and FEI did little to address the immediate issues at Guachalá. As a result of the massacre, the FEI and PCE began to take a more active interest in private haciendas. Ironically, the hacienda's actions also further pushed agricultural workers into the PCE / FEI camp. Who else would defend workers imprisoned in Quito, provide housing for visiting family members, and assist with burying massacre victims?[45]

Perhaps the biggest shortcoming for Guachalá was the failure to keep this protest in the private arena; the issues that it sparked quickly spread far beyond the hacienda's internal control mechanisms. The massacre marked a shift in spreading Indigenous protests away from core areas of leftist influence. Polarizing strikes began to pop up in new areas. On the Candelaria hacienda in Cayambe, rather than negotiating demands for higher salaries, better working conditions, overtime and vacation pay, and an end to diezmos and primicias, the owners sent in the police to imprison the syndicate's leaders. Similar actions took place at the powerful Jarrín family's San Antonio hacienda where workers still fought for many basic rights, including an end to free work requirements, payment for women's labor, and provision of tools. The local syndicate claimed that the hacienda owed workers seven years of back pay, and it called for an increase in salaries.[46] Supporting their struggle, the Federación de Trabajadores de Pichincha (FTP, Pichincha Workers Federation) called on the ministries of work and government to protect the workers at San Antonio. Well-established agricultural syndicates at Pesillo and La Chimba sent telegrams to the Minister of Social Welfare and the National Congress declaring their intentions to strike if the conflict at San Antonio was not immediately settled.[47] Indigenous organizations increasingly took over solidarity roles that urban colleagues previously had provided.

Leftist Politics

With the passing of the first generation of urban marxists such as Paredes, Chávez, and Rodríguez, who had intimate knowledge of and close contact with Indigenous activists, a new generation of leaders emerged who lacked the same level of interest and involvement with rural struggles. The Communist Party continued to support the demands of hacienda workers who labored "as beasts of burden, suffering inhumane treatment from mayordomos, administrators, and renters."[48] From the floor of the Senate, the PCE secretary-general Pedro Saad advocated distributing Asistencia Pública lands to huasipungueros in order to attend to their needs.[49] Saad, however, was from the coast and did not have the same intimate contact with highland Indigenous communities as previous leaders. In addition, Raquel Rodas describes Saad as more conciliatory to traditional class enemies and less radical than the previous leader Ricardo Paredes. This alienated Cacuango, and she was tempted to leave the party, but Paredes urged her to stay while also noting that a true communist never gives up but rather stays in the struggle come what may.[50]

Already in the 1940s, communist statements had increasingly begun to emphasize an anti-imperialist agenda of national sovereignty over that of Indigenous rights. In particular, the PCE aggressively denounced the 1942 Río Protocol that ceded half of Ecuador's territorial claims in the eastern Amazon to Peru, and challenged proposals to sell the Galapagos Islands to the United States for use as a military base.[51] Rhetorical statements struggled to keep Indigenous issues in the public eye. In the 1948 elections, the PCE denounced the conservative presidential candidate Manuel Elicio Flor for his "defense of the interests of large landholders who oppress the Indians." The communists presented an alternative platform that included agrarian reform and the development of cooperatives to "protect Indians and peasants, abolishing exploitative feudal vestiges." The communists called on "workers, peasants, Indians, servants, teachers, artisans, etc., to defend their conquests, the Labor Code and social laws, to not permit their destruction."[52] A resolution from the fourth party congress in 1949 advocated an "anti-imperialist agrarian revolution" that would give land to the "peasant masses and agricultural workers." It advocated eliminating "feudal obstacles that weigh heavily on Indians and peasants," and breaking up state-owned haciendas into experimental farms and cooperatives. It placed importance on the mobilization of "rural masses, Indians, montuvios, salaried agricultural workers, and peasants, in a struggle for their lives and land." The resolution ended with an acknowledgment that too often such political statements were not put into action, and it called for the party to become "an authentic guide of all oppressed people of Ecuador" in a struggle for "a society without classes, without exploitation, without oppression of any type."[53] Political divisions between liberals and leftists allowed the conservative Camilo Ponce Enríquez to gain the presidency in 1956. In office, Ponce accused the communists of "under the pretext of raising the Indians' condition, abusing their ignorance and turning them into cannon fodder." Ecuador, he claimed, had become "one of communism's prime targets in South America."[54] Since he did not believe Indians could struggle for themselves, their protests must be the result of "actions instigated by 'expert communist agitators.'"[55]

Although communist leaders continued to embrace the rhetoric of a worker-peasant alliance, Indigenous peoples played a shrinking role in this process. Part of the decline was due to demographic shifts from the "Indigenous" highlands to the "peasant" coast, as well as from "Indigenous" rural areas to "mestizo" urban areas. *El Pueblo* dedicated more attention to agrarian reform issues, but increasingly these focused on coastal plantations with few Indigenous workers, and eventually the newspaper moved its editorial offices from Quito to Guayaquil. By the 1970s, the PCE had a strong presence among peasants, but mostly among mestizos on the coast.[56] Galo Ramón blames the left's increasing distance from Indigenous communities on a mechanical implementation of Soviet ideas that advocated a vertical relationship between the party and the masses.[57] This was perhaps the beginning of ideological and strategic divisions between Indigenous communities and urban communists that later led to a widely held stereotype of leftist paternalistic attitudes toward, and strategic usurpation of, Indigenous movements.

Nevertheless, the PCE continued to shape Indigenous discourse, and the discussions were not always unilateral and univocal. An example of this give and take emerged in the drafting of the party platform for the sixth congress in 1957. The Central Committee distributed a preliminary document that minimized Indigenous concerns.[58] A month before the congress, Indigenous leaders met at party headquarters and proposed various changes that appeared in the final draft.[59] Some of the editing was rather cosmetic, such as adding references to Indians in a discussion of the feudal exploitation of the peasantry. What is noteworthy, though, was the addition of a new section on social classes, with a special mention of "Ecuadorian Indians who occupy a special place within the peasant masses." The statement asserted that "this Indian mass unquestionably has a series of national elements, a language, Kichwa and other autochthonous tongues, a tradition, their own cultural manifestations." They were denied education in their own language and, through literacy restrictions, the right to vote. These small changes added up to altering a document from one that minimalized the importance of Indigenous struggles to making an Indigenous consciousness central to the communist struggle.[60] If previously communists had shaped Indigenous discourse, now the reverse was true with Indigenous activists shaping a leftist agenda.

Echoing Mariátegui's strategies from the 1920s, the PCE's secretary-general Pedro Saad advocated engaging rural communities "with their own language, Kichwa for the Indians, in order to arrive at an understanding with them in order to bring a message of faith, freedom, and independence which is the program of the party."[61] According to Agustín Cueva, although the marxist left "exhibited great revolutionary fervor," it remained a "very limited nuclei of intellectuals and students, disconnected from the working class, the peasantry, and the people generally."[62] The party's work needed to extend beyond a few radical leaders in order to became a true mass organization. This could be accomplished through resurrecting the newspaper *Ñucanchic Allpa* and developing a network of peasant cells. The left continued to see Indians as "natural allies" with the working class in a march toward revolutionary changes in society.

If Indigenous peoples struggled to remain present in communist discourse, they had virtually disappeared in other leftist groups. In a lengthy report to the PSE party congress two weeks after the Guachalá massacre, the secretary-general Manuel Agustín Aguirre made no reference to these events.[63] Subsequent statements advocating "the incorporation of the Indian into the [national] culture" reflected a strongly assimiliationist tone that failed to embody Indigenous needs or concerns.[64]

Even while leftist political party discourse shifted away from ethnic issues, Indigenous movements expanded and matured. Under the leadership of the FEI, Indigenous movements broadened out from public haciendas to private estates and diversified away from key economic issues of salaries and working conditions to embrace land as a central demand. The communist leader Jorge Rivadeneyra characterized a 1960 strike at Pesillo for higher wages and better working conditions as very carefully planned and executed. For the first time, the protesters had organized strike committees with established communication links designed to stop work on the hacienda and prevent provocations or retaliations. After only twelve hours on strike, the workers gained concessions including a raise in salaries, a health post, paid vacations, the rehiring of seventeen milkmaids, and a sports field. Rivadeneyra described the strike leader Amadeo Alba as "not vacillating for an instant, discussing issues as equals with the owners, demonstrating that Indians are also human beings" who "have a right to a dignified life and do not tremble in the face of danger, not even in the face of death." Following the example of the workers at Pesillo, Rivadeneyra predicted a "vertiginously quick" victory and liberation for the peasantry.[65]

Rural protests also underwent a noticeable shift from an emphasis on salaries and work conditions to land reform. Economic petitions did not entirely disappear. In 1959, workers on the Chaupi hacienda in Pesillo successfully complained to the labor inspector to address salaries, mistreatment, and abuses.[66] For the most part, however, demands increasingly focused on agrarian reform. Although land had always been important, leaders introduced the concept of land *ownership,* which subsequently became a defining characteristic of Indigenous struggles. "For the first time in our history," the PCE stated in 1952, "the Indian and montuvio understand with clarity that their happiness depends on the delivery of the land for which they struggle."[67] The Communist Party's 1956 electoral platform, featuring a graphic of a communist worker with a hammer and anvil breaking the chains of Africans and Indigenous peoples, advocated ending the huasipungo system, raising the salaries of agricultural and Indigenous workers, and giving Asistencia Pública land to Indians and peasants.[68] Both urban leftists and Indigenous activists demanded breaking up government-owned haciendas and giving the land to Indigenous peasants, either individually or as cooperatives. Communists had a lasting influence on how rural communities conceptualized their struggles for land.

SIX

Agrarian Reform?

Ten days before José María Velasco Ibarra assumed the executive office for the fourth time in August 1960, police wounded two people when they evicted hundreds of peasants in Milagro who had invaded parcels of land shouting "vivas" to Cuba, Fidel Castro, and agrarian reform.[1] In October 1960, peasants on the Atapo and Quinchocajas haciendas presented the labor ministry with demands for a raise in salary, end of abuses, and a normalization of work requirements.[2] Two months later, five hundred Indigenous workers reportedly chanting "vivas" to Cuba and Russia rose up on the Carrera hacienda. Complaining that they had not been paid in four months, the Indians declared the land to be theirs, and suggested that the hacendado Altamirano leave before he was killed. In response, Altamirano fled the estate and accused three communist leaders from Quito of instigating the revolt. The government sent in thirty police to quell the uprising.[3] Similar uprisings occurred in January 1961 on the La Clemencia hacienda in Imbabura and on Villanueva in Guayas, and in March another in Loja demanded expropriation of hacienda land.[4] In one of the most successful protests during this period, peasants took over the Tenguel hacienda in March 1962 and forced the United Fruit Company to sell it to the Ecuadorian government.[5]

These revolts were only a few of the many powerful rural uprisings during the early 1960s, all of which reflect changes in the dynamics, discourse, and strategies in Ecuador's Indigenous and peasant movements. The FEI leader Carlos Rodríguez recalled that after lagging in the mid-1950s, rural organizing efforts peaked between 1958 and 1963. During this period, the federation delivered three hundred petitions to the Labor Inspector in the Ministry of Social Welfare, with many coming from Cayambe. From May 1958 to April 1961, the Labor Inspector reported 173 labor conflicts with 77 of these on haciendas. About one fourth of the protests took place in Cayambe, especially in the perpetually conflictive zone of Pesillo. From May 1962 through April 1963, the government counted forty-four more agricultural conflicts throughout the highlands.[6] Later Indigenous organizations applauded the FEI for "powerfully raising the struggle for land" and putting itself at the front of the fight.[7] This growth in protests took place in the context of economic changes with manufactured imports surpassing raw material exports such as bananas, coffee, and cacao, leading to an increased dependency on foreign loans and investment.

Open revolts often came only after peons believed that they had exhausted legal appeals with the government. Many protests were against nonpayment of salaries, although from that starting point, demands often extended into a broad range of other issues. Osvaldo Albornoz Peralta lists seven principal demands: land, defense of huasipungo plots, improvements in wages, reduction in the workload, suppression of nonremunerative work requirements (huasicamas, chagracamas, milkmaids), provision of tools, and better treatment.[8] Despite this range of issues, activists increasingly pushed agrarian reform as the primary and most critical demand.

Federación Nacional de Campesinos e Indios

By the late 1950s, the PCE secretary-general Pedro Saad recognized that the FEI and its sister CTE affiliate the Federación de Trabajadores Agrícolas del Litoral (FTAL, Federation of Coastal Agricultural Workers) had become moribund. Hundreds of delegates from agricultural unions, peasant groups, and comunas formed the FTAL in September 1954, but a lack of economic resources limited its effectiveness.[9] After an initial period of intensive activity, the FEI had also ceased to be effective and had not held a congress since 1952. In an attempt to reactivate the peasant struggle and build a stronger and more unified movement, Saad advocated merging the two into one federation tentatively called the Federación Nacional de Campesinos e Indios (National Federation of Peasants and Indians).[10] This was a return to the CTE's plans in 1944 for a unified National Peasant and Indian Federation, although distinct economic and ethnic situations on the coast and in the highlands had led to the formation of two organizations.

In October 1960, the CTE brought together 350 delegates representing 130 organizations and 200,000 peasants and Indians from the highlands and coast for the Primera Conferencia Nacional Campesina (First National Peasant Conference). Under the theme "land to those who work it," the CTE president Víctor Zúñiga called the meeting "with the principal objective of discussing the problem of agrarian reform."[11] César Muñoz, head of the peasant secretariat of the CTE, served as president of the meeting, and Amadeo Alba, an Indigenous leader from Cayambe, was one of three vice presidents. The conference advocated an agrarian reform that included the extension of credit, technical assistance, housing, health care, and roads. More broadly, delegates discussed improvements for the lives of peasants, elimination of feudalism, development of national industry, nationalization of the irrigation system, and free distribution of water to peasants. Even as the peasant movement moved forward with its demands for agrarian reform, it did not discard ethnic aspects of the struggle. Delegates called for recognition of "Quechua together with Spanish as an official language and its use for teaching in highland schools."[12] Given that language was a primary marker of ethnic identity, the preservation of Kichwa represented a rejection of liberal assimilationist ideologies. In addition, they advocated universal suffrage and the popular election of local officials. Illustrating that Indigenous and peasant struggles were not isolated from broader national and international issues, delegates declared their solidarity with the Cuban Revolution.[13]

Three delegates presented conference findings to the National Assembly and called on Velasco Ibarra to implement an effective agrarian reform program. Representing Cayambe's peasant syndicates, Miguel Lechón eloquently argued for an agrarian reform that would benefit those who worked the land. It should not only involve "the distribution of land, but also the creation of schools for the education of children, because it is not acceptable that in the twentieth century Indians and peasants remain ignorant." Neptalí Ulcuango added that the traditional policy of sending landless Indians and peasants to colonize faraway lands was not an acceptable form of agrarian reform; they wanted the lands that they were working. The coastal peasant leader Neptalí Pacheco added that their clamor was for peace, work, land, and liberty, and in the process they would destroy the landholding structures that held the peasantry in misery.[14]

The conference delegates decided that both the FTAL and the FEI were to meet at the beginning of 1961, followed by a national peasant congress to organize a new Federación Nacional Campesina del Ecuador (National Peasant Federation of Ecuador).[15] Nevertheless, this new federation failed to materialize. Pointing to the direction taken by Indigenous struggles in the 1960s, instead of working more closely with coastal montuvio peasants the highland Indians acquired a stronger and more acutely developed sense of ethnic identity.

Agrarian Unrest

On February 5, 1961, two thousand Indians on the Columbe Grande hacienda in Chimborazo complained that the hacienda owner had not paid them and appeared to have no intention of doing so. Police suppressed the unrest, resulting in two Indians killed, three policemen injured, and over sixty Indians arrested. One day earlier, the Ministry of Social Welfare had met with leaders from fifteen haciendas in a failed attempt to solve the problems peacefully. The FEI, the CTE's Peasant Commission, the FTP, and Telmo Hidalgo, the functional senator for highland workers, all came to the defense of the arrested Indians. These allies helped counter the government's attacks, leading the governor of Chimborazo to encourage landowners to bring workers' accounts up to date. Supporters also presented the president with demands to withdraw the police, pay wages, abolish feudalistic labor requirements (including the huasicama, cuentayo, and chagracama), and give land to huasipungueros. Velasco Ibarra justified police actions as necessary to preserve order, and he told the assembled labor leaders that the prosecution of abuses should be pursued through legal means rather than an uprising. Nevertheless, he ordered the imprisoned workers released and launched an investigation into abuses on the haciendas. "We should put those who abuse Indians in jail," the president stated, "but I feel impotent to take the radical measures that you want" because "of the environment in our country." Velasco Ibarra repeatedly appealed to popular concerns, but he failed to follow through with concrete policies to benefit the subaltern masses.[16]

Wealthy property owners and their conservative allies challenged the legitimacy of rural protests, arguing that they were due to the intervention of "known communist agitators." The Frente Anticomunista Ecuatoriano (Ecuadorian Anti-Communist Front) declared that the FEI leader Carlos Rodríguez was the "principal communist agitator and direct cause of the incident" at Columbe. He had organized the Indians into a military regiment, named Manuel Agualsaca as colonel, and gave ranks to other workers. Columbe was a testing ground for an international communist conspiracy backed by Cuba's Fidel Castro to take over Ecuador, and the government had done nothing to stop this. Neighboring hacendados complained that communists without provocation stirred up violence on their estates. The Anti-Communist Front found the calls for social justice unconvincing and denounced Indigenous demands as hypocritical. The rebels had called for the police to withdraw their forces only because it would provide an opening to relaunch the insurrection. Other demands (payment of salaries, elimination of labor requirements, land) were "in the clouds," impossible to realize, and provided an excuse for more agitation. The communists played on Indigenous ignorance with promises of owning the haciendas, using this as a pretext to collect money from the workers. The anti-communists also accused the agitators of stirring up racial hatred by counseling the workers to "kill the hacienda owners, the whites, Columbe's administrator, and to abuse the owner's wife."[17]

The charges of savage Indians wanting to kill white landholders and rape their women were overstated, but such statements indicate the persistent presence of fear and racism. It did not help that the Ministry of Welfare expressed similarly exaggerated fears. Despite their best efforts, the ministry warned, "in a very short period of time the country could find itself in a situation of an Indigenous revolution, inspired by Chinese communist revolutionary formulas that could destroy the democratic institutions that govern our country." The ministry urged the congress to take immediate measures to destroy clandestine organizational efforts and prevent thousands of Indigenous peoples from falling victim to communist ploys.[18] These heightened fears reflect the effectiveness of aggressive leaders who kept applying pressure on the government.

Agrarian Reform Proposals

The 1954 agricultural census revealed Ecuador's extreme imbalance in land ownership.[19] For decades, liberals, conservatives, socialists, and Indigenous organizations had advanced agrarian reform proposals without success. For example, in 1951 the Functional Senators for the Working Class presented legislation to the National Assembly to distribute Asistencia Pública lands to hacienda workers. Although it gained congressional approval, President Velasco Ibarra killed the project.[20] In 1956, leftist legislators once again presented congress with petitions from Indigenous workers to split up government-owned haciendas.[21] The goal was to destroy the hacienda system along with its feudalistic modes of production and give the land to peasants.[22] Increasingly the left embraced agrarian reform as its cause célèbre. Rather than challenging the existing land tenure system by redistributing hacienda land, the government historically had opted to colonize allegedly unused lands in the Amazon as a means of relieving land pressure in the highlands.[23] In 1957 the Ministry of Agriculture formed the Instituto Nacional de Colonización (National Colonization Institute) to relocate highland peasants on Tsáchila Indian land at Santo Domingo de los Colorados on the western slopes of the Andes. These limited reforms failed to satiate the peasant thirst for land or satisfy leftist political demands. The triumph in 1959 of the Cuban Revolution sent shockwaves throughout Latin America, and its subsequent radical agrarian reform program convinced many elites of the critical importance of modifying the land tenure system in order to prevent another such "disaster."

Sensing that an agrarian reform program was imminent, forward-thinking hacendados began to give their workers land in order to control the process. Emilio Bonifaz, owner of the expansive Guachalá hacienda, was one of the first to give land voluntarily to his workers. On October 2, 1959, he granted land titles to twenty families at Pitaná, the site of the 1954 massacre, although Galo Ramón makes the point that the hacienda distributed *bad* land. Hacendados kept the core irrigated and fertile sections, and only gave away poor, eroded, useless lands. The reforms were also designed to undercut radical organizing efforts. For his noble efforts, Bonifaz received a medal of agricultural merit. His actions gave the Guachalá hacienda a reputation as one of the leading modernizing forces in Ecuadorian agrarian polices and created a model that other hacendados emulated.[24] In total, from 1959 to 1964 there were 3,019 cases of landowners liquidating huasipungos through private initiative, with the majority of these located in Pichincha.[25]

Scholars have hotly debated whether Ecuador's agrarian reform legislation was due to peasant and Indigenous pressures on the government for land, or rather a result of the modernizing influence of enlightened landowners. Osvaldo Barsky originally presented the thesis that modernizing landowners initiated the agrarian reform process because they were eager to rid themselves of the burden of providing for huasipungueros on their estates. Moving to mechanized production and wage labor, they believed, would increase their profit margins. Andrés Guerrero, on the other hand, argued that agrarian reform was a result of peasant actions and the class struggle between peasants and landowners that finally forced hacendados to give in to their demands. To focus primarily on the actions of landowners, as Barsky does, was not only to deny agency to rural actors but also to misrepresent what actually was happening with this historical process in Ecuador.[26] Fernando Velasco echoes that "from the beginning of 1960 there was a noticeable rise in social agitation in the countryside. In the Sierra and on the Coast the number of syndicates rose and petitions, strikes, and all sorts of demands and complaints became more common. It was a state of general effervescence, impelled and articulated fundamentally by the Communist Party through the Ecuadorian Federation of Indians in the Sierra and the Federation of Coastal Agricultural Workers."[27]

In the face of pressure from below, members of the Ecuadorian elite began to advocate for change in the country's land tenure patterns to prevent a class struggle and to terminate obsolete institutions that were seen as impeding the modernization of the country. Many hacendados, however, gave land to their workers only *after* protests such as a 1961 FEI march on Quito.[28] As Leon Zamosc concludes, "It was class conflict, and not the mere rationale of capitalist production, that motivated some modernizing landowners" to favor agrarian reform legislation.[29] Land distribution was costly, but not nearly as expensive as if a successful revolt were to result in the complete expropriation of the hacienda.[30] Hacendado actions were deliberate and self-serving rather than altruistic. Any gains were not gifts from modernizing landowners but the result of long and intense Indigenous struggles in alliance with urban leftists.

Francisco Gangotena similarly underscores that peasants, not hacendados, had taken the initiative on the Galte and Pull haciendas. In 1951, a new owner attempted to move from the traditional huaspungo model to a more modern and efficient wage labor system. While on the surface Indigenous challenges to this change could be seen as a conservative reaction of peasants clinging to tradition, it was the radical leadership affiliated with the FEI and PCE that led this as a struggle for social justice within the framework of building a class consciousness. Not only had internal unrest "pushed the landlords against the wall," but rural communities pressed their concerns with a unified voice. Written complaints were always signed by a "peasant group" and presented in the name of the community.[31]

Activists naturally championed their role in forcing agrarian reform concessions from the government. "It is not an exaggeration," Albornoz Peralta stated, "that most of the demands which they have achieved, particularly land rights and the formation of cooperatives in Cayambe, are the result of the struggle of the Ecuadorian Federation of Indians and its valiant directors."[32] Saad similarly emphasized the role of the FEI and the PCE in forcing the government to cede land to huasipungueros.[33] Indians shared a similar voluntarist attitude. "Land, culture, rights of freedom of thought, organization, and action," Neptalí Ulcuango declared, "were not a gift from the master, government, legal system, nor did they fall from the sky." Rather, these were triumphs of the Indian struggle, and because of this, Indians should never think of themselves as anything less than the elite bosses and government officials.[34] Indigenous workers did not gain reforms by passively waiting for the landowners or government to act, nor were reforms the results of passive resistance, as implied in James Scott's model of "the weapons of the weak." As the famed abolitionist Frederick Douglass once stated, "Power concedes nothing without a demand. It never has and it never will."[35] Land transfers were a direct result of continual organizational pressure from below.

Agrarian reform was one of the hottest topics in the 1960 elections. The PCE denounced the miserable state in which the conservative president Camilo Ponce Enríquez had left the country. "Enormous masses of Indians and peasants," the party declared, "live in worse conditions than animals." Nor did the leading candidates Galo Plaza and José María Velasco Ibarra provide viable alternatives, for both were part of a reactionary oligarchy that favored a "continuation of the feudal regime that maintains Indians oppressed like beasts." Instead they called for an agrarian reform that would give land to peasants and end feudal labor relations for the Indians.[36] Nevertheless, Velasco Ibarra gained rural support because of his promises to promulgate agrarian reform legislation. "Peasants wanted land," Velasco Ibarra noted. "People called for nationalization. Politicians talked of a new future."[37] According to John Uggen, the leftist candidacy of Antonio Parra had forced him into this position. After his election, Velasco Ibarra backed away from these promises. From the PCE's perspective, the populist leader "had stolen and then betrayed" their program.[38]

Caught between an unwillingness to promulgate agrarian reform legislation and an inability to contain rural protest, in November 1961 Velasco Ibarra was forced out of office (for the third time without completing his term) after only fourteen months in power. His vice president, Carlos Julio Arosemena Monroy, who assumed power, was a millionaire from Guayaquil. Both his father and grandfather had previously also served as chief executive. Despite a reputation for leaning to the left, Arosemena selected a fairly conservative cabinet and governed as a moderate.[39] As with his predecessor, he was increasingly torn between popular demands for labor and land reforms and the interests of international capital.

The 1961 FEI March

Mounting pressure for agrarian reform culminated in a massive march on December 16, 1961. The FEI and the CTE peasant commission organized twelve thousand Indians and peasants who peacefully descended on Quito to seek redress for their grievances. Dressed in traditional ponchos, skirts, and hats, men and women cascaded like an avalanche through the streets of the capital for more than one and a half hours, carrying signs demanding bread, justice, education, and land, and shouting in Spanish and Kichwa their demands for agrarian reform and an end to the huasipungo system. Andrés Guerrero describes this rally as "undoubtedly the largest urban protest march of Indigenous peasants in Ecuadorian history."[40] The FEI demanded an increase in wages, elimination of feudal work demands, land for huasipungueros, irrigation, schools, and universal suffrage. Although the march focused on economic and political issues, an undercurrent of ethnicity flowed through the event. One banner stated, "We have been exploited for four centuries"—thereby rhetorically tracing the roots of exploitation to the Spanish conquest. Other banners supporting Fidel Castro and the Cuban Revolution highlighted the movement's leftist tendencies. Signs proclaiming "Tierra o Muerte" ("land or death") echoed Emiliano Zapata's agrarian struggle in the Mexican Revolution.[41]

The FEI cultivated support from broader popular movements for a radical and democratic agrarian reform that would bring progress to Ecuador. Student organizations canvassed the streets of Quito in an effort to drum up support for the march.[42] The FTP offered its "class solidarity" by providing food and housing and arranging Christmas treats for the children.[43] The Partido Socialista Revolucionario (PSR, Revolutionary Socialist Party), one of the most radical of the leftist parties in the 1960s, encouraged the FEI to pass resolutions on agrarian reform that "would be revolutionary and reach for solutions to the Ecuadorian problem."[44]

President Arosemena, together with his leftist ministers of social welfare, treasury, and defense, led the march through Quito's streets. Speaking in a driving rain to the assembled crowd at Plaza Bolívar, Arosemena criticized previous governments for not paying attention to Indigenous demands. The FEI president Miguel Lechón highlighted patterns of abuses and low salaries on haciendas, and he proclaimed that Ecuador should follow the example of the recently triumphant Cuban Revolution. He called for education, medical attention, land, water, electricity, and the infrastructure necessary to change land tenure patterns. Finally, the CTE president and PSR member Víctor Zúñiga addressed the crowd.[45]

In reflecting echoes of the march on the national consciousness, editorials in El Comercio called for a rethinking of racial prejudices against Indigenous workers. Indians are human beings, the paper editorialized, "with rights and not only obligations. They are capable of progress like any other men, and can form a creative and positive force" in improving the prosperity of the country. Still reflecting paternalistic attitudes, the editorial called for the government to educate Indians in order to improve their mental abilities and consciousness so that they would assimilate into the national culture and contribute to social progress.[46] Even a landowner association took out a half-page advertisement in El Comercio calling for a solution to the country's agricultural problems, although it emphasized that calls for agrarian reform should not provide cover for "known political agitators" to "disturb the public peace."[47] Popular actions had shifted elite discourse away from the blatant racist reactions that organizers had faced three decades earlier when they first attempted organize a national federation.

Jaime Galarza Zavala polemically argued that "it was clear that the Indian constitutes a fundamental force in the Ecuadorian revolution, the iron fist that will shatter the feudal regime."[48] The journalist Lilo Linke wondered "how much longer Indians and mestizos will wait. It cannot be too difficult to get them marching again, the next time perhaps in a not so humble mood."[49] Although the marxist left was electorally weak, it exerted considerable influence over popular movements, and Indigenous activists continued to collaborate closely with these allies.

The December 16 rally was the opening salvo for the third FEI congress, whose principal objective was to demand a just, radical, and democratic agrarian reform. The march was so successful that it overshadowed the succeeding congress in both contemporary journalistic accounts as well as in subsequent historical memories to the point that little record of its proceedings remain. Apparently this was the first congress since 1952. If statements from the CTE are accurate, they pressed the FEI to meet after a gap of almost a decade.[50] The historical record does not shed light on why this was termed the third congress, since the FEI had already held a third congress in 1948 and a fourth in 1952. The FEI claims not to have any organizational archives, and this awkward numbering system may simply be a reflection of poor recordkeeping in an organization that relied largely on memory and oral traditions.[51] Were the two previous congresses so unsuccessful that they simply had been forgotten? This was a period of transition from a first-generation leadership to that of a second generation, and perhaps the congresses were insignificant details that had not been passed along. Or, perhaps more sinisterly, it reflects an underlying division in FEI's leadership with two different groups organizing events under the federation's banner. There is little evidence to support any of these interpretations. Nevertheless, the march and congress do indicate that the FEI was emerging out of dormancy, becoming in the 1960s the most militant and active that it had been since its founding almost twenty years earlier. Continuing previous leadership patterns, Miguel Lechón who like Gualavisí and Cacuango came out of militant Indigenous movements in Cayambe, now served as president as well as sitting on the Central Committee of the PCE. Luis Bolívar Bolaños Sánchez, a white lawyer from Quito, a member of the Central Committee of the PCE, and the organizational secretary of the CTE, was the secretary-general. Over the next decade, Lechón assumed a frequent visual presence in the communist party newspaper *El Pueblo* and became a common fixture at marches, representing the Indigenous face of demands for effective agrarian reform legislation. He readily mixed leftist idioms and ethnic references into his speech, with statements such as, "Indians of the Indian-peasant race were massacred, compañero."[52]

In the face of "considerable pressure," Arosemena promised to execute an agrarian reform law. Immediately after the march, the government announced that with all urgency it was drafting an emergency law to grant huasipungueros titles to their lands.[53] Nevertheless, despite Arosemena's promises, agrarian reform was not immediately forthcoming. The proposal to abolish the huasipungo system stalled when it met opposition from the agricultural association, which had just congratulated the FEI on its congress. Elites went on a counteroffensive, responding with an alternative project that proposed minor reforms in order to stabilize and solidify the existing economic order.[54] It was not until the following September that the socialist deputy Alfredo Pérez Guerrero finally presented congress with a proposal to abolish the huasipungo system.[55] Indigenous peasants knew from experience not to wait passively for the promised reforms but rather to keep pressure on those in power. The march represented a watershed, but it was not the end of the struggle for agrarian reform.

Despite common perceptions of Arosemena as a leftist sympathizer, his tenure in office resulted not only in no agricultural reform legislation but also increased repression of rural movements.[56] The CTE and FEI pointed to repressive measures that wealthy landowners took against peasant movements under the guise of fighting communism. The owner of the Cunuyacu hacienda in Tungurahua, Miguel Chico, burned Segundo Punina's hut and executed Segundo Benjamín Toalombo. The property owners in Cayambe arrested Julio Chicaiza, a leader of the Peasant League in Juan Montalvo, and sent a group of hoodlums to shoot at Rubén Rodríguez's house. The administrators on the Pesillo hacienda burned the hut of the worker Honorio Cacuango and killed a sheep belonging to another worker. A priest and a mayordomo savagely beat a worker from the Tigua cooperative whom they accused of being a "communist Indian."

The most serious threats were on the Columbe Grande hacienda, the site of a powerful uprising the previous February. Claiming rumors of communist plans to burn the hacienda, landowners threatened local leaders, FEI organizers, and even political activists who no longer lived in the area. The FEI and CTE pointed to the source of the violence. "In response to the just and minimal demands of the workers on the haciendas who ask for their salaries, tools, and human treatment," their statement read, "the exploiters only raise the argument of brute force, assassinations, fires, tortures, jailings, and firings." They declared that despite these threats "the peasant organizations will redouble their struggle and unity, and defeat the landowner's violence." They called on other popular movements to "lend solidarity to their brothers in the countryside."[57] The Unión Revolucionaria de Juventudes Ecuatorianas (URJE, Ecuadorian Youth Revolutionary Union) responded with a forceful denunciation of the provocations at Columbe Grande. They declared that "only the combative action of the people will lead to agrarian reform."[58] The URJE statement confirmed elite fears that Indigenous protests were mobilizing other sectors of the popular movement that, in turn, lent visibility and legitimacy to rural demands.

In May 1962, Pesillo Indians petitioned the government for five hundred hectares of land to distribute to those without huasipungo plots and to increase the size and quality of the plots already established. In a break from the tradition that gave land only to men, the activists asked that widows be allowed to remain on their dead husbands' plots. The Indians requested that huasipungueros be allowed to retire after thirty years, demanded that fired workers be rehired, and called for an end to obligatory service requirements. In response, authorities jailed the syndicate leader Amadeo Alba. The strike was strategically planned during harvest, which helped the syndicate win its wage and land demands.[59]

Hidden in this story are indications of broad shifts in land tenure, service tenancy, and economic relations on haciendas that changed Indigenous struggles. Fifty years earlier, the government rewarded Aquiles Jarrín for drawing additional workers onto the hacienda.[60] Now there was a labor surplus and huasipungo plots became a treasured commodity. Access to land assumed more importance than salaries and working conditions. Peloso notes how the introduction of machinery in Peru drove down labor costs as "plantation owners no longer felt the need to give way to tenant demands for space and privilege."[61] Indians increasingly needed to develop new strategies to realize their goals.

On August 15, 1962, police massacred thirteen and injured twenty Salasacas who fought for water rights from the Pachanlica River in Tungurahua. This inhumane treatment profoundly moved public opinion. Several weeks later, with photos and a front-page story, El Comercio reported that Salasacas dressed in their traditional white pants and black ponchos presented a petition directly to congress in Quito. Together with the local parish priest Antonio Michelena, they decided to remain until their concerns were addressed. "We are poor," Manuel Caizabancha nervously stated, "and need water to survive." Angel Saquil added that they were thirsty not only for water but also for a teacher and education for their children. Their presentation deeply moved the deputies, who responded with a standing ovation in homage to the victims of the massacre. They approved a resolution that denounced the massacre, initiated an investigation, provided 100,000 sucres of indemnification for the families of the victims, and requested a study of the irrigation system. More than anything, the dramatic testimonies forced the congress to move ahead with discussions to abolish the huasipungo system.[62] Even the conservative El Comercio editorialized in favor of these reforms.[63]

Urban leftists continued to support the rural struggles. In 1962, Nela Martínez helped found the Unión Revolucionaria de Mujeres del Ecuador (URME, Revolutionary Union of Ecuadorian Women), and the first issue of the union's periodical Nuestra Palabra featured Martínez's biography of the

Dolores Cacuango, 1968. Photo by Rolf Blomberg.
Courtesy of the Archivo Blomberg, Quito, Ecuador.

"unforgettable" Dolores Cacuango and her struggles against elite domination.[64] The dramatic increases in Indigenous activism posed a serious threat
to elite hegemony, and rumors began to circulate of a right-wing conspiracy
to overthrow Arosemena's government. Finally, Arosemena's overtures to
the left, his support for the revolutionary Cuban government, and his problems with drinking led to a military coup on July 11, 1963. The military junta
declared that the coup was "necessary to stop the terrorist and subversive
wave that today shakes the country."[65] A month earlier, fascist groups condemned Neptalí Pacheco León, Carlos Rodríguez, Jorge Rivadeneira, and
Bolívar Bolaños for introducing propaganda from Cuba and for arming
peasant leaders to push the FTAL and FEI to militant action. Their actions
went against the "profound Christian sentiments of the Indian."[66] Further
motivating the coup, a growing sentiment within the military feared that a
return to power in the 1964 elections of either the populist Velasco Ibarra or

the conservative Ponce Enriquez would lead to more chaos and a strengthening of the left.[67]

The coup was a momentary blow to Ecuador's popular movements, as it imprisoned hundreds of political activists, forced others into hiding, drove the PCE underground, and disrupted internal organizational structures. The repression was particularly vicious in Pesillo and in Milagro where the PCE had gained significant support. The military closed the Indigenous schools that the FEI had set up in Cayambe in 1945. Tránsito Amaguaña and Amadeo Alba were arrested and remained in prison for eighteen months. Uggen notes that "no political party, except the PCE, was willing to articulate peasant demands, and they were declared illegal."[68] The FEI never recovered from these repressive actions, and the coup represented the beginning of the end for the federation as the primary Indigenous organization in Ecuador. On the coast, the military also invaded and collapsed organizing efforts on the Tenguel hacienda, which workers had taken over the previous year. Finally, the coup brought an end to the longest sequence of constitutional governments up to that point in Ecuador's history.[69] Much like the 1925 July Revolution that took place in the context of a collapsing cacao economy, this break in the constitutional order came in the wake of declining banana exports.

Agrarian Reform and Colonization Law

On July 11, 1964, the first anniversary of taking power, the military government promulgated the Ley de Reforma Agraria y Colonización (Agrarian Reform and Colonization Law) and established the Instituto Ecuatoriano de Reforma Agraria y Colonización (IERAC, Ecuadorian Institute of Agrarian Reform and Colonization). Under John F. Kennedy's Alliance for Progress program, Ecuador was one of eleven Latin American countries between 1960 and 1964 to implement agrarian reform programs. With the left's voice muted, these reforms favored modernizing agrarian capitalists and did little to address underlying social and economic inequalities.

The purpose of the law was "to correct defects in the current agricultural structure through better distribution and utilization of the land." It proposed improving conditions for agricultural workers through "the abolition of defective modes of tenure and work such as the huasipungo." Landowners were given a twelve-month period to phase out the huasipungo system. No longer could they pay agricultural workers with scrip or in kind with land or water rights; instead, workers were to be paid entirely in cash. The ex-huasipungueros were to receive their small plots, and they were to have continued access to water, firewood, and other hacienda resources, although landowners often managed to skirt this aspect of the law. Plots were to go to the male head of family, although women sometimes gained access to them after the death of the holder. Traditional laborers including huasicamas, cuentayos, and milkmaids were now to be paid, although activists continued to struggle for equal pay for women's work, paid vacations, and other benefits that the labor code stipulated.[70] Gaining rights for women was an important achievement after years of struggle for the recognition of their role in Indigenous communities.

The agrarian reform program sought to eliminate leftist influences in rural organizing efforts. The law specifically outlawed land invasions and excluded from its benefits anyone who occupied land in a violent or clandestine manner. Furthermore, the law placed cooperatives under the administrative control of the agrarian reform institute.[71] The message from IERAC was clear: the law of agrarian reform was a blessing that liberated people from their miserable condition. A propaganda pamphlet stated: "We owe all this to the military government that gave agrarian reform to the peasants. We will not forget it."[72] The junta's strategy was to co-opt key issues of Ecuador's popular movement. Thus IERAC "became a competitor of the PCE, but with the superior resources of the national government."[73] Activists represented a threat to elite privilege, and the government fought to control them.

The agrarian reform law made little progress in addressing the underlying structural problems that rural peoples faced. Despite the rhetoric of improving peasants' lives, the law fostered capitalist penetration in the countryside, a concentration of land holdings, and the development of agribusiness. Article four promised to guarantee the rights of agricultural workers, but the law failed to define what those rights were and how they would be protected. The law set a cap on land ownership at one thousand hectares, but this limited only the very largest estates. Furthermore, the government never seriously enforced this provision. Its ideological orientation was toward modernization, with a goal to make agricultural production more efficient rather than redistributing land. In contrast, Indians received small, marginal plots not suitable for intensive cultivation. M. R. Redclift observes that some landowners welcomed the end of the huasipungo system because free wage-labor could be exploited more cheaply.[74] Former huasipungueros became an inexpensive, unskilled labor force without access to hacienda resources. William Thiesenhusen notes that "the *minifundismo* created by the abolition of the huasipungo system was as bad or worse than *huasipungaje* itself."[75] In the end, the government expropriated relatively little land. From 1964 to 1970, only 10.2 percent of highland peasant families (27,087 families in total) received land, and the IERAC redistributed only 8.5 percent (125,231 hectares) of the land belonging to haciendas larger than five hundred hectares. Rather than eliminating poverty and discrimination, it simply reorganized and entrenched economic and racial subordination. The legislation proved to be reform in name only with no real redistribution of power or economic wealth.[76]

The military government's promises of agrarian reform also failed to put an end to endless Indigenous revolts. On August 3, 1964, two months after the promulgation of the law, 150 Kayambis from El Chaupi, Moyurco, and San Pablourco on the Pesillo hacienda demanded justice from the current renter, Wilson Monge. Elites accused communists of inciting the uprising and identified the well-known communist leader Jorge Rivadeneyra as the primary instigator. Authorities noted that a current of subversion ran through the workers, and that precautions should be taken because it was harvest time. Although the situation remained tense, the following day the Indians returned to work. Monge informed the police that he had concrete information that the workers were planning another strike that would stop the harvest and cause landowners serious economic damage.[77] Agrarian reform had failed to stop rural organizing efforts.

Experts advocated using Pesillo as a model for reforms that might be implemented on other haciendas. Some Indigenous leaders had long requested that the hacienda be converted to a cooperative rather than broken up into small private holdings.[78] Under this pressure, in 1966 IERAC divided Pesillo into a pilot program with two worker-managed cooperatives, "Atahualpa" and "Simón Bolívar."[79] The cooperatives for the most part met with failure because government officials had not considered local needs. Many people resented that they were essentially working for yet another landowner, this time IERAC. Many activists believed that the land should be given to them without cost or obstacles. The agrarian reform legislation did not provide for leadership training, thus resulting in poor administration. Members often did not understand a cooperative's potential benefits for accessing credit and other resources. Furthermore, as the FEI president Manuel Escobar noted, the cooperatives were chronically underfunded and bureaucratic red tape needlessly complicated the process of gaining financing.[80]

Some Indigenous intellectuals criticized the formation of cooperatives as an attempt to disrupt traditional forms of social organization, introduce foreign structures, and impose state policies on Indigenous communities. Nepalí Ulcuango argued that cooperatives did not work because they were part of a capitalist system that was foreign to Indigenous realities. Never, he stressed, "would the cooperative system benefit rural peoples."[81] Not all families joined the cooperatives, which led to discord and tension between community members. Cooperative legislation continued to divide Indigenous movements along the lines of the 1937 comunas law between those rooted in the former hacienda system and the "traditional" or "free" communities organized as comunas.[82] Tránsito Amaguaña noted that although "the cooperatives did not solve the basic problems which peasants faced and furthermore led to new conflicts," at least with the cooperatives "the peasants no longer had to work for the master nor for the government, but rather worked for themselves and their families."[83] But the internal contradictions proved to be too great. In the 1980s, the Simón Bolívar cooperative divided its land among its members and formally dissolved. The promise of the cooperative structure remained a frustrated and unrealized dream.

Ultimately, the military dictatorship was unable to solve the growing economic and social problems that had plagued previous civilian administrations. In March 1966, in the face of growing student and worker demonstrations, the military junta turned the government back to civilian control. Rather than halting dissent, the transition triggered another round of protests, with at least twenty-nine peasant actions in the following nine months.[84]

With a return to civilian government, militants attempted to rebuild the FEI and restore it to its previous position of prominence. The federation regained a strong presence in zones that formed its traditional base of support, particularly on government-owned haciendas in Chimborazo, Cotopaxi, and Pichincha. In October 1966, the FEI held its first congress in almost five years. At the inaugural session in the Salón de la Ciudad in Quito, president Miguel Lechón told 350 delegates in Kichwa that their struggle was not only on behalf of peasants, but for all Ecuadorians. He called for a true agrarian reform program "so that Ecuadorian land would be for Ecuadorians," and he demanded that "the next government give us an authentic agrarian reform law that will liberate us." The secretary-general Bolívar

Bolaños angrily denounced the program as a fraud and called for an authentic agrarian reform program led by a popular revolutionary government. The congress called for a reorganization of IERAC in order to incorporate representation from the FEI and FTAL. Although the main issue was with the slow-moving and incomplete agrarian reform program, Lechón also called for schools that would end high illiteracy rates in rural communities. Amadeo Alba, the first vice president of the congress, called for unity in the face of the problems that Indians faced. The session ended with Lechón leading a homage to the elderly Dolores Cacuango for her lifetime of service to the cause.[85]

As with previous meetings, the congress triggered a significant increase in activism as militants returned to their home communities rededicated to the struggle for an authentic agrarian reform that responded to the needs of the rural masses. An uprising at Colta in Chimborazo successfully extracted concessions from IERAC.[86] In a well-coordinated campaign under the leadership of Alba, Lechón, and Ulcuango, together with the advisors Bolaños and Colón Narváez, one thousand Indians took over the Pisambilla, Moyurco, El Chaupi, San Pablourco, and Pesillo haciendas in Cayambe. Together with labor leaders from the FTP, the FEI met in Quito with Juan Casals, the director of IERAC. A newspaper report observed that "they aspire to be owners of the land and work in freedom" rather than continue under the control of the IERAC.[87]

To regain control the government sent in military troops, arrested Narváez and Bolaños, and used the air force to conduct aerial surveillance to uncover clandestine meetings.[88] Forty years after the formation of the first peasant syndicates in Cayambe, many of the organizational dynamics remained similar to those of the previous era. Indians fought for control over local affairs, the government sent in the armed forces to suppress their uprisings, and supportive urban leftists faced criminal prosecution. In the 1920s, local activists dressed Chávez as an Indian; once again they used this tactic to prevent Bolaños's arrest. But now, rather than relying on outside mediators, the FEI made its own public statements. The group invited the press to tour Cayambe with FEI leaders to observe their realities. Journalists representing elite interests could hardly believe that Indians were capable of claiming a leading role in these movements, and as a result they tended to minimize the importance of their actions.[89] Nevertheless, "the FEI had a lot of power," as Javier Herrán, a Spanish priest who worked for years with rural movements in Cotopaxi and Cayambe, later noted. "They became the protagonist of the first law of agrarian reform."[90] The federation gained more prestige when Colón Narváez began working as its representative inside IERAC. The PCE called for party members to support him in the face of conservative reactions that sought to limit his influence among the masses because he would "guarantee the struggle for peasant objectives."[91]

On May 1, 1968, the PCE championed Indigenous participation in its annual May Day march. The FEI brought in eight thousand workers with their own style and agenda, including a casket and demands to bury IERAC's nonfunctioning agrarian reform apparatus. In a speech at the rally, Neptalí Ulcuango called for "the need for a revolutionary change in the political-economic-social structure" of the country.[92] Workers on the Pull hacienda subsequently struck for back payment and for the return of their huasipungo plots. Ambrosio Lasso launched a "solidarity strike" on the Galte and other neighboring haciendas. These prolonged strikes spread across several haciendas and paralyzed production including the milking of cows and the planting and harvesting of potatoes and barley. The work stoppage, as Paola Sylva notes, "represented true challenges to the power of the landowners." It "considerably weakened the image of the landowners, often forcing them to make concessions."[93] At Pesillo, workers gained concessions on salaries, housing, education, health, sports facilities, tools, the return of fired workers to their positions, and the acquisition of land titles for ex-huasipungueros.[94] The protest wave culminated in a July 1968 massacre of eight landless workers and injuries to twenty-two others who had occupied land on the Santa Ana hacienda in Loja to press their demands with the landowner and government.[95]

Velasco Ibarra won the presidency in 1968 for the fifth and final time. In another seeming repeat of history, rather than ruling on behalf of the masses who had placed him in power he repressed leftist protests. In 1970, he suspended the constitution and declared himself dictator. Once again, the military stepped in and appointed General Guillermo Rodríguez Lara as dictator. The "Revolutionary and Nationalist Government of the Armed Forces" came to power just as Ecuador entered an oil boom, the third export-driven economic boom of the twentieth century following cacao in the 1920s and bananas in the 1950s. The nationalist dictatorship attempted to use oil revenues to fund social services. Similar to how the previous military government implemented an agrarian reform program in 1964, this new dictatorship decreed Ecuador's second agrarian reform law in 1973 a year after taking power. Its assimilationist thrust treated rural inhabitants as peasants rather than as Indians. "There is no more Indian problem," Rodríguez

Lara stated when challenged about the unique needs of Indigenous peoples. "We all become white when we accept the goals of the national culture."[96]

Communists continued to press for deeper agrarian reforms to address the needs of agricultural workers, including giving land to those who worked it, suppressing feudalistic labor demands, extending affordable credit lines, organizing cooperatives, raising salaries, providing housing, and raising the prices of agricultural commodities.[97] As in 1964, the new law favored modernization, development, and efficiency rather than the redistribution of land. Statistically, the reform resulted in little positive gain for Indigenous workers. In 1974, 50.2 percent of tillable land (and largely the best land) remained in the hands of estates larger than one hundred hectares. From 1954 to 1974, the average landholding size for a peasant fell from 1.71 to 1.5 hectares. Until 1982, agrarian reform laws affected only about 15 percent (about half a million hectares) of agricultural land in the highlands. Such statistics led Manuel Chiriboga to conclude that the 1973 agrarian reform law "was an insignificant advance" over the previous 1964 law.[98] Although the legislation had ended the huasipungo system, it did not end great inequalities in land ownership or address social and economic injustices in the countryside.[99] Tránsito Amaguaña contended that the agrarian reform legislation had "not satisfied the needs of the peasants, but it permitted capitalist penetration of agriculture."[100]

With a deteriorating economic situation, labor unions staged a general strike in 1975, and peasant organizations increased their calls for agrarian reform. Rather than meeting popular demands, the military regime became increasingly conservative and antagonistic to the left. In 1976, a military triumvirate replaced Rodríguez in what represented a rightward power shift that further increased political repression. This closed peasant hopes to gain access to land and caused the popular movement to lose force.[101] By the early 1980s, agrarian reform had come to a standstill. Facing this reality, Indigenous activists developed new strategies to confront their continued subjugation.

SEVEN

Return of the Indian

On September 26, 1974, Lázaro Condo died in the midst of a confused confrontation between the police and Indigenous members of the comuna Toctezinín in Chimborazo. With the authorization of the agrarian reform institute, the Indians had occupied a disputed plot of land that Amalia Merchán claimed belong to her hacienda. The Indigenous rights organization Ecuarunari, barely two years old, came to help organize the occupation. Merchán convinced Governor Américo Alava to send police to evict the protesters. The police fired tear gas at the Indians, including women, the elderly, and children. Condo, watching this confrontation, demanded that the officials respect the human dignity of the protesters. The police turned their rage on him, shooting him in the leg and in the head. The mayordomo Jorge Bermeo continued to beat him while he was down. The police took him to the provincial capital of Riobamba, but he bled to death along the way.[1]

Condo is remembered as one of Ecuador's primary Indigenous heroes and martyrs. His assassination coincided with a shift in the content, discourse, and strategies of Indigenous movements. Together with civil rights, student demands, and gender issues, popular movements increasingly pushed the politics of ethnic identities to the forefront. The anthropologist Muriel Crespi observes "that this new political configuration is triggering change in Indian ethnic identification" and their relations with the white world.[2] Xavier Albó terms this resurgence of ethnic discourse "the return of the Indian."[3]

New ethnic federations, as well as the formation of cooperatives and

Kayambis celebrate the 2003 Inti Raymi (Sun Festival) in the town of Ascazubi.
Photo by Marc Becker.

associations that enjoyed government support, led to a decline in peasant syndicates as a viable form of political organization on haciendas.[4] Unlike many earlier leaders, Condo was not a huasipunguero. Rather, he was a comunero—part of a free Indigenous community that previously had not actively participated in the creation of peasant syndicates and the FEI. Instead of assimilating huasipungueros into mestizo society, agrarian reform policies removed Indigenous workers from the tightly controlled domains of hacienda systems that had inadvertently "encouraged the proliferation of 'Indian' organizations that stressed cultural difference from a dominant white-mestizo society."[5] Ending the hacienda system forced racism into the public arena, thus leading to heightened political mobilizations. New issues gained dominance, including a defense of native cultures and languages (which emphasized the importance of bilingual education) and human rights (including a struggle against cultural and racial discrimination). Growing educational and economic opportunities provided Indigenous peoples with less incentive to discard their ethnic identities.[6]

Changes in the Catholic Church also inspired increased organizational activity. Notably, progressive sectors of the Catholic Church rather than the Communist Party came to Condo's defense. Monsignor Leonidas Proaño, known as the Bishop of the Indians, joined Ecuarunari in energetically condemning the military government for the brutal murder.[7] Proaño's declaration reflected broader shifts within the church. The Second Vatican Council (1962–1965) provided political openings in what traditionally had been a very conservative institution, leading to declarations from the 1968 Latin American Bishops Conference in Medellín, Colombia, that affirmed the commitment of the church to the task of liberating people from neocolonialism and "institutionalized violence." In what became known as the "preferential option for the poor," the bishops committed themselves to a struggle for social justice. This led to a split between the traditional priests who retained their long-term and close association with landed elites and accused activists of being "Indian communists thieves of the land," and a younger generation of priests allied with the "church of the poor" who helped out with Indigenous struggles.[8] Progressive religious activists grounded in the Brazilian educator Paolo Freire's participatory methodology of "listening, seeing and acting" helped "awaken" subalterns in a struggle for social justice.[9] The new "popular church" represented a rupture in the triumvirate power alliance that the conservative church hierarchy had traditionally maintained with wealthy landholders and government officials. These theological shifts helped draw Indigenous protests away from leftist influences. A new generation of leaders constructed Indigenous identities in a manner that fostered the formation of ethnic federations.

Decline of the FEI

Although the FEI continued to function as an organization, by the 1970s its public presence and political significance was considerably lessened.[10] Tránsito Amaguaña observed that after the FEI gained what had become its principal demand (land reform), it began to lose power and influence.[11] Estuardo Gualle, secretary-general of the FEI during the 1970s and 1980s, commented that when agrarian reform legislation in the 1960s terminated the huasipungo system, many peasants left the land to work in the city and the organization's base of support evaporated.[12] The once-strong peasant movement lost its national presence and instead became regionalized and isolated.[13] The FEI did not adapt well to a new political context and changing agrarian order. "This organization that supported the struggle and even emerged from these struggles," Ulcuango reflected, no longer had the force and power that it once did.[14]

A variety of factors contributed to the demise of the FEI. A study of peasant movements notes that while the FEI was "the first peasant organization with an almost national structure" and remained "an important part of the history of peasant movements" for leading the fight for agrarian reform, a new situation of capitalist development "demanded new ideas and new forms of organization."[15] Breaking up Asistencia Pública haciendas, the traditional stronghold for the FEI, weakened the federation. Although very limited, promulgating agrarian reform stole much of the rhetorical thunder from its demands. The FEI seemingly was unable to move beyond the issue of land, and its growing reliance on outsiders gave increasing credibility to competing organizations' claims that it was subject to non-Indian concerns. The first generation of leaders, including Gualavisí, Cacuango, Paredes, and Chávez, were now passing from the scene. The FEI's success in forcing through a program of agrarian reform and then its difficulties in adapting to a new environment engendered a new generation of Indigenous activists. In a growing anti-communist atmosphere, these activists opted for other seemingly less radical, Catholic-based federations. Furthermore, the PCE no longer emphasized Indigenous issues as it had done decades earlier.[16]

In 1968, the PCE celebrated Ricardo Paredes's seventieth birthday, noting that the "syndicalist organizations, particularly those of the Indians, will want to pay tribute." The celebration, however, was held on the coast in Guayaquil, the current location of the party's headquarters and far from Indigenous communities in the highlands. No Indigenous leaders attended the ceremony, and the FEI limited itself to a telegram of congratulations.[17] From an institutional perspective, this is a noted contrast from 1926 when Paredes and Gualavisí participated as equals in the founding of the party. Instead, the following year activists in Cayambe held their own ceremony honoring Paredes's lifetime of labor on behalf of Indigenous causes.[18] Rather than being fresh and dynamic, communist rhetoric increasingly merely mimicked earlier proclamations. A statement at the eighth party congress in 1968 spoke of Indigenous peoples possessing "national elements" including their own language, traditions, and cultures, but these words were largely copied from their last congress—which took place eleven years earlier. Indigenous issues were subordinated to the development of a worker-peasant alliance. "The definitive solution to the Indigenous problem," the statement

Funeral of Dolores Cacuango, April 24, 1971. Photo by Rolf
Blomberg. Courtesy of the Archivo Blomberg, Quito, Ecuador.

read, was a "democratic agrarian reform." In reflecting a liberal assimilationalist mindset, these reforms would "bring [to] Indians all of the elements of modern culture, giving them what is necessary to improve their
economic situation and to increase their consumer relationships with the
domestic market."[19] Although at Pesillo (a strong base of support for the
FEI) 72 percent of the Indigenous workers still belonged to the PCE, the
party no longer was the strong ally of rural social movements that it once
had been.[20]

Rather than radicalizing the party, the triumph of the Cuban revolution in
1959 divided an already fragmented left into pro-Soviet, pro-China, and pro-
Cuba wings, weakening organizations allied with the traditional Communist Party.[21] Competing leftist factions criticized the PCE for having lost its
revolutionary fervor and began to champion peasant and Indigenous issues
more loudly and clearly than did the PCE. The maoist Partido Comunista

Marxista-Leninista del Ecuador (PCMLE, Marxist-Leninist Communist Party of Ecuador) advocated a more radical position of discarding government-run agrarian reform programs.[22] Echoing the thoughts of José Carlos Mariátegui and Ernesto Che Guevara, Joaquín Aymara of the Partido Socialista Revolucionario (PSR, Revolutionary Socialist Party) argued that in the absence of an urban industrialized proletariat, the Ecuadorian revolution would happen in the countryside. "The problem of the Ecuadorian Indian," he wrote, "is the problem of the distribution of land." In drawing parallels to the Cuban Revolution, Aymara argued that "the day the Indigenous peasantry rises up in arms it will become an invincible revolutionary agent."[23] While these alternative voices and trends ultimately strengthened Indigenous movements, multivocality also chipped away at the FEI's authority to speak for all Indigenous peoples.

Members and supporters of the FEI desperately fought to maintain the organization's viability. In 1968, the federation resurrected its bilingual newspaper *Ñucanchic Allpa* for a third and final time. An editorial note stated that "after a long interruption," *Ñucanchic Allpa* had reappeared as "the voice of the Indian masses of Ecuador." In an attempt to consolidate its influence, it welcomed the FTAL to its pages. "In *Ñucanchic Allpa,*" the editors wrote, "rural comrades will find not only valiant denunciations of abuses against them, but also information on rural struggles and an orientation for their organization so that they may obtain their demands."[24] Reflecting pressing issues of the time, it dedicated extensive coverage to problems with the 1964 agrarian reform law.[25]

Although non-Indians had always played important roles in rural struggles, white urban men became more prominent in the federation. For example, in 1968 a delegation of three members of the FEI's executive committee—the honorary president Ricardo Paredes, Colón Narváez, and Luisa Gómez—met with President Otto Arosemena Gómez to present a statement denouncing problems with the Tigua cooperative and the suppression of schools in Chimborazo.[26] All three had long been supportive of Indigenous struggles, but what is notable is the absence of any Indigenous activists in what previously had always been shared spaces. Similarly, in 1970 the CTE Executive Committee member Narváez represented the FEI in Moscow, and Bolaños took Soviet trade unionists on a tour of Cayambe.[27] The left drafted statements without fully incorporating or considering Indigenous perspectives. "The agrarian question" became "an urban, or national, or 'proletarian' question." As the anthropologist William Roseberry notes, "It was a question posed *about* the peasantry, not necessarily *of* or *by* them, and it was most frequently posed by urban intellectuals and activists."[28]

Antonio Quinde, a long-time Indigenous activist from Cañar, remembered that the FEI was the only organization that represented Indigenous peoples but that its structure was increasingly alienating for its members. "In a FEI Congress," Quinde recounted, "Bolaños would read ten to fifteen pages, and the Indigenous peoples would not understand anything and fall asleep." Once Bolaños finished his discourse, strategically placed university students would shout their "vivas" and approve the document "while in their sleepy state the Indigenous peoples would also applaud and say 'approved.'" This led Quinde to leave the FEI "because this is no way to treat a human being, and worse Indigenous peoples."[29] The Kayambi leader Neptalí Ulcuango similarly complained that Bolaños alienated many activists who had been very active both within the Indigenous movement as well as other allies. "I do not know whether these were involuntary or intentional errors," Ulcuango recounted, but it was "since then that the FEI bit by bit began to decline to the point of disappearing."[30] It is this memory of increasing paternalism possibly complicated by interpersonal conflicts, rather than earlier patterns of actively struggling together as equals, that led to increased tension between Indigenous movements and the left.

In 1972, the FEI held its fifth congress, its first in almost six years. Retaining the symbiosis of having a white urban intellectual paired with a rural Indigenous activist from Cayambe, Estuardo Gualle replaced Bolaños as secretary-general of the organization and Manuel Escobar replaced Miguel Lechón as president. A resolution from the congress began with the statement that "in our country, subjugated to the oppression and exploitation of imperialism and of local oligarchies allied with capitalist monopolies, the struggle for social and national liberation is historically unavoidable." Agrarian reform formed a fundamental part of this "anti-imperialist, anti-feudal, democratic national revolution" to "transform economic and social structures" in order to "benefit the peasant masses." In particular, the FEI pointed to the need to break up large estates, give land to those who worked it, and form cooperatives. In addition, the FEI demanded water, housing, the elimination of debts, access to markets, schools, medical treatment, electricity, better salaries, fair prices, affordable credit, and technical assistance. Finally, the statement ended with a call for democracy, a strengthening of the worker-peasant alliance, international solidarity, and for "peace and friend-ship among people."[31]

On one level, this document is not significantly different from other Indigenous resolutions. Calls for agrarian reform and access to water had long been central demands and would continue to be so for the rest of the twentieth century. An end to abuses, higher salaries, improved medical care, and schooling were also virtually universal demands. Nevertheless, the tone and framing of this resolution reveals significant shifts. It includes only two explicit usages of ethnic language, first in a demand for land for "Indians and peasants" and later in a call to dismiss debts against "Indigenous peoples and poor peasants." Another demand called for primary education in "autoch-thonous languages." Ultimately, the marginalization of explicitly ethnic ref-erences is not that significant; rather, it is largely a reflection of current language sentiments that preferred the usage of the more complimentary term campesino instead of the derogatory term indio. What is notable, however, is how the arguments were framed. While about half of this 1972 document concerned some aspect of agrarian reform removed from explicit ethnic or Indigenous concerns, the founding 1944 FEI mission statement demanded "the economic emancipation of Ecuadorian Indians" as it called to "raise the Indians' cultural and moral level while conserving whatever is good in their native customs."[32]

While new organizations sought to "awaken" the ethnic conscience of Indians, the FEI increasingly appealed to the class consciousness of a rural proletariat. The FEI began to sign statements with language such as, "for the liberation of the peasants."[33] An FEI leader noted that "Indian is for us not so much a biological as a social concept. There are no sharply defined racial groups in Ecuador." He concluded by saying that "what we are trying to create is class consciousness, not race consciousness." The Swedish journal-ist Sven Lindqvist found it difficult to untangle the two concepts. "Race and class are so interwoven," he stated, "that social indignation constantly as-sumes overtones of racial struggle."[34] This perhaps represents a low point in the FEI's trajectory as part of an explicitly Indigenous movement, but it has come to be seen as representative of its entire history. The federation con-tinued to limp along for decades as a shadow of its former self, applauding the efforts of Indigenous heroes such as Fernando Daquilema, Ambrosio Lasso, and Dolores Cacuango, and continuing to make calls for agrarian reform.[35]

At the PCE's ninth congress in November 1973, the secretary-general Pedro Saad again criticized the FEI and FTAL, as he had in the early 1960s, for their failure to "realize the old and correct position of the formation of only one peasant organization" built in the context of a strong worker-peasant alliance. They continued to follow "old work methods tinted with legalism that does not permit a more energetic deployment of mass action."[36] Osvaldo Albornoz Peralta also complained that excessive legalism had become an "obstacle to the politicization of the peasants" with Indigenous leaders working with urban lawyers but "leaving the great masses on the margins, or at least with a passive and insufficient level of participation."[37] Jaime Galarza similarly notes that while previously the FEI "represented a great effort and a deeply felt hope" in a struggle against feudal exploitation, it was weakened through excessive legalism and repression during the military dictatorships. Several factors hindered the success of peasant uprisings—a lack of clear objectives, a lack of support from urban areas, and military inexperience. "Their rebuilding," Galarza noted, "is today slow and laborious." But every defeat can also provide lessons, and Galarza was optimistic that the struggle would continue.[38]

Javier Herrán faulted the FEI for its increasingly vertical control of peasant organizations from urban centers, especially when it attempted to extend its work into new areas. Rather than solving rural problems, the federation became more interested in "maintaining the people in permanent movement so that on May 1 they could fill the streets of Quito." Herrán also criticized the FEI's lack of "a cultural or anthropological analysis of Indigenous peoples, and a failure to tie their proposals to Indigenous realities." Nevertheless, he concedes that Catholic organizations "did not do anything new or different from the FEI," as he focused his criticism on failures in their organizational structures rather than in their ideology or political agenda.[39] Subsequent Indigenous federations such as CONAIE also criticized the FEI for being too narrowly focused on the highland region; for being under the control of external, non-Indigenous agents such as socialists, communists, and labor leaders; and for emphasizing class issues to the exclusion of ethnic identities.[40]

In illustrating how completely class had become the dominant paradigm and had erased memories of earlier histories of ethnic organizing, Crawford Young maintained in his 1976 seminal work *The Politics of Cultural Pluralism* that political movements had not been based on the mobilization of Indigenous racial or ethnic solidarity, but instead organizations examined the world through the lens of social class influenced by marxism. "Indians are and must be peasants," Young writes. "They cannot be incorporated with the framework of protest as Indians, or Quechua."[41] With class discourse in ascendancy and a growing perception of "Indian" as a derogatory label, the FEI's utilization of ethnic constructs became increasingly rare. The FEI staked out ideological territory in the popular movement halfway between an urban mestizo labor movement and an ethnic-based Indigenous movement. The FEI president Manuel Escobar noted that "in the struggle of the popular sectors, we are different, we are Indians."[42] Although Escobar spoke as an Indian, the nature of the demands for which he struggled indicates that his ethnicity was almost incidental to (or perhaps deeply imbedded within) his economic and class-based demands. He emphasized agrarian reform issues, including the need for cooperatives, credit, and land titles. What unified peasants and Indians was a common struggle for land. It was ultimately class demands that lent strength and force to Indigenous struggles.

Academics have been particularly harsh in criticizing the FEI.[43] Jorge León attacks the federation for embracing "an exclusively class analysis, excluding ethnic issues."[44] Leon Zamosc criticizes "its excessive legalism and lack of radicalism, which are attributed to a narrow conception of the character of the anti-feudal struggle" as well as a lack of "a clear demand to eliminate the hacienda system."[45] Amalia Pallares characterizes the federation as "too isolated and bureaucratic and having little local presence in the highlands."[46] Unfortunately, these perspectives come from the vantage point of the 1980s, which in retrospect tends to underscore the federation's shortcomings. Many of the criticisms focus on the later part of the FEI's history after it had achieved many of its original objectives and was in decline. Examining the federation's evolution from its roots in the 1920s and 1930s highlights its surprisingly innovative and effective engagements with pressing issues.

Elites held a similar view of Indigenous movements. Seemingly unaware that the FEI had always maintained very close relations with the PCE, El Comercio lamented in 1966 that it had become "entirely dominated and directed by marxist agents." Unfortunately, the newspaper continued, "several authentically Indigenous leaders appear to have been contaminated by communism, and naively believe in the promises to return their 'ancestral lands.'"[47] Manuel Chiriboga also assailed the organization's centralized character and its clientalistic relations with urban agents. He denounced the Communist Party for training the FEI's leaders and defining its ideology and goals.[48]

To complicate matters further, urban leftists overstated the importance of their role in forging Indigenous organizations. In 1986, Central Committee members announced that "Communists are active among the Indians." The party proudly noted its role in forming early peasant unions in the 1930s, and the necessity "to defend Indian communities and the lands belonging to them and to bring about an agrarian reform that would end the latifundium system."[49] The party's secretary-general claimed that "no other political party in the country has defended the Indigenous movement as much as ours."[50] In Indigenous testimonies, however, local activists made it clear that they began the organizing themselves and actively sought out the urban leftists to assist them. The communists increasingly viewed themselves as paternalistically providing a vanguard role for isolated Indigenous groups unable to defend their own interests. At the same time, urbanization and a growing radical youth movement meant that in the eyes of the PCE the FEI had been surpassed in importance.[51]

In the 1980s, with the FEI eclipsed by new ethnic-based organizations, President Manuel Escobar noted that the federation continued to struggle for land, defend Indigenous cultures, and fight against landlord abuses. Even after gaining control of hacienda land through the formation of cooperatives, Escobar indicated that many structural barriers remained that prevented the full realization of Indigenous goals. Hacendados still held political power in Ecuador and made it difficult for Indians to access credit and other necessities. "We are the owners of Ecuador," Escobar stated, "not the creoles who came to live here." Indians needed to continue organizing to gain political power.[52] White allies like the secretary-general Estuardo Gualle also continued to work in rural communities, suffering repression for their efforts. In 1983, two people beat Gualle in Chimborazo, leaving him with fractures on his face and body. The government quickly released the perpetrators, thereby indicating their complicity in the attack.[53] Similar to responses to earlier leftist allies, the government feared Gualle's support of Indigenous concerns and denounced his actions as inciting rural protests.[54]

In 1986 on the occasion of the sixtieth anniversary of the formation of the PCE, Albornoz Peralta stated that this "Federation that today has declined in importance hopefully will study the new situation facing the peasant movement and will follow the route which Gualavísi and other founders laid out and return to its previous strength."[55] At the FEI's seventh congress in 1989, organizers lamented that it had not been able to hold a congress in almost a decade. The executive committee had ceased to function, and many of its leaders and members had left for other organizations. The federation needed a congress in order to receive reports from its directors and to select a new executive committee that could carry the work forward. Organizers proposed a thirty-one-point program that championed democratic agrarian reform to grant land to peasants, provide technical assistance and credit for development, support the establishment of cooperatives, raise salaries, and provide schools and health care. In addition, the platform called for the recognition of Ecuador as "a multinational and multicultural country," as well as "safeguarding the ethnic personality of Indian peoples . . . defending their beautiful ancestral culture." A hope was that the congress would not only develop a work plan to restructure and strengthen the federation, but would build unity with the movement in establishing a single peasant union.[56]

Half a century after its founding, the FEI met once again at its eighth congress in 1995. The federation maintained that the country's deep economic and political crisis "demonstrated today more than ever the validity of the positions that the FEI has taken since its founding." It linked neocolonial dependency to racial discrimination and the need "to create a new power that represents the interests of the people and embraces the plurinational and pluricultural character of the Ecuadorian nation." In an attempt to remain relevant in a changing political situation, the FEI moved beyond issues of agrarian reform. "The Indigenous movement can no longer be considered exclusively from an agricultural viewpoint," the FEI stated. Strengthening ties with other social movements would build "a large popular civic movement that would allow us to open a path to a new society" and construct a popular government that "recognizes our legitimate rights as citizens of the Ecuadorian nation."[57] The formerly formable federation struggled to remain relevant in the face of changing realities.

Significantly, activist organizations tend to be more kind to the FEI than to outside observers. Indeed, even as the federation was in decline, CONAIE stated that the FEI was "one of the first organizations to use the name Indian and to demand payment for the work of Indigenous men and women on haciendas, and also to seek land for our people."[58] Similarly, Ecuarunari remembered that the FEI had fought for land, for an end to feudal labor relations and to racial discrimination, and for a better life overall. "The seed it sowed in the fertile ground," Ecuarunari notes, "has blossomed" in the work of subsequent organizations.[59]

As with most organizations, the FEI had outlived its usefulness. Or, perhaps more accurately, popular movements had outgrown the FEI. The anthropologist Marc Edelman notes "that peasant movements often rose and fell fairly rapidly" in Costa Rica, and "that this wasn't necessarily such a bad thing."[60] It reflected a typical and healthy evolution of ideologies and strategies. The FEI provided a critical base, and later organizers looked back at the federation as "for a long time representing the struggle of Indigenous peoples, it was the example, the seed, the birth of new organizations."[61] As Pichincha's provincial branch of Ecuarunari stated, "the founding of Ecuarunari in no sense was meant to counteract the FEI."[62] The legacy of the federation's struggles for land and ethnic rights continued to be important as new organizations took over the leadership of Indigenous movements in Ecuador.

Amazon

One of the earliest and best-organized of the new Indigenous organizations that emerged in the 1960s was the Federación de Centros Shuar (Shuar Federation). The Shuar, located in Ecuador's southeastern Amazon and thus far from the FEI's traditional base among Indigenous workers on highland haciendas, organized their federation in 1964 to advocate for self-determination, economic self-sufficiency, defense of their lands, bilingual education, health care, and civil rights. Ernesto Salazar notes that Salesian missionaries "planned and carried out" the establishment of the federation in order to protect the Shuar from colonist encroachment.[63] International influences proved conducive to mobilizing the Shuar and building it into a model for subsequent organizations.[64] Although the Shuar's goals were similar to those of earlier highland organizations, they emerged out of dramatically different cultural and economic contexts. Indigenous federations responded to a state presence, and this happened more slowly on the Amazonian margins of western domination.

In 1969, Josefina missionaries helped found the Federación Provincial de Organizaciones Campesinas de Napo (FEPOCAN, Provincial Federation of Peasant Organizations of Napo) in the northern Amazon to shield Indigenous communities from more radical leftist influences.[65] The role of Salesian and Josefina missionaries illustrates a reliance of Indigenous organizations on external support. The communist leader Ricardo Paredes notes that "there was no clash between Indigenous religiosity and communist ideologies because their Christian beliefs were superficial and were not completely opposite of their communist beliefs. They believed more deeply in their own gods."[66] Rather, secular leftists and religious activists competed for subaltern allegiance, representing two alternative trends in the evolution of Indigenous movements. As could be expected, leftists were as critical of "the Shuar who fell under the dependency of an Italian Catholic order, the Salesian Mission" as were Catholics of the FEI for its alliance with the communists.[67]

FENOC

Parallel to its work in the Amazon, the Catholic Church organized two new competing peasant-Indigenous federations in the highlands. The first was the Federación Ecuatoriana de Trabajadores Agropecuarios (FETEP, Ecuadorian Federation of Agricultural Workers), founded in 1965 at the eighth congress of the Confederación Ecuatoriana de Obreros Católicos (CEDOC, Ecuadorian Confederation of Catholic Workers). The Conservative Party founded CEDOC in 1938 with the goal of stopping communist influence in labor movements and emphasizing a conservative religious spirit in Ecuador's workers. The stated purpose of FETEP was to assist agricultural workers in the transition from the huasipungo system. The Catholic Church sought to form a parallel organization to the FEI in order "to restrict communist influence in peasant sectors."[68] The FEI condemned FETEP as an attempt to divide the peasant movement and stop its revolutionary tendencies.[69] At its third congress in 1968, FETEP transformed itself into the Federación Nacional de Organizaciones Campesinas (FENOC, National Federation of Peasant Organizations) as it broadened its mission to address other issues facing rural communities.

In 1972, the peasant movement overtook FENOC and converted it into a force for revolutionary change in Ecuadorian society. As a result, FENOC began to present itself as a classist peasant organization fighting for agrarian reform. It called for a unity of worker and peasant struggles, a role for peasants in crafting agrarian policies, respect for Indigenous cultural forms, and the construction of a revolutionary party that would struggle for the construction of a socialist society.[70] It adopted standard labor organizing strategies that included strikes, lawsuits, and occupations of lands. Osvaldo Barsky notes that FENOC had "achieved a strong level of national development, and its positions were more radical than those of the FEI," including its use of land invasions as a mechanism to force transformations in the agrarian system.[71] Roberto Santana criticized both the FEI and FENOC for being cut from the same leftist cloth. "Syndicalism of a marxist tendency as

Federación Nacional de Organizaciones Campesinas Indígenas y Negras (FENOCIN) in an October 2002 march against the Free Trade Area of the Americas (FTAA) in Quito. Photo by Marc Becker.

well as a leftist Christian tendency," he wrote, "present the same results that are far from being satisfactory."[72] Secretary-General Mesías Tatamuez noted that "FENOC has a clear political position in the struggle for socialism," because it favored unification of the left in a search for social justice.[73]

At its fifth congress in 1977 FENOC declared, "We peasants have gained consciousness and experience. We no longer need leaders who come from the cities."[74] The FENOC leader Alberto Andrango noted that Indigenous peasants experienced a double exploitation, for being both poor and Indian. He constructed FENOC's fight for land rights as fundamental to preserving ethnic identities because it allowed people to remain in their home communities rather than migrating to urban areas where they would be assimilated into the mestizo population.[75] Reflecting the growing importance of ethnicity to peasant movements, in 1988 the organization changed its name to FENOC-I (Federación Nacional de Organizaciones Campesinas-Indígenas, or National Federation of Peasant-Indigenous Organizations) and finally in

1999 to FENOCIN (Federación Nacional de Organizaciones Campesinas Indígenas y Negras, or National Federation of Indigenous, Peasant, and Black Organizations). Because it worked on a national level with many different rural communities, and because not all of these communities were ethnically Indigenous, FENOC sometimes was not viewed as an explicitly *Indigenous* organization, although it played a significant role in those struggles. By the end of the twentieth century it was often overshadowed by CONAIE, but in rural communities it remained an important and powerful force for social justice.

Ecuarunari

In 1972, Ecuarunari (Ecuador Runacunapac Riccharimui, a Kichwa phrase that means "to awaken the Ecuadorian Indians") grew out of progressive sectors of the Catholic Church in the context of a struggle between conservatives and Christian Democrats for control of CEDOC and its peasant wing FENOC. Ecuarunari unified eleven highland organizations, plus two additional organizations on the coast and in the Amazon. Priests working in rural communities proposed the formation of Ecuarunari with two goals in mind: "That it be Indigenous and that it provide an alternative to the traditional Indigenous movement of the FEI, controlled by the Ecuadorian Communist Party."[76] Later, CONAIE characterized Ecuarunari as "the first truly Indigenous organization in the highlands."[77] Of the three federations (FEI, FENOC, Ecuarunari), Ecuarunari was commonly seen as the most "ethnic," as it "planted for the first time specific demands such as respect for their cultures, traditions, languages, natural authorities, etc.," even though the FEI had campaigned for similar issues in the 1940s.[78] This does not mean it did not also rely on outside allies or build on previous organizing efforts. Bishop Proaño was an early partisan for Ecuarunari. The church lent Tepeyac, a training institute for Indigenous leaders located at the Monjas Corral hacienda that had previously belonged to the Riobamba dioceses, to found the new federation. The Cañar activist Antonio Quinde argued that religious support was necessary because the FEI had adapted an organizing model that relied on white outsiders to guide the federation's labors. "We Indigenous peoples did not know anything about administering an organization," Quinde stated. "In this area we were blind because we had not even participated in the FEI." Increasingly, Indigenous activists wanted their own organization "because we saw that the struggle was not only for land, but also for education, cultural identity, and dignity."[79] In the early years, priests controlled local organizations and framed discussions within the context of reflections on biblical texts.[80] As with other organizations, Indigenous activists soon gained control over the federation.

The long-time activist Neptalí Ulcuango, who played a central role in the FEI in Cayambe in the 1950s, emphasized a continuity in the transition from the FEI to Ecuarunari. "Ecuarunari was born as a valid alternative to the Ecuadorian Federation of Indians when it disappeared in 1970," but it organized among the same people who had been active in the FEI.[81] In addition, CONAIE acknowledged that "the birth of Ecuarunari in no sense was meant to counteract FENOC or the FEI."[82] Similar to FENOC but more closely associated with ethnic organizing efforts, Ecuarunari sought to "awaken" the conscience of Indians and open their eyes to "oppression and exploitation in order to struggle for our rights, which we have been denied throughout history since the Spanish Conquest."[83] Its goals were to defend rights to education, health care, and basic services, as well as to struggle against the oppression, exploitation, and discrimination faced by peasants and Indigenous peoples.[84] Ecuarunari promoted grassroots cooperatives and associations, and it functioned as a development organization on projects to modernize agriculture and develop bilingual education.

Ideologically, Ecuarunari was influenced partially by the example of the Cuban Revolution, and perhaps even more so by liberation theology and the 1968 Latin American Bishops Conference. From its beginning, Ecuarunari engaged in political struggles with the government. In 1973, a year after its founding, landlords killed one of the organization's leaders, Cristóbal Pajuña, in Tungurahua. A year later the military dictatorship killed Lázaro Condo in Chimborazo.[85] In 1977, police assassinated Pablo Robalino, the president of the Simón Bolívar comuna in Pichincha, who had been petitioning IERAC for land from a neighboring hacienda.[86] In Cotacachi, police tortured and killed Rafael Perugachi, who had intervened when the police beat another Indian.[87] Ecuarunari emerged as an activist organization through baptism by fire.

Class and ethnicity have been competing themes throughout Ecuarunari's history, and the federation has been commonly described as "a bit Indigenous and a bit classist."[88] Ecuarunari opposed traditional leftist politics that subordinated ethnic concerns to those of peasants in general, thereby ignoring the cultural and linguistic aspects of Indigenous society. During its first phase (1972–1977), Ecuarunari emphasized an Indigenous consciousness. At the organization's third congress in 1977, the federation experienced a definite ideological shift toward a class-based conception of the peasant-Indigenous movement.[89] During a 1977 strike, Ecuarunari called for an increase in wages, the right to strike, agrarian reform, and the nationalization of primary industries. The platform did not include any overtly ethnic demands.[90] At the organization's fourth congress in 1978, Ecuarunari defined itself as "a national peasant and Indigenous organization that searches for total and radical change in the current situation of marginalized, oppressed, and exploited peoples." Furthermore, it was "an anti-imperialist organization that struggles for a definitive liberation of our country, for a society without exploitation" and "for the unity of Indigenous peoples and all exploited sectors of our country."[91] In the 1980s, Ecuarunari began to shift back to a more ethnic position, thereby reflecting a growing emphasis on an "Indian" identity as a force for social justice.

Still, Ecuarunari assumed positions consistent with a leftist ideology. It routinely defended the Cuban revolution, condemned the U.S. invasion of Grenada in 1983, and supported revolutionary struggles in Central America in the 1980s. The Cuban and Nicaraguan revolutions were "expressions and syntheses of a future toward which we are advancing: the new society."[92] Ecuarunari even advocated a "struggle for the formation of a socialist state."[93] Many of its goals and objectives were not unlike those of the FEI. Some leaders expressed the need to "build unity with other peasant organizations, with urban workers, with all exploited people, in order to struggle for a free country."[94] In creating an ideological framework for their struggle, not only did they rely on the example of Andean Indigenous leaders such as Rumiñahui, Túpac Amaru, and Daquilema, but also Latin American mestizo and leftist leaders including José Martí and Augusto César Sandino. Because of these ideological influences, Ecuarunari emerged at the end of the twentieth century as one of the most militant Indigenous organizations in Ecuador.

Whereas Francisco Ron interprets Ecuarunari's move toward a class analysis as a positive development that broadened its social base, Roberto Santana believes that these were "politics of integration" that diminished the importance of ethnic identity among Ecuador's Indigenous peoples and weakened the movement.[95] Ecuarunari's history reveals multiple influences and strands of thought that are interwoven to form a strong and dynamic Indigenous movement. Its trajectory manifests the importance of building alliances with other actors; illustrates how Indigenous movements negotiated competing forms of identity; and demonstrates how it emerges out of a previous history of rural organizational struggles and strategies.

Peasant-Indigenous Alliances

The three main peasant-Indigenous organizations (FEI, FENOC, and Ecuarunari) had a complicated relationship with one other, sometimes coordinating activities but at other times fiercely competing for the allegiance of the same Indigenous base. In 1972, they unified forces in the Frente Unido de Reforma Agraria (FURA, United Front for Agrarian Reform). This coalition demanded a return of lands to peasant communities, suppression of feudalistic labor demands, support for agricultural cooperatives, provision of technical assistance, and payment of higher salaries. The FURA organized a series of marches and peasant congresses, beginning with a 1972 demonstration in Guayaquil. The act of holding the march on the mestizo coast away from the "Indigenous" highlands reflected a shift in discourse away from ethnicity. Even when the FEI activists Lechón and Gualle organized and led FURA marches in the heavily Indigenous areas of Zumbahua, Cañar, and Riobamba, Indigenous issues were not specifically part of the agenda.[96]

In 1973, the FURA mobilized five thousand people in Quito, fifteen thousand in Cuenca, and fifty thousand in Guayaquil in massive marches for agrarian reform. At the Guayaquil march, Lechón supported the anti-imperialist impulses of Guillermo Rodríguez Lara's new military government as he called for a resolution of labor conflicts and liquidation of large estates. Much like Arosemena a decade earlier, General Rodríguez spoke to the cheering crowd as he promised a new agrarian reform law. The FURA marches culminated in the I Encuentro Nacional Campesino por la Reforma Agraria (First National Peasant Encounter for Agrarian Reform) in Quito. Its call for "an authentic and radical agrarian reform" that incorporated and responded to peasant needs and demands was partially realized when Rodríguez promulgated new legislation in October. As with the first agrarian reform law, the apparent realization of the organization's primary demand undermined the FURA's strength and it began to fall apart.[97] Some members of the alliance became increasingly frustrated with the PCE's efforts to dominate organizing efforts. In response, FENOC found their attempts to be "a dividing force that does not lead to an integration of peasant mobilization" and ultimately hurt the efforts to form a national-level organization.[98] Nevertheless, for a short time the FURA represented a remarkable unification of diverse ideological trends in Ecuador's Indigenous and peasant movements.

In 1978, FEI, FENOC, and Ecuarunari resurrected their cooperative efforts in the Frente Unico de Lucha Campesina (FULC, United Front for Peasant Struggle) whose chief objective remained petitioning for an effective agrarian reform. The FULC criticized the agricultural ministry for being under the domain of large landholders, and it called instead for an agrarian reform under peasant control. These efforts acquired increased urgency when a 1979 agrarian development law threatened to end land distribution and consolidate large modernizing estates. The agrarian reform program had caused "peasants and Indigenous peoples to abandon the countryside and to sink into subemployment in the cities."[99] The FULC demanded "a real and true agrarian reform that not only gives land, but also raises workers' salaries, lends technical and agricultural assistance, provides sufficient financing to cover production demands, organizes the sale of products, and creates gathering points to market products.[100] It supported the leftist electoral coalition Frente Amplio de Izquierda (FADI, Broad Leftist Front) as the best way to gain political space to organize for democratic freedoms, higher salaries, lower prices, and better agrarian reform legislation.[101]

Reflecting a growing ethnic consciousness, the coalition soon changed its name to the Frente Unico de Lucha Campesina e Indígena (FULCI, United Front for Peasant and Indigenous Struggle). It continued to focus its efforts on agrarian reform, but it also called for an investigation of those responsible for massacres of peasants, a return to democratic governance, universal suffrage, expanded educational opportunities for Indigenous peoples, and promotion of the role of women.[102] Unfortunately, the FULCI realized limited success and soon disappeared, partially due to the failure of the FEI and FENOC to support the coalition.[103]

In 1979, the populist Jaime Roldós Aguilera won Ecuador's first presidential elections in ten years. The promulgation of a new constitution gave illiterates the right to vote, extending citizenship rights to many Indigenous peoples for the first time. In his inaugural address, Roldós recognized ethnic diversity in Ecuador, and in Kichwa he proclaimed that he spoke "for all people who live in this country."[104] Exploiting this political opening, on October 16, 1980, FENOC and Ecuarunari led a "Marcha Nacional Campesina Indígena" (National Peasant Indigenous March) that called for changes to the agrarian reform law, expulsion of the Summer Institute of Linguistics, nationalization of petroleum reserves, and formation of a bilingual educa-tion program. About ten thousand people joined this massive mobilization, the largest demonstration in Quito in years, illustrating the rising power of the peasant-Indigenous movement. Representing a spirit of unity across class and ethnic divides, they named the march "Martyrs of Aztra" to honor those massacred in a sugar mill strike three years earlier. After the march, activists presented congress with their demands to reorganize IERAC.[105]

In the 1980s, under the leadership of Blanca Chancoso, Ecuarunari con-tinued this pattern of working with other peasant organizations.[106] At its sixth congress in 1981, Ecuarunari adapted the slogan, "Peasant-Indigenous Unity Against Hunger and Governmental Deceptions."[107] In 1982, Chancoso organized with FENOC the Primer Encuentro Nacional Campesino Indígena (First Peasant and Indigenous National Encounter) in Quito. The objectives of the meeting were to promote unity between peasant and Indigenous groups and to present a unified face to the government. Reflecting an orientation toward peasant issues, the meeting's slogans were "agrarian reform with peasant control" and for "bread, land, and a free country." About one hundred assembled delegates condemned the government for favoring large landholders and for the imperialistic nature of rural develop-ment programs. The assembly presented a right to land as "fundamental for the development of a nationality, of our culture, our language," and key to a political struggle "against imperialism and for an authentic democracy." Delegates advocated the creation of a Coordinadera Nacional Campesina e Indígena (National Peasant and Indigenous Coordinating Body) to unify their efforts.[108] Although the FEI's secretary-general Gualle and the local activist Pedro Quinatoa from FEI-Cayambe attended the meeting, the fed-eration no longer was one of the primary organizers on par with FENOC and Ecuarunari. The CTE's coastal peasant affiliate FTAL took the FEI's place on the meeting's final statement.

Two years later FENOC organized a Segunda Convención Nacional Cam-pesina e Indígena (Second Peasant and Indigenous National Convention), al-though this time the FEI was the co-organizer and Ecuarunari did not partici-pate. Continuing their attempts to forge a peasant-Indigenous alliance, the participants formed a Coordinadora Campesina e Indígena (Peasant and Indigenous Coordinating Body). The meeting's resolutions highlighted op-position to the agrarian reform programs and the neoliberal economic policies of the incoming conservative president León Febres Cordero. The secretary-general of FENOC, Mesías Tatamuez, served as president of the

Coordinating Body. He emphasized that its primary objective was the defense of an agrarian reform that would improve conditions in the countryside. The organization also called for the expulsion of World Vision and the Summer Institute of Linguistics—the Christian missionary groups criticized as agents of imperialism that undermined local cultures.[109] Perhaps more notable, however, was the lack of strong ethnic language in the document. A split between those who favored alliances with leftist and popular organizations and those who emphasized ethno-nationalist identities began to divide the Indigenous movement. The Coordinating Body held a third meeting a year later at Chordelég in Azuay, but soon thereafter it apparently disappeared in the face of the ascendancy of alternative ideological trends in the peasant-Indigenous movement.[110]

Ethnic rights movements did not emerge out of a political vacuum; rather, they grew out of decades of organizing against centuries of oppression. Observers often interpret new ethnic-rights movements as a deliberate shift away from a class-based analysis of society. Nevertheless, ethnic identities had long played a key role in rural movements. Ricardo Paredes and the Socialist Party in the 1920s explicitly included Indigenous peoples in their organizing strategies. In addition, new ethnic federations maintained dynamic relations with outside supporters, including leftist political parties and labor unions, while they continued to place a strong emphasis on economic and class issues. This history challenges an ungrounded assumption that many on the left have "anti-race predilections" that led them to ignore if not snub Indians and their social movements.[111] Far from ignoring race or embodying racist attitudes, the left played a fundamental role in how Indigenous peoples organized and presented their demands, and how they struggled for their rights. Carlos Iván Degregori cautions that ethnic movements "do not always arise in the same manner, present the same characteristics, or evolve in the same way."[112] The FEI, FENOC, and Ecuarunari emerged out of different contexts and would respond in different ways, but together they built a remarkably strong Indigenous movement in Ecuador.

Pachakutik

In June 1990 a powerful Indigenous uprising, the largest in Ecuador's history, paralyzed the country for a week. Indigenous peoples across the country united in defense of common political goals to an extent never before seen. The pan-Indigenous federation CONAIE emerged at the forefront of protests that called for land, economic development, education, and recognition of Indigenous nationalities. "The uprising marked a decisive change in the future of our movement," CONAIE's vice president, Luis Macas, declared. "We have achieved a political space; we have entered into the political scene of the country."[1] This movement to redefine Indigenous peoples' roles in society had profound implications that threatened Ecuador's power base of white elites.

Indigenous militants began to refer to this uprising as a *pachakutik*. The historian Nils Jacobsen defines this term as "the Andean notion of a turning point of cosmic dimensions and the beginning of a new era through which what was below would be on top and vice versa."[2] It was not only a rupture, but also a force "that was capable of restoring order."[3] Pachakutik has long been a concept that drove millenarian revolts in the southern Andes. It was the name of the ninth and one of the most famous Inka rulers who in 1438 began an imperial expansion out of the Cuzco Valley. The term had rarely been used in the north, but now it was introduced into the language of Ecuador's Indigenous rights movements. Macas gave this name to his eldest son, and militants in the Amazon launched a new political party in 1995 under the name.[4] The anthropologist Norman Whitten rooted its use in millennial concepts located "between a remembered past and an imagined future" in which "oppression is remembered, and movements toward collective self-determination are enacted."[5] Kichwa intellectuals appropriated this term to press forward with the deep changes sweeping through Ecuador.

Scholars commonly interpret contemporary Indigenous movements emerging out of this pachakutik as "new" in that they were primarily concerned with legal reforms, struggles over territory and resource use, and interactions with non-Indigenous organizations and social movements.[6] New social movements differ from traditional political parties or labor unions in that they respond to a specific crisis rather than engaging in a project of historical transformation (such as taking over state structures). Rather than being rooted in a class analysis, new social movement theorists point to "ethnicity, gender, and sexuality as the definers of collective identity."[7] Critics, however, question what is so new about these movements. "Old" social movements did not entirely ignore identity politics, and "new" movements have not discarded a class consciousness. Rather, social movements reveal a strong continuity in goals, strategies, and tactics. More important is to understand how various forms of identity (including class, ethnicity, and gender) interact with each other in specific historical contexts.[8]

In Ecuador, an Indigenous movement that scholars have championed as a classic example of a new social movement found itself engaging in street demonstrations, running for electoral office, and even overthrowing governments—the most traditional strategies of the "old" style movements. In the 1990 uprising, Indigenous activists presented a broad range of demands, with the symbolically most important being the constitutional recognition of Ecuador as a plurinational state. Far from the limited goals of identity politics, Indigenous demands hit at the heart of how elites had structured the state. Activists had long used many of these tactics. For example, the blocking of roads was a common component of 1970s labor strikes.[9] A new generation of Indigenous organizations that captivated the attention of many people did not emerge out of a vacuum. It was an extension of long struggles, often fought in collaboration with sympathetic supporters, to gain a voice in how society would be structured and who it would benefit.

CONAIE

Building on earlier initiatives, in August 1980 Amazonian Indigenous organizations formed the Confederación de Nacionalidades Indígenas de la Amazonía Ecuatoriana (CONFENIAE, Confederation of Indigenous Nationalities of the Ecuadorian Amazon). The pan-Amazonian federation struggled for social, political, and economic equality for Indigenous communities, and to gain respect for their cultures within the Ecuadorian state. Several months later, Ecuarunari joined CONFENIAE to form the Consejo Nacional de Coordinación de las Nacionalidades Indígenas del Ecuador (CONACNIE, National Coordinating Council of Indigenous Nationalities of Ecuador). Both new federations represented the ascendancy of an organizing strategy based primarily on ethno-nationalist discourse, and the consolidation of the third part of what Guerrero and Ospina point to as the triple origins of Indigenous movements. Instead of relying on the political left or on progressive sectors of the Catholic Church, CONFENIAE and CONACNIE cultivated political alliances with transnational advocacy networks and nongovernmental organizations to facilitate the linkage of Indigenous organizations to global struggles.[10] In a partial explanation of these shifts, the CONACNIE leader Manuel Imbaquingo complained that "several years ago Indigenous organizations were strong," but imperialism had infiltrated the organizing efforts in a variety of ways, including through religious sects, such that it "has caused us to fight one community against another . . . which has weakened us."[11]

"If we do not reinforce our unity," CONACNIE observed, "there is a danger that various maneuvers would divide us and we would lose our presence." For this reason, it was important to build "only one national organization for the various Indigenous nationalities in the country."[12] In order to realize success, it was "indispensable to unite the double dimension of our struggle" through recognition of "the double character of our problems: as members of a class and as part of different Indigenous nationalities."[13] This theme was reiterated in CONACNIE's second meeting in April 1984, which emphasized a "consciousness of their class position" while at the same time reaffirming an identity as peoples and nationalities.[14] The coordinating council met with limited success, and it betrayed ideological differences—including tension between ethnic-oriented Amazonian organizations and highland groups grounded in class politics—that would continue to plague efforts to build a unified national movement. Focusing on the "double dimension" of class and ethnic aspects of the Indigenous struggle ultimately did more to forge a coalition between highland and lowland activists than to bridge divides between Indigenous and other popular organizations.[15]

Scholarship on race and ethnicity (as well as gender) has moved far beyond seeing these concepts as fixed, biological, primordial, and essentialized, and instead understands them as fluid, changeable, negotiable social constructs. Pallares observes that this transformation "did not mean an abandonment of class demands, but rather a rearticulation of material demands into the political ideologies and practices of indianismo."[16] Reducing the complexities and subtleties of human interactions into a sterile model of class versus ethnicity misses the complex interplay between various types of identities. As Pallares notes, "double consciousness is characterized by the inevitable and constituting presence of two forms of consciousness that are shaping each other." Identities are defined and refined through interactions with the dominant culture. Race, as Elizabeth Kuznesof notes, "was not only a social construct, but it was constantly reconstructed."[17] The goal should not be eschewing one form of consciousness for another but allowing multiple forms of consciousness to transform each other.[18] It is in the process of reconstructing these identities to confront new and changing situations that Indigenous cultures were able to survive and flourish in the face of external domination.

Meeting at the Nueva Vida (New Life) camp outside Quito in November 1986, five hundred delegates representing nine Indigenous nationalities and twenty-seven organizations formed CONAIE to replace CONACNIE. Ecuarunari and CONFENIAE joined a much smaller coastal organization called the Coordinadora de Organizaciones Indígenas de la Costa Ecuatoriana (COICE, Coordinating Body of Indigenous Organizations of the Ecuadorian Coast) to combine all Indigenous peoples into one large pan-Indian movement dedicated to defending Indigenous concerns and agitating for social, political, and educational reforms. Their demands included land, funds for economic development, respect for Indigenous languages, development of bilingual education, recognition of traditional medicine, and, finally, reestablishment of diplomatic relations with the revolutionary Sandinista government in Nicaragua.[19] Further, CONAIE emerged at a point of growing unity within popular movements with Indigenous organizations working more closely with labor federations in campaigns of common interest.[20]

Since CONAIE was organized as an overtly and explicitly Indigenous organization, observers tend to interpret it as a triumph of ethnic discourse over class analysis. The sociologist Alicia Ibarra argues, however, that this has always been a false dichotomy and CONAIE represents a successful fusion of class and ethnic perspectives.[21] At its second congress in November 1988,

CONAIE declared itself to be an "organization of oppressed and exploited people," and it defined its struggle as "anti-colonial, anti-capitalist, and anti-imperialist." It continued to call for agrarian reform as well as for unity of the popular movement.[22] In addition to land issues, CONAIE also critiqued industrialization, unemployment, housing, education, health, and racial discrimination. Further, CONAIE rejected the "racist" position of positing an Indigenous against mestizo struggle that "in its most extreme position advocated the expulsion of the invaders and a return to Tawantinsuyu." Rather, CONAIE advocated a "third way" in which the struggle acquired a "double dimension" of organizing on a class basis together with other popular movements to transform society as well as independent ethnic organizations in defense of Indigenous cultures.[23] Leon Zamosc notes that "the Ecuadorian case calls attention to the fact that class conflict continues to be a relevant factor in Latin American politics." Rather than limiting the struggle to ethnic rights, "the Indian movement has transcended them, involving itself in broader battles over social issues and becoming a player in the contest for political power."[24]

Social movement theorists recognize that material needs can play an important role in mobilizing a movement, but that an ideological framework is also necessary to solidify coherent actions.[25] While ethnicity has proven capable of engaging and mobilizing people, it alone has been less successful at maintaining a level of organizational energy over the long haul. Increasingly, analysts acknowledge how "the privileging of identity construction has . . . obscured the material conditions and structural challenges that shape social movement dynamics."[26] Indigenous movements could succeed only inasmuch as they were able to blend class and ethnic elements. Indeed, CONAIE was most successful when it embraced rather than denied the class nature of Indigenous oppression. While the FEI overtly used class discourse to challenge a history of racial discrimination, CONAIE exploited ethnic identities to press an economic agenda. Class and ethnicity appeared at the same time to be mutually conflictive and reinforcing.

Indigenous Nationalities

Beginning in the 1970s, academic and activist debates evolved from the question of whether to pursue class or ethnic-based strategies of organization to the question of whether to construct Indians as a class, ethnic group, community, people, or nationality. In 1973, the anthropologist Gladys Villavicencio asked almost incidentally if commercial success in Otavalo was leading to the formation of an Indigenous nationality.[27] In 1979, after returning from the Soviet Union, Ileana Almeida published an essay in which she presented Indigenous peoples in the Andes as a Quechua nationality. Drawing on a marxist analysis, she argued that a common history, territory, economy, culture, and language all meant that Indigenous peoples formed a true nationality. Furthermore, in an argument that CONAIE subsequently would make, nations did not necessarily coincide with states, for several nationalities were included within the Ecuadorian state.[28] Later Almeida expanded on this concept to note two contrasting constructions of nationality—one being a homogenizing influence that emanated from the dominant classes, and the other representing an anti-colonial movement for national liberation that emerged out of Indigenous and other popular struggles that respected and embraced cultural diversity.[29] José Sánchez Parga proposed that Indigenous movements had a "triple dimension." In addition to class and ethnicity, they also included a nationalist orientation, including citizenship demands, with each aspect informing the other two. Rather than being opposed to each other, class, ethnicity, and nationalism formed a trinity that could not be divided.[30]

The concept of "Indigenous nationalities" had never completely disappeared since the communists introduced it in the 1930s. In the 1944 Constituent Assembly, Ricardo Paredes as representative of the "Indigenous race" argued that Indigenous histories, languages, territories, and cultural institutions made for distinct nationalities.[31] At its 1957 congress, the PCE noted that Indigenous peoples possessed "national elements," a sentiment that the party's secretary-general, Pedro Saad, articulated in his own statements.[32] In a 1977 interview, the communist militant César Endara observed the double character of Indigenous exploitation in that "in addition to economic exploitation they were also exploited nationally."[33] Similarly, the newly founded communist–affiliated coalition FADI called for the defense of "the specific rights of Indigenous communities and national groups in the country (Kichwa, Shuar, Cofan, etc.)."[34] With Almeida's essay, this concept gained newfound resilience, and other leftists began to speak of "the existence of oppressed Indigenous nationalities within the State."[35] At a 1982 congress, the labor federation CEDOC voted to send "revolutionary greetings to Ecuador's Indigenous nationalities" who "for many years have been fighting for their inalienable rights."[36] The following year, FADI's vice president, Rafael Quintero, again embraced the Indigenous movements, whose participants now expressed their demands "not only as peasants, but also as peoples and nationalities."[37] Similarly FENOC, the more "peasant" of the Indigenous organizations, called for a defense of "our rights as peoples and nationalities."[38] In 1985, the PSE proposed a Law of Indigenous Nationalities to the national congress.[39] The conceptualization of Indigenous peoples as nationalities gained resilience from the political left more quickly than it did within Indigenous communities. Unlike the assumption of many academics, Indigenous leaders did not reclaim this identity on their own but rather it was a contribution from marxist intellectuals.[40]

The formation of CONFENIAE in 1980 took place in the midst of a shift in language as a new generation of Indigenous activists began to embrace this discourse. "We have claimed the term nationalities," the Indigenous intellectual Alfredo Viteri observes, "as a category that includes all of the different Indigenous groups."[41] The First Regional Conference of Indigenous Nationalities of the Ecuadorian Amazon that founded CONFENIAE in August 1980 was originally to be called the First Regional Conference of Indigenous Organizations of the Ecuadorian Amazon. The decision to change the name reflected an increased concern with petitioning for territorial and political rights as nationalities. The statutes set out by CONFENIAE declared the organization's intent to "defend and value the cultures of Indigenous nationalities in the Ecuadorian Amazon."[42] Local Amazonian federations also shifted their discourse to reflect these changes, moving from employing the language of "Indigenous classes" in the 1970s to "Indigenous federations" in the 1980s and to "ethnic nationalities" in the 1990s."[43] In a 1984 essay, the Shuar intellectual Ampam Karakras advocated that Indigenous peoples conceptualize themselves as "Indian nationalities" with all of the corresponding economic, political, cultural, and linguistic aspects. "We want to use our own names, maintain our own identity and personalities," Karakras wrote.[44] As the political scientist José Antonio Lucero ascertains, "indigenous activists in Ecuador have taken a term from the lexicon of Marxist and European thought and 'Indianized' it."[45]

In 1988, CONAIE presented its conceptualization of Indigenous nationalities to the Indigenous Affairs Commission of the National Congress. In the proposed Law of Indigenous Nationalities, CONAIE declared that the republic of Ecuador was a plurinational state, and it argued that the government must recognize Indigenous territoriality, organization, education, culture, medicine, and judicial systems.[46] Further, CONAIE argued that their proposal would not establish separate states for the various ethnic groups, as elites feared, but rather it would "reflect the reality of the country and the continent in respect to different national cultures and to the reestablishment of social, political, and economic equality."[47] Santana notes that Indigenous demands had not been a serious threat to elites as long as they only demanded respect for their cultures, but engaging in a discourse of Indigenous nationalities seemed to imply autonomy, self-determination, and territorial rights that presented a more serious challenge to the dominant culture.[48] Despite elite fears, Indigenous demands were not secessionist. Rather than seeking a separate state, they sought respect for their cultures within existing state structures. While opponents argued that multiculturalism was a threat to society, the political scientist Melina Selverston-Scher contends that diversity, not homogeneity, was critical for stable democracy.[49] Ecuador's national problems, CONAIE asserted, were not the result of the presence of distinct ethnic groups, but rather existed because of socioeconomic inequalities. The solution was to be found in reclaiming their "true historic and cultural roots" and their "identity as people with a history and a future."[50] As the anthropologist Suzana Sawyer notes, "nation *is* a politically charged and volatile category," and Indigenous success in subverting this imagery enabled ethnic groups "to challenge exclusionary state rule and dominant notions of the nation."[51]

The call to recognize Ecuador's plurinational character became CONAIE's key and most contentious demand. Lucero observes that nationalities "are not naturally existing units but rather the products of politics." Indigenous movements can embrace a variety of mechanisms for advancing their agenda, including organizing themselves as ethnic communities (pueblos), federations, cooperatives, or comunas. In this context, "nationality became the discursive vehicle for CONAIE's alternative democratic political project." Rather than falling back on a "tradition" or even reflecting an existing reality, nationalities formed part of a strategy to construct active political subjects. The success of CONAIE in this project was not so much because "nationalities" reflected reality but because they were able to mobilize around this discourse. That discourse succeeded, Lucero contends, because it was rooted in a trajectory of civil society rather than in "the clientelistic dynamics of party politics" as developed in Bolivia, and probably to a lesser extent in Peru.[52]

In employing the discourse of nationalities as an organizing tool, whether consciously or not, CONAIE built on a long, rich tradition. Given its roots in leftist discourse, it should come as no surprise that at its seventh congress in

1989 the FEI also declared Ecuador to be "a multinational and multicultural country." It argued that the 1917 Bolshevik Revolution was the first to "resolve the problem of the nationalities" and affirmed the need to fight for the "recognition of a multinational state."[53] Six years later, at its eighth congress, the FEI presented a powerful argument for why Ecuador must be recognized as a plurinational state. The country embodied a society with a rich "diversity of cultures, languages, and peoples with distinct historical origins." Spanish colonization and subsequent governments had excluded this diversity in their attempts to construct a unitary "Ecuadorian nationality" under a centralized state structure. The FEI called for the full participation of Indigenous nationalities in government so that they would have a voice in policies that affected them.[54]

Galo Ramón sees two distinct trends in Indigenous identity in Ecuador: the first emphasized specific local ethnic identities and the second constructed a unified pluriethnic identity.[55] Building plurinational identities presents certain challenges. "A movement unified through a plurality of differences," the historian Chad Black writes, "always walks a tenuous line, marginalizing voices within while protesting such marginalization from without."[56] Furthermore, as Carol Smith points out in the case of Maya identities in Guatemala, fragmented identities can ensure the survival of Indigenous cultures. "Throughout history," she notes, "Indian communities have maintained themselves through diversity, which has prevented them from forming a united Indian nation that could proclaim its own national sovereignty." She continues by stating that "this 'weakness' has also been the source of Indian cultural 'strength,' since no centralized power in Guatemala has ever found a single cultural source or symbol to destroy through which Indian culture *in general* would be eradicated."[57] Understanding fragmented (or local) identities as a tool of resistance brings into question whether forming Indigenous nationalities was a worthwhile goal, or whether achieving that goal would only facilitate repression. It was this minefield of ethnic identities and politics that activists needed to navigate for Indigenous movements to flourish.

After years of agitation, activists scored a partial victory in 1998 when politicians revised the first article of the constitution to recognize Ecuador's "pluricultural and multiethnic" nature but then stopped short of using the contentious term "plurinational." A subsequent section on collective rights implicitly recognized this ideological construction with the statement that "Indigenous peoples, who self-define as nationalities of ancestral races, and

The Kayambi intellectual Pedro Guaña in the 2004 Inti Raymi (Sun Festival) in the city of Cayambe. Photo by Marc Becker.

Negro or Afro-Ecuadorian peoples, form part of a united and indivisible Ecuadorian state."[58] The desire to have Ecuador formally recognized as a plurinational state remained an illusive goal.

Levantamientos

On June 4, 1990, CONAIE launched a nationwide *levantamiento* (uprising) that blocked roads in order to paralyze the transport system, thereby effectively cutting off the food supply to cities and shutting down the country for a week. Sometimes called the "levantamiento indígena de Inti Raymi"— because the uprising took place just before the traditional June solstice "Sun Festival" celebrations—it thrust Indigenous activists as actors onto the national stage. Frustrated by stagnated talks with the government over bilingual education, agrarian reform, and demands to recognize Ecuador's plurinational nature, CONAIE decided at its fifth assembly in April 1990 to launch the uprising to force the government to negotiate their demands.[59]

Starting in the central and northern highlands, it spread across the country as a decentralized phenomenon with local activists taking individual initiatives to press their demands. Clashes between police and Indigenous peoples blocking roads led to the detention of several leaders and the death of Oswaldo Cuvi from Riobamba. "The history of our country is the history of 500 years of Indigenous resistance," CONAIE stated at the beginning of the uprising, exploiting rhetorical openings provided by the approaching October 12, 1992, quincentennial of Columbus's voyage to the Americas. "The Indigenous Uprising demonstrates the continuity of a struggle begun by Rumiñahui, Tupac Amaru, and other leaders who fought to recover the lands belonging to our forefathers."[60]

For much of Latin America the 1980s had been a "lost decade," with the economic growth of the 1970s coming to a screeching halt as hyperinflation, spiraling unemployment, and a crushing debt crisis unraveled elite dreams of joining the industrialized First World. For many popular sectors that never enjoyed the benefit of the "boom," the 1980s represented a "gained decade" as neighborhood, women's, peasant, environmental, and—more than any other—Indigenous social movements experienced growing political strength and legitimacy.[61] An ability to engage diverse political, social, and economic issues on local, regional, national, and international levels helped build Indigenous movements to their strongest and most active point. The consolidation of organizational structures placed Indigenous peoples in a strong position. The 1990 uprising introduced a decade of greatly intensified Indigenous activism and visibility.

"Without planning or foresight," Leon Zamosc notes, "CONAIE found itself the only popular organization that could represent the distressed rural population of the Sierra."[62] With CONAIE's lead, Indigenous movements presented the government with a list of "sixteen points" that revolved broadly around cultural issues (such as support for traditional medicine and bilingual education programs), economic concerns (negotiating debts, accessing credit, and budgeting for economic development programs in Indigenous communities), and political demands (ending political control over local communities and amending the first article of the constitution to declare Ecuador to be a plurinational and multicultural state).[63] Members of other Indigenous organizations, including FEI and FENOC, joined the uprising.[64] Observers noted that the growth of Indigenous consciousness was likened to the "awakening of a sleeping giant."[65] The uprising represented a true pachakutik.

The concerns of the Indigenous movements' rank and file were often much more immediate and pragmatic than the leadership's rhetorical posturing implied. Unable to wait for CONAIE's formal protest, on May 28—a week before the uprising was to begin—two hundred activists from six highland provinces occupied the historic Santo Domingo cathedral in the middle of colonial Quito and demanded the resolution of seventy-two land disputes.[66] The anthropologist Lynn Meisch maintains that "the demand for genuine land reform . . . is the glue that binds the indigenous movement. Many *indígenas* do not have a clue, and could care less, about the rest of CONAIE's agenda."[67] Long after agrarian reform programs were to have solved the land problem, one study listed 217 agrarian conflicts during the 1980s.[68] At its second congress in 1988, CONAIE declared the agrarian reform agency IERAC to be "public enemy number one of Indigenous peoples" for its failure to resolve these issues and consistently favoring non-Indigenous concerns.[69] "Not one hacienda in 1992" ("1992 Ni una hacienda en el Ecuador") and "Without land there is no democracy" became common protest slogans. "The demand for rights to land and territoriality are historic," Macas noted. "It is nothing new." He then proceeded to observe that "in reality this is our principal demand." Finally, echoing statements from Mariátegui in the 1920s, he stated: "There will be no solution to the Indigenous problem unless there is a solution to the land problem."[70] Emphasizing the depth of this issue, protestors noted that for Indigenous communities land "is not only a means of production, it is a fundamental base for their culture and life."[71] Exemplifying continuity, many grassroots demands were still fundamentally the same as those that drove the FEI and earlier movements. Similar to how rural protests forced agrarian reform legislation in the 1960s, one of the most concrete outcomes of the 1990 levantamiento was to place agrarian issues back on the negotiating table. Even in an increasingly urbanized country, land conflicts were still intense even to the point of death squads executing Indigenous leaders. In the northern province of Imbabura in March 1991, landowners assassinated Julio Cabascango—the third local leader to be killed in six months in ongoing agrarian conflicts.[72]

Many times, as demonstrated by the seemingly spontaneous occupation of the Santo Domingo church, leaders found themselves playing catch-up with their bases. Even before the uprising started, local activists increasingly pressed militant actions. On May 19, Indigenous community members around Lake San Pablo in Otavalo occupied the La Clemencia hacienda.[73] Grassroots pressure forced CONAIE to speed up the timing of their planned uprising, fearing that otherwise they would lose their legitimacy as representing Ecuador's Indigenous movement.[74] But, as Sawyer notes, far from being spontaneous, most successful protests were highly orchestrated events intended to influence specific policies.[75] Leaders had requested audiences with President Rodrigo Borja, and they only moved to direct actions when the government refused to meet.[76] Finally on June 8, CONAIE's aggressive actions pressed the government to the negotiating table. Indigenous protestors abandoned their roadblocks and the military released its detainees. Three weeks later, CONAIE announced that it would suspend the dialogue "until the government gives a definitive response to the problem of lands." Other unresolved issues included economic reforms, the institution of bilingual education, and the recognition of Ecuador as a plurinational country.[77] For the next several years, the government and CONAIE alternated between the negotiating table and rhetorical positioning that occasionally led to street protests.

The 1990 levantamiento took advantage of openings that Borja's (1988–1992) centrist government had created for Indigenous peoples. The previous conservative government of León Febres Cordero (1984–1988) had implemented neoliberal economic policies and assumed dictatorial attitudes as it applied repressive measures against popular movements. In contrast, Borja's election raised grassroots expectations. The new president met with Indigenous organizations and attempted to address their concerns. In the years leading up to the 1990 uprising, he employed favorable rhetoric in speeches, proclaiming that "Ecuador is a plurinational and multicultural country." Indigenous nationalities, he noted, had been here "many years before we invented our states."[78] Taking advantage of these apertures and apparent official legitimization of their self-conceptualization as Indigenous nationalities, militants pressed for even more rights. "We peasants and Indigenous nationalities are the most affected by the economic crisis and the government's social policies," activists declared on the eve of the uprising. "Borja has not complied with his electoral promises."[79] Borja believed that he had done more than any other government to support Indigenous demands, and he felt betrayed when they rebelled against him.[80] The uprising underscores Crane Brinton's argument in *The Anatomy of Revolution* that revolts do not emerge out of oppression and deprivation, but rather a failure to realize rising aspirations.

The uprising caught the urban marxist left, which a decade earlier had largely dismissed Ecuador's rural population as a significant force in a social revolution, off guard. Only three years earlier, Barbara Schroder noted that "although indigenas have gained some representation in national-level labor organization, they are all but invisible in political parties and in the Ecuadorian state."[81] Alicia Ibarra, who previously had emphasized the class nature of Indigenous movements, now recognized the potential for identity politics to mobilize the masses for social change. "It had an immense capacity to convoke people to action," Ibarra stated. "It demonstrated a high level of organization and consolidation of the movement. It was a call to recognize that in Ecuador there were still Indians with a voice that cannot be ignored or quieted."[82] With the left in disarray after the fall of the Soviet Union and the Berlin Wall, the PCE recognized the strategic opening and jumped at the opportunity to ally with a strong and well-organized social movement. Ecuador, the PCE noted, had a plurinational society comprised of a diversity of cultures, languages, and peoples with different historical origins, and it called for the "constitutional establishment of the rights of Indigenous nationalities and ethnic groups."[83] A new ethno-nationalist discourse emerged out of the ideological spaces created by these broader political shifts. Rather than the left rescuing Indigenous identities from the dustbin of history, it was Indigenous mobilization that provided leftist ideologies with a continuing relevance to Ecuador's social movements.

In response to Indigenous demands, CONAIE explicitly cultivated the external support of labor and peasant unions, the church, and students.[84] The bishop of Riobamba issued a statement supporting the uprising, condemning the oppression and exploitation that Indigenous peoples faced, and celebrating the "human values and rights of the Indigenous nationalities and ethnicities of our country." In response, local landed elites accused the church of instigating protest movements, even while the bishop emphasized that the uprising had been an entirely Indigenous decision.[85] "It is the task of the working class," the PCE noted in El Pueblo shortly after the levantamiento, "to deepen the process of unity and struggle with this reborn Indigenous movement." The party continued by stating: "The true realization of a plurinational and multiethnic state can only be achieved with the unified struggle of all popular sectors."[86] Cristobal Tapuy, the president of CONAIE, echoed this sentiment with a call for "the unity not only of Indian peoples, because not only we Indians are exploited, but also of workers, peasants, Blacks, and students."[87] Further, CONAIE noted that in the face of the crisis that Ecuador faced, "popular and Indigenous organizations see the importance of together strengthening our struggles of resistance."[88] Similar to the FEI and other earlier organizations, CONAIE reached out to popular organizations to work together to achieve common goals. Now, however, instead of the left attempting to organize subalterns, this relationship was reversed with Indigenous organizations setting the agenda for the rest of the popular movement. Thus CONAIE saw power in unity, and alliances with non-Indigenous sectors became critical as it pressed its demands with the government.

In a seeming parallel with the January 1931 strike at Pesillo that was followed with an Indigenous congress in February, a month after the Inti Raymi uprising CONAIE joined with the South American Indian Information Center (SAIIC) and the Organización Nacional Indígena de Colombia (ONIC, National Indigenous Organization of Colombia) to organize the First Continental Conference on Five Hundred Years of Indigenous Resistance. Four hundred representatives from 120 Indigenous nationalities and organizations throughout the Americas gathered in Quito on July 17 to 23, 1990, to form a united front against oppression, discrimination, and exploitation. Working together with other marginalized sectors of society, Indigenous peoples demanded complete autonomy and self-government, including respect for customary law and traditional justice systems within their own communities. Participants appealed for "complete structural change" that would "be achieved only after the rejection of the capitalist system" and through participation in a struggle "geared toward the construction of a new society, pluralistic, democratic and based on popular power."[89]

When the dust cleared, observers questioned what concrete objectives the uprising had achieved. Even two years later, not one of the land conflicts that CONAIE had presented to the government had been resolved.[90] Nevertheless, the uprising had resulted in a seismic shift in consciousness. "We are no longer the same," an Indigenous leader from Cotopaxi observed. "Now we hold our heads high."[91] Much like the 1931 strike at Pesillo, the 1990 uprising introduced a decade of incredibly heightened activism with Indigenous peoples playing a key role in political developments. A year later, Indigenous activists returned to Quito and occupied Congress to demand constitutional reforms, ratification of the International Labor Organization Convention 169 concerning the rights of Indigenous peoples, and amnesty for one thousand Indigenous activists charged in the previous year's uprising.[92] The following year, the quincentennial triggered another round of protests and road blockages.[93]

Building on this momentum, the Organización de Pueblos Indígenas de

Pastaza (OPIP, Organization of Indigenous Peoples of Pastaza) presented the government with a plan for handing over control of 90 percent of the land (including petroleum deposits) in the Amazonian province of Pastaza. Borja responded by denouncing what he saw as an attempt to dismember "our national territory" and create "a 'parallel state' within Ecuador's borders, in which national laws would have no power over 'traditional rights.'" The CONAIE vice president Luis Macas denied that they were trying to "erode Ecuadorian sovereignty," declaring instead a desire "to develop our communities in a collective form."[94] Land was a commodity of interest to colonists, but territory was "an ancestral space where culture develops," and it was that ethnic use of land that they sought to protect. Two years of governmental inaction led to an April 1992 *caminata* (march) from the Amazon to Quito. Inspired by female elders and drawing on the historical legacy of Jumandi's 1578 revolt, two thousand Kichwa, Shuar, and Achuar peoples walked 240 kilometers in thirteen days to demand "the legalization of the territories they inhabit, and that the national constitution be reformed to reflect the plurinational and multicultural reality of Ecuador." They emphasized their desire to "protect the forest from the irrational exploitation of oil resources and guarantee the development of our culture, language and laws." They were joined in the highlands by the Salasaca, their "mountain brothers," who enthusiastically provided them with material and moral support, and together they continued on to Quito. President Borja announced that he would be "pleased" to receive the Indians when they arrived in Quito. He initially agreed to their demands for control over territory, but later he refused to hand over land titles—citing concerns for "national security" along the contested border with Peru.[95] In response, a delegation of Indigenous leaders met with congressional deputies to demand constitutional reforms.[96] Sawyer calls the caminata "a crucial juncture in the process of indigenous nation building." The caminata provided an opportunity to weave "indigenous rights together with local understandings of identity and place," leading to "a unique moment of indigenous agency."[97]

In June 1994, peasant and Indigenous groups unified in "La Movilización por la Vida" ("The Mobilization for Life"). Similar to the Article 27 revisions that triggered the Zapatista uprising in Mexico earlier that year, the government of the conservative president Sixto Durán Ballén (1992–1996) proposed a new law that would allow communally held land to be sold or mortgaged, thus turning it into a commodity that could be taken away from Indigenous peoples. Not only would this new law bring an end to thirty years of agrarian reform, it would also implement neoliberal policies that included the privatization of water rights, the auctioning of state-owned land, and the intensification of the export of agricultural commodities. Agricultural reforms "have not resolved the problem of Indigenous People and Nationalities," CONAIE complained. Rather, they were " 'agrotechnical' capitalist reforms that responded to the economic and political interests of national and foreign exploiters" and failed to take into account the need for a true and comprehensive development plan.[98] An umbrella group called the Coordinadora Agraria Nacional (CAN, National Agrarian Coordinator) argued that because of its impact on rural populations, the proposed legislation should be submitted to extensive debate. When Durán Ballén refused to listen to criticisms, activists blocked roads and paralyzed the country for ten days. The government declared a state of emergency and threatened military action to end the protests. Despite what was one of the largest and most successful protests in Ecuador's history, Durán Ballén proceeded to promulgate a new law of agrarian development that created the Instituto Nacional de Desarrollo Agrario (INDA, National Institute of Agrarian Development) to replace IERAC. Nevertheless, the protests had strengthened inter-ethnic Indigenous-peasant coalitions to challenge neoliberal policies. This mobilization revealed that land rights continued to be a central demand for Indigenous organizations and remained a defining characteristic of Indigenous movements.[99]

In 1995, Amazonian leaders founded the Movimiento Unidad Plurinacional Pachakutik–Nuevo País (MUPP–NP, Pachakutik Movement for Plurinational Unity–New Country) to campaign for political office. This political movement emerged out of years of debate on the roles of Indigenous peoples in electoral politics, including whether Indigenous organizations should put forward their own candidates and issues, or whether they should support existing parties that "understand and guarantee the fundamental rights of the Indigenous population."[100] After gaining the right to vote in 1979, Indigenous peoples tended either to vote for leftist or center-leftist candidates or not to vote at all, arguing that "elections do not interest us because we do not identify with any of the candidates."[101] Activists debated whether to found an "Indian Political Front" or "Ecuadorian Indian Party," with some arguing that organizing separately would marginalize Indigenous peoples from the broader popular movement. The FENOC leader Alberto Andrango maintained that "we have to unite ourselves as poor people

The Indigenous leader Blanca Chancoso leads a march against the Free Trade Area of the Americas (FTAA) at the 2004 Americas Social Forum in Quito.
Photo by Marc Becker.

without forgetting that we are Indigenous." He advocated working with the political left to advance not only Indigenous concerns "but also those of other popular classes." Andrango twice won a position on the city council in his native Cotacachi as the leader of a local Indigenous organization and a candidate of the Socialist Party.[102] Reflecting its historical roots, the FEI supported the communist-affiliated FADI coalition and called on peasants to vote for this list. The first self-identified Indigenous person elected to congress, however, was Manuel Naula from Chimborazo in 1984 on the center-left Izquierda Demócratica (ID, Democratic Left) ticket.[103]

As Indigenous activists became better organized and more assertive, they increasingly ran into conflicts with their traditional allies on the left who expected them to play the role of a junior partner in a coalition. As a result, they resisted forwarding the names of Indigenous activists as candidates. Women faced similar problems, and Indigenous women were completely excluded. Community members complained that political parties only paid attention to them, including the running of Indigenous candidates, to gain votes. "We are a step for those who are going up," they observed. "No party has taken our interests seriously."[104] The CONAIE leader Blanca Chancoso (whom Xavier Albó terms a later-day Dolores Cacuango)[105] also complained that political parties ignored Indigenous issues. "They would speak for us," she noted, "but it was out of the question for an Indian to be in the leadership."[106] The CONAIE leader Luis Maldonado criticized the left for acting the same as the political right, only showing up during campaigns to make promises that were promptly forgotten once in office. The parties were opportunistic: they took measures to improve their electoral position, but refused to use their positions of power to denounce killings of Indigenous leaders. This was part of a broader crisis in the left, because "in Ecuador there is a divide between the left and popular organizations."[107] Even with this tension, Karakras contended that Indigenous movements "could not support the right, because they are the ones who . . . have exploited the popular sectors, and in particular the Indigenous population."[108]

The Pachakutik movement represented the emergence of a third option between joining leftist coalitions or creating ethnic parties, with Indigenous peoples working together as equals with other popular movements to form a new political movement. Pachakutik was an explicit reversal of a policy that CONAIE adopted at its third congress in 1990 not to participate in elections because neither the political system nor political parties were functioning in a way that represented people's interests.[109] Increasingly, however, Indigenous activists believed it was time not only for them to make their own politics but also to make good politics that would benefit everyone. Structured as a political *movement* rather than political *party*, Pachakutik was organized in a horizontal, democratic, and inclusionary fashion. It explicitly identified itself as part of the new Latin American left that embraced principles of community, solidarity, unity, tolerance, and respect. Pachakutik opposed the government's neoliberal economic policies and favored a more inclusive and participatory political system. It represented a culmination of CONAIE's drive to insert Indigenous peoples directly into debates, giving them a voice and allowing them to speak for themselves.[110]

Pachakutik experienced moderate success on both local and national levels in its first electoral contest in 1996, including the election of six Indigenous deputies to congress and Auki Tituaña as mayor of Cotacachi in Imbabura. Luis Macas won a post as a national deputy in the National Assembly, becoming the first Indigenous person elected to a nationwide

Luis Macas speaking at the 2004 Continental Summit of Indigenous Nations and Peoples of the Americas in Quito. In 1996, Macas won a post as a national deputy in the National Assembly, thereby becoming the first Indigenous person elected to a nationwide office. Photo by Marc Becker.

office. Macas's victory, as the journalist Kintto Lucas noted, was due to his success "in combining the indigenous vote . . . with the vote of progressive and left-wing sectors."[111] Andrés Guerrero points to Pachakutik as a watershed in the evolution of Indigenous movements, with them no longer being "an extra-state organism and beginning to function in the political arena."[112] Pachakutik had become a significant power bloc in national politics.

Abdalá Bucaram, one of the wealthiest people in Ecuador and a populist cut from the same cloth as Velasco Ibarra, won the presidency in 1996 largely on campaign promises of aiding the poor. Once in office, however, he implemented neoliberal reforms that included raising transportation and cooking-gas prices that hurt the poor but benefitted the wealthy elite. Within six months, Bucaram's economic policies and rampant corruption alienated his power base, leading to a mass uprising on February 5, 1997, that evicted him from power.[113] This brought to an end the longest chronological succession of uninterrupted constitutional rule in Ecuador's history (1979–1997), returning the country to the status quo of frequent and extra-constitutional changes of power. During the next eight years, eight chief executives held power.

The last coup of the twentieth century in Latin America occurred in Ecuador on January 21, 2000, when an alliance of lower-ranking military officials and Indigenous leaders evicted Jamil Mahuad from power. Faced with soaring inflation and a free-falling economy, Mahuad proposed replacing the sucre with the U.S. dollar as legal tender. Critics, including Indigenous peasants and poor urban workers, denounced this sacrifice of national sovereignty that could only undermine their standard of living. The CONAIE president Antonio Vargas, Colonel Lucio Gutiérrez, and the former supreme court president Carlos Solórzano—symbolizing a union of Indians, soldiers, and the law—formed a new body, the Government of National Salvation. Several hours later, General Carlos Mendoza replaced Gutiérrez in the Junta, but then resigned, thereby collapsing the provisional government and handing power over to Vice President Gustavo Noboa. After taking power Noboa proceeded with a plan to convert sucres to dollars, a plan so radical that it did not even enjoy the support of the International Monetary Fund.[114] In a repeat of the fall of Bucaram three years earlier, the oligarchy took advantage of Indigenous movements to grab power for themselves.

Instead of being protagonists, Indians seemingly demonstrated Barrington Moore's allegation that the success of peasant revolutions "has been of a strictly negative sort. The peasants have provided the dynamite to bring down the old building. To the subsequent work of reconstruction they have brought nothing."[115] José Antonio Lucero observes that with CONAIE's participation in attempts to gain state power their strategies had apparently shifted from organizing broad sectors of civil society to engaging in "palace revolutions and elite pacts" that made it look more like a traditional political actor.[116] Opportunistic leaders often with sectarian interests collaborated with the government, resulting in advocacy for reformist rather than revolutionary (in the sense of a pachakutik) policies. Indigenous movements had learned the importance of unifying with other social movements, but now they were attempting to navigate the uncertain terrain of working with political parties and governments. After the failure of the coup, Vargas stated that "we were betrayed by a treacherous clique of generals and admirals, but our struggle is not over, and we may have to be even tougher when we mobilize again."[117] In an echo of Túpac Katari's statement centuries earlier,

Indigenous peoples left Quito declaring that they would be back, and they would be millions.

Vargas declared that "what occurred on January 21 was a rehearsal."[118] A year later, Indigenous peoples were once again on the streets of Quito demanding changes in government, though this time the levantamiento failed.[119] Long-term divisions within the Indigenous movement emerged in these conflicts. Vargas, in what his opponents viewed as an opportunistic posturing, left CONAIE for the Federación Ecuatoriana de Indígenas Evangélicos (FEINE, Ecuadorian Federation of Evangelical Indians). There he created a new ethnic party called Amauta Jatari to campaign for the presidency in 2002, but in the end he finished last in a field of eleven candidates with less than 1 percent of the vote. Instead, Vargas's former co-coup plotter Lucio Gutiérrez won the presidency largely on the basis of support in rural Indigenous communities. Acknowledging this base, Gutiérrez named the long-time CONAIE leaders Luis Macas and Nina Pacari to the ministerial posts of agriculture and foreign affairs. When, similar to previous populist leaders, Gutiérrez ignored his Indigenous base and implemented neoliberal policies, Pachakutik left his government. After the split with Pachakutik, Vargas joined the Gutiérrez government as minister of social welfare. With Gutiérrez's popularity in a free fall, massive street demonstrations in Quito in April 2005 removed him from power and placed Vice President Alfredo Palacios in office. Unlike previous uprisings, Indigenous movements played a minor role in Gutiérrez's removal, with those allied with FEINE coming to his support. Out of these divisions, a grassroots movement reemerged that emphasized deeper involvement in the struggle against neoliberal economic policies, racial discrimination, and a lack of democracy.[120] Indigenous peoples took the lead in grassroots political battles, including opposition to Ecuador's participation in the Free Trade Area of the Americas (FTAA).[121] These subaltern mobilizations represented a continued rebirth of Indigenous movements and provided hope for the future.

Pablo Dávalos notes that these protests were "part of a long and complex political process of the Ecuadorian Indigenous movement that incorporates a series of qualitative transformations throughout the decade of the 1990s." He points to this as a watershed moment when Indians moved from being a "counter force" that relied on external strategies typical of a social movement to being political actors in their own right.[122] Indigenous organizations moved from struggling for higher salaries and better working conditions to presenting demands for land reform and finally to championing

The Argentine Nobel Peace Prize winner Adolfo Pérez Esquivel and the Bolivian Indigenous leader Evo Morales join Leonidas Iza and other CONAIE leaders in an October 2002 march against the Free Trade Area of the Americas (FTAA) in Quito. Photo by Marc Becker.

political claims of territoriality and issuing calls to reform the constitution to reflect the country's plurinational and multicultural reality. They had demonstrated that they were "the only popular sector capable of winning real gains."[123] Indeed, the January 2000 coup closed not only a decade but an entire century of extraordinary political developments during which Indigenous peoples acquired new forms of leadership, introduced new discourses, placed themselves on the center stage of popular movements, inserted their demands in such a way that they could not be ignored, and transformed the political landscape of the country.

From the FEI to CONAIE

A comparison of CONAIE with earlier Indigenous organizing efforts, particularly the FEI, provides a window into continuities and changes during

An Indigenous woman participant in an October 2002 march against the Free Trade Area of the Americas (FTAA) in Quito. Photo by Marc Becker.

the twentieth century in Ecuador's Indigenous movements. Women continue to play central roles in Indigenous struggles, often in the front lines of protests. Nina Pacari, Blanca Chancoso, and other women remain central to organizational structures, though perhaps in relatively fewer numbers than earlier in the century. As more Indians became part of mainstream Ecuadorian society, gender roles increasingly reflected those of the dominant society. Unique gendered ideologies, such as gender complementarity, became less apparent. The gendered characteristics of Indigenous movements changed in ways that may not necessarily be a positive development in comparison to earlier in the twentieth century.

Forty years earlier the FEI, like CONAIE, conceptualized and presented itself as a national organization. Like the FEI, CONAIE encountered various problems in solidifying a "truly national" organization. Both federations faced difficulty in reaching beyond their bases of support in certain communities. Deep political, cultural, and economic differences continued to divide Indigenous communities, peoples, and nationalities. By the end of the century, CONAIE dominated Indigenous discourse in a way similar to how the FEI did at midcentury. Nevertheless, CONAIE now represented only one of multiple organizational trends in Ecuador's Indigenous-peasant movements. FENOC, for example, alternatively cooperated and competed with CONAIE for the allegiance of Indigenous peasants. FEINE, with its base in evangelical communities in Chimborzo, also joined the struggle for social equality and solidarity.[124] Religious workers presented the politically conservative FEINE as an alternative to the leftist-oriented CONAIE, much as FENOC and Ecuarunari were created as alternatives to the FEI. In the 1980s, Ecuarunari's secretary-general Manuel Imbaquingo contended that FEINE would never work together with other peasant-Indigenous organizations "because their political line is religious, whereas ours is classist."[125] All Indigenous organizations, however, seem to drift leftward. In the 1990s, FEINE increasingly coordinated efforts with CONAIE and FENOC and sometimes the FEI as they worked toward common goals. The values of cultural diversity that Indigenous movements professed to embrace were also embodied, at their most successful points, in the multivocal nature of Indigenous organizations. There was not only one model for organizing a social movement, and logically one can expect to observe a "multiplicity of actors, spaces, and voices that constitute contemporary indigenous struggles."[126] It would be a mistake to conceptualize this history as that of a single unified Indigenous movement, for in reality Ecuador had numerous Indigenous movements representing competing interests, concerns, and cultures. Diversity and multi-vocality, rather than homogeneity, became a characteristic of strong and dynamic Indigenous rights movements.

Supporters often depict CONAIE as a more authentically Indigenous organization than the FEI—that is, less dependent on non-Indians and in more control of their own ideological agenda. Perhaps in learning from the FEI's experience, CONAIE fostered this autonomous image by banning partisan political propaganda and keeping political parties at arm's length in order to undercut accusations that outside agitators had organized their events. While strategically necessary, it hides the reality that social movements always operate in a broader political environment. Kevin Healy notes that "the return to liberal democracy from authoritarian rule, the proliferation of non-governmental development organizations (NGO's), the emergence of an indigenous intelligentsia, the active role of international environmental organizations and the increasingly progressive position and involvement of sectors of the Catholic church are factors contributing to this ferment over indigenous political, environmental, educational and cultural rights." Healy emphasizes that CONAIE would not have realized its success "without the support of non-indigenous middle-class political actors." He argues that an "ability to cultivate and utilize a number of national and international allies for institutional support" is "one measure of this new organizational effectiveness and dynamism."[127] Building alliances does not mean selling out a movement, but it is crucial for a successful organizing strategy.

The CONAIE leader Luis Macas acknowledges that "the struggles of the indigenous movement are always aligned to the larger context," and that they share common demands and objectives and must be understood in that context.[128] He denied that Indigenous peoples sought to separate themselves from broader social movements, but rather that they must operate in an atmosphere of equality and mutual respect with others struggling for social justice.[129] To argue with integrity for a plurinational state requires respecting and cultivating alliances with other non-Indigenous cultural traditions and social movements. Andrango notes that "we have our own needs as Indigenous peoples . . . but that does not mean that we march alone, isolated."[130] Viewed from the perspective of the development of Indigenous movements throughout the twentieth century, CONAIE's reliance on outside supporters becomes a logical action with clear precedence, tracing back to Indigenous participation in the foundation of the socialist party and leftist support for rural organizing efforts in the 1920s. Recognizing this external support does not deny Indigenous agency, nor does it negate the validity of either the FEI or CONAIE, but rather points to the importance of allies in realizing organizational objectives.

Not only did CONAIE demonstrate continuity with earlier organizations in its cultivation of external support from non-Indigenous allies, it also formulated a political ideology that had much in common with leftist movements. In one of its first public actions, CONAIE joined labor unions in the 1987 May Day march. "From the beginning," the historian Chad Black notes, "CONAIE sought to cultivate and maintain public solidarity with the worker's movement, aligning itself with the progressive political tradition."[131] It postured an anti-imperialist position that denounced economic, political, ideological, and technological dependence on outside forces and advocated moral, political, and material solidarity for other movements. Further, CONAIE expressed its solidarity to those who lived under "colonial and neo-colonial systems as well as people who suffer economic blockades and military invasions from imperialist forces," a clear reference to the situation in Cuba.[132] These proclamations are similar to those of the earlier international leftist movements that supported the Bolshevik Revolution or Augusto César Sandino's struggle against the U.S. Marines in Nicaragua. Even CONAIE's position on the "Indian Question" echoed what Mariátegui wrote in the 1920s that the situation of the Indigenous masses could not be solved through moral appeals to conscience, religious conversions, or education, but rather their problems were rooted in the nature of the land tenure system.[133] Indeed, CONAIE stated that the dispossessed position of Indigenous peoples in Ecuador was "not solely a pedagogical, ecclesiastical, or administrative problem as the dominant sectors would have it, but rather it is fundamentally an economic-political structural problem."[134] Only through fundamental economic change and land reform would social change take place.

Pacari contends that Indigenous ethnic identities are not against class struggle but instead are complementary to it. Although Indigenous peoples are peasants and workers, they also have their own characteristics and customs. Pacari calls on the left to recognize and respect these differences as they organize together, and not to subjugate Indigenous peoples to a proletarian ideology that would depersonalize and assimilate them, deny their unique history, and eventually end their identity as a people.[135] Zamosc notes that "class was a fundamental factor in the struggles of the 1990s" and that Ecuador's "Indian movements cannot be seen as purely ethnic phenomena."[136] Ethnicity became a rallying cry for what were essentially class demands, and contrasting class with ethnic identity results in a false dichotomy.

Pacari points to a critical difference between earlier organizations such as the FEI and later ones such as CONAIE. The early organizations tended to focus on issues of wages, land, and even cultural issues such as bilingual education, but "without a broader political perspective." Pacari further contends that "while these concrete demands remain central concerns of the indigenous movement, they are now accompanied by demands of a more political stripe: the right to self-determination, the right to our cultural identity and our languages, and the right to develop economically according to our own values and beliefs." Specifically, CONAIE added to the Indigenous movement a new political demand of "the construction of a plurinational state that tolerates and encourages diversity among different groups in society." Nevertheless, she concedes that, "in the highlands, traces of indigenous organization can be detected in the Ecuadorian Indigenous Federation (FEI)."[137]

Not only did CONAIE draw on a long leftist history of social mobilization, but it also made extraordinary contributions to leftist thought and action. It defined the struggle as a "frontal assault on the repressive national and international hegemonic economic, political, and ideological capitalistic system that hinders the self-determination and economic and political independence of Indigenous peoples and nationalities and other social sectors." The organization's goal was not simply to take control of state power, but "the transformation of the nature of the current power of the hegemonic uninational state that is exclusionary, anti-democratic, and repressive." In its place, activists would construct "a humanistic, plurinational new society."[138] Indigenous political maturity and organizational structures, Alicia Ibarra notes, have been of "incalculable value" in advancing Ecuador's popular struggles.[139]

Even when organized explicitly as ethnic organizations, in protest marches Indigenous peoples still fell back on old slogans such as "Hasta la victoria siempre" ("Toward victory always") and "Luchando creando poder popular" ("Struggling creating popular power") that leftist parties and labor unions had repeatedly used for years. Organizations effectively combined class and ethnic symbols in their discourse. In a call to the congress for a provincial Indigenous organization, César Pilataxi noted that popular movements were in a state of crisis because they had lost "their means of struggle–class solidarity." In order to regain the initiative, the movement would have to join Túpac Amaru, Fernando Daquilema, Che Guevara, and Fidel Castro in a struggle for freedom and socialism.[140] Grassroots organizations often moved seamlessly between class, ethnic, and nationalist ideologies and identities. The provincial Federación Indígena y Campesina de Imbabura (FICI, Indigenous and Peasant Federation of Imbabura) chose a name that bridged ethnicity and class to signify its "political alliance with exploited classes as well as leftist political forces." It engaged an "anti-capitalist and anti-imperialist" struggle for national liberation "as Indian nationalities."[141] For their part, leftists insisted that they still had important contributions that they could and should make to Indigenous movements.[142] Indigenous organizations never made a clean break with their leftist past, nor have urban leftists discarded a long reliance on ethnic discourse. Nor would there be any clear purpose for doing so.

Notes

I. WHAT IS AN INDIAN?

1. The use of a capital "I" in reference to Indigenous peoples is intentional and based on (and in respect for) a preference specified by the board of directors of the South and Meso American Indian Rights Center (SAIIC) as a strong affirmation of their ethnicities. It is not intended to essentialize identities; indeed, the use of the plural "peoples" recognizes a broad diversity not only in Ecuador but throughout the Americas. These identities, as this book illustrates, were socially constructed, variously produced, historically contingent, and differently experienced. There are important legal and political distinctions between terms such as *campesinos* (peasants), *pueblos* (peoples), ethnic groups, communities, and nationalities in referring to the Indigenous inhabitants of the Americas, but for the most part an analysis of this language extends beyond this text. As Mercedes Prieto notes, historically "there was no single or normalized expression to refer to the indigenous population; ambiguity was prevalent" (Prieto, "A Liberalism of Fear," 62). The conflictive and ambiguous nature of language is a common problem for all who write about colonized peoples. Historically, *indio* (Indian) has been a derogatory term, but native peoples in the Americas increasingly have subverted the colonial term in their liberation struggles. It is used in that spirit here.

2. See, for example, Albó, "El retorno del Indio"; Almeida, *Sismo étnico en el Ecuador*; Cornejo Menacho, ed., *INDIOS*; León Trujillo, *De campesinos a ciudadanos diferentes*; Meisch, "We Will Not Dance on the Tomb of Our Grandparents"; Mor-

eno Yánez and Figueroa, *El levantamiento indígena del inti raymi de 1990*; and Zamosc, "Agrarian Protest and the Indian Movement in the Ecuadorian Highlands."

3. CONAIE, *Las nacionalidades indígenas en el Ecuador*, 147.

4. See the electronic appendix http://www.yachana.org/indmovs/ for a list of these revolts.

5. Scott, *Weapons of the Weak*.

6. Moreno Yánez, *Sublevaciones indígenas*, 152–202.

7. Ibarra, "Cambios agrarios y conflictos étnicos en la sierra central," 178, 257–60.

8. Gerlach, *Indians, Oil, and Politics*, xv.

9. Jenkins, *Re-thinking History*, 7.

10. Mallon, *Peasant and Nation*; Joseph and Nugent, eds., *Everyday Forms of State Formation*; Guardino, *Peasants, Politics, and the Formation of Mexico's National State*.

11. Guerrero Cazar and Ospina Peralta, *El poder de la comunidad*, 22.

12. Ibarra, *"Nos encontramos amenazados por todita la indiada"*; Sattar, "An Unresolved Inheritance."

13. Glave, "The 'Republic of Indians' in Revolt," 518–19.

14. Gow, "Yawar Mayu," 149.

15. Albornoz Peralta, *Las luchas indígenas*, 33–35; CEDEP, *Lorenza Abimañay*; Romo-Leroux, *Movimiento de mujeres en el Ecuador*, 69–70.

16. Ulcuango, "Antecedentes a la organización indígena en la provincia," 5–6; Ecuarunari, *Historia de la nacionalidad y los pueblos quichuas del Ecuador*, 365; Lucía Lechón, in Yánez, *Yo declaro con franqueza*, 65.

17. Taylor, *Drinking, Homicide, and Rebellion in Colonial Mexican Villages*, 116.

18. Rafaela Herrera, "La india del diablo," *El Comercio*, October 7, 1984, Suplemento Domingo; Rodrigo Granizo Romero, "La india del diablo," *El Comercio*, April 1, 1985.

19. Costales, *Fernando Daquilema*, 168–69.

20. O'Connor, *Gender, Indian, Nation*, chapter 5.

21. Navarro and Sánchez Korrol, *Women in Latin America and the Caribbean*, 62–63.

22. Stark, "El rol de la mujer en los levantamientos campesinos de las altas llanuras del Ecuador," 48–53; Moscoso, "Mujer indígena y sociedad republicana," 239.

23. Crespi, "Mujeres campesinas como líderes sindicales," 169.

24. Silverblatt, *Moon, Sun, and Witches*; also see Allen, *The Hold Life Has*, 78–85.

25. O'Connor, "Helpless Children or Undeserving Patriarchs?"; O'Connor, "Widows Rights Questioned," 96, 105.

26. Rodríguez, "Acción por el Movimiento de Mujeres," 16.

27. Dore, *Myths of Modernity*, 149.

28. Eric Van Young observes that a "hacienda is hard to describe, but you know it

when you see it" (Van Young, "Mexican Rural History since Chevalier," 25). To further complicate the matter, the word "hacienda" can have multiple meanings. In Ecuador, it is sometimes used to refer to the economic enterprise of the land's owner or renter; to the administrative center that included the main house where the landholder lived; or to all of the enterprise's land and resources. The term is generally used here in the broadest sense to mean the extensive landholdings of the estate as well as the associated administrative apparatus. For a summary of hacienda administrative structures, see Lyons, *Remembering the Hacienda*, 76–82.

29. Bonifaz, "Origen y evolución de una hacienda histórica: 'Guachalá' II," 342–43.

30. Guerrero, *La semántica de la dominación*.

31. Hassaurek, *Four Years among the Ecuadorians*, 174.

32. "Decreta de 12 abril de 1899," in Rubio Orbe, *Legislación indigenista del Ecuador*, 65–67.

33. Sáenz, *Sobre el indio ecuatoriano y su incorporación al medio nacional*, 130–31.

34. Lyons, *Remembering the Hacienda*, 231–33.

35. "Ley de cultos," Decreto no. 1, *Registro Oficial* 3, no. 912 (October 14, 1904): 9381–83.

36. "Ley de Beneficencia," Decreto no. 2, *Registro Oficial* 3, no. 789 (October 19, 1908): 4164–65.

37. Pérez Guerrero, "La télesis social y la raza india," 160.

38. *Huasipungo* (sometimes spelled "guasipungo") is a Kichwa term comprised of *huasi* (house) and *pungo* (door), but the roots of this term have been lost. The term is unique to Ecuador, although the system it represents is not. Rural workers engaged in similar debt-peonage (or perhaps more accurately share-tenancy) labor relations were called *terrazueros* (Colombia), *inquilinos* (Chile), *yanacunas* (Peru), *colonos* (Bolivia), etc. See Oberem, "Contribución a la historia del trabajador rural de américa latina," 301.

39. Buitrón, *Condiciones de vida y trabajo del campesino de la provincia de Pichincha*, 70; Albó, "Andean People in the Twentieth Century," 783.

40. Pallares, "From Peasant Struggles to Indian Resistance," 129.

41. NACLA, "Gaining Ground," 14.

42. Guerrero, "The Construction of a Ventriloquist's Image," 555–90.

43. Ruiz Hernández and Burguete Cal y Mayor, "Indigenous People without Political Parties," 24–25.

44. The almost absolute historical nature of this rural / urban Indian / mestizo division (even as an increasing number of Indigenous peoples migrated to urban centers) is reflected in the lack of the words "city" and "countryside" in the Indigenous Kichwa language. Rather, these concepts are expressed by *runa llacta* ("place of the

people"—i.e., Kichwa people) and *mishu llacta* ("place of the *mestizos*"). Kichwa (commonly spelled Quichua in the historical record) is the Ecuadorian variant of Quechua, the largest surviving Indigenous language and cultural group in the Americas that stretches across the Andean highlands from Colombia to Chile and includes between eight and twelve million speakers.

45. Albornoz Peralta, *Las luchas indígenas*, 113; Ulcuango in Yánez del Pozo, *Yo declaro con franqueza*, 174.

46. Selverston, "The Politics of Culture," 134.

47. Roper, Perreault, and Wilson, "Introduction," 9. Also see, among many others, Selverston, "The Politics of Culture," 135; and Albó, "El retorno del Indio," 305.

48. "VI asamblea general de la Federación Provincial de Centros Shuaras de Morona Santiago, Sucúa, enero 20–22, 1969," Centro Documentación Abya-Yala, Quito, Ecuador.

49. Perruchon, *I Am Tsunki*, 153.

50. Boughton, "The Communist Party of Australia's Involvement in the Struggle for Aboriginal and Torres Strait Islander People's Rights," 284.

51. Zinn, *You Can't Be Neutral on a Moving Train*, 52.

52. Sánchez Parga, "Entre Marx y Rumiñahui," 81.

53. Guerrero Cazar and Ospina Peralta, *El poder de la comunidad*, 26–27.

54. Suárez, *Contribución al estudio de las realidades entre las clases obreras y campesinas*, 32–35.

55. Larson, *Trials of Nation Making*, 124.

56. Weismantel, *Cholas and Pishtacos*.

57. Hall, "Subjects in History," 298.

58. Albó, "El retorno del Indio," 308.

59. Delgado-P., "Ethnic Politics and the Popular Movement," 82.

60. Ramos, "Cutting through State and Class," 274.

61. Santana, *¿Ciudadanos en la etnicidad?*, 17.

62. Ramón, *El regreso de los runas*, 197, 205.

63. Albó, "Andean People in the Twentieth Century," 824.

64. Almeida, "Consideraciones sobre la nacionalidad Kechwa," 13, 14.

65. Ibarra, *Los indígenas y el estado en el Ecuador*.

66. Postero and Zamosc, "Indigenous Movements and the Indian Question in Latin America," 12.

67. Pallares, *From Peasant Struggles to Indian Resistance*, 34. Chad Black makes a similar argument in "The Making of an Indigenous Movement."

68. Wade, *Race and Ethnicity in Latin America*, 78, 79.

69. Kuznesof, "Ethnic and Gender Influences on 'Spanish' Creole Society in Colonial Spanish America," 160, 168.

70. hooks, *Teaching to Transgress*.

71. McClintock, *Imperial Leather*, 5.

72. Mattiace, *To See with Two Eyes*, 28–29.

73. Schryer, *Ethnicity and Class Conflict in Rural Mexico*, 22.

74. Rubin, *Decentering the Regime*, 2.

2. SOCIALISM

1. PSE, *Labores de la Asamblea Nacional Socialista*, 33. The complicated issues of terminology around the use of the term "campesino" extend well beyond the scope of this discussion. Chad Black (personal communication) suggests that "maybe we need to think of the term *campesino* as being multivocal—when marxist ideologues used it, they were thinking in production terms, whereas when others used it, *campesino* was just a trope for *indígena*." Also see Becker, "Peasant Identity, Worker Identity."

2. Endara, "La fundación del partido," 48.

3. PSE, *Labores de la Asamblea Nacional Socialista*, 29, 52.

4. Ibid., 4. It was not until after Indians gained the right to vote in 1979 that bourgeois parties in Ecuador began to court them in their electoral strategies.

5. Andrews, *Afro-Latin America*, 84.

6. Olesen, *International Zapatismo*, 114.

7. Rosenthal, "The Arrival of the Electric Streetcar and the Conflict over Progress in Early Twentieth-Century Montevideo," 321.

8. Drake, *The Money Doctor in the Andes*, 135.

9. Robalino Dávila, *El 9 de julio de 1925*, 14.

10. Coronel Valencia, "Hacia un 'control moral del capitalismo,' " 61–62.

11. Paredes, "El movimiento obrero en el Ecuador," 79.

12. Borja y Borja, *Las constituciones del Ecuador*; Milk, "Growth and Development of Ecuador's Worker Organizations," 99; Schodt, *Ecuador*, 69; Paz y Miño Cepeda, *Revolución Juliana*.

13. Cueva, *The Process of Political Domination in Ecuador*, 125–27.

14. Milk, "Growth and Development of Ecuador's Worker Organizations," 91.

15. Rosenthal, "Controlling the Line, 2.

16. Guevara, *Puerta de El Dorado*, 336–40.

17. "Los sucesos de Leito," *El Comercio*, September 27, 1923, 1. Also see "¿Hasta cuando

han de existir los comuneros?" *El Comercio,* September 22, 1923, 1; "Los sucesos de Leito," *El Comercio,* September 24, 1923, 1; "¿Que hacer de las quinientas families de Leito?" *El Comercio,* September 25, 1923, 1; "Vagos y mendigos," *El Comercio,* September 26, 1923, 1; Ibarra, "Cambios agrarios y conflictos étnicos en la sierra central (1820–1930)," 196–201; Restrepo Jaramillo, *El rey de la leña,* 153; and Albornoz Peralta, *Las luchas indígenas,* 59–62.

18. Kulikoff, *The Agrarian Origins of American Capitalism,* 264, 269.

19. Paige, *Coffee and Power,* 361.

20. Drake, *The Money Doctor in the Andes,* 8.

21. TSE, *Elecciones y democracia en el Ecuador,* 187.

22. See, for example, PSE, *Estatutos* (1933), 24; and Jaramillo Alvarado, *El indio ecuatoriano,* vol. 2, 153.

23. Prieto, "A Liberalism of Fear," 125, 122–23.

24. "Indagación de abusos contra unos indígenas," *El Comercio,* November 10, 1932, 2; "Queja del senador por la raza india por abusos con los indígenas en Cariamanga," *El Comercio,* November 13, 1932, 5.

25. Miller, "The Suffrage Movement in Latin America," 169. Notably, Amy Lind provides an alternative interpretation of this history when she argues that women played an important role in shaping political discourse and that women's suffrage was an important gain for social movements. See Lind, *Gendered Paradoxes,* 29.

26. Elías Muñoz Vicuña placed the founding of this organization in the month of January of 1926. See Vicuña, *Historia del movimiento obrero del Ecuador,* 25. In the 1940s, a local official would claim that "no Indigenous community in any sense exists in the parroquia," revealing the contested nature of identity and its relation to political struggle. See letter from F. Barrera A., Jefe Político del Cantón Cayambe, to Ministro de Gobierno y Justicia, Cayambe, October 21, 1942, Oficio no. 267. Thanks to Galo Ramón for providing a copy of this document.

27. Salamea, "Transformación de la hacienda y los cambios en la condición campesina" (1978), 52. The U.S. ambassador William Dawson gives the membership number as one thousand in a letter to Secretary of State, Washington, no. 176, March 9, 1931, National Archives Records Administration (hereafter NARA), Record Group (hereafter RG) 59, 822.00B / 28, p. 3, College Park, Maryland.

28. "El dueño de Changalá acude a la junta de gobierno," *El Comercio,* February 25, 1926, 1.

29. "La razón y la fuerza," *El Comercio,* March 8, 1926, 1.

30. "Se atacó a la policía de Cayambe," *El Comercio,* November 6, 1926, 1. On the 1926 uprising at Changalá, see "El pueblo de Cayambe ataca Changalá," *El Comercio,*

February 24, 1926, 3; Albornoz Peralta, "Jesús Gualavisí y las luchas indígenas en el Ecuador," 160–67; and Maldonado, *El Cantón Cayambe*, 103–5.

31. Feierman, *Peasant Intellectuals*, 4.

32. Neptalí Ulcuango, interviewed by Mercedes Prieto, July 7–8, 1977; Ricardo Paredes, interviewed by Mercedes Prieto, April 20, 1977, Prieto Collection.

33. Letter from Juan Francisco Sumárraga to Director, Junta Central de Asistencia Pública, March 21, 1946, in Comunicaciones Recibidas (Received Communications, hereafter CR), Segundo Semestre, Segundo Parte, 1946, 1555, Archivo Nacional de Medicina del Museo Nacional de Medicina "Dr. Eduardo Estrella," Fondo Junta Central de Asistencía Pública, Quito, Ecuador (hereafter JCAP). The author is deeply indebted to this archive's former director, Dr. Eduardo Estrella, and its current director, Dr. Antonio Crespo, for their kindness and support of this investigation.

34. For a basic biographical treatment of Gualavisí's life, see Albornoz Peralta, "Jesús Gualavisí," 155–88. For more on Gualavisí's role as a peasant intellectual in framing protest, see Becker, "Indigenous Communists and Urban Intellectuals in Cayambe."

35. For biographies of Lame, see Castillo-Cárdenas, *Liberation Theology from Below*; and Castrillón Arboleda, *El indio Quintin Lame*.

36. Martínez, *Yo siempre he sido Nela Martínez Espinosa*, 187. A photo in Muñoz Vicuña, *Masas, luchas, solidaridad*, 91, of a Central Committee meeting in Quito, July 26–28, 1947, shows seventeen people, of which Cacuango is one of three women and the only Indigenous person. Also see Rodas Morales, *Dolores Cacuango*; Rodas Morales, *Crónica de un sueño*; Albornoz Peralta, *Dolores Cacuango y las luchas indígenas de Cayambe*; and Martínez, "Dolores Cacuango."

37. Luxemburg, "The Junius Pamphlet," 304.

38. Tránsito Amaguaña, interviewed by Andrés Guerrero on September 17, 1976, Prieto Collection.

39. Yánez, *Yo declaro con franqueza*, 265.

40. See Escuela de Formación de Mujeres Lideres "Dolores Cacuango," http://mujer kichua.nativeweb.org/.

41. Bulnes, *Me levanto y digo*, 31–40; Yánez, *Yo declaro con franqueza*; Rodas Morales, *Tránsito Amaguaña*.

42. Gallegos Lara, *Biografía del pueblo indio*, 62–67.

43. Gangotena, "Peasant Social Articulation and Surplus Transference," 113.

44. Gallegos Lara, *Biografía del pueblo indio*, 62–67.

45. Gangotena, "Peasant Social Articulation and Surplus Transference," 48; Sylva Charvet, *Gamonalismo y lucha campesino*, 163, 128, 200.

46. Letter from Julio E. Moreno, Ministerio de Gobierno, to Contralor General, September 10, 1929, Oficio no. 690, Ministerio de lo Interior, Sección Gobierno, Libro de Varios Autoridades, Julio a Setiembre 1929, no. 3, 438, Archivo General del Ministerio de Gobierno, Quito, Ecuador; Agustín Vega Tipan, María Vega, Pedro Toaquiza et al., "Tremenda matanza indígena en Tigua," *La Hoz* 1, no. 2 (September 11, 1930): 2; Fiallo and Ramón, *La lucha de las comunidades indígenas del cantón Pujilí,* 3–4; Colvin, *Arte de Tigua,* 19.

47. Costales, *Fernando Daquilema,* vi.

48. Albornoz Peralta, "Jesús Gualavisí," 185.

49. Gow, "Yawar Mayu," 272, 273; Rivera Cusicanqui, *Oppressed but Not Defeated,* 47–48. In Mexico, Barry Carr similarly traces how "a new historical actor, the Mexican Communist party," provided "a vehicle for the politicization of a small but important group of peasants." See Carr, *Marxism and Communism in Twentieth-Century Mexico,* 91.

50. Albornoz Peralta, "Jesús Gualavisí," 166.

51. "Encendiendo la Antorcha," *La Antorcha* 1, no. 1 (November 16, 1924): 1; "Al gobierno," *La Antorcha* 2nd ser., 1, no. 1 (March 24, 1925): 1; "El socialismo en el Ecuador," *La Antorcha* 1, no. 12 (January 31, 1925): 5. Also see Alexander, *Organized Labor in Latin America,* 125; Martz, "Marxism in Ecuador," 4–5.

52. "Manifiesto a la nación," *La Antorcha* 2nd ser., 1, no. 7 (May 1, 1925): 1. See Vasconcelos, *The Cosmic Race.*

53. Stutzman, *"El Mestizaje."*

54. Haywood, *Black Bolshevik,* 121, 122, 133.

55. Albornoz Peralta, "Jesús Gualavisí," 167, 182.

56. "Abusos de Gamonalismo," *La Vanguardia* 1, nos. 9–10 (March 1, 1928): 13.

57. Prieto, "A Liberalism of Fear," 158.

58. "El socialismo en las escuelas," *El Comercio,* May 16, 1928, 1.

59. De la Cadena, *Indigenous Mestizos,* 119.

60. Langer, "Andean Rituals of Revolt," fn. 33; Albó, "Andean People in the Twentieth Century," 782.

61. Albó, "Andean People in the Twentieth Century," 776.

62. Jorge Carrera Andrade, "El calvario indígena," *La Vanguardia* 1, nos. 7–8 (February 29, 1928): 12.

63. "Proletarios de todos los paises, unidos!" (Spanish) and "Tucuy llactacunapac huacchacuna, shuclla tucuichic!" (Kichwa). See *Frente Obrero* 1, no. 3 (October 1934): 1. Other Communist Party activists also advocated the publication of literature in Indigenous languages, including Guaraní and Kichwa. See *Los partidos comunistas de América del Sur y del Caribe y el movimiento sindical revolucionario,* 51.

64. This is similar to what Blanca Muratorio observed with protestant missionaries in the Colta region of Chimborazo, where external intervention provided resources and facilitated the consolidation of group interests that led to the strengthening of ethnic identities and class consciousness. See Muratorio, "Protestantism and Capitalism Revisited" and Muratorio, "Protestantism, Ethnicity, and Class in Chimborazo."

65. Uggen, "Peasant Mobilization in Ecuador," 14.

66. Conferencia de Cabecillas Indios, "Indicaciones," Ñucanchic Allpa 1, no. 8 (March 17, 1936): 2; "Convocation of Congress of Agricultural Laborers and Peasants," attached to Letter from William Dawson to Secretary of State, Washington, no. 170, February 27, 1931, NARA RG 59, 822.00B/27, p. 2. Also see "Autoridades, curas, tinterillos y ladrones explotan a los campesinos," El Pueblo, May 1, 1954, 6.

67. Larson, "Andean Communities," 14.

68. Olesen, International Zapatismo, 213.

69. Many Central American solidarity activists experienced this in the 1980s, especially in Salvadorian sister cities in which people from radically different cultures and socioeconomic classes developed peer and mutually supportive relationships in a common struggle to stop Ronald Reagan's imperialistic policies.

70. Luis Catucuamba, interviewed by Mercedes Prieto, August 6, 1977, and Neptalí Ulcuango, interviewed by Mercedes Prieto, July 7–8, 1977, Prieto Collection; Manuel Catucuamba in Yánez, Yo declaro con franqueza, 183; Miguel Lechón in ibid., 185.

71. Pilo de la Peña, "Los indios aspiran socialimente," La Antorcha 1, no. 3 (November 29, 1924): 3.

72. Ricardo A. Paredes, "El pueblo de Cayambe," Germinal, February 26, 1926, 1; Paredes, "El movimiento obrero en el Ecuador," 80; "El asunto de Changalá," El Comercio, March 6, 1926, 6; Endara, "La fundación del partido," 55.

73. Gould and Lauri-Santiago, " 'They Call Us Thieves and Steal Our Wage,' " 233.

74. "El partido comunista organizador y defensor de los indios," El Pueblo, June 2, 1951, 6. The Secretary General of the PCE in the 1980s also noted that the party came of age through organizing Indians in Cayambe. Maugé, "Las tareas actuales de nuestro movimiento," 223.

75. Rodas Morales, Nosotras que del amor hicimos, 80. Academics working on contemporary Indigenous movements are often unaware of this long history. For example, Tanya Korovkin refers to the founding of the FEI almost twenty years later as the rural communities' "first brush with the political left." See "Indigenous Movements in the Central Andes," 145.

76. PSE, Labores de la Asamblea Nacional Socialista, 74. The proposal passed.

77. Ibid., 28–29, 33; also see Rodas Morales, *Nosotras que del amor hicimos,* 45.

78. Published newspaper notes (possibly from *El Comercio*) on Gómez's death dated Quito, November 23, 1976 (FEI), and Quito, November 25, 1976 (PCE), both located in Prieto Collection.

79. Paredes, "El movimiento obrero en el Ecuador," 77, 81.

80. Communist International, *The Revolutionary Movement in the Colonies,* 6.

81. Burns, *The Poverty of Progress,* 152.

82. Paredes, "VI World Congress," 1177.

83. Communist International, *The Revolutionary Movement in the Colonies,* 59.

84. "Reivindicaciones mínimas propugnados por el Comité Central del Partido Comunista," *Campamento* 2, no. 63 (November 23, 1933): 3.

85. Carr, *Marxism and Communism in Twentieth-Century Mexico,* 32.

86. Brysk, "Acting Globally," 32.

87. PSE, *La primera Conferencia del Consejo Central Ampliado del Partido Socialista Ecuatoriano,* 12.

88. "El P.S.E. haciendose comunista," *La Hoz* 1, no. 8 (December 20, 1930): 1. The PCE sometimes claimed that their party was not founded in May 1926 with the PSE, but on September 22, 1925, as the Sección Comunista de Propaganda y Acción Lenin (Communist Section of Lenin Propaganda and Action) under the guidance of the Mexican diplomat Rafael Ramos Pedrueza, whom Plutarco Elías Calles had exiled to Ecuador. See "Rafael Ramos Pedrueza," *El Pueblo,* April 20, 1968, 2; and "47 aniversario," *El Pueblo,* September 23, 1972, 2.

89. "El partido comunista organizador y defensor de los indios," *El Pueblo,* June 2, 1951, 6. The word "tribe," like the word "Indian," was a pejorative term for Amazonian Indians. Communist use of the term can alternatively be interpreted as a reflection of mestizo racism and cultural insensitivity, or an indication of concern for disenfranchised populations that extended much more broadly than any other political discourse of the time, or perhaps a combination of the two.

90. Ortiz Villacís, *La ideología burguesa en el Ecuador,* 119–20; PCE, "Saludo del Comité Central del P.C.E. al camarada Pedro A. Saad," 19.

91. "Ricardo Paredes, Candidato del Partido Comunista," Imprenta La Económica, [1933], Muñoz Collection. See the electronic appendix http://www.yachana.org/indmovs/ for the text of this platform.

92. "Manifiesto del Bloque Obrero-Campesino" (Quito, May 2, 1932), Hojas Volantes, 1921–1932, D. Polit Partid., p. 247, Biblioteca Ecuatoriana Aurelio Espinosa Pólit (hereafter BEAEP), Cotocollao, Ecuador; cf. Communist International, *The Revolutionary Movement in the Colonies,* 59.

93. El Comité de Lucha Popular, "Manifiesto al Pueblo," Imprenta Sucre, August 29, 1933, Hojas Volantes, 1933–1938, p. 48, BEAEP. *Montuvios* were poor mestizo peasants who worked on export-oriented plantations on the coast.

94. "Grave cisma se produjo en el Partido Socialista Ecuatoriano," *El Día*, December 24, 1930, 1; Charles A. Page, "Memorandum with Regard to Communism in Ecuador," attached to letter from William Dawson to Secretary of State, Washington, no. 150, January 29, 1931, NARA RG 59, 822.00B / 24, p. 20.

95. PSE, *Estatutos* (1933), 9.

96. PSE, *Estatutos* (1936), 4.

97. PSE, *Estatutos* (1939), 2.

98. Ricardo Paredes, interviewed by Mercedes Prieto, April 20, 1977, Prieto Collection.

99. Monroy, *El convento de la Merced de Quito de 1534–1617*, 220; Ramón, *El regreso de los runas*, 152.

100. "Aviso," Decreto no. 24, *Registro Oficial* 3, no. 949 (November 29, 1904): 9682.

101. Crespi, "Changing Power Relations," 224.

102. Basile and Paredes, *Algunos factores económicos y geográficos*, 26.

103. Ibid, 29.

104. JCAP, *Informe presentado por el Director de la Junta Central de Asistencia Pública de Quito al Ministerio del Ramo*, 72. The minister of social welfare also advocated breaking up the government-owned haciendas both because the renters were not motivated to make the necessary improvements and as a way to terminate worker protests. See Durango, *Informe del Ministro de Previsión Social*, 59.

105. Cliche, *Anthropologie des communautés andines équatoriennes*.

106. Carr, *Marxism and Communism in Twentieth-Century Mexico*, 88.

107. The use of the "ethnic" name El Inca is curious given that located on the margins of the Inka conquest few Indigenous activists in Ecuador appealed to the legacy of Tawantinsuyu in their struggle for social justice. This may point to a socialist influence. Ricardo Paredes, like José Carlos Mariátegui in Peru, applauded the agrarian socialist legacy of the Inkas, which he saw as still apparent in Indigenous communistic traditions and institutions. See Paredes, "El movimiento obrero en el Ecuador," 81.

108. CONAIE, *Nacionalidades indígenas*, 30; Conferencia de Cabecillas Indios, "Indicaciones," *Ñucanchic Allpa* 1, no. 8 (March 17, 1936): 2; Neptalí Ulcuango, interviewed by Mercedes Prieto, July 7–8, 1977, Prieto Collection; Virgilio Lechón in Yánez, *Yo declaro con franqueza*, 154–55.

109. Neptalí Ulcuango in Yánez, *Yo declaro con franqueza*, 163–64. The following year, Valladares was accused of shooting another worker on the hacienda. See "Un

indígena de Pesillo ha sido gravemente herido," *El Día,* February 24, 1931, 8; "Se ha sindicado a Valladares en el crimen de Pesillo," *El Día,* February 27, 1931, 8.

110. See Ibarra, *Los indígenas y el estado en el Ecuador,* xxiii.

111. Letter from Carlos Torres L. and Gustavo Araujo Z. to José Rafael Delgado, August 17, 1930, in CR, Julio-Diciembre 1930, 732, JCAP; Letter from José Rafael Delgado to the Director de la Asistencia Pública, September 9, 1930, in CR, Julio-Diciembre 1930, 733, JCAP. Although in public pronouncements elite figures usually were careful to employ the polite term *indígena* (Indigenous), in private communications Delgado and others freely used the more casual and derogatory term *indio* (Indian), thereby revealing underlying racist attitudes. Activists at La Chimba apparently formed Pan y Tierra in the aftermath of a massive strike at Pesillo and Moyurco in December 1930 and January 1931. See Comité de Huelga, "La huelga de los sindicatos 'Tierra Libre' y 'El Inca': Los crímenes de los latifundistas, authoridades y servidumbre," Quito: Imprenta "Nueva Era," March 18, 1931, Hojas Volantes, 1931–1940, p. 9, BEAEP; Letter from José Rafael Delgado to the Junta de Asistencia Pública, January 24, 1931, in CR, Enero-Junio 1931, 890, JCAP. Delgado claimed that he always kept the JCAP informed of socialist agitation, but the only document preserved in the JCAP archives in Quito about these early organizational efforts is the September 1930 letter regarding the formation of El Inca. Mercedes Prieto determined that all three organizations appeared between 1927 and 1931, although she does not document these events. See Prieto, "Haciendas estatales," 113. Neptalí Ulcuango states that El Inca was founded in 1925 (interviewed by Mercedes Prieto, July 7–8, 1977, Prieto Collection). He lists the syndicate's leaders as Juan Albamocho, Florencio Catucuamba, Venancio Amaguaña, Neptalí Ulcuango (his father), Rosa Alba (his grandmother), Ignacio María Alba, Mercedes Cachipuendo, Segundo Lechón, Víctor Calcán, "and others." Ulcuango, "Antecedentes a la organización indígena en la provincia," 7. Of the subsequent organizations, Virgilio Lechón named Pío Campués, Francisco Nepas, and Tránsito Amaguaña as important leaders at La Chimba. Dolores Cacuango was the most important leader at Moyurco, as well as Ramón Alba, Miguel Lechón, Clotilde Tarabata, and Virgilio Lechón. Virgilio Lechón in Yánez, *Yo declaro con franqueza,* 83. As these syndicates were never legally registered with the government and were largely the creation of nonlettered peasants, no written organizational records exist that can be used to trace their history.

112. Letter from Augusto Egas to Sr. Ministro de lo Interior y Policía, September 2, 1930, in Libro de Oficios que dirige la Junta de Asistencia Pública (or Comunicaciones Dirigidas, Sent Communications, hereafter CD), 1930, 353, JCAP; letter from Augusto Egas to the Jefe Político of Cayambe, September 2, 1930, in CD, 1930, 353,

JCAP; letter from Augusto Egas to the Ministro de Previsión Social y Asistencia Pública, September 3, 1930, in CD, 1930, 354, JCAP; letter from Augusto Egas to the Ministro de Previsión Social, September 24, 1930, in CD, 1930, 379–80, JCAP. Also see a letter from the Ministro de Previsión Social y Trabajo to the Jefe Político of Cayambe, October 16, 1930, in CR, Julio-Diciembre 1930, 559, JCAP.

113. "El terror de los campos," *La Hoz* 1, no. 2 (September 11, 1930): 6.

114. "Formación del socorro Obrero y Campesino," *La Hoz* 1, no. 2 (September 11, 1930): 6.

115. "El gobierno de Ayora permite abusos imperdonables," *La Hoz* 1, no. 2 (September 11, 1930): 1.

116. Reprinted from *La Choza* (Partido Socialista Ecuatoriano), November 15, 1930, in Solórzano, *Nuestra gente*, 15–16.

117. Ricardo Paredes, interviewed by Mercedes Prieto, July 7, 1977, Prieto Collection.

118. Carr, *Marxism and Communism in Twentieth-Century Mexico*, 43.

119. Klehr, Haynes, and Firsov, *The Secret World of American Communism*, 8.

120. Wasserstrom, "Indian Uprisings under Spanish Colonialism," 54.

121. Landsberger, "The Role of Peasant Movements and Revolts in Development."

122. Crespi, "Mujeres campesinas como líderes sindicales," 163.

123. "La Asamblea General de Campesinos de los Canones Yaguachi y Milagro, a los Obreros y Campesinos en general," Imp. del C.C. del P.S., Muñoz Collection.

124. Uggen, "Peasant Mobilization in Ecuador," 15.

125. Ulianova,"El levantamiento campesino de Lonquimay y la Internacional Comunista," 193–94.

126. Buitrón, "Situación económica y social del indio Otavaleño," 61.

127. For example, see Meisch, *Andean Entrepreneurs*, 202; and Kyle, *Transnational Peasants*, 159.

128. "Los atropellos y robos en Chimba," *Ñucanchic Allpa* 1, no. 8 (March 17, 1936): 4. For an analysis of this newspaper, see Becker, "La historia del movimiento indígena escrita a través de las páginas de *Ñucanchic Allpa*."

129. Nepalí Ulcuango in Yánez, *Yo declaro con franqueza*, 81; Tránsito Amaguaña, interviewed by Andrés Guerrero on September 17, 1976; Tránsito Amaguaña, interviewed by Mercedes Prieto on November 26, 1977, Prieto Collection; Rodas Morales, *Nosotras que del amor hicimos*, 82.

130. Van Cott, "Indigenous Peoples and Democracy," 5. Without presenting any evidence, Allen Gerlach distorts the history of these organizations as the work of non-Indians uninterested in "the preservation of Indian culture, language, communities and traditional territory." See Gerlach, *Indians, Oil, and Politics*, 61.

131. Mariátegui, "The Indigenous Question in Latin America," 108.

132. Martínez, "La condición actual de la raza indígena en la provincia de Tungurahua," 221. An alternative interpretation would be that San Juan simply provided a convenient cover for outsiders to enter a community and to organize when everyone was together for the celebration.

133. Ramos, "Cutting through State and Class," 273.

134. de la Cadena, *Indigenous Mestizos*, 140, 187, 193, 312.

135. Weismantel, *Cholas and Pishtacos*, 271.

136. CONAIE, *Nacionalidades indígenas*, 223, 261, 281.

137. Mariátegui, "The Indigenous Question in Latin America," 37, 34; Martínez, "Dolores Cacuango," 23.

138. Nils Jacobsen notes a similar phenomenon for Peru in *Mirages of Transition*, 338.

139. Quijano, *Problema agrario y movimientos campesinos*, 58, 61.

140. Albó, "Bases étnicas y sociales para la participación Aymara," 416.

141. Prieto, "A Liberalism of Fear," 252–53.

142. Letter from William Dawson to Secretary of State, Washington, no. 176, March 9, 1931, NARA RG 59, 822.00B/28, p. 2. The United States was interested in uncovering foreign, particularly Soviet, support for these movements but was never able to do so.

143. Letter from Harold D. Clum, American Consul, Guayaquil, to Secretary of State, Washington, no. 463, February 12, 1930, NARA RG 59, 822.00B/11, p. 2.

144. Letter from William Dawson to Secretary of State, Washington, no. 96, December 30, 1930, NARA RG 59, 822.00B/17, p. 4.

145. Albornoz, *Informe del Ministerio de Gobierno y Previsión Social a la nación*, 3–7.

146. Charles A. Page, "Memorandum with Regard to Communism in Ecuador," attached to letter from William Dawson to Secretary of State, Washington, no. 150, January 29, 1931, NARA RG 59, 822.00B/24, p. 20.

147. Ibid., p. 15–17.

148. Letter from Augusto Egas to José Rafael Delgado, September 2, 1930, in CD, 1930, 352, JCAP; letter from Augusto Egas to the Ministro de Previsión Social y Asistencia Pública, September 3, 1930, in CD, 1930, 354, JCAP; letter from Augusto Egas to the Jefe Político of Cayambe, September 3, 1930, in CD, 1930, 355, JCAP.

3. STRIKE!

1. Quoted in Brinton, *The Anatomy of Revolution*, 33.

2. Sawyer, *Crude Chronicles*, 87.

3. Foweraker, "Popular Movements and Political Change in Mexico," 5.

4. Postero and Zamosc, "Indigenous Movements and the Indian Question in Latin America," 8.

5. Letter from Augusto Egas to Sr. Intiendente General de Policía, December 26, 1930, in CD, 1930, 471, JCAP; letter from Augusto Egas to Sr. Ministro de Gobierno, January 7, 1931, in CD, 1931, 6, JCAP; "La sublevación de los indígenas de una hacienda," *El Comercio,* December 31, 1930, 1; "Los indígenas de Pesillo y Moyurco se han sublevado," *El Día,* December 31, 1930, 1. In an examination of events leading up to a failed 1932 peasant uprising, the historians Jeffrey Gould and Aldo Lauri-Santiago note that "the decisive role of rural subaltern groups in transforming the leftist agenda make 1929–1931 El Salvador, along with 1933 Cuba, stand out in the history of the Latin American left." See Gould and Lauri-Santiago, " 'They Call Us Thieves and Steal Our Wage,' " 225. A similar list is presented in *Los partidos comunistas de América del Sur y del Caribe y el movimiento sindical revolucionario,* 6. To this list, we should add the contemporary events in Ecuador.

6. "Pliego de peticiones que los sindicatos 'El Inca' y 'Tierra Libre' situados en la parroquia Olmedo, presentan a los arriendatarios de las haciendas donde trabajan," *El Día,* January 6, 1931, 1. See the electronic appendix http://www.yachana.org/indmovs/ for a list of these demands.

7. Prieto, "Condicionamientos de la movilización campesina," 42.

8. L. V., "El problema de tierras en el Ecuador," *La Antorcha* 2nd ser., 1, no. 2 (March 30, 1925): 4–5; "Manifiesto a la nación," *La Antorcha* 2nd ser., 1, no. 7 (May 1, 1925): 1.

9. Letter from Augusto Egas to José Rafael Delgado, September 2, 1930, in CD, 1930, 352, JCAP; letter from Augusto Egas to Sr. Ministro de Gobierno, January 7, 1931, in CD, 1931, 6, JCAP.

10. El Comité de Lucha Popular, "Manifiesto al Pueblo," Imprenta Sucre, August 29, 1933, Hojas Volantes, 1933–1938, p. 48, BEAEP.

11. Mariátegui, "The Anti-Imperialist Point of View," 42–43.

12. Escobar, "La FEI," 49.

13. Botero, *Indios, tierra y cultura,* 70.

14. Carr, *Marxism and Communism in Twentieth-Century Mexico,* 82, 101.

15. "Se soluciona el problema creado por los indígenas sublevados en las haciendas Pesillo y Moyurco," *El Comercio,* January 8, 1931, 1. In a letter to JCAP, Delgado noted that he had raised salaries, including that of milkmaids, from fifteen to twenty centavos and was now paying day laborers forty centavos for an eight-hour day. Letter from José Rafael Delgado to the Junta de Asistencia Pública, January 24, 1931, in CR, Enero-Junio 1931, 891, JCAP. The agreement is also discussed in a

letter from the Secretaria de Policía to the Jefe Político, January 7, 1931, in CR, Enero-Junio 1931, 894, JCAP.

16. Letter from A. Batallas, Comisario del Trabajo, to Ministro de Gobierno y Previsión Social, Quito, January 24, 1931, Ramón Collection; "Regresa de Cayambe el Piquete del Yaguachi," *El Día,* January 16, 1931, 4.

17. Ignacio María Alba et al., "La verdad en el asunto de los indígenas de las haciendas de Pesillo," *El Día,* March 28, 1931, 5; Virgilio Lechón and Manuel Catucuamba in Yánez, *Yo declaro con franqueza,* 78.

18. Letter from Augusto Egas to Sr. Ministro de Gobierno y Provision Social, January 27, 1931, in CD, 1931, 38, JCAP; "Arrendatarios de la Asistencia Pública," *El Comercio,* January 30, 1931, 2; JCAP, *Informe de la Dirección de la Junta Central de Asistencia Pública,* 52.

19. Letter from Augusto Egas to Sr. Ministro de Gobierno, January 7, 1931, in CD, 1931, 7, JCAP.

20. Comité de Huelga, "La huelga de los sindicatos 'Tierra Libre' y 'El Inca': Los crímenes de los latifundistas, authoridades y servidumbre," Quito: Imprenta "Nueva Era," March 18, 1931, Hojas Volantes, 1931–1940, p. 9, BEAEP.

21. Labriolle, "Acotaciones: Peligro comunista," *El Comercio,* January 10, 1931, 3.

22. JCAP, *Informe de la Dirección de la Junta Central de Asistencia Pública,* 50–52.

23. "Las comunidades indígenas revoltosas," *El Comercio,* January 30, 1931, 3.

24. "Normas para el trabajo rural," *El Día,* January 6, 1931, 3; "Varios millares de indígenas se han concentrado en Cayambe para asistir al primer congreso de campesinos del Ecuador," *El Día,* January 30, 1931, 1.

25. Comité de Huelga, "La huelga de los sindicatos 'Tierra Libre' y 'El Inca,'" BEAEP.

26. "Convocation of Congress of Agricultural Laborers and Peasants," attached to Letter from William Dawson to Secretary of State, Washington, no. 170, February 27, 1931, NARA RG 59, 822.00B / 27.

27. Ibid.

28. "El Congreso de Obreros Agrícolas y Campesinos," *La Hoz* 8 (December 20, 1930): 4.

29. "Varios millares de indígenas se han concentrado en Cayambe para asistir al primer congreso de campesinos del Ecuador," *El Día,* January 30, 1931, 1.

30. "Los representantes de 100 mil indios viajan para el 1er. Congreso de los Campesinos que se reunirá en Cayambe," *El Comercio,* January 31, 1931, 1; Letter from William Dawson to Secretary of State, Washington, no. 158, February 7, 1931, NARA RG 59, 822.00B / 17, p. 6; Prieto, "Condicionamientos de la movilización

campesina," 55. *El Día* mentioned an obviously inflated figure of ten thousand delegates. See "Crónicas de Cayambe," *El Día*, February 6, 1931, 2.

31. "Siguen llegando a Cayambe gentes de diversas procedencias para la celebración del Primer Congreso de Campesinos del Ecuador," *El Día*, January 31, 1931, 1; "Puntos que serán discutidos en el primer congreso de campesinos q' se realizarán en el Cantón Cayambe," *El Comercio*, February 1, 1931, 1.

32. Letter from William Dawson to Secretary of State, Washington, no. 158, February 7, 1931, NARA RG 59, 822.00B / 17, p. 7.

33. "Varios personas fueron capturados por hallarse comprometidas en el movimiento comunista de Cayambe," *El Comercio*, February 2, 1931, 1. Those arrested included Luis Chávez, Alejandro J. Torres, Manuel Viteri (the secretary general of the party), Ricardo Paredes, Cerveleón Gómez Jurada, Juan Bustamante, Gustavo Araujo, and Leonardo Muñoz.

34. "Los concurrentes al congreso de campesinos que iba a reunirse en Cayambe desisten de sus propositos," *El Comercio*, February 3, 1931, 1; "Se han descubierto documentos de propaganda comunista que se ligan directamente con la fracasada reunión del congreso de campesinos," *El Comercio*, February 4, 1931, 1, 4. The following day *El Comercio* printed the text of an extensive State Council debate with Angel M. Paredes raising these issues in front of the government. See "El Dr. Angel M. Paredes denuncia ante el consejo de estado la violación de garantias constitucionales con motivo del congreso de campesino," *El Comercio*, February 5, 1931, 1, 4. Ironically, less than half a year earlier the JCAP had contracted the services of Ricardo Paredes, a medical doctor, to work with sick children. See letter from Augusto Egas to Sr. Tesorero de JCAP, August 5, 1930, in CD, 1930, 315, JCAP; "Fue puesto en libertad el doctor Ricardo Paredes," *El Día*, February 20, 1931, 4.

35. "La declaración rendida por el Sr. Luis F. Chavez como secretario general del comité organizador del congreso de obreros agrícolas y de campesinos," *El Día*, February 20, 1931, 2; Letter from William Dawson to Secretary of State, Washington, no. 158, February 7, 1931, NARA RG 59, 822.00B / 17, p. 6.

36. Guerrero, "The Construction of a Ventriloquist's Image," 589–90.

37. "Los concurrentes al congreso de campesinos que iba a reunirse en Cayambe desisten de sus propositos," *El Comercio*, February 3, 1931, 1; "Diversas actividades gubernativas y medidas tomadas ayer en relación con el proyecto de primer Congreso de Campesinos en Cayambe," *El Día*, February 3, 1931, 1; "Se han descubierto documentos de propaganda comunista que se ligan directamente con la fracasada reunión del congreso de campesinos," *El Comercio*, February 4, 1931, 1,

4. Pointing to a certain racist disregard for the individual identity of Indigenous peoples, a similar report in *El Día* also misspelled Gualavisí's name as "Gualavasí." See "En Cuenca se ha capturado gran cantidad de propaganda comunista y algunos manifestos sobre el proyectado congreso de Cayambe," *El Día*, February 4, 1931, 1; letter from Augusto Egas to the Ministro de Gobierno y Asistencia Pública, March 10, 1931, in CD, 1931, 79, JCAP.

38. Franck, *Vagabonding down the Andes*, 40, 209.

39. Paz y Miño, *Monografía de la provincia de Pichincha*, 18–19. Juan José Perugachi, Secretario de la Tenencia Política de Olmedo, describes the trip by mule in an interview by Mercedes Prieto on October 27, 1976, Prieto Collection.

40. Dirección General de Obras Públicas, *Informe de la Dirección General de Obras Públicas*, 3, 7.

41. Drake, *The Money Doctor in the Andes*, 165; Clark, *The Redemptive Work*, 42; Ojeda, "Efectos del ferrocarril en la agricultura y la ganadería," 647–56. Also see Rosenthal, "Controlling the Line."

42. For example, see the responses to Daquilema's 1871 uprising in Riobamba. Letter from Rumsey Wing to Mr. Fish, Quito, December 23, 1871, in *Foreign Relations of the United States, 1872* (New York: Kraus Reprint Corporation, 1966), 173.

43. Dirección General de Obras Públicas, *Informe de la Dirección General de Obras Públicas*, 100–101.

44. Bustamente and Manuel Madrid, *Monografía de la provincia de Pichincha*, 71, 221. Similar developments also led to a more immediate state presence in other contentious areas, such as Milagro on the coast and the Zumbahua hacienda in the highlands. Weismantel observes that today the provincial capital city "Latacunga is only two hours from Zumbagua, but in living memory it was an arduous two-day trek, with a long, cold night spent in the *páramos* of Tigua"; Weismantel, *Food, Gender, and Poverty in the Ecuadorian Andes*, 48. Also see Uggen, "Peasant Mobilization in Ecuador," 42, 75.

45. Mariátegui, "The Indigenous Question in Latin America," 36–37.

46. Rosenthal, "Streetcar Workers and the Transformation of Montevideo," 492.

47. Uggen observes the same phenomenon on the Ecuadorian coast. See Uggen, "Peasant Mobilization in Ecuador," 25.

48. Garfield, *Indigenous Struggle at the Heart of Brazil*, 161.

49. Albornoz, *Informe del Ministerio de Gobierno y Previsión Social a la nación*, 69. Although the workers federation Sociedad Artística e Industrial del Pichincha created this center, the welfare ministry claimed to support it in order to prevent it from turning into a center of subversive propaganda.

50. Albornoz Peralta, *Historia del movimiento obrero ecuatoriano*, 44.

51. "141 peones de Cayambe han venido a esta ciudad intempestivamente abandonando sus faenas del campo," *El Comercio,* March 13, 1931, 1; "Ayer fueron apresados 156 indígenas de las haciendas de Cayambe," *El Día,* March 13, 1931, 8; "No se efectuó la audiencia del presidente con los indígenas de Cayambe," *El Día,* March 14, 1931, 1; "Se les obligará a salir de las haciendas de Cayambe a los indígenas," *El Día,* March 17, 1931, 1.

52. Bulnes, *Me levanto y digo,* 14.

53. Moscoso, "Estado, comunidad y levantamientos indígenas en las provincias del Azuay y Cañar, 1830–1930," 56.

54. Subcomandante Insurgente Marcos, "A Year of the Zapatista Government (March 17, 1995)," in *Our Word Is Our Weapon,* 246.

55. Letter from Augusto Egas to the Ministro de Gobierno y Asistencia Pública, March 10, 1931, in CD, 1931, 79, JCAP.

56. "La situación económica de los indígenas de Pesillo," *El Comercio,* March 24, 1931, 1, 2; letter from Augusto Egas, Segundo D. Rojas V., and Ernesto Robalino to Sr. Ministro de Gobierno y Asistencia Pública, April 30, 1931, CR, Enero-Junio 1931, JCAP, 896–901; "Hoy parten a Cayambe el director de la Asistencia Pública y el jefe de investigaciones," *El Día,* March 19, 1931, 8; "El resultado de las negociaciones de Cayambe," *El Día,* March 24, 1931, 8.

57. Letter from Augusto Egas, Segundo D. Rojas V., and Ernesto Robalino to Ministerio de Gobierno y Asistencia Pública, April 30, 1931, in CR, Enero-Junio 1931, 900, JCAP; "La situación económica de los indígenas de Pesillo," *El Comercio,* March 24, 1931, 2.

58. Ignacio María Alba and others, "La verdad en el asunto de los indígenas de las haciendas de Pesillo," *El Día,* March 28, 1931, 5.

59. "Se ha producido un levantamiento de los indígenas en la hacienda Tanlahua en la prov. de Bolívar," *El Comercio,* May 25, 1931, 1; "El gobierno ha despachado una comisión de confianza para conferenciar con los indígenas," *El Comercio,* May 26, 1931, 1; "Los indígenas de la provincia de Bolívar," *El Comercio,* May 26, 1931, 3; "Tranquilidad en los indígenas de la hda. Talahua," *El Comercio,* May 28, 1931, 3; Albornoz Peralta, *Las luchas indígenas,* 68.

60. Oficio from Jefe Político of Otavalo to the Governor of the Province of Imbabura, August 21, 1931, No. 345, in CR, 1925–1931, 196–197, Jefatura Política, Otavalo. Thanks to Kenny Kincaid for bringing this event to my attention.

61. Letter from Augusto Egas to José Rafael Delgado, September 2, 1930, in CD, 1930, 352, JCAP; Letter from Augusto Egas to Sr. Ministro de Gobierno, January 7, 1931, in CD, 1931, 6, 9, JCAP.

62. Letter from Miguel A. Albornoz, Ministro de Gobierno y Previsión Social, to

Director, Junta Central de Asistencia Pública March 17, 1931, Oficio no. 627, in CR, Enero-Junio 1931, 767, JCAP.

63. José Rafael Delgado, "La tranquilidad en las haciendas de Cayambe," *El Comercio,* March 27, 1931, 8.

64. "La situación económica de los indígenas de Pesillo," *El Comercio* (Quito), March 24, 1931, 1. These leaders from Pesillo included Vicente Amaguaña, Juan Albamocho, Gaspar Alba, Florencio Catucuamba, José Cacuango (all with huasipungos), Ignacio Alba, Segundo Lechón, José María Amaguaña, Venancio Amaguaña, and Pascual Albamocho (without huasipungos). Two huasipungueros from La Chimba (Florentino Nepas and Antonio Nepas) and four from Moyurco (Virgilio Lechón, Juan de Dios Quishpe, Benjamin Campués, and Rafael Catucuamba) were also expelled. Another leader, Manuel Quinchiguango, was no longer working on the hacienda. In fact, many of the strike leaders were not huasipungueros but arrimados (relatives of huasipungueros who did not have a labor contract but lived on the hacienda with family members and helped out with assigned tasks).

65. Neptalí Ulcuango, interviewed by Mercedes Prieto, July 7–8, 1977, Prieto Collection.

66. Luis Catucuamba in Yánez, *Yo declaro con franqueza,* 178; Martínez, "Dolores Cacuango," 23.

67. Neptalí Ulcuango in Yánez, *Yo declaro con franqueza,* 82. On organizational efforts at Yanahuaico, see Becker, "Comunas and Indigenous Protest in Cayambe, Ecuador."

68. Tránsito Amaguaña, interviewed by Mercedes Prieto on November 26, 1977, Prieto Collection.

69. Prieto, "Condicionamientos de la movilización campesina," 54. Neptalí Ulcuango claims that landholders paid authorities to side with them. See interview by Mercedes Prieto, July 7–8, 1977, Prieto Collection.

70. Martínez, "Dolores Cacuango," 23.

71. Prieto, "Condicionamientos de la movilización campesina," 58.

72. "Our huasipungo! Our huasipungo!"

73. See Sáenz, *Sobre el indio ecuatoriano,* 54–56, as well as chapter three ("El problema del Indio," 101–62) in which he discusses questions of land and labor in the highlands. Also see Prieto, "Haciendas estatales," 68.

74. Buitrón, *Condiciones de vida y trabajo del campesino de la provincia de Pichincha,* 38. The hacendado Emilio Bonifaz similarly complained that Indigenous peoples did not have an "economic mentality" that would lead them to work harder and earn more money. See Bonifaz, *Sobre la pobreza del campesino del callejón interandino,* 24. An alternative explanation, of course, for the workers' preference for the

huasipungo system is that due to the seasonal nature of wage labor, peons might actually earn much less than a huasipunguero as well as not have the built-in safety net of the subsistence agricultural production of the huasipungo plot.

75. Cornell University, *Indians in Misery*, 147.

76. Bauer, "Rural Workers in Spanish America."

77. Gibson, *The Aztecs under Spanish Rule*, 249.

78. Bauer, "Rural Workers in Spanish America," 41–42. Also see Knight, "Mexican Peonage." Recently Elizabeth Dore has challenged what has become the dominant interpretation that peonage led to capitalist transition. She argues instead that it impeded economic development and that introducing a gender analysis reveals how patriarchal authority assured the continuance of labor coercion. See Dore, *Myths of Modernity*, 164–65.

79. Hassaurek, *Four Years among the Ecuadorians*, 171. For a broader analysis of how mid-nineteenth-century liberal agrarian policies facilitated this development in Ecuador, see Williams, "Popular Liberalism and Indian Servitude," 711.

80. Peloso, *Peasants on Plantations*, 158, 167.

81. Letter from José Rafael Delgado to the Director of the Junta de Asistencia Pública, April 23, 1931, in CR, Enero-Junio 1931, 893, JCAP.

82. Transcribed oficio of Sr. Intendente Accidental de Policía de Pichinga, April 21, 1931, in CR, Enero-Junio 1931, 711, JCAP; letter from Julio Miguel Páez to the Junta de Asistencia Pública, April 25, 1931, in CR, Enero-Junio 1931, 776, JCAP; transcribed petition to Ministro de Gobierno, May 18, 1931, in CR, Enero-Junio 1931, 769, JCAP; letter from Augusto Egas to the Ministro de Gobierno y Asistencia Pública, May 26, 1931, in CD, 1931, 170, JCAP.

83. Albornoz, *Informe del Ministerio de Gobierno*, 190–94.

84. "Nuevo levantamiento de los indios de Cayambe se ha estado preparando," *El Comercio*, August 16, 1931, 1.

85. Augusto Egas to Sr. Ministro de Gobierno y Asistencia Pública, Quito, March 31, 1932, in CD, 1932, 107, JCAP. Also see Becker, "Coaliciones interétnicas en los años treinta."

86. "Los concurrentes al congreso de campesinos que iba a reunirse en Cayambe desisten de sus propositos," *El Comercio*, February 3, 1931, 1; "Diversas actividades gubernativas y medidas tomadas ayer en relación con el proyecto de primer Congreso de Campesinos en Cayambe," *El Día*, February 3, 1931, 1; Augusto Egas to the Ministro de Gobierno y Asistencia Pública, Quito, March 10, 1931, in CD, 1931, 79, JCAP; General Jaramillo, Intendencia General de Policía de la Provincia de Pichincha to the Director of the Junta de Asistencia Pública, Quito, April 1, 1931, in CR, Enero-Junio 1931, 506, JCAP.

87. For basic biographical data on Rodríguez, see Rodríguez Rojas, "Datos biográficos del Señor Rubén Rodríguez Mera"; and Cifuentes Navarro, "Rubén Rodríguez." The enduring significance of Rodríguez's influence on Cayambe was reflected in the 1996 race for the presidency of the Municipality of Cayambe when Fausto Jarrín invoked Rodríguez's name, implying that he was continuing the political project of the earlier leader.

88. Augusto Egas to Sr. Don Heriberto Maldonado, Quito, June 25, 1935, in CD, 1934–1935, 355, JCAP; Heriberto Maldonado to Director de la Junta Central de Asistencia Pública, Quito, June 27, 1935, in CR, Enero-Junio 1935, 862, JCAP; "Various personas fueron capturados por hallarse comprometidas en el movimiento comunista de Cayambe," *El Comercio,* February 2, 1931, 1.

89. "Los indígenas de las haciendas de beneficencia de Bolívar producen agitaciones como las de Cayambe," *El Comercio,* April 30, 1931, 1; "Levantamiento general de indígenas iniciado cn Quinua Corral tiene sobresaltados a los agricultores," *El Comercio,* May 12, 1931, 1. Also see "Los indígenas de las haciendas Quinua-Corral y El Espino resuelven acer un paro gral. de sus labores," *El Comercio,* May 9, 1931, 5; "Cada vez más alarmante la actitud de los indígenas de las haciendas de Quinua Corral y El Espino en Bolívar," *El Comercio,* May 13, 1931, 1.

90. "Diez mil indios de Latacunga se dice que amenazan una propiedad perteneciente al Sr. Aresio Paz," *El Comercio,* May 9, 1931, 5.

91. "Amotinamiento de indígenas en la sección Palmira," *El Comercio,* November 10, 1932, 5; Albornoz Peralta, *Las luchas indígenas,* 68–69.

92. Albornoz Peralta, *Las luchas indígenas,* 69–71; CONAIE, *Nacionalidades indígenas,* 299–300.

93. "Producese levantamiento de indios en una hacienda del Chimbrazo," *El Comercio,* February 27, 1935, 1, 3; Albornoz Peralta, *Las luchas indígenas,,* 71–72.

94. "Indígenas de Pull establecerán colonia en Saloya," *El Día,* October 5, 1935, 8; Joaquín Gallegos Lara, "La libertad de Ambrosio Lasso," *Ñucanchic Allpa* 1, no. 8 (March 17, 1936): 1. The use of the term "massacre" is not hyperbolic but a reflection of contemporary usage. Legal definitions vary, but a massacre generally refers to the premeditated and indiscriminate killing of multiple innocent civilians at one time.

95. PCE, *Abajo las maniobras dictatoriales de Velasco Ibarra,* 1.

96. Albornoz Peralta, *Las luchas indígenas,* 71–74.

97. Gangotena, "El 'coronel' Ambrosio Laso"; Comité Central del PCE, *Exposición a la Corte Suprema,* 4; "Anuncia levantamiento indígena d' una hacienda en el Chimborazo," *El Comercio,* April 2, 1936, 4; Gallegos Lara, *Biografía del pueblo indio,* 66.

98. Telegrams from Minister in Ecuador to Secretary of State, no. 45, September 28,

1935, NARA RG 59, 822.00 Revolutions / 70:Telegram and no. 50, October 8, 1935, NARA RG 59, 822.00 Revolutions / 74:Telegram.

99. Federico Páez, "Ley orgánica del trabajo," *Registro Oficial* 1, no. 112 (February 11, 1936): 344.

100. "Ley de tierras baldías y colonización," *Registro Oficial* 1, no. 187 (May 12, 1936): 112–20; Federico Páez, "A la nación" (Quito: Imprenta Nacional, March 6, 1936), Hojas volantes, 1869–1960, p. 102, BEAEP.

101. PSE, *Estatutos* (1939), 3, 8.

102. "Ley de Organización y Régimen de las Comunas" (Decreto no. 142), *Registro Oficial* 558 (August 6, 1937): 1517–19. Data on specific comunas are kept in the archive of the Dirección Nacional de Desarrollo Campesino, Ministerio de Agricultura, Quito, Ecuador. For more context on legislative debates around comuna legislation, see Prieto, "A Liberalism of Fear," 152–55. Also see Becker, "Comunas and Indigenous Protest in Cayambe, Ecuador."

103. "Proyecto de ley sobre comunidades indígenas," *El Comercio*, April 2, 1936, 8.

104. CONAIE, *Nacionalidades indígenas*, 127; Striffler, *In the Shadows of State and Capital*, 64.

105. "Estatuto Jurídico de las Comunidades Campesinas" (Decreto No. 23), *Registro Oficial* 39 and 40 (December 10 and 11, 1937): 2388–90.

106. Ministerio de Prevision Social y Trabajo, *Código del Trabajo*, Artículo 375, 228.

107. Letter from Gonzalo Oleas to Director de la Junta Central de Asistencia Pública, Quito, March 6, 1939[?], in CR, Primer Semestre, 1939, 957, JCAP. See Becker, "Indigenous Struggles for Land Rights on the Zumbahua Hacienda in Twentieth-Century Ecuador."

108. "Quejas de los indígenas de diferentes provincias," *Ñucanchic Allpa* 2nd ser., 15 (May 28, 1940): 4.

109. Letter from J. Humberto Correa, Inspector Provincial de Pichincha, to Señor Administrador de la Hacienda "Guachalá," January 5, 1944, AH / BC, 7 / XI / 22.

110. "Patronguna, Peonguna," *Ñucanchic Allpa* 2nd ser., 16 (November 5, 1944): 2, 5.

111. Malo, *Memoria*, 11–12; Bulnes, *Me levanto y digo*, 34.

112. Letter from Augusto Egas to Sr. Ministro de Gobierno, January 7, 1931, in CD, 1931, 9, JCAP.

113. Harvey, *The Chiapas Rebellion*, 11.

114. Virgilio Lechón, interviewed by Mercedes Prieto, March 4, 1978, Prieto Collection.

115. Neptalí Ulcuango, in Yánez, *Yo declaro con franqueza*, 174.

116. Ramón, "Cayambe," 165.

117. Clark, "Indians, the State and Law," 67. Clark also notes that "paradoxically, these forms of resistance also implied a recognition and legitimization of the state. In

cases like this the complexity of the dialectic of resistance and accommodation in situations involving domination is made evident" (70).

4. FEDERACIÓN ECUATORIANA DE INDIOS

1. Rodas Morales, *Nosotras que del amor hicimos,* 60. For an extended discussion of this uprising and the subsequent constitutional changes, see Becker, "State Building and Ethnic Discourse in Ecuador's 1944–1945 Asamblea Constituyente." To put the May Revolution in a broader historical context, it is well to remember that a general strike in El Salvador during the same month of May 1944 led to Maximiliano Hernández Martínez's removal from power, and that a similar uprising in Guatemala in June 1944 forced Jorge Ubico to resign, which opened the way for Juan José Arévalo and Jacobo Arbenz's progressive reforms. See Parkman, *Nonviolent Insurrection in El Salvador.*

2. For a discussion of the founding of the CTE, see Milk, *Movimiento obrero ecuatoriano el desafío de la integración.*

3. CONAIE later applauded these early efforts as establishing "the bases for constructing an organization on a regional and national level." See CONAIE, *Nacionalidades indígenas,* 31.

4. "Una tarea imperiosa," *Frente Obrero* 1, no. 3 (October 1934): 4.

5. Ulianova,"El levantamiento campesino de Lonquimay y la Internacional Comunista," 212.

6. Carr, *Marxism and Communism in Twentieth-Century Mexico,* 105.

7. PCE, *Abajo las maniobras dictatoriales de Velasco Ibarra,* 6.

8. Presídium de la Conferencia de Cabecillas Indígenas, "Hoy se Clausura la Conferencia de Cabecillas Indígenas" (Quito: Editorial de El Correo, November 7, 1935), Hojas Volantes, 1933–1938, p. 298, BEAEP (see the electronic appendix http://www.yachana.org/indmovs/ for a copy of this document); "Sensacionales denuncias se harán ante el congreso indígena," *El Día,* November 7, 1935, 7. Other than these two documents, apparently little information beyond that preserved in the oral tradition remains of this meeting. Interview with Nela Martínez, Quito, April 27, 1996. Mercedes Prieto searched without success for information on this meeting. See Prieto, "Haciendas estatales," 119.

9. Albornoz Peralta, "Jesús Gualavisí," 175; "El partido comunista organizador y defensor de los indios," *El Pueblo,* June 2, 1951, 6.

10. "Organización y Peticiones de Indios," *Ñucanchic Allpa* 1, no. 8 (March 17, 1936): 1.

11. "De Cayambe," *El Comercio,* April 6, 1936, 7.

12. "Actitud terrorista del Inspector de Trabajo," *El Comercio,* December 23, 1935, 7.

13. "El pueblo Cayambeño contra los gamonales," *Ñucanchic Allpa* 1, no. 8 (March 17, 1936): 1, 4.

14. Aguilar Vazquez, *Informe a la nación*, 37.

15. Conferencia de Cabecillas Indios, "Indicaciones," *Ñucanchic Allpa* 1, no. 8 (March 17, 1936): 2.

16. The construction of "Indigenous nationalities" in the 1930s has been almost completely forgotten in Ecuador, with scholars commonly tracing its roots back only to the 1970s. For example, see Ibarra, "Intelectuales indígenas, neoindigenismo, e indianismo en el Ecuador," 83. The anthropologist Ileana Almeida later noted that sympathetic leftists had brought back this concept of nationalities from the Soviet Union in the 1970s and introduced it to the fledgling organizations in Ecuador. See Selverston-Scher, *Ethnopolitics in Ecuador*, 23. An earlier, though negative, construction of Indigenous nationalities came in 1916 when the hacendado Nicolás Martínez argued that "independent nations" needed to disappear in order for Indians to be civilized and become full citizens. See "La condición actual de la raza indígena en la provincia de Tungurahua," 218. Also see Becker, "Mariátegui, the Comintern, and the Indigenous Question in Latin America."

17. *Los partidos comunistas de América del Sur y del Caribe y el movimiento sindical revolucionario*, 33. Also see Communist International, *The Revolutionary Movement in the Colonies*, 58.

18. Presídium de la Conferencia de Cabecillas Indígenas, "Hoy se Clausura la Conferencia de Cabecillas Indígenas."

19. Comité Central del PCE, *Exposición a la Corte Suprema*, 9.

20. Conferencia de Cabecillas Indios, "Indicaciones," *Ñucanchic Allpa* 1, no. 8 (March 17, 1936): 2.

21. "Indígenas de Cayambe forman el primer Comité Antifascista del campo en Yanahuaico," *Antinazi* 2, no. 24 (August 17, 1943): 2; "Comité indígena antifascista se organizó en Juan Montalvo," *Antinazi* 2, no. 25 (September 5, 1943): 2; Movimiento Antifascista del Ecuador (MAE), "Informes y resoluciones: Conferencia Provincial Antifascista de Pichincha, Septiembre 20–27 de 1943," 28, 32, facsimile edition in Mériguet, *Antinazismo en Ecuador*, 283, 284; and Martínez, "Prologo," in Mériguet, *Antinazismo en Ecuador*.

22. "Los obreros textiles de la República constituyen la Federación Nacional del Trabajo," *Ñucanchic Allpa* 1, no. 8 (March 17, 1936): 4.

23. James, *The Black Jacobins*, 283.

24. "Indians in the National Congress of Workers," *Boletín Indigenista* (Instituto Indigenista Interamericano, Mexico) 4, no. 3 (September 1944): 199.

25. "Solemne inauguración del Congreso de Trabajadores del Ecuador," *El Comercio*,

July 5, 1944, 1; "Congreso Nacional de Trabajadores eligió presidente al Sr. Pedro Saad," *El Comercio*, July 6, 1944, 4; "Numerosas ponencias aprobadas por el Congreso Obrero del Ecuador," *El Comercio*, July 9, 1944, 5; "Congreso de Trabajadores eligió representantes a la Asamblea Constituyente," *El Comercio*, July 10, 1944, 1, 6.

26. CTE, "Estatutos de la Confederación de Trabajadores del Ecuador," 199–200.

27. "Esta noche se inaugura el congreso indígena ecuatoriano," *El Día*, August 6, 1944, 8; "Anoche se inauguró el primer congreso indígena ecuatoriano," *El Comercio*, August 7, 1944, 4; "Delegados al congreso indígena estan en Quito," *El Día*, August 7, 1944, 7.

28. "Ponencias aprobadas por el Congreso Indígena reunido en esta Capital, del 6 al 9 de Agosto retropróximo," *Ñucanchic Allpa* 2nd ser., 16 (November 5, 1944): 5.

29. Endara, "La fundación del partido: Una experiencia testimonial," 56.

30. Selverston, "The Politics of Culture," 138; Pallares, *From Peasant Struggles to Indian Resistance*, 13. Deborah J. Yashar and Donna Lee Van Cott also dismiss the federation as "largely nonindigenous" and "led and organized by non-Indians," reflecting a general lack of knowledge of the history and significance of the organizations. See Yashar, *Contesting Citizenship in Latin America*, 101; Van Cott, *From Movements to Parties in Latin America*, 103. This assumption seems to follow Marx's argument that since the French peasantry were "incapable of asserting their class interest in their own name" that "they cannot represent themselves, they must be represented." See Marx, *The Eighteenth Brumaire of Louis Bonaparte*, 124.

31. Martínez, *Yo siempre he sido Nela Martínez Espinosa*, 146.

32. Crespi, "Mujeres campesinas como líderes sindicales," 151.

33. "Hora social en homenaje a delegados indígenas," *El Día*, August 8, 1944, 3; "Congreso indígena," *El Día*, August 9, 1944, 2; "Sesion de clausura del congreso de indígenas se llavará a cabo hoy," *El Comercio*, August 9, 1944, 12; "El primer congreso indígena del Ecuador," *Ñucanchic Allpa* 2nd ser., 16 (November 5, 1944): 2.

34. "La elección de representantes al Congreso Indigenista de Méjico y las calumnias de 'El Comercio,'" *Ñucanchic Allpa*, 2nd ser., 15 (May 28, 1940), 3.

35. "Statutes of the National Indian Institute," *Boletín Indigenista* 3, no. 3 (December 1943): 242–57; "Inauguración del Instituto Indigenista Nacional," *El Comercio*, October 28, 1943.

36. "A New Department of Indian Affairs," *Boletín Indigenista* 3, no. 2 (June 1943): 87–91; "The Establishment of a National Indian Institute," *Boletín Indigenista* 3, no. 3 (September 1943): 159.

37. Santana, *¿Ciudadanos en la etnicidad?* 146.

38. De la Cadena, *Indigenous Mestizos*, 132.

39. Larson, *Trials of Nation Making*, 173.

40. Milk, "Growth and Development of Ecuador's Worker Organizations," 60. Also see Segundo Congreso Obrero, "Programa, reglamento y proyectos," 232.

41. Colloredo-Mansfeld, "'Dirty Indians,'" 193. Also see Pío Jaramillo Alvarado's prologue in Maiguashca, *El indio.*

42. Prieto, "A Liberalism of Fear," 62–63.

43. Blanco, *Land or Death,* 131.

44. Ramos, "Cutting through State and Class," 273.

45. Perreault, "Shifting Ground," 4.

46. FEI, *Estatutos,* 3. The Ministry of Social Welfare and Labor accepted the new organization's statutes on January 29, 1945, a fact that has led some historians to mistakenly give 1945 as the founding year of the FEI. Even the FEI's website (http://www.cte-ecuador.org/FEI.php) gives this as the founding date. See the electronic appendix http://www.yachana.org/indmovs/ for a copy of this document.

47. "Competition in Indian Arts and Arts Using Indian Motives," *Boletín Indigenista* 6, no. 1 (March 1946): 28–33. The FEI statutes stipulated that all of its affiliates should celebrate this date. See FEI, *Estatutos,* 8. For a while, this Indigenous art exhibit became an annual event. See "Sobre arte indígena," *Surcos,* April 27, 1948, 5, 8.

48. See, for example, Perreault, "Development Identities," 404; de la Pena, "Etnicidad, ciudadanía y cambio agrario," 45.

49. Barth, *Ethnic Groups and Boundaries;* Nagel, *American Indian Ethnic Renewal,* 32.

50. Ramón, "Cayambe," 166.

51. Lurie, "The Contemporary American Indian Scene," 419–20.

52. Howard, "Pan-Indian Culture of Oklahoma," 215.

53. Lurie, "The Contemporary American Indian Scene," 419–20.

54. Thomas, "Pan-Indianism," 77, 84. Also see Hertzberg, *The Search for an American Indian Identity.*

55. Nagel, *American Indian Ethnic Renewal,* 12.

56. Cornell, *The Return of the Native,* 107.

57. Nagel, *American Indian Ethnic Renewal,* 19.

58. Talbot, "Free Alcatraz," 88.

59. CONAIE later noted how literacy and training in the Spanish language affected the nature of Indigenous leadership. See CONAIE, *Nacionalidades indígenas,* 278.

60. See Dandler and Torrico, "From the National Indigenous Congress to the Ayopaya Rebellion"; and Gotkowitz, "'Under the Dominion of the Indian.'"

61. Foerster and Montecino Aguirre, *Organizaciones, lideres y contiendas mapuches,* 251.

62. Santana, *¿Ciudadanos en la etnicidad?* 128–29. Galo Ramón similarly maintains that the left was only interested in huasipungueros and not free Indigenous

communities because the former were more similar to the working class. See Ramón, "La comunidad indígena ecuatoriana," 72. An alternative interpretation is that the FEI deliberately organized huasipungueros precisely because they believed engaging in wage labor on haciendas would cultivate a class consciousness. Indians in "free" communities were less likely to interact with others in a way that engendered a class consciousness. Instead, organizations emphasizing ethnic identities later emerged out of these communities.

63. "Doctor Ricardo Paredes," *Ñucanchic Allpa* 2nd ser., 16 (November 5, 1944): 1; "Delegados al congreso indígena estan en Quito," *El Día*, August 7, 1944, 7.

64. Ricardo Paredes in "Actas de la Asamblea Constituyente de 1944," vol. 3, 325–30 (September 21, 1944), Archivo Palacio Legislativo (hereafter APL), Quito, Ecuador; Vega Ugalde, *La Gloriosa*, 117. Also see "El partido comunista organizador y defensor de los indios," *El Pueblo*, June 2, 1951, 6; Cueva, *The Process of Political Domination in Ecuador*, 37; and Muñoz, *Testimonio*, 86–88.

65. Jesús Gualavisí and Luis Alvaro, "A los indios ecuatorianos," *Ñucanchic Allpa* 2nd ser., 4, no. 18 (October 5, 1946): 1.

66. FEI, *Estatutos*, 10. The 1945 Constitution, which was in effect for a little over a year, provided for a functional deputy for Indian organizations and required this deputy to be involved in related activities. This concession, however, was struck from the subsequent 1946 Constitution. See Borja y Borja, *Las constituciones del Ecuador*, 569, 570.

67. Decades later, CONAIE also encountered similar governmental resistance to the idea of establishing itself as the exclusionary organizational representative of Indigenous concerns in Ecuador. See CONAIE, "Anteproyecto de ley de nacionalidades indígenas del Ecuador," 208. Jose Antonio Lucero develops the theme of representation in "Arts of Unification."

68. Warren, *Indigenous Movements and Their Critics*, 19–20.

69. Fiallo and Ramón, *Lucha de las comunidades indígenas del cantón Pujilí*, 1. Similar dynamics were at work in the United States. As white communists became involved in the "Negro Question," black activists shaped the party as much as they were shaped by it. See Maxwell, *New Negro, Old Left*.

70. FEI, *Estatutos*, 8.

71. "La Federación Indígena del Ecuador," August 31, 1944, Hoja Volante, Muñoz Collection (see the electronic appendix http://www.yachana.org/indmovs/ for a copy of this document). The Assembly also condemned the attack. See "Actas de la Asamblea Constituyente de 1944," vol. 2, Sesión del 28 de agosto de 1944, APL; "La Asamblea Nacional siguió estudiando la expedición de la nueva Carta Política," *El Comercio*, September 6, 1944, 3.

72. Jesús Gualavisí and Luis Alvaro, "A los indios ecuatorianos," *Ñucanchic Allpa* 2nd ser., 4, no. 18 (October 5, 1946): 4.

73. Comité Ejecutivo de la Federación Indígena, "Manifiesto que el Comité Ejecutivo de la Federación Indígena dirige al pueblo ecuatoriano" (Cayambe, February 1945), Ramón collection. See the electronic appendix http://www.yachana.org/indmovs/ for a copy of this document.

74. "La Federación Ecuatoriana de Indios," December 4, 1946, Hojas Volantes 1946–1950, No. 39, BEAEP. See the electronic appendix http://www.yachana.org/ind movs/ for a copy of this document. Indicating the FEI's close connection with the PCE, four days later Ricardo Paredes in the name of the PCE also published a statement calling for freedom for the imprisoned leaders. See Ricardo A. Paredes, Secretario General, Partido Comunista del Ecuador, "Un nueva ola de terror contra las fuerzas democráticas se ha iniciado ¡Detengamosla!," Quito, December 8, 1946, Hojas Volantes, 1941–1965, p. 108, BEAEP.

75. Rodríguez, "Acción por el Movimiento de Mujeres," 23. Also see Martínez, *Yo siempre he sido Nela Martínez Espinosa*; and Becker, "Race, Gender, and Protest in Ecuador."

76. At the end of the twentieth century, Thomas Olesen similarly points to the skills (particularly the use of the Internet) that intermediaries brought to the neo-Zapatista uprising in southern Mexico that contributed to their success in gaining visibility and political space. See Olesen, *International Zapatismo*, 13, 213.

77. "Ñucanchic Allpa organizador y guía de los indios ecuatorianos," *Ñucanchic Allpa* 2nd ser., 4, no. 18 (October 5, 1946): 1.

78. Luis Catucuamba in Yánez, *Yo declaro con franqueza*, 181.

79. "El problema del indio, problema nacional," *Ñucanchic Allpa* 2nd ser., 16 (November 5, 1944): 2.

80. "Victoria de los trabajadores de Chaupi-Muyurco," *El Pueblo*, February 21, 1959, 7.

81. "Se agudizan las represiones en el campo," *El Pueblo*, October 25, 1952, 3; "Persecuciones y atropellos a los indios de Hacienda Pisambilla," *El Pueblo*, May 26, 1956, 4.

82. Martínez, *Yo siempre he sido Nela Martínez Espinosa*, 110.

83. "Datos biográficos del Secretario Gral. del Partido Comunista del Ecuador Ricardo Paredes," *El Pueblo*, June 2, 1951, 3; "Modesto Rivera," *El Pueblo*, June 2, 1951, 6.

84. An exception perhaps was in Cayambe where a statement from the Tierra Libre syndicate in Moyurco in January 1944 indicates continual high levels of Indigenous agitation for higher salaries, fewer labor demands, an end to abuse, etc. See "La voz de los indios," *Surcos*, February 1, 1944, 5.

85. "Dueños de haciendas de Chimborazo no cumplen la leyes del trabajo," *El Comer-*

cio, August 26, 1944, 1; "Abastos municipales en Cayambe proporcionan beneficios a los pobladores," *El Comercio,* August 26, 1944, 11; "Indígenas de la provincia del Chimborazo están abandonando los trabajos de cosechas," *El Día,* August 26, 1944, 1, 2; "Peones de haciendas de Chimborazo se han levantado en actitud belicosa," *El Comercio,* August 27, 1944, 16; "Peones de las haciendas piden liquidación de cuentas," *El Comercio,* August 31, 1944, 12; "Se hace gestiones que vuelvan al trabajo indígenas de Chimborazo," *El Comercio,* October 20, 1944, 12; "Provocadores siguen azuzando a indígenas," *El Comercio,* November 8, 1944, 1; "Varias peticiones hicieron en Cayambe al Presidente de la Rep. Dr. Velasco," *El Comercio,* December 31, 1944, 12; "Versión oficial de levantamiento de los indígenas en el anejo Sanguicel," *El Comercio,* January 13, 1945, 1, 11; "Comuneros se resisten a desocupar una hacienda situada en el cantón Pangua," *El Comercio,* January 25, 1945, 12; "Prodújose levantamiento de indígenas de cantón Cayambe conta la autoridad," *El Comercio,* January 30, 1945, 1, 2; "No ha habido cl tal levantamiento de indígenas en Cayambe, díjose oficialmente," *El Día,* January 30, 1945, 1, 6; "Cabecillas provocaron levantamiento de los indígenas en el cantón Colta," *El Comercio,* February 8, 1945, 10; "La Asamblea reconsieró ayer otros artículos de la Constitución Política," *El Comercio,* February 14, 1945, 10; "Sobre los agitadores en Chimborazo," *El Comercio,* February 20, 1945, 1, 3.

86. Letter from J. A. Jalevalel, Personero Auxiliar to Director, JCAP, in Correspondencia Recibida, Segundo Semestre, Segundo Parte, 1946, 1554, JCAP.

87. Burns and Burns, *A People's Charter,* 462, 13.

88. Comité Ejecutivo de la Federación Indígena, "Manifiesto que el Comité Ejecutivo de la Federación Indígena dirige al pueblo ecuatoriano" (Cayambe, Febrero de 1945), Ramón Collection; "El indio frente a la cultura," *Ñucanchic Allpa* 2nd ser., 4, no. 18 (October 5, 1946): 2; "Programa de reinvindicaciones para los indios ecuatorianos," *Ñucanchic Allpa* 2nd ser., 4, no. 18 (October 5, 1946): 3.

89. Letter from Luis Coloma Silva, Director, to Modesto Rivera, Secretario General de la Federación Ecuatoriana de Indios, Quito, February 10, 1950, Oficio no. 72-SIA, Comunicaciones Dirigidas, Departamento de Haciendas, D y R, Enero-Junio 1950, JCAP; letter from José R. Chiriboga Ch., Director de Asistencia Pública, to Modesto Rivera, Secretario General de la Federación Ecuatoriana de Indios, Quito, October 2, 1953, Oficio no. 42-SE, Comunicaciones Dirigidas, Departamento de Haciendas (DH), 1953, JCAP.

90. Foweraker and Landman, *Citizenship Rights and Social Movements,* 1.

91. Although its statutes indicated that the FEI was to hold an organizational congress every year, in reality these meetings happened much less frequently. This was in

large part due to the difficulties in bringing people together, given the lack of resources and Ecuador's weak communications infrastructure. Since it took thirteen years to found the FEI, it was perhaps unrealistic to expect to hold subsequent congresses on an annual basis.

92. FEI, *Segundo congreso de indios ecuatorianos* (see the electronic appendix http:// www.yachana.org/indmovs/ for a copy of this document); "El II congreso de indios ecuatorianos," *Surcos*, March 2, 1946, 8; "Second Congress of Ecuadorian Indians," *Boletín Indigenista* 6, no. 1 (March 1946): 32–35. The FEI's statutes created the Comité Central de Defensa Indígena to engage legal issues related to the Indigenous movement, with the main goal "to carry out the economic emancipation of the Ecuadorean Indians" (FEI, *Estatutos*, 8; also see Gangotena, "The Socio-Economic System of an Ecuadorean Indian Community," 30).

93. "Misión de la Federación Ecuatoriana de Indios," *Ñucanchic Allpa* 2nd ser., 4, no. 18 (October 5, 1946): 4. See the electronic appendix (http://www.yachana.org/indmovs/) for a copy of this document.

94. "Inauguración del Segundo Congreso d' Indios en el teatro Sucre," *El Día*, February 7, 1946, 2; "Hoy se inaugurará el Segundo Congreso Indigenista," *El Día*, February 8, 1946, 6; "Después de tomar varias resoluciones el Congreso dará hoy término a sus labores," *El Día*, February 11, 1946, 1, 6; "Ponencia creando Consejo Nacional de Educación Indígena conoció el Congreso," *El Día*, February 13, 1946, 1. Quito's conservative newspaper *El Comercio* did not report on the FEI congress.

95. "El II congreso de indios ecuatorianos," *Surcos*, March 2, 1946, 8.

96. "Misión de la Federación Ecuatoriana de Indios," *Ñucanchic Allpa* 2nd ser., 4, no. 18 (October 5, 1946): 4.

97. Letter from C. Aníbal Maldonado, Administrador, to Jefe, Departamento de Haciendas, Asistencia Pública, October 10, 1946 (Oficio no. 27), in CR, 1946, JCAP.

98. Jesús Gualavisí and Luis Alvaro, "A los indios ecuatorianos," *Ñucanchic Allpa* 2nd ser., 4, no. 18 (October 5, 1946): 4; "Misión de la Federación Ecuatoriana de Indios," *Ñucanchic Allpa* 2nd ser., 4, no. 18 (October 5, 1946): 4.

99. Rodas Morales, *Nosotras que del amor hicimos*, 63.

100. "La segunda sesión del Congreso Nacional de Trabajadores fue muy borrascosa," *El Comercio*, November 5, 1946, 12.

101. Jesús Gualavisí and Luis Alvaro, "A los indios ecuatorianos," *Ñucanchic Allpa* 2nd ser., 4, no. 18 (October 5, 1946): 4.

102. "El Congreso Nacional de Trabajadores realizó el nombramiento de comisiones," *El Comercio*, November 6, 1946, 12. The others were Neptalí Pacheco León, a peasant leader from the coast, and Francisco T. Castro.

103. "Cooperativa Tigua," *Registro Oficial* 1, 237 (March 16, 1945): 2039; Miguel A. Zambrano, "Indian Agricultural Cooperative," *Boletín Indigenista* 11, no. 3 (September 1951): 217.

104. "La cooperative Tigua," *Ñucanchic Allpa* 2nd ser., 4, no. 18 (October 5, 1946): 2.

105. Ramón, "La comunidad indígena ecuatoriana," 28.

106. "Conferencia de dirigentes indígenas se reunirá esta noche," *El Comercio,* April 19, 1947, 11.

107. "Día del Indio celebró con interesante programa el Normal 'Juan Montalvo,' " *El Comercio,* April 20, 1947, 3.

108. "Las cotizaciones a la F.E.I.," *Ñucanchic Allpa* 2nd ser., 5, no. 20 (March 1948): 3.

109. "Importancia del próximo Congreso de la Federación de Indios," *Ñucanchic Allpa* 2nd ser., 5, no. 20 (March 1948): 1; Modesto Rivera, Jesús Gualavisí, and Dolores Cacuango, "Convocatoria al Congreso de la Federación Ecuatoriana de Indios," *Ñucanchic Allpa* 2nd ser., 5, no. 20 (March 1948): 4; "Ayer se inauguró el III Congreso de la Federación Ecuatoriana de Indios; Tomó la palabra el Ministro de Previsión," *El Comercio,* April 20, 1948, 12; "Sobre arte indígena," *Surcos,* April 27, 1948, 5, 8. On the Bureau of Indian Affairs, see "Se ha creado Junta de Cuestiones Indígenas," *El Comercio,* October 17, 1947, 3; and Carlos Julio Arosemena, "Junta de Cuestiones Indígenas y Campesinas," *Registro Oficial* 1, no. 25 (October 16, 1947): 230–31.

110. Ejecutivo del Comité Central del Partido Comunista del Ecuador, "Nuestra solidaridad con las luchas del campesinado," *El Pueblo,* August 15, 1953, 5.

111. Santana, *¿Ciudadanos en la etnicidad?* 126.

112. Letter from Federico B. Jarrín, Jefe Político del Cantón Cayambe, to Ministro de Gobierno, Cayambe, November 18, 1947, Oficio no. 204, Ramón Collection.

113. "El partido comunista, vanguardia de la lucha campesina," *El Pueblo,* June 2, 1951, 6; "El XXV aniversario de la fundación del Partido Socialista del Ecuador," *El Pueblo,* June 2, 1951, 7.

114. "Una nueva farsa con los trabajadores agrícolas," *Surcos,* May 29, 1948, 5.

115. Ibid.

116. "Infundada fué la noticia de que rebelión indígena se preparaba en Pesillo," *El Comercio,* May 4, 1948, 12; "Piden sancionar a quienes alarman con rumor de levantamientos indígenas," *El Comercio,* May 5, 1948, 9; "Indígenas de Olmedo reclaman contra el despojo de terrenos que usufructuaban," *El Comercio,* June 2, 1948, 9.

117. Neptalí Ulcuango, interviewed by Mercedes Prieto, July 7–8, 1977, Prieto Collection; Virgilio Lechón, interviewed by Andrés Guerrero on September 8, 1976, Prieto Collection; Virgilio Lechón in Yánez, *Yo declaro con franqueza,* 199, 224; Neptalí Ulcuango in Yánez, *Yo declaro con franqueza,* 226; Luis Catucuamba in

Yánez, *Yo declaro con franqueza*, 229. In 1898 the government had declared these payments voluntary, but the failure to implement this law testifies to the continuing power of the haciendas. See Juan Freile-Granizo, "Leyes Indigenistas: Compilación," *Sarance* 19 (1994): 240.

118. Amauta, "Legislación protectora de indios," *Surcos*, May 29, 1948, 8.

119. "Una nueva farsa con los trabajadores agrícolas," *Surcos*, May 29, 1948, 5. Also see Prieto, "Condicionamientos de la movilización campesina," 67.

120. "Arrendatario de una hacienda impone a los huasipungueros duros trabajos; Presentan reclamación al Ministerio del Ramo," *El Comercio*, September 15, 1949, 8; J. A. Tapia Vargas, "Desmintiendo las calumnias de un comunista," *El Comercio*, September 24, 1949, 8.

121. Dolores Cacuango, "Federación Ecuatoriana de Indios," *El Día*, September 27, 1949, 8; Humberto Navarro, "Confederación de Trabajadores del Ecuador," *El Día*, September 28, 1949, 2.

122. José Antonio Tapia Vargas, "Desplantes del Comunismo Criollo," *El Comercio*, September 28, 1949, 8.

123. Maynard, "Indian-Mestizo Relations," 34. In Australia, Bob Boughton similarly notes that "anti-communist sentiment was more often used to justify attacks on Aboriginal rights." See Boughton, "The Communist Party of Australia's Involvement in the Struggle for Aboriginal and Torres Strait Islander People's Rights," 284.

124. "Levantamiento indígenas," *Surcos*, February 27, 1945, 4.

125. CONAIE, *Nacionalidades indígenas*, 147–48.

5. GUACHALÁ

1. Gow, "Yawar Mayu," 121.

2. See Coronel and Salgado, *Galo Plaza Lasso*.

3. "Congreso extraordinario de la Federación de Indios se inaugurará hoy en el Normal Juan Montalvo," *El Comercio*, November 18, 1950, 18; "Se inauguró el Congreso de la Federación Ecuatoriana de Indios en esta capital," *El Comercio*, November 19, 1950, 13; "Con asistencia del presidente de la república se clausuró el tercer congreso de indígenas," *El Comercio*, November 21, 1950, 14. The FEI leaders also took advantage of this meeting to discuss other organizational matters, including concerns regarding Indigenous education.

4. The growing importance and legitimacy of the FEI was further demonstrated in 1952 when Quito's mayor granted the organization land in the Marín to build a "Casa del Indio" (Indian House) that was to include a lunch room, dormitory,

"and other services fundamental to the welfare, progress, and education of the Ecuadorian Indian." The FEI had been planning this house since its second congress in February 1946, and it was still trying to build it in 1968. See "La Casa del Indio Ecuatoriano," *Ñucanchic Allpa* 2nd ser., 5, no. 20 (March 1948): 4; "La Casa del Indio se construirá en esta ciudad; El Municipio cedió en solar para este objeto," *El Comercio*, July 11, 1952, 7; "Delegación de la FEI denuncia al presidente de la república graves incorrecciones del IERAC otros problemas indígenas," *Ñucanchic Allpa* 3rd ser., 1 (April 18, 1968): 3.

5. "Se inauguró el Congreso de la Federación Ecuatoriana de Indios en esta capital," *El Comercio*, November 19, 1950, 13; "Con asistencia del presidente de la república se clausuró el tercer congreso de indígenas," *El Comercio*, November 21, 1950, 14; "Prodújose ayer levantamiento indígena en Licto y Columbe," *El Comercio*, November 30, 1950, 14. Galo Plaza discusses his efforts to calm Indian fears of the census in *Problems of Democracy in Latin America*, 35 36; also see Clark, "Race, 'Culture,' and Mestizaje." The 1962 agricultural census once again triggered uprisings in the central highlands. See Albornoz Peralta, *Las luchas indígenas*, 87–88. The anthropologist Peter Wogan reports that resistance to censuses in the Indigenous community of Salasaca was so great that the government was unable to complete any of its five censuses during the second half of the twentieth century. See Wogan, *Magical Writing in Salasaca*, 61. For an analysis of issues related to the construction of race, classification of Indigenous peoples, and Indigenous resistance in the context of the 1950 census, see Prieto, "A Liberalism of Fear," 217–32.

6. "La Federación Ecuatoriana de Indios y su VI Congreso," *El Pueblo*, August 16, 1952, 4; "El VI Congreso de la Federación Ecuatoriana de Indios reclama unidad de los trabajadores para conquistar su liberación social y nacional," *El Pueblo*, September 6, 1952, 4; Albornoz Peralta, *Las luchas indígenas*, 116. The reference to this as the sixth congress in *El Pueblo* appears to be an error.

7. "Los terratenientes desatan persecución contra los dirigentes campesinos," *El Pueblo*, May 29, 1954, 6; Neptalí Ulcuango, interviewed by Mercedes Prieto, July 7–8, 1977, Prieto Collection.

8. "Gamonales y autoridades arnistas atropellan a indígenas de Galte," *El Pueblo*, January 10, 1953, 4.

9. "Los campesinos de Galte obtienen gran victoria," *El Pueblo*, August 15, 1953, 5–6; Albornoz Peralta, *Las luchas indígenas*, 77. Also see "Telegrama de Cayambe," *El Pueblo*, September 5, 1953, 8.

10. Ejecutivo del Comité Central del Partido Comunista del Ecuador, "Nuestra solidaridad con las luchas del campesinado," *El Pueblo*, August 15, 1953, 5; "Modesto Rivera exige desde la Cárcel sanción para los asesinos," *El Pueblo*, August 29, 1953, 8;

"Los disturbios en la hacienda La Merced dejaron saldo de 2 muertos y 14 heridos," *El Comercio*, August 8, 1953, 16; "Cura de Píntag y tres sindicados por los sucesos de La Merced rinden declaración," *El Comercio*, August 9, 1953, 19; "Otra victima de disturbios en la hacienda La Merced falleció," *El Comercio*, August 12, 1953, 16; Albornoz Peralta, *Las luchas indígenas*, 77–79; "Continúan atropellos en Hda. La Merced," *El Pueblo*, December 12, 1953, 8; "Ecuador," *Hispanic American Report* (Hispanic American Studies, Stanford University) 6, no. 9 (October 1953): 25.

11. "El latifundio de la Asistencia Pública, terrateniente amenaza incendiar chozas de los indios," *El Pueblo*, March 20, 1954, 6; "En hacienda Pesillo," *El Pueblo*, April 10, 1954, 6; "Victoriosas luchas de los campesinos," *El Pueblo*, November 29, 1958, 6.

12. "Gamonal roba a los indios en Cotopaxi," *El Pueblo*, April 5, 1952, 3.

13. "Desalojo de campesinos en Guamote," *El Pueblo*, May 26, 1956, 4.

14. For a survey of the history of Guachalá, see Emilio Bonifaz's two-part essay "Origen y evolución de una hacienda histórica" in the *Boletin de la Academia Nacional de Historia*, as well as Diego Bonifaz, *Guachalá*, and Ramón's *Resistencia andina*. Documents outlining Guachalá's history are in the Archivo Histórico del Banco Central del Ecuador (hereafter AH / BC), Fondo Neptalí Bonifaz.

15. See, for example, a letter from J. Humberto Correa, Inspector Provincial de Pichincha, to Señor Administrador de la Hacienda "Guachalá," January 5, 1944, AH / BC, 7 / XI / 22.

16. "Lo que los indígenas no dijeron por presión de la policía," *El Pueblo*, January 16, 1954, 6.

17. El Comité Ejecutivo de la Federación Ecuatoriana de Indios, "La Federación de Indios frente a sucesos de Guachalá," *El Pueblo*, January 16, 1954, 6.

18. "Indígenas de hacienda 'Guachalá' obtenen mejoras," *El Pueblo*, October 10, 1953, 5.

19. Interview with Marieta Cárdenas in Salamea, "Transformación de la hacienda y los cambios en la condición campesina," 67.

20. Interview with José Pacheco in Salamea, "Transformación de la hacienda y los cambios en la condición campesina," 68.

21. "Falleció ayer otro indígena víctima de acontecimientos en la hacienda Cayambe," *El Pueblo*, January 13, 1954, 16; César Troya Salazar, "Alrededor de los sucesos registrados en la hacienda 'Guachalá,'" *El Pueblo*, January 15, 1954, 11. Emilio Bonifaz similarly later complained that workers at Guachalá saw hacienda resources as belonging to them. See *Los indígenas de altura del Ecuador*, 71–72.

22. "Falleció ayer otro indígena víctima de acontecimientos en la hacienda Cayambe," *El Pueblo*, January 13, 1954, 16; "Dos indígenas de la hacienda 'Guachalá' fueron muertos por la policía," *El Pueblo*, January 11, 1954, 3. This narrative summary is

extracted largely from mainstream newspaper reports, supplemented with a series of stories in the January 16, 1954, issue of the Communist Party newspaper *El Pueblo*. Both Salamea and Albornoz Peralta briefly describe the uprising, although both fail to provide much detail or interpretation.

23. "Los testigos y sindicados de los sucesos de Guachalá rindieron sus declaraciones," *El Pueblo*, January 12, 1954, 14.

24. "Sindicados por los sucesos de la hacienda Guachalá son enviados a cárcel pública," *El Pueblo*, January 15, 1954, 3.

25. "Masacre en Guachalá," *El Pueblo*, January 16, 1954, 1, 6.

26. El Comité Ejecutivo de la Federación Ecuatoriana de Indios, "La Federación de Indios frente a sucesos de Guachalá," *El Pueblo*, January 16, 1954, 6.

27. "Contra el terror sangriento en los campos," *El Pueblo*, January 23, 1954, 8.

28. Albornoz Peralta, *Las luchas indígenas*, 80–81.

29. Interview with Pompeyo Andrade in Salamea, "Transformación de la hacienda y los cambios en la condición campesina," 69–70.

30. Jaramillo Alvarado, *El indio ecuatoriano*, 197–99.

31. "Lo que los indígenas no dijeron por presión de la policía," *El Pueblo*, January 16, 1954, 6. The injured were Rosa Collago, Cuito Limaico, Luis Quishpe, Pablo Collago, Cruz Collago, Nicolás Quishpe, Rafael Acero, Nicolás Quishpe, Justo Pacheco, Carlos Quishpe, and San Antonio.

32. Ejecutivo del Comité Central del Partido Comunista del Ecuador, "Acompañemos en su ultimo camino al valiente luchador Emilio Quishpe" (Editora Quito, January 16, 1954), Hojas Volantes, 1951–1960, vol. 2, p. 97, BEAEP. Similar language appears in the editorial "¡Contra la explotación feudal, por la tierra para los campesinos!" *El Pueblo*, January 16, 1954, 3.

33. Comité Provincial de Pichincha del Partido Comunista del Ecuador, "Se habla de victima a Pedro Saad, interpelante al Ministro de Gbno" (Editoria Quito, September 1953), Hojas Volantes, 1951–1960, vol. 2, p. 90, BEAEP; Comité Provincial de Pichincha del Partido Comunista del Ecuador, "A cerrar el paso al facsismo y a impedir la explotación del pueblo" (Editorial Quito, September 1953), Hojas Volantes, 1951–1960, t. 2, p. 91, BEAEP.

34. Ponce Enríquez, *Informe a la nación*, 1954, 23, 28–29.

35. "Lo que los indígenas no dijeron por presión de la policía," *El Pueblo*, January 16, 1954, 6. The twelve detainees were Pedro Pacheco, Andrés Pacheco, Justo Pacheco, José Cruz Farinango, Nicolás Pacheco, Miguel Collago, Elías Quishpe, José Manuel Quishpe, Abel Pacheco, Fermín Quishpe, Esteban Collago, and Rubén Rodríguez. In Ecuador, as in most of Latin America, prisons often did not provide meals for inmates but rather relied on families to bring in food from the outside.

36. "Contra el terror sangriento en los campos," *El Pueblo*, January 23, 1954, 8. The PCE and CTE demanded Rodríguez's release. See "Masacre en Guachalá," *El Pueblo*, January 16, 1954, 6; and El Comité Ejecutivo de la CTE, "La C.T.E. respalda a los compañeros de Guachalá," *El Pueblo*, January 16, 1954, 8.

37. "¡Contra la explotación feudal, por la tierra para los campesinos!," *El Pueblo*, January 16, 1954, 3.

38. El Comité Ejecutivo de la CTE, "La C.T.E. respalda a los compañeros de Guachalá," *El Pueblo*, January 16, 1954, 8.

39. Interview with Marieta Cárdenas in Salamea, "Transformación de la hacienda y los cambios en la condición campesina," 67–68.

40. El Comité Ejecutivo de la Federación Ecuatoriana de Indios, "La Federación de Indios frente a sucesos de Guachalá," *El Pueblo*, January 16, 1954, 5–6.

41. J. Orión Llaguno, "Como robaron Guachalá a los indios," *El Universo*, January 14, 1954.

42. "Guachalá: Proeza de los sanguinarios," *Surcos*, February 1954, 4.

43. Interview with Marieta Cárdenas in Salamea, "Transformación de la hacienda y los cambios en la condición campesina," 67.

44. Interview with Pompeyo Andrade in Salamea, "Transformación de la hacienda y los cambios en la condición campesina," 69, 176.

45. Interview with Marieta Cárdenas in Salamea, "Transformación de la hacienda y los cambios en la condición campesina," 67–68.

46. "Victoriosas luchas de los campesinos," *El Pueblo*, November 29, 1958, 6.

47. Comité Ejecutivo de la Federación de Trabajadores de Pichincha, "Respaldemos la huelga de la Hda. San Antonio" (Quito, September 16, 1958), Hojas Volantes, 1951–1960, t. 2, p. 244, BEAEP.

48. "Trabajadores exijen la parcelación de las haciendas de la Asistencia Pública," *El Pueblo*, October 20, 1956, 4.

49. "Tierras de la Asistencia Pública deben ser parceladas," *El Pueblo*, August 23, 1952, 1.

50. Rodas Morales, *Dolores Cacuango*, 158; Rodas Morales *Nosotras que del amor hicimos*, 85.

51. "Manifiesto del Partido Comunista del Ecuador en el VIII aniversario del protocolo del Río de Janeiro" (Quito, January 29, 1950), Hojas Volantes, 1946–1950, t. 1, p. 253, BEAEP; "El XXV aniversario de la fundación del Partido Socialista del Ecuador," *El Pueblo*, June 2, 1951, 7. Also see "El protocolo de Río de Janeiro y el Partido Comunista del Ecuador," *Surcos*, November 15, 1943, 4.

52. Comité Ejecutivo del Partido Comunista del Ecuador, "El Partido Comunista frente al problema electoral" (Quito, May 17, 1948), Hojas Volantes, 1946–1950, p. 154, BEAEP; Comité Central del Partido Comunista del Ecuador, "El Partido

Comunista y el gobierno de Plaza-Sotomayor" (Quito, September 1, 1948), Hojas Volantes, 1946–1950, p. 172, BEAEP.

53. PCE, *Por la paz por la democracia y el progreso,* 29, 31, 35–36, 39.

54. Merlo Vasquez, *Informe a la nación, 1958,* 17; Tad Szulc, "Reds in Ecuador Accused of Plot," *New York Times,* May 15, 1959, 4.

55. Guerrero Arias, *El saber del mundo de los condores,* 53.

56. PCE, *Documentos IX Congreso,* 114.

57. Ramón, "La comunidad indígena ecuatoriana," 28.

58. "Democracia, independencia y bienestar para el pueblo del Ecuador (Programa inmediato del Partido Comunista del Ecuador)," *El Pueblo,* December 22, 1956, 3–5; and PCE, *Proyecto de programa inmediato del Partido Comunista del Ecuador.*

59. "Conferencia campesina de Pichincha, Imbabura y Cotopaxi," *El Pueblo,* May 6, 1957, 6.

60. PCE, *Democrácia, independencia y paz para el pueblo del Ecuador,* 14. Also see Albornoz Peralta, "Sobre algunos aspectos del problema indígena," 64.

61. Saad, "Sobre la alianza obrero campesina," 52–56. For a critical analysis of Saad's position, see Ramón, "La comunidad indígena ecuatoriana," 26–27. Cf. Mariátegui, "The Indigenous Question in Latin America," 37. Emerging out of a similar situation, militant Indians in Chile similarly formed a National Federation of Peasants and Indians with the encouragement of leftists to fight for agrarian reform and other concerns. See Foerster and Montecino Aguirre, *Organizaciones, líderes y contiendas mapuches,* 299.

62. Cueva, *The Process of Political Domination in Ecuador,* 48.

63. Aguirre, *Informe al XX Congreso del Partido Socialista Ecuatoriano.* In fairness, this document may have been drafted before the massacre and in advance of the congress.

64. Aguirre, *Teoría y acción socialistas,* 19, 20.

65. Jorge Rivadeneyra, "Victoria campesina en Pichincha," *El Pueblo,* April 2, 1960, 6.

66. "Los trabajadores de Chaupi han presentado un reclamo," *El Pueblo,* February 7, 1959, 7; "Victoria de los trabajadores de Chaupi-Muyurco," *El Pueblo,* February 21, 1959, 7.

67. "Liquidemos el feudalismo," *El Pueblo,* February 17, 1952, 4.

68. Comité Central del PCE, *Por un gobierno democrático al servicio del pueblo,* 9.

6. AGRARIAN REFORM?

1. "Ecuador," *Hispanic American Report* (Hispanic American Studies, Stanford University) 13, no. 8 (August 1960): 546. Steve Striffler discovered through oral life

histories that no one present during a strike at Tenguel remembered cheering for Cuba and Russia, and that the press intentionally reported the protests as such in order to delegitimize them as the work of outside agitators. See Striffler, "Communists Communists Everywhere!" Anti-communism has commonly been used to justify attacks on aboriginal rights; see Boughton, "The Communist Party of Australia's Involvement in the Struggle for Aboriginal and Torres Strait Islander People's Rights," 284. On the other hand, forty years later the Indigenous organization Ecuarunari championed both Hugo Chavez's Bolivarian Revolution in Venezuela as it took an increasingly socialist turn as well as the Indigenous socialist Evo Morales's electoral victory in Bolivia, recognizing each of these events as the embodiment of subaltern aspirations throughout Latin America. See, for example, Humberto Cholango, "ECUARUNARI respalda revolución bolivariana: En Venezuela está en juego el futuro de los pueblos que luchan por su soberanía," Quito, August 12, 2004, http://www.ecuarunari.org/ven12ago4.html; and Patricio Zhingri T., "El triunfo de Evo Morales en Bolivia es el triunfo de los movimientos sociales y del movimiento indígena," Quito, December 19, 2005, http://www.ecuarunari.org/19dico5.html. Such statements point to the continuing importance of leftist roots and alliances for many Indigenous movements.

2. "Trabajadores de Hda. Atapo presentaron pliego de peticiones," *El Comercio,* October 20, 1960, 24; "Pliego de peticiones presentan trabajadores de Hda. Quinchocajas," *El Comercio,* October 21, 1960, 16.

3. "500 indígenas atacaron la hacienda Carrera, Cayambe," *El Comercio,* December 20, 1960, 25; "Jefe de la Policía informa que hay normalidad en la Hda. Carrera," *El Comercio,* December 21, 1960, 32.

4. "Comuneros vecinos a Hda. La Clemencia tomaron posesión de las tierras," *El Comercio,* January 28, 1961, 12; "Demanda reinvindicatoria de la Hcda. La Clemencia se tramita," *El Comercio,* February 9, 1961, 20; "Grupo de campesinos intentó invadir la hacienda Villanueva," *El Comercio,* February 9, 1961, 20; "Campesinos acusados de asaltar hacienda están presos: Gquil.," *El Comercio,* February 11, 1961, 12; CEDEP, *Luchas campesinas,* 14; Vela Monsalve, *Las tácticas del comunismo,* 50.

5. See Striffler, "Communists Communists Everywhere!" 107–20; and Striffler, *In the Shadows of State and Capital,* 94–104.

6. Barsky, *La reforma agraria ecuatoriana,* 329; Cordero Crespo, *Informe a la nación, 1959,* 3–5; Crespo Ordoñez, *Informe a la nación, 1960,* 1–3; Baquero de la Calle, *Informe a la nación, 1960–1961,* 14–17. Uggen similarly lists twenty-six strikes and land invasions, many of them organized with the support of the PCE, from 1960 to 1963; see Uggen, "Peasant Mobilization in Ecuador," 173, 178–79.

7. Ecuarunari, *Historia de la nacionalidad y los pueblos quichuas,* 24.

8. Albornoz Peralta, *Las luchas indígenas*, 117–23.

9. Muñoz Vicuña, *Historia del movimiento obrero del Ecuador*, 52; Redclift, *Agrarian Reform and Peasant Organization in the Ecuadorian Coast*, 114–16.

10. Saad, *La reforma agraria democratica*, 106; Saad, "Sobre la alianza obrero campesina," 52–53.

11. "Hoy instálase acto público de Reunión Nacional Campesina," *El Comercio*, October 15, 1960, 9.

12. "Resolución de la Primera Conferencia Nacional Campesina," October 16, 1960, Prieto Collection.

13. "CTE formuló proyecto sobre reforma agraria," *Surcos*, December 1960, 4; "Primera Conferencia Nacional de Campesinos inauguróse ayer," *El Comercio*, October 16, 1960, 3; "Conferencia campesina propone bases para la Reforma Agraria Ncnal.," *El Comercio*, October 24, 1960, 2.

14. "Senado recibió a delegados de la Conferencia Nacional de Campesinos del Ecuador," *El Comercio*, October 18, 1960, 3.

15. "CTE formuló proyecto sobre reforma agraria," *Surcos*, December 1960, 4.

16. "2.000 indígenas se amotinaron: Columbe," *El Comercio*, February 6, 1961, 1, 10; "Agitadores están azuzando a los indígenas en Columbe, dice Ministro de Gobierno," *El Comercio*, February 7, 1961, 28; "Solicitan a Ministro de Gobierno libertad de varios indígenas," *El Comercio*, February 8, 1961, 28; "63 indígenas están presos por levantamiento: Columbe," *El Comercio*, February 9, 1961, 28; "FTP demanda investigación imparcial de sucesos con campesinos de Chimborazo," *El Comercio*, February 11, 1961, 2; "Amplia investigación sobre levantamiento indígena de Columbe está realizándose," *El Comercio*, February 11, 1961, 12; "Establécese que dos indígenas murieron en alzamiento-Columbe," *El Comercio*, February 12, 1961, 28; "Dr. Velasco ordenó libertad de indígenas presos por el levantamiento de Columbe," *El Comercio*, February 13, 1961, 1, 10; Erickson et al., *Area Handbook for Ecuador*, 145–46; Albornoz Peralta, *Las luchas indígenas*, 84–87.

17. El Frente AntiComunista Ecuatoriano, "Columbe, primer tanteo para el push comunista de este año" (Quito: La Prensa Católica, 1961), Hojas Volantes, 1951–1960, p. 398, BEAEP.

18. Baquero de la Calle, *Informe a la nación, 1960–1961*, xxv.

19. División de Estadística y Censos, *Primer censo agropecuario nacional*. For an analysis of the agrarian census, see Saunders, "Man-Land Relations in Ecuador."

20. "Trabajadores exijen parcelacion de la Asistencia Pública," *El Pueblo*, October 20, 1956, 4. Paola Sylva Charvet lists twelve such agrarian reform proposals between 1940 and 1962 in *Gamonalismo y lucha campesino*, 93.

21. "Trabajadores exijen parcelacion de la Asistencia Pública," *El Pueblo*, October 20,

1956, 4. Also see "A la parcelación de haciendas de la Asistencia Pública para sus propios trabajadores," *El Pueblo,* October 20, 1956, 1, 3; "Trabajadores agrícolas piden la parcelacion de haciendas," *La Tierra,* October 19, 1956; and "La FTP solicita al Congreso aprobar el decreto de parcelación de la haciendas de la Asistencia Pública," *Diario del Ecuador,* October 23, 1956.

22. Aguirre, *Teoría y acción socialistas,* 28, 33.

23. For example, see "Ley de tierras baldías y colonización," Decreto no. 223, *Registro Oficial* 1, no. 187 (May 12, 1936): 112–20.

24. Jaramillo, *El indio ecuatoriano,* 198; Salamea, "Transformación de la hacienda y los cambios en la condición campesina," 66–76; Salamea, "La transformación de la hacienda y los cambios en la condición campesina," 261–62; Guerrero, *Haciendas, capital y lucha de clases andina,* 137; Bonifaz, "Guachalá, pt. II, " 347; Ramón, "Cayambe," 167; Zamosc, *Peasant Struggles and Agrarian Reform,* 14; Barsky, *Reforma agraria,* 72–78.

25. Velasco, *Reforma agraria y movimiento campesino indígena de la sierra,* 82.

26. Barsky, *Reforma agraria.* Also see the various essays collected in Guerrero, *De la economía a las mintalidades;* and *Haciendas, Capital y lucha de clases andina.* Chiriboga's essay "La reforma agraria en el Ecuador y América Latina," 30–36, is a good short introduction to agrarian reform debates. Also see Leon Zamosc, *Peasant Struggles and Agrarian Reform.*

27. Velasco, *Reforma agraria,* 77.

28. Ibid., 82.

29. Zamosc, *Peasant Struggles and Agrarian Reform,* 19.

30. Guerrero, *Haciendas, capital y lucha de clases andina,* 99, 139.

31. Gangotena, "Peasant Social Articulation and Surplus Transference," 88–89. Also see Sylva, *Gamonalismo y lucha campesino,* 162.

32. Albornoz Peralta, "Jesús Gualavisí," 181.

33. Saad, *La nueva ley de reforma agraria del Ecuador,* 48–49.

34. Ulcuango, "Antecedentes," 8–9.

35. Douglass, *Frederick Douglass,* 367.

36. PCE, *Manifiesto del Partido Comunista del Ecuador sobre las elecciones de 1960,* 3, 7, 13.

37. Velasco Ibarra quoted in Gerassi, *The Great Fear in Latin America,* 144.

38. Uggen, "Peasant Mobilization in Ecuador," 171, 178.

39. "Ecuadorean Chief Is Reported Out," *New York Times,* November 8, 1961, 1, 14; Paul P. Kennedy, "Arosemena Takes Oath in Ecuador," *New York Times,* November 10, 1961, 1, 3.

40. Guerrero, *Haciendas, capital y lucha de clases andina,* 97. In a related article, Guerrero discusses changes in ethnic identity in Ecuador from this march to the 1990

Indigenous levantamiento. See Guerrero, "La desintegración de la administración étnica en el Ecuador."

41. "III Congreso de Federación Ecuatoriana Indigenista se inaugura hoy en esta ciudad," *El Comercio,* December 16, 1961, 1, 14; "Grandiosa marcha de la Reforma Agraria y el III Congreso de la F.E.I.," *El Comercio,* December 16, 1961, 19; El Comité Ejecutivo Nacional, La Comision Nacional Campesina de la CTE, "III Congreso de la Federación Ecuatoriana de Indios y Gran Concentración de la Sierra para exigir la Reforma Agraria Radical y Democrática," *Mañana,* December 7, 1961, 2.

42. "Cooperan para Tercer Congreso de Federación Ecuatoriana Indígena," *El Comercio,* December 12, 1961, 15.

43. "FTP respalda a los campesinos que vendrán a Congreso," *El Comercio,* December 15, 1961, 3.

44. "III Congreso de Federación Ecuatoriana Indigenista se inaugura hoy en esta ciudad," *El Comercio,* December 16, 1961, 1, 14.

45. "Ecuador," *Hispanic American Report* (Hispanic American Studies, Stanford University) 15, no. 1 (January 1962): 56; "El Dr. Arosemena expone su decisión de actuar para la eliminación de huasipungos," *El Comercio,* December 17, 1961, 1, 3.

46. "El problema indígena," *El Comercio,* December 17, 1961, 4.

47. "La Camara de Agricultura de la I Zona," *El Comercio,* December 16, 1961, 18.

48. Galarza Zavala, *El yugo feudal,* 173.

49. Linke, "Ecuador's Politics," 65.

50. See El Comité Ejecutivo Nacional de la Confederación de Trabajadores del Ecuador, "Tierra para los campesinos," *Mañana,* December 14, 1961, 19.

51. As evidence of the numbering being a simple clerical error, the 1952 congress had also erroneously been reported as the sixth. See "La Federación Ecuatoriana de Indios y su VI Congreso," *El Pueblo,* August 16, 1952, 4.

52. Miguel Lechón in Yánez, *Yo declaro con franqueza,* 184.

53. "Prepárase Proyecto de Ley de Emergencia; Se liquidará el problema de huasipungos," *El Comercio,* December 19, 1961, 1, 13; "Elaborado el proyeco de decreto ley de emergencia para abolir el huasipungero," *El Comercio,* December 27, 1961.

54. Barsky, *Reforma agraria,* 136.

55. "C. de Diputados discutió en primera proyecto de Ley de supresión de huasipungo," *El Comercio,* September 7, 1962, 1, 12. Also see Barsky, *Reforma agraria,* 130–34.

56. Uggen, "Peasant Mobilization in Ecuador," 182.

57. Comite Ejecutivo de la Confederación de Trabajadores del Ecuador; Comité Ejecutivo de la Federación Ecuatoriana de Indios, "Los terratenientes desatan la

violencia contra los campesinos" (Quito, February 28, 1962), Hojas Volantes, 1961–1970, p. 110, BEAEP.

58. El Consejo Provincial de URJE del Chimborazo, "Al pueblo ecuatoriano" (1962), Hojas Volantes, 1961–1970, p. 187, BEAEP.

59. "Boletín de la Federación Ecuatoriana de Indios," *El Pueblo*, May 12, 1962, 7; Crespi, "Patrons and Peons, 185.

60. Contrato de arrendamiento a Aquiles Jarrín Espinosa, Quito, February 28, 1913, Archivo National de Historia (hereafter ANH), Quito, Ecuador, EP / P3a, vol. 161, t. 1, 228.

61. Peloso, *Peasants on Plantations*, 130–31.

62. "C. de Diputados discutió en primera proyecto de Ley de supresión de huasipungo," *El Comercio*, September 7, 1962, 1, 12; Albornoz Peralta, *Las luchas indígenas*, 88–90; Poeschel-Renz, "*No quisimos soltar el agua.*"

63. "La tierra y el hombre," *El Comercio*, September 8, 1962, 4.

64. Martínez, *Yo siempre he sido Nela Martínez Espinosa*, 113–21; Martínez, "Dolores Cacuango."

65. "Junta militar asume el poder," *El Comercio*, July 12, 1963, 1. The *New York Times* and the socialist newspaper *Weekly People* noted that Arosemena's drinking was just an excuse, and the coup had been planned in advance because of his failure to take action against "terrorism and Communist-inspired subversion." See Richard Eder, "Ecuador's Junta Seeks Brief Rule," *New York Times*, July 14, 1963, 21; "U.S. Likes Ecuador 'Revolution,' " *Weekly People*, July 27, 1963, 1.

66. Movimiento ARNE, Jefatura de Información, "Panorama Actual del Comunismo en el Ecuador," June 6, 1963, 1, Partido Comunista. Misc. 1, BEAEP.

67. Kofas, "The IMF, the World Bank, and U.S. Foreign Policy in Ecuador, 1956–1966," 73.

68. Uggen, "Peasant Mobilization in Ecuador," 241.

69. "Las autoridades continúan en tarea de aislar a los comunistas en todo el país," *El Comercio*, July 15, 1963, 1, 8; "La Junta Military declara fuera de Ley al comunismo," *El Comercio*, July 19, 1963, 1, 3; Striffler, "Communists Communists Everywhere!" 107–20; Striffler, *In The Shadows of State and Capital*, 109. To date, 1979–1997 is the longest period of constitutional rule, and it came to an end when popular protests forced Abdala Bucaram, a populist leader much like Velasco Ibarra, from power.

70. "Ley de Reforma Agraria y Colonización," Decreto Supremo No. 1480, *Registro Oficial* 297 (July 23, 1964).

71. Ibid., 24.

72. IERAC, *Historia de un arrimado*. Also see IERAC, *Historia de un Huasipunguero*.

73. Uggen, "Peasant Mobilization in Ecuador," 209–10.

74. Redclift, *Agrarian Reform*, 26–27.

75. Thiesenhusen, "Land Reform in Latin America," 211.

76. Velasco, *Reforma agraria*, 98; Redclift, *Agrarian Reform*, 166.

77. "Prodújose levantamiento de indígenas en la hacienda El Chaupi del Cantón Cayambe," *El Comercio*, August 4, 1964, 24; "Indígenas que se levantaron en El Chaupi tornaron a sus labores," *El Comercio*, August 5, 1964, 28; "Se denució un posible paro de actividades en 5 haciendas en Cayambe," *El Comercio*, August 7, 1964, 28.

78. "El campesinado exige la parcelación de las haciendas estatales," *El Pueblo*, January 19, 1957, 4.

79. Junta Nacional de Planificación y Coordinación Económica, *Solicitud de crédito no. 1–63 que el Gobierno del Ecuador presenta al Banco Interamericano de Desarrollo para al recolonización de las haciendas*.

80. Escobar, "La FEI," 48–49.

81. Guaña, Camino, and Ulco, *Inti Raymi Cayambi*, 116; Neptalí Ulcuango, interviewed by Mercedes Prieto, July 7 and 8, 1977, Prieto Collection.

82. Ramón, "La comunidad indígena ecuatoriana," 77.

83. Rodas Morales, *Tránsito Amaguaña*, 38.

84. Uggen, "Peasant Mobilization in Ecuador," 235.

85. "Iniciose Congreso de Federación de Indios," *El Comercio*, October 22, 1966, 17; "Congreso de Federación de Indios del país pide escuelas y colegios," *El Comercio*, October 22, 1966, 12; El Comité Ejecutivo, "La Federación Ecuatoriana de Indios (FEI) al país," *El Comercio*, November 3, 1966, 1, 10. Following the numbering of the 1961 meeting, FEI called this their fourth congress rather than the more proper sixth.

86. "Indígenas habríanse levantado," *El Comercio*, November 10, 1966, 14; "No hubo muertos en el levantamiento de indígenas de Colta," *El Comercio*, November 11, 1966, 48.

87. "La Federación de Indios pide reorganización y fiscalización de IERAC," *El Comercio*, October 29, 1966, 14; "Indígenas de Pesillo tratan de posesionarse de varias haciendas," *El Comercio*, October 29, 1966, 14.

88. "Vigilancia policial y aérea por temor de un levantamiento indígenas," *El Comercio*, October 30, 1966, 3; "Dos dirigentes de Fed. de Indios fueron detinidos, pero luego salieron libres," *El Comercio*, October 31, 1966, 16.

89. "Peligro de levantamiento indígena en Pisambilla," *El Comercio*, November 1, 1966, 11; "Federación de Indios informa ocupación militar de Cayambe," *El Comercio*, November 1, 1966, 13; El Comité Ejecutivo, "La Federación Ecuatoriana de Indios (FEI) al país," *El Comercio*, November 3, 1966, 1, 10. For an example of the glowing press reports on IERAC's advances in Cayambe that appear aimed at undermining

leftist political activity, see "La distribución de tierras de Pesillo realízase con éxito," *El Comercio,* November 3, 1966, 1, 14; and "IERAC completa programa de integración campesina y social en hacienda Pesillo," *El Comercio,* November 6, 1966, section 3, 2.

90. Herrán quoted in Tibán, Llaquiche, and Alfaro, *Historia y proceso organizativo,* 48.

91. "Solidaridad de los obreros con los campesinos e indios," *El Pueblo,* March 23, 1968, 4; "La CTE, la FEI, la FTAL y la campaña rabiosa de los directivos de IERAC," *El Pueblo,* April 6, 1968, 6.

92. "FEI entierra al IERAC," *El Pueblo,* May 11, 1968, 9.

93. Sylva, *Gamonalismo y lucha campesino,* 126–27. See also Gangotena, "Peasant Social Articulation and Surplus Transference," 76.

94. Conflicto de Trabajo Hcda "San Pablo-Urco" (1968), Prieto Collection.

95. Galarza, *Los campesinos de Loja y Zamora,* 117, 173–74.

96. Whitten, *Sacha Runa,* 268.

97. Saad, *La realidad agropecuaria del Ecuador,* 79–81.

98. Chiriboga, "Los programas de desarrollo económico y social y la población indígena," 125.

99. FENOC, "La situación de los campesinos en el país," 376–77.

100. Rodas Morales, *Tránsito Amaguaña,* 37.

101. Ibarra, *Los indígenas y el estado en el Ecuador,* 97–98.

7. RETURN OF THE INDIAN

1. Ecuarunari, *Historia de la nacionalidad y los pueblos quichuas,* 70–76; López Cando, Martínez Espinoza, and Castillo Castillo, *Pilahuín,* 96.

2. Crespi, "St. John the Baptist," 478.

3. Albó, "El retorno del Indio," 299–345.

4. Almeida and Prieto, "Modalidades organizativas," 36.

5. Pallares, *From Peasant Struggles to Indian Resistance,* 43.

6. Belote and Belote, "Drain from the Bottom," 45.

7. Botero, *Movilización indígena, etnicidad y proceso de simbolización en Ecuador;* Ecuarunari, *Historia de la nacionalidad y los pueblos quichuas,* 75–76.

8. CONAIE, *Nacionalidades indígenas,* 195. The Peruvian theologian Gustavo Gutiérrez was the first to articulate a basis for identifying with popular struggles. See his *Theology of Liberation.*

9. Pallares, *From Peasant Struggles to Indian Resistance,* 151.

10. Chiriboga, "Transformaciones Agrarias," 125; Almeida and Prieto, "Modalidades organizativas," 36.

11. Rodas Morales, *Tránsito Amaguaña*, 39.

12. Gualle, "FEI." Indeed, this period did see a growing rural-urban migration.

13. CEDEP, *Viva la huelga*, 6.

14. Neptalí Ulcuango in Yánez, *Yo declaro con franqueza*, 176.

15. CEDEP, *Luchas campesinas*, 12. The same argument is made in CONAIE, *Nacionalidades Indígenas*, 213. Also see Galarza Zavala, "La vida misma," 96.

16. For an example, see Comité Central del Partido Comunista del Ecuador, "Adelante hacia otras victorias decisivas (Manifiesto del Partido Comunista del Ecuador)" (Guayaquil: Editorial Huancavilca, March 31, 1966), Hojas Volantes, 1885–1973, p. 142, BEAEP.

17. "Septuagésimo cumpleaños del c. Ricardo Paredes," *El Pueblo*, March 2, 1968, 2; "Homenaje del Partido al Camarada Ricardo Paredes," *El Pueblo*, March 23, 1968, 2, 8.

18. "Homenaje a Ricardo Paredes al cumplir 70 años de edad y al dejar su labor de Cayambe," Prieto Collection.

19. PCE, *Programa y estatutos*, 12, 38.

20. Rivera, "El caso del Portento," 75.

21. Bonilla, *En busca del pueblo perdido*, 34, 72. In the 1930s the left had already been divided into communist, socialist, and vanguardist wings representing different histories and traditions.

22. Fiallo and Ramón, *Lucha de las comunidades indígenas del cantón Pujilí*, 5.

23. Aymara, *¿Cuál es la vía revolucionaria en el Ecuador?* 4–5.

24. "Vuelve Ñucanchic Allpa para defender a las masas campesinas del Ecuador," *Ñucanchic Allpa* 3rd ser., 1 (April 18, 1968): 6.

25. Miguel Lechón, "La FEI denuncia las atrocidades del IERAC," *Ñucanchic Allpa* 3rd ser., 1 (April 18, 1968): 1–3.

26. "Delegación de la FEI denuncia al presidente de la república graves incorrecciones del IERAC otros problemas indígenas," *Ñucanchic Allpa* 3rd ser., 1 (April 18, 1968): 3.

27. Richard F. Staar et al., eds., *Yearbook on International Communist Affairs* (1970), 291.

28. Roseberry, "Beyond the Agrarian Question in Latin America," 323.

29. Ecuarunari, *Historia de la nacionalidad y los pueblos quichuas*, 352.

30. Neptalí Ulcuango, interviewed by Mercedes Prieto, July 7 and 8, 1977, Prieto Collection.

31. "La Federación Ecuatoriana de Indios F.E.I. Frente a la Reforma Agraria y los cambios de estructura, Plataforma de Lucha," *El Pueblo*, July 29, 1972, 8, 7. See the electronic appendix http://www.yachana.org/indmovs/ for a copy of this document.

32. FEI, *Estatutos*, 3.

33. El Comité Ejecutivo, "La Federación Ecuatoriana de Indios (FEI) al país," *El Comercio*, November 3, 1966, 1, 10.

34. Lindqvist, *The Shadow*, 120. Lindqvist describes the leader (whom he does not name but probably was Bolívar Bolaños) as "a lawyer with Indian features, but speaking only Spanish."

35. "Cayambe: Terrateniente burla acta transaccional," *El Pueblo*, July 22, 1972, 7; "Federación Ecuatoriana de Indios," *El Pueblo*, August 12, 1972, 1; "Boletin de la FEI: Mision Andina quiere arrebatar tierras comunales," *El Pueblo*, September 23, 1972, 6; "La FEI saluda a los indígenas en su día," *El Comercio*, April 19, 1973, 10.

36. PCE, *Documentos IX Congreso*, 66–67, 108.

37. Albornoz Peralta, *Las luchas indígenas*, 125.

38. Galarza Zavala, *El yugo feudal*, 32, 173.

39. Tibán, *Historia y proceso organizativo*, 47–48.

40. CONAIE, *Nacionalidades indígenas*, 32.

41. Young, *The Politics of Cultural Pluralism*, 459. Young also notes that these are human constructions; "Society probably does tend to become what men think that it is."

42. Escobar, "La FEI," 49.

43. Andrés Guerrero is an exception in pointing to the FEI as a "notable" precursor that led "important mobilizations and accomplished significant gains in land during the agrarian reform program." See Guerrero, "Poblaciones indígenas, ciudadanía y representación," 103.

44. León, "Las organizaciones indígenas," 381, 382–83.

45. Zamosc, *Peasant Struggles and Agrarian Reform*, 12.

46. Pallares, *From Peasant Struggles to Indian Resistance*, 150.

47. "La operaciones del comunismo," *El Comercio*, November 6, 1966, section 3, 1.

48. Chiriboga, "Transformaciones agrarias," 125.

49. Garaycoa and Veintimilla, "Defending Democracy and Fighting for the Working People's Rights," 97.

50. Maugé, "Las tareas actuales de nuestro movimiento," 229, 232.

51. Since its founding in 1966, the *Yearbook on International Communist Affairs* had mentioned the FEI every year. Its last mention in 1978 observed the increasing unimportance of the organization to the PCE. Staar, *Yearbook on International Communist Affairs* (1978), 374.

52. Escobar, "La FEI," 48–49.

53. "Denuncian ataque físico a dirigente indígena: C.T.E.," *El Comercio*, August 24, 1983.

54. "Tres haciendas fueron invadidas en Cayambe," *El Tiempo*, October 22, 1983; "Dos

funcionarios del IERAC secuestrados," *Hoy,* October 27, 1983; "Comuneros de Cayambe secuestraron a dos funcionarios del IERAC," *El Comercio,* November 27, 1983.

55. Albornoz Peralta, "Jesús Gualavisí," 182.

56. FEI, *VII Congreso Federación Ecuatoriana de Indios;* FEI, *Por una F.E.I. poderosa y combativa.*

57. FEI, *VIII Congreso Ordinario,* 1–2, 8–9.

58. Ecuarunari-CONAIE, "Lineamientos políticos generales del movimiento indígena en el Ecuador," 40.

59. Ecuarunari, *Historia de la nacionalidad y los pueblos quichuas,* 24, 25.

60. Edelman, *Peasants Against Globalization,* 35.

61. Ecuarunari, *Historia de la nacionalidad y los pueblos quichuas,* 24.

62. CONAIE, *Nacionalidades indígenas,* 149.

63. Salazar, "The Federación Shuar and the Colonization Frontier," 593–94; Also see Federación de Centros Shuar, *Federación de Centros Shuar.*

64. Brysk, *From Tribal Village to Global Village,* 68.

65. CONAIE, *Nacionalidades indígenas,* 45–55; Perreault, "Shifting Ground," 190–258; Wilson, "Indigenous Federations, NGOs, and the State," 106–38.

66. Ricardo Paredes, interviewed by Mercedes Prieto on July 7, 1977, Prieto Collection.

67. Galarza Zavala, *Los campesinos de Loja y Zamora,* 34.

68. CONAIE, *Nacionalidades Indígenas,* 203, 207, 214.

69. Gualle, "FEI," 42.

70. FENOC, *FENOC y la movilización campesina,* 42.

71. Barsky, *La reforma agraria,* 222.

72. Santana, *¿Ciudadanos en la etnicidad?* 127–28.

73. Tatamuez, "FENOC," 39.

74. *Informe del 5to. Congreso Nacional de la FONOC* (Quito, Oct. 1977), reprinted in FENOC, "La situación de los campesinos en el país," 381.

75. Andrango, "Contra la discriminación y la pobreza," 50–51.

76. Ecuarunari, *Historia de la nacionalidad y los pueblos quichuas,* 49.

77. CONAIE, *Nacionalidades indígenas,* 128.

78. ALAI, "CONAIE," 9.

79. Ecuarunari, *Historia de la nacionalidad y los pueblos quichuas,* 354.

80. Ibid., 52.

81. Ibid., 367.

82. CONAIE, *Nacionalidades indígenas,* 149.

83. Federación Pichincha Riccharimui, *500 años de resistencia indígena y popular,* 3.

84. Mullo, "El movimiento indígena en la provincia de Pichincha," 33; Federación Pichincha Riccharimui, *500 años de resistencia indígena y popular*, 3.

85. Mullo, "El movimiento indígena en la provincia de Pichincha," 35; Ecuarunari, *Historia de la nacionalidad y los pueblos quichuas*, 70–76; López Cando, Martínez Espinoza, and Castillo Castillo, *Pilahuín*, 96.

86. "Noticiero Indigenista," *América Indígena* 37, no. 1 (January-March 1977): 211–12.

87. Pallares, *From Peasant Struggles to Indian Resistance*, 82–82; Ecuarunari, *Historia de la nacionalidad y los pueblos quichuas*, 83–84.

88. "Un poco indígena y un poco clasista." Marcía Silva de Acosta, "Ecuador: ¿Un estado multnacional?" *El Comercio*, July 11, 1989.

89. Ron Proaño, "Las movilizaciones campesinas en Ecuador," 13.

90. Pallares, *From Peasant Struggles to Indian Resistance*, 211.

91. Ecuarunari, "El movimiento campesino indígena," 45, 46.

92. Ibid., 50, 48.

93. Ramón, "Estado plurinacional," 9.

94. Federación Pichincha Riccharimui, *500 años de resistencia indígena y popular*, 3.

95. Santana, "El caso de Ecuarunari," 35; Santana, *Campesinado indígena y el desafío de la modernidad*, 166.

96. "Sin vacilaciones reforma agraria democrática," *El Pueblo*, August 19, 1972, 1; "El FURA y la reforma agraria," *El Pueblo*, September 2, 1972, 10; "FURA del Chimborazo," *El Pueblo*, September 30, 1972, 8.

97. "Gigantesca concentración campesina por la reforma agraria democrática (Guayaquil)," *El Pueblo*, June 9, 1973, 5–6; "Las luchas obreras, campesinas, y populares," *El Pueblo*, July 14, 1973, 4; FENOC, *FENOC y la movilización campesina*, 21; CEDEP, *Luchas campesinas*, 23.

98. CEDEP, *Luchas campesinas*, 16. Activists never seemed to question the usefulness of a national federation, although a historical argument could be built that such centralization makes movements more susceptible to co-optation.

99. Ecuarunari, "El movimiento campesino indígena 'Ecuarunari,' " 44.

100. Federación Pichincha Riccharimui, *500 años de resistencia indígena y popular*, 7.

101. FENOC, "Manifiesto campesino"; FENOC, "Consejo Nacional de la FENOC"; CONAIE, *Nacionalidades indígenas*, 220.

102. CONAIE, *Nacionalidades indígenas*, 220–21; Macas, "Los Saraguros," 56; CEDEP, *Luchas campesinas*, 44.

103. Ecuarunari, *Historia de la nacionalidad y los pueblos quichuas*, 110.

104. "Corto mensaje en quichua dirigió presidente Roldós," *El Comercio*, August 11, 1979, A16. The Indigenous organization Ecuarunari criticized Roldós's symbolic

action as a reactionary ploy to halt the growing leftist influence on Indigenous movements. See Ibarra, *Los indígenas y el estado en el Ecuador,* 108–9 n.41.

105. "El pueblo salio, Roldos se escondió," *Lucha Campesina* 11 (November 1980): 6–7; CEDEP, *Luchas campesinas,* 31–32; Ecuarunari, *Historia de la nacionalidad y los pueblos quichuas,* 98–103; "Parlamento recibió a concentración de campesinos de FENOC," *El Comercio,* October 18, 1980.

106. Albó, "Andean People in the Twentieth Century," 832.

107. Ecuarunari-CONAIE, "Lineamientos políticos generales del movimiento indígena en el Ecuador," 41.

108. "Primer Encuentro Unitario Campesino-Indígena," *Lucha Campesina* 17 (May 1982): 6–9; CEDEP, *Luchas campesinas,* 44.

109. "Acuerdos de la Segunda Convención Nacional Campesina e Indígena," *Lucha Campesina* 34 (July 1984): 4–5; "Forman coordinadora campesina indígena," *Hoy,* July 17, 1984. In the late 1980s, FENOC still called for the formation of an organization alternatively called the Coordinadora Nacional Campesino-Indígena (National Peasant-Indigenous Coordinating Body) or the Central Unica Campesina (United Peasant Central). See FENOC, "Organizaciones," 52.

110. "Tercer Encuentro de Organizaciones Campesinas," *El Mercurio* (Cuenca), July 25, 1985.

111. Warren, "Socialist Saudades," 227.

112. Degregori, "Ethnicity and Democratic Governability in Latin America," 204.

8. PACHAKUTIK

1. Macas, *Levantamiento indígena,* 3.

2. Jacobsen, *Mirages of Transition,* 240. Because Kichwa was an Indigenous language transcribed into Western script, this word has several alternate spellings, most notably *pachacuti.* "Pacha" means time or land, and "kutik" return to; hence, the word implies a return in time or a cultural rebirth. See Perreault, "Development Identities," 409.

3. Ossio, "Cosmologies," 556.

4. Beck and Mijeski, "Barricades and Ballots."

5. Whitten, *Millennial Ecuador,* x.

6. Roper, Perreault, and Wilson, "Introduction," 6.

7. Buechler, "New Social Movement Theories," 441, 442.

8. Hellman, "The Riddle of New Social Movements"; Edelman, *Peasants Against Globalization,* 19–20.

9. CEDEP, *Viva la huelga,* 34.

10. Guerrero and Ospina, *El poder de la comunidad,* 26–27; CONAIE, *Nacionalidades indígenas,* 99; Martin, *The Globalization of Contentious Politics,* 91.

11. "Pueblos indios seguimos existiendo," *Hoy,* April 13, 1984.

12. Ecuarunari-CONAIE, "Lineamientos políticos generales del movimiento indígena en el Ecuador," 42.

13. CONAIE, *Nacionalidades indígenas,* 261.

14. "II Encuentro de Nacionalidades Indígenas," *Punto de Vista* 3, no. 137 (May 2, 1984): 4.

15. Pallares, *From Peasant Struggles to Indian Resistance,* 179.

16. Ibid., 199.

17. Kuznesof, "Ethnic and Gender Influences," 168.

18. Pallares, *From Peasant Struggles to Indian Resistance,* 182. A century earlier, W. E. B. Du Bois similarly wrote of a double consciousness of "two souls, two thoughts, two unreconciled strivings" within African descendants in the United States that divided their identities while they tried to merge their double selves "into a better and truer self." See Du Bois, *The Souls of Black Folk,* 11.

19. CONAIE, *Nacionalidades indígenas,* 269–72.

20. "Hoy primera marcha unitaria por 10 de mayo," *Hoy,* May 1, 1987.

21. Ibarra, *Los indígenas y el estado en el Ecuador,* xiv, xxv.

22. Fander Falconi, "El reto histórico de las nacionalidades," *Hoy,* November 17, 1988.

23. CONAIE, *Nacionalidades indígenas,* 223, 261, 281.

24. Zamosc, "The Indian Movement in Ecuador," 132.

25. Selverston-Scher, *Ethnopolitics in Ecuador,* 102.

26. Roper, Perreault, and Wilson, "Introduction," 10–11. In a dissenting view, Roberto Santana argues that CONAIE weakened Indigenous movements by utilizing class-based strategies to advance an ethnic agenda. See Santana, "Actores y escenarios étnicos en Ecuador."

27. Villavicencio, *Relaciones interétnicas en Otavalo-Ecuador,* 6, 283.

28. Almeida, "Consideraciones sobre la nacionalidad Kechwa," 15–16.

29. Almeida, "La cuestión indígena como cuestión nacional," 26.

30. Sánchez Parga, "Etnia, estado y la 'forma' clase," 59; Sánchez Parga, *Presente y futuro de los pueblos indígenas,* 82. Also see Sánchez Parga, ed., *Etnia, poder y diferencia en los andes septentrionales.*

31. "Actas de la Asamblea Nacional Constituyente de 1944," vol. 1, 720 (August 22, 1944), APL.

32. PCE, *Democrácia, independencia y paz para el pueblo del Ecuador,* 14. See Saad, "La cuestión agraria," in *Obras escogidas,* 9; and Saad, "Sobre la alianza obrero campesina," 53.

33. César Endara in Yánez, *Yo declaro con franqueza,* 27.

34. FADI, *Documentos del proceso de constitución del Frente Amplio de la Izquierda de Ecuador (FADI) y primera declaración pública.*

35. "El campesinado indígena y el estado," 8. Also see Fiallo and Ramón, *La lucha de las comunidades indígenas del cantón Pujilí,* 10.

36. CEDIS and CEDOC, *XIV Congreso Nacional CEDOC,* 47.

37. Quintero, "La cuestión de la tierra," 120.

38. FENOC, "Organizaciones," 49.

39. Santana, *¿Ciudadanos en la etnicidad?* 46–47, 264.

40. For example, see Guerrero and Ospina, *El poder de la comunidad,* 26.

41. Viteri, "Los pueblos de la Amazonía se unen," 46.

42. CONAIE, *Nacionalidades Indígenas,* 116.

43. Perreault, "Shifting Ground," 225; Perreault, "Development Identities," 394.

44. Karakras, "Las nacionalidades indias y el estado ecuatoriano," 106.

45. Lucero, "Arts of Unification," 200.

46. CONAIE, "Anteproyecto de ley de nacionalidades indígenas del Ecuador, 1988," 202–12. For an examination of how the constructions "nacionalidades indias" and "pueblos indígenas" subsequently evolved, see Guerrero and Ospina, *El poder de la comunidad,* 186.

47. CONAIE, "500 años de resistencia india," 117.

48. Santana, *¿Ciudadanos en la etnicidad?* 281.

49. Selverston-Scher, *Ethnopolitics in Ecuador,* 10.

50. CONAIE, "500 años de resistencia india," 118.

51. Sawyer, "The 1992 Indian Mobilization," 78.

52. Lucero, "Locating the 'Indian Problem,'" 36, 34; Lucero, "Arts of Unification," 172.

53. FEI, *VII Congreso Federación Ecuatoriana de Indios,* 10–11, 5.

54. FEI, *VIII Congreso Ordinario,* 2–3.

55. Ramón, "Política e interculturalidad indígena," 216–18.

56. Black, *The Making of an Indigenous Movement,* 38–39.

57. Smith, "Conclusion," 282–83.

58. "Constitución Política de Ecuador, 1998," http://www.georgetown.edu/pdba/Constitutions/Ecuador/ecuador98.html.

59. "Levantamiento indígena prepara CONAIE," *Punto de Vista* 9, no. 418 (May 21, 1990): 5; Macas, *Levantamiento indígena,* 16; Almeida, "El levantamiento indígena como momento constitutivo nacional," 17.

60. "Uprising in Ecuador," *SAIIC Newsletter* 5, no. 3–4 (December 1990): 19. Also see the special issue "Victorioso levantamiento indígena," *Punto de Vista* 9, no. 421 (June 11, 1990).

61. Ramón, *Actores de una década ganada.*

62. Zamosc, "Agrarian Protest and the Indian Movement," 62.

63. Several different versions of the "sixteen points" exist, and some of them are collected in the electronic appendix (http://www.yachana.org/indmovs/).

64. "Evaluación del levantamiento indio: Cuidado con el buey manso," *Punto de Vista* 9, no. 424 (July 2, 1990): 7.

65. Healy, "Allies and Opposition Groups to the 1990 Indigenous Political Mobilizations in Ecuador and Bolivia," 20.

66. "Ayuno en templo de Santo Domingo: 'Ni una hacienda en el 92,'" *Punto de Vista* 9, no. 421 (June 11, 1990): 4–5; Field, "The Land Issue in the Ecuadorian Highlands," 17.

67. Meisch, "We Will Not Dance on the Tomb of Our Grandparents," 58.

68. Dubly and Granda, *Desalojos y despojos*.

69. Santana, *¿Ciudadanos en la etnicidad?* 65.

70. Macas, *Levantamiento indígena*, 10.

71. "Evaluación del levantamiento indio: Cuidado con el buey manso," *Punto de Vista* 9, no. 424 (July 2, 1990): 6.

72. "Noticiero Indigenista," *América Indígena* 51, no. 2–3 (April-September 1991): 377.

73. "Recuperan tierras del antepasados," *Punto de Vista* 9, no. 419 (May 28, 1990): 5.

74. León, "Versiones de los protagonistas," 124; Black, "The Making of an Indigenous Movement," 163.

75. Sawyer, "The 1992 Indian Mobilization," 68.

76. "Evaluación del levantamiento indio: Cuidado con el buey manso," *Punto de Vista* 9, no. 424 (July 2, 1990): 6.

77. "Suspendido diálogo entre la CONAIE y el gobierno," *Punto de Vista* 9, no. 424 (July 2, 1990): 4.

78. Black, *The Making of an Indigenous Movement*, 31; Macas, *Levantamiento indígena*, 12.

79. Coordinadora Popular, "Manifiesto a la opinión pública," *Punto de Vista* 9, no. 417 (May 14, 1990): 9.

80. Black, "The Making of an Indigenous Movement," 134–35.

81. Schroder, "Ethnic Identity and Non-Capitalist Relations of Production in Chimborazo, Ecuador," 136. As one example of this marginalization, Indigenous participation in labor strikes is almost entirely ignored in CEDEP, *Viva la huelga*.

82. Ibarra, "Los indios del Ecuador y su demanda frente al Estado," 79.

83. PCE, *Por la reconstitución histórica de la izquierda*, 14. Also see Staar, *Yearbook on International Communist Affairs* (1991), 80.

84. Macas, *Levantamiento indígena*, 16.

85. "Iglesia de Riobamba apoya levantamiento indio," *Punto de Vista* 9, no. 423 (June 25, 1990): 5.

86. "El encuentro continental de pueblos indios y las libertades que persigue," *El Pueblo*, July 23–29, 1990, 8.

87. "Somos raíces y aquí estamos luchando," *El Pueblo*, July 23–29, 1990, 8.

88. "El porque de la ingobernabilidad," *Nacionalidades Indias*, April 1994, 1.

89. CONAIE, *Declaration of Quito*; Draper, "Minga in Ecuador."

90. "Diálogos: mucho ruido, pocos resultados," *Punto de Vista* 11, no. 513 (April 6, 1992): 2.

91. "A un año del levantamiento indígena," *Punto de Vista* 10, no. 470 (May 27, 1991): 8.

92. "24 horas en el interior del Congreso," *Punto de Vista* 10, no. 471 (June 3, 1991): 8–11.

93. "Por 500 años: Presencia y movilización indígena y popular," *Punto de Vista* 12, no. 540 (October 13, 1992): 12–13.

94. Field, "Ecuador's Pan-Indian Uprising," 43.

95. SAIIC, "March on Quito: Amazon Indians Demand to be Heard," *SAIIC Newsletter* 6, no. 3 (spring-summer 1992): 4–7; SAIIC, "Ecuador Government Refuses to Fulfill Their Promise to Amazon Marchers," *Urgent Action Bulletin*, May 13, 1992, South and Meso American Indian Rights Resource Library (SAIIC), Oakland, California; "11 de abril, marcha indígena: Por tierra y dignidad," *Punto de Vista* 11, no. 513 (April 6, 1992): 8–10; "Marcha indígena: ¡Adelante!" *Punto de Vista* 11, no. 515 (April 20, 1992): 8–13; "Misión cumplida," *Punto de Vista* 11, no. 516 (April 27, 1992): 8–12; Veilleux, "Ecuador"; Sawyer, "The 1992 Indian Mobilization"; Sawyer, *Crude Chronicles*, 27–56; Whitten, Whitten, and Chango, "Return of the Yumbo."

96. "Indios presentaron reformas constitucionales," *Punto de Vista* 11, no. 517 (May 4, 1992): 3.

97. Sawyer, "The 1992 Indian Mobilization," 77, 65.

98. CONAIE, *Proyecto político*, 31.

99. The new law is published in INDA, "Reglamento organico y funcional del Instituto Nacional de Desarrollo Agrario." The alternative proposal is published in CAN, *Proyecto de ley agraria integral*. For a summary of the uprising from one of its leaders, see Macas, "La ley agraria y el proceso de movilización por la vida." Also see Sawyer, *Crude Chronicles*, 149–81; and Treakle, "Ecuador."

100. Karakras, "CONACNIE," 48.

101. José Sánchez-Parga, "¿Por qué no votan los indígenas?" *Hoy*, September 22, 1991; Chiriboga and Rivera, "Elecciones de Enero de 1988 y participación indígena."

102. Andrango, "Como indígenas tenemos nuestros planteamientos políticos," 294–95. Amalia Pallares explores this complicated relationship between Indigenous organizations and the political left in Cotacachi in *From Peasant Struggles to Indian Resistance*, 72–109. In Bolivia, the formation of Indigenous parties achieved mini-

mal electoral success, seemingly reinforcing Andrango's argument that it was better to work in coalition with existing leftist parties rather than creating new ones. See Calla Ortega, "Hallu hayllisa huti." Indigenous-based political parties for the first time made a significant impact in Bolivia in 2002, seemingly reflecting a broader regional shift in Indigenous political participation. See Van Cott, "From Exclusion to Inclusion"; and Van Cott, *From Movements to Parties in Latin America*.

103. "Gobierno del FADI asegurará la tierra al que la trabaja, dijo René Maugé en Cayambe," *El Pueblo*, December 9–15, 1983; Vicente Olmedo, "Afirma el primer legislador indígena, 'No soy un diputado folklórico': Manuel Naula," *Hoy*, December 10, 1984.

104. CONAIE, *Nacionalidades indígenas*, 176. The local Indigenous leader Alberto Andrango makes the same points in "Como indígenas tenemos nuestros planteamientos políticos."

105. Albó, "Andean People in the Twentieth Century," 832.

106. ALAI, "La CONAIE," 9. Also see Ecuarunari, *Historia de la nacionalidad y los pueblos quichuas*, 147, 357.

107. Maldonado, "CONAIE," 93; Maldonado, "Indígenas y elecciones 1992," 306.

108. Karakras, "CONACNIE," 48.

109. "Participación en elecciones provoca controversia indígena," *Punto de Vista* 11, no. 517 (May 4, 1992): 7–10; Maldonado, "Indígenas y elecciones 1992," 305.

110. Lucas, *We Will Not Dance on Our Grandparents' Tombs*, 118. For more on Pachakutik, see their Web sites at http://www.pachakutik.org.ec/ and http://www.diputadospk.org/.

111. Lucas, *We Will Not Dance on Our Grandparents' Tombs*, 5.

112. Tillería, "Andrés Guerrero redefine el Estado-Nación," 11. Also see Andolina, "The Sovereign and Its Shadow."

113. Torre, "Populism and Democracy"; Barrionuevo Silva, *Constituyente de los pueblos*; Gerlach, *Indians, Oil, and Politics*, 81–113; Andolina, "The Sovereign and Its Shadow."

114. Walsh, "The Ecuadorian Political Irruption"; Lucas, *We Will Not Dance on Our Grandparents' Tombs*; O'Connor, "Indians and National Salvation"; Salots Galarza, ed., *La rebelión del arcoiris*; Gerlach, *Indians, Oil, and Politics*, 163–203; Fitch, "Post-Transition Coups."

115. Moore, *Social Origins of Dictatorship and Democracy*, 480.

116. Lucero, "Crisis and Contention in Ecuador," 67.

117. Larry Rohter, "Bitter Indians Let Ecuador Know Fight Isn't Over," *New York Times*, January 27, 2000, A3.

118. Gerlach, *Indians, Oil, and Politics*, 201.

119. Chiriboga, "El levantamiento indígena ecuatoriano de 2001"; and García, "¿Un levantamiento indígena más?"

120. Simbaña, "Lecciones de marzo y julio."

121. Becker, "Ecuador," 1.

122. Dávalos, "Movimiento indígena ecuatoriano," 112; Dávalos, "Ecuador," 28.

123. Lucas, *We Will Not Dance on Our Grandparents' Tombs*, 44.

124. See http://www.feine.org.ec/; and Jarrín Cuvi, "Protestantism, the Indigenous, and Political Participation in Ecuador."

125. Imbaquingo, "Ecuarunari," 45.

126. García and Lucero, "'Un País Sin Indígenas,'" 159. See Lyons, *Remembering the Hacienda*, 210, for other examples of multiple responses to oppression.

127. Healy, "Allies and Opposition Groups," 1–3.

128. Luis Macas, "Foreword," in Selverston-Scher, *Ethnopolitics in Ecuador*, xiii.

129. ALAI, "La CONAIE: Un paso a la autodeterminación," 10.

130. Andrango, "Como indígenas tenemos nuestros planteamientos políticos," 252.

131. Black, *The Making of an Indigenous Movement*, 29.

132. CONAIE, *Proyecto político*, 14, 27.

133. Mariátegui, "The Problem of the Indian," in *Seven Interpretive Essays on Peruvian Reality*, 22.

134. CONAIE, *Proyecto político*, 5.

135. Bulnes, *Me levanto y digo*, 61–62.

136. Zamosc, "The Indian Movement in Ecuador," 144, 145. In a manner similar to how Joan Scott argues that gender is not synonymous with women, increasingly academics have come to see that ethnicity is not synonymous with Indigenous, and it is not the presence of ethnic identities that makes Ecuador such a fascinating case study. See Scott, "Gender," 1054. An argument similar to the one that Anne McClintock makes "that feminism is as much about class, race, work and money as it is about sex" can be made that Indigenous movements are as much about power as culture. See McClintock, *Imperial Leather*, 7.

137. Pacari, "Taking on the Neoliberal Agenda," 25, 24.

138. CONAIE, *Proyecto político*, 7.

139. Ibarra, *Los indígenas y el estado en el Ecuador*, xxvi.

140. Federación Pichincha Riccharimui, "Hacia el XII Congreso de la Federación Pichincha Riccharimui!"

141. CONAIE, *Nacionalidades indígenas*, 136, 143.

142. Ibarra, *Los indígenas y el estado en el Ecuador*, 246.

Glossary

(Kichwa terms are in italics)

Apegado Literally "stuck-on," a landless person often living alongside a road. This term included Indigenous workers who assisted with the harvest on a hacienda and, in exchange, were allowed to collect leftovers in the field from the harvest and sometimes received a small cash payment for their services.

Arrimado An Indian who did not have a labor contract with the hacienda, but lived with a relative who did and helped cultivate that person's huasipungo plot. This person was obliged to help with tasks on the hacienda, and earned a small wage for doing so.

Campesino Literally a person from the countryside (*campo*), usually indicating someone (often an Indian) who works the land for a living. Campesino is sometimes translated into English as "peasant."

Chagra A small plot of farmland, usually belonging to an Indian or mestizo.

Chagracama A person assigned the duty of protecting a hacienda's crops from birds and other predators. Often an Indian who was injured, too young, or too old and could not work in the fields; a chagracama was liable for any crop losses.

Comuna Established by a 1937 law, comuna refers to a community that held resources (often pasture land and water) communally.

Concertaje A system of contracted debt that held Indian laborers (conciertos) to a hacienda under threat of prison. Conciertos received access to a small plot of land in exchange for their labor, and their children inherited their debts. In essence, the Indigenous laborers become property of the hacienda owner and would be purchased and sold together with the hacienda. This system was outlawed in 1918, but in essence it continued in the huasipungo system.

Concierto A person, usually an Indian, who contracted the debt in the system of concertaje.

Cuentayo A person, usually an Indian, who cared for the animals on a hacienda, and whose work included milking the cows, taking the animals to pasture, and other tasks related to the care of livestock. Possibly derived from the Spanish *cuenta*, meaning to account for livestock on the hacienda. Also sometimes called a *huagracama*.

Diezmos A theoretically voluntary 10 percent tithe on crops, animals, and other products that the Spanish crown and later the Catholic Church charged the Indians as a tax.

Doctrina Basic religious instruction that landowners imparted to their Indian workers.

Faena An assigned task for an agricultural worker on a hacienda.

Gamonal A derogatory term imported from Peruvian indigenistas for a large landholder or local boss.

Hacendado The owner of a hacienda, also sometimes called an *amo* or *patrón* by the Indians.

Hacienda A landed estate, usually in the highlands, dedicated to production for an internal market. Also called *latifundio*.

Huasicama From the Kichwa *huasi* (house) and *cama* (keeper), a domestic servant who took care of household duties in the house of the hacienda owner, either on the hacienda or in the city.

Huasipungo The service tenancy relationship that bound Indian workers to a hacienda after the abolishment of concertaje in 1918. Huasipungo also refers to the small plot of land that an Indian was allowed to use on the hacienda. Sometimes spelled *guasipungo,* this is a Kichwa term comprised of *huasi* (house) and *pungo* (door), but its roots have been lost.

Huasipunguero The Indian who contracted a debt with a landowner within the huasipungo system. This person had access to a small plot of land in exchange for working on the hacienda.

Indigenismo Ideology of white, urban intellectuals (called indigenistas) who paternalistically sought to implement assimilationalist policies that they believed would help Indians.

Indio suelto An Indian who occasionally worked as a day laborer on a hacienda for a cash wage, but was not bound to the hacienda. Also called a *peón libre.*

Jefe político A representative of the central government on a regional cantonal level who was often white or mestizo and performed a variety of judicial and administrative duties.

Jornalero A day laborer on a hacienda who was paid a small wage in cash and sometimes with food.

Kichwa The language of most Indians in the Ecuadorian highlands, also known as Runa Shimi (the language of people). Traditionally spelled "Quichua," and part of the large Quechua Andean language group.

Mayordomo Usually a mestizo who supervised the day-to-day agricultural work on a hacienda.

Mestizo A person who represented a mixing of European and Indigenous cultures and often played the role of broker between white and Indigenous worlds.

Minga Communal work party organized for public works projects.

Montuvio Poor mestizo peasants on the coast who tended to be mobile, migrating among export-oriented plantations during harvests and to urban areas in search of employment.

Obraje Colonial textile workshop, notorious for extremely abusive working conditions.

Pachakutik A cosmic reversal, a revolution.

Páramo High-altitude pasture lands.

Parroquia A civil parish, the most local administrative division in Ecuador, with the larger units being cantons and provinces.

Patrón Landowner, master. See hacendado.

Peón Peon; unskilled worker or field laborer.

Peón libre An Indian who occasionally worked as a day laborer on a hacienda for a cash wage but was not bound to the hacienda. Also called a *peón suelto* or *indio suelto.*

253

Primicias A theoretically voluntary contribution of the first fruits of a harvest that the church charged the Indians.

Quichua See *Kichwa*.

Raya A line or hatch mark in a hacienda accounting book that represented one day of labor for a worker.

Sindicato Syndicate, peasant union.

Socorro A loan that a concierto or huasipunguero received from a hacendado to cover expenses related to an illness, wedding, or funeral.

Suplido An advance of goods such as clothing, food, or seed received by a huasipunguero from a hacienda owner and charged against future wages or service.

Tawantinsuyu Land of four quarters, the Inka name for their empire

Tarea An assigned task for an agricultural worker on a hacienda, remunerated on a piecework basis.

Teniente político A representative of the central government on a local parroquia level who was often white or mestizo and performed a variety of judicial and administrative duties.

Tinterillos Semiprofessional or petty lawyers who exploited their privileged position to mediate legal or cultural conflicts in rural communities.

Biographies

Alba, Amadeo (1928–?). An Indigenous leader from the cooperative "Atahualpa" on the Pesillo hacienda in Cayambe. He attended Neptalí Ulcuango's bilingual school and became involved in political struggles from a young age. In the early 1960s, he traveled to Cuba where he studied for a month and met with revolutionary leaders. He was repeatedly imprisoned for his actions as a communist and peasant leader in Cayambe.

Alba, Ignacio. A leader in the early organization of syndicates on the Pesillo hacienda in the 1920s, and later a leader of the cooperative at San Pablourco.

Albamocho, Juan. A leader from Pucará on the Pesillo hacienda in the 1920s and 1930s. He was particularly combative, and the landlords often selected him for repressive acts, including evicting him from his huasipungo in April 1931.

Alfaro, Eloy (1842–1912). A military general who led a liberal revolution that placed him in power on June 5, 1895. He began a process of liberal reforms that included the confiscation of church-owned lands and the secularization of education. He was overthrown in a military coup in 1911 and assassinated in Quito on January 28, 1912.

Alvaro, Luis F. A secretary-general of the Comité Central de Defensa Indígena, a participant in the founding of the FEI, and an alternative to Ricardo Paredes for the position of functional representative for the Indigenous race to the 1944 National Assembly. As secretary-general of the FEI in 1946, he worked closely with President Jesús Gualavisí.

Amaguaña, Tránsito (1909–). A principal Indigenous leader from La Chimba in northern Cayambe. In 1931, she was evicted along with her family from their house in Pesillo.

She went to live in Yanahuaico and later moved to La Chimba when she married Manuel Túqueres. She spent her entire life organizing strikes, unions, and bilingual schools.

Arosemena Monroy, Carlos Julio (1919–2004). Velasco Ibarra's vice president in 1960 who took power when the president resigned in 1961, only subsequently to be overthrown himself in a 1963 military coup. Although he gained some leftist and peasant support, he was unable to implement their primary demand of agrarian reform.

Bolaños Sánchez, Luis Bolívar. A lawyer from Quito and a member of the Central Committee of the PCE. He was also the organizational secretary of the CTE and the secretary-general of the FEI in the 1960s, during which time he worked closely with President Miguel Lechón.

Bonifaz Jijón, Emilio (1914–1994). The eldest son of Neptalí Bonifaz and the owner of the Guachalá hacienda in the 1950s. He initiated a process of landlord-guided agrarian reform, and he was an amateur sociologist who wrote racist books about the Indians on his hacienda.

Bonifaz Ascásubi, Neptalí (1870–1952). The owner of the Guachalá hacienda at the height of its operations, the founder of the Central Bank, and a presidential candidate in 1931.

Cacuango, Dolores (1881–1971). One of the first Indigenous leaders from Cayambe and a founder and president of the FEI. Cacuango was born at San Pablourco on the Pesillo hacienda, and at the age of fifteen she was sent to Quito to work as a domestic worker for the hacienda owner. The contrast she observed in the lifestyles between the landholders and peons led her to dedicate her life to struggle for Indigenous rights. She never had an opportunity to attend school and never learned to read and write, but she struggled to assure that others would have that opportunity. Under her guidance, the first Indigenous bilingual schools were established in Cayambe. During the May 1944 Revolution, she led an assault on the army base in Cayambe. She was a communist leader and suffered imprisonments and other abuses because of her political activities.

Catucuamba Cacuango, Luis (1924–). An Indigenous leader and the son of Dolores Cacuango. He taught at the Yanahuaico Indigenous school from 1945 until 1963 when a military coup shut down the independent bilingual schools.

Chávez Obregón, Luis Felipe (1882–1938). A socialist lawyer who supported Indigenous struggles in Cayambe in the 1930s and provided housing in Quito.

Chávez Molineros, Luis Fernando (1909–?). A son of Luis Felipe Chávez who helped organize the 1931 Primer Congreso de Organizaciones Campesinos in Cayambe. Often called Luis F. Chávez (hijo).

Daquilema, Fernando (1845?–1872). The leader of an 1871 revolt at Chimborazo.

Delgado, José Rafael. A renter of the Pesillo hacienda from 1921 until the government resumed direct administration in 1945.

Egas, Augusto. The director of the Junta Central de Asistencia Pública in the 1930s.

Escobar, Manuel. A leader of cooperatives at Pesillo in the 1960s who was elected president of the FEI in 1972.

Gómez de la Torre, Luisa María (1887–1976). A militant in the PCE, AFE, and the FEI, and a teacher who helped found bilingual schools in Cayambe in the 1940s.

Gualavisí, Jesús (1867–1962). Born on the Changalá hacienda in the parroquia of Juan Montalvo, Gualavisí organized the first peasant syndicate in Cayambe in 1926. He was the only Indigenous representative at the founding of the Ecuadorian Socialist Party in 1926, and became actively involved in communist politics. He helped found the FEI in 1944 and served as its first president.

Gualle Bonilla, Estuardo. The secretary-general of the FEI in the 1970s and 1980s.

Jaramillo, Juan Genaro (1895–1958). A socialist lawyer from the 1920s and 1930s who helped early Indigenous activists in Cayambe.

Jarrín Espinosa, Aquiles. A civic leader in Cayambe and a renter of the Pesillo hacienda from 1913–1921.

Lasso, Ambrasio (1905–1970). The leader of an uprising on the Pull hacienda in Chimborazo in 1935. Subsequently he served as the leader of the Peasant Syndicate of Galte and led a successful 1968 strike that won salaries and access to land.

Lechón, Miguel (1922–?). An Indigenous leader from Cayambe and the president of the FEI from 1961 to 1971. He was also a member of the PCE and he traveled to Cuba in 1962 for the third anniversary of the revolution. He administered the Rumiñahui Cooperative on the Moyurco hacienda after agrarian reform in the 1960s.

Lechón, Virgilio (1904–1985). An Indigenous leader who was repeatedly imprisoned for his political actions. He had a huasipungo in Chaupi on the Pesillo hacienda but was evicted for leading a strike in 1931. After living in Yanahuaico and Cariacu, he later acquired another huasipungo in Moyurco.

Macas, Luis (1950–). A Saraguro from southern Ecuador who served as president of CONAIE and as a deputy to the National Assembly in the 1990s.

Maldonado Estrada, Luis. A socialist leader who supported Indigenous movements in the 1920s and 1930s. He later served as secretary-general for the PSE and as a delegate to the National Assembly.

Martínez, Nela (1912–2004). A writer and member of the PCE since 1934, Martínez edited the *Ñucanchic Allpa* newspaper for the FEI, founded the AFE, and led the 1944 May Revolution. She worked closely with Dolores Cacuango and Luisa Gómez de la Torre in Indigenous struggles and bilingual education programs.

Muñoz, Leonardo J. (1898–1988). A founder of the Socialist Party and the owner of a bookstore in Quito.

Narváez Duque, Colón. A member of the CTE executive committee, an advisor to the FEI in the 1960s, and a representative to the agrarian reform agency IERAC.

Pacheco León, Neptalí. A coastal peasant leader and member of the Communist Party.

Páez, Julio Miguel. A renter of the Moyurco and San Pablourco haciendas from 1921 to 1945 and an ally with José Rafael Delgado against Indigenous organizations.

Paredes, Angel Modesto. A lawyer, professor, author, and politician, he was a founder of the Socialist Party and a brother of Ricardo Paredes.

Paredes, Ricardo (1898–1979). A medical doctor and journalist from Riobamba. Paredes helped found the Ecuadorian Socialist Party in 1926. He was a delegate to the sixth congress of the Communist International in the Soviet Union in 1928. In 1931 he converted the PSE into the Ecuadorian Communist Party. He served as its secretary-general for more than twenty years, and he edited the newspapers *La Antorcha*, *El Pueblo*, and others. He was a presidential candidate for the Communist Party several times and served in the 1944–1945 National Assembly as the Functional Representative for the Indigenous Race. He maintained personal contacts with Indigenous leaders in the canton of Cayambe and helped found the FEI in 1944.

Perugachi, Juan José (1900–?). Founder of the town of Olmedo, where he was the Teniente Político and the secretary of the Tenencia Política.

Rivadeneyra Altamirano, Jorge. A 1960s guerrilla leader who supported Indigenous movements at Pesillo and elsewhere.

Rivera, Modesto. A member of the PCE since the early 1930s, he became secretary-general of the FEI in 1948 and secretary of Peasant and Indian Organizations for the CTE in the 1950s. He was a close collaborator with Dolores Cacuango in defending Indigenous rights.

Rodríguez, Carlos. An urban communist supporter of the FEI in the 1960s.

Rodríguez Mera, Rubén (1904–1973). A teacher and a local communist leader in Cayambe. Rodríguez was a member and president of Cayambe's municipal council. He also ran unsuccessfully several times for the position of deputy in the national congress. He was a strong supporter of Indigenous rights and helped found the FEI. Like other leaders, he was imprisoned for his political activism.

Saad Niyaim, Pedro Antonio (1909–1982). A lawyer from Guayaquil, he was a founder of the CTE, functional representative for coastal workers in the National Assembly in the 1940s and 1950s, and secretary-general of the PCE from 1952 until 1981.

Saez, Alejo (1866–1909). An Indigenous leader born in Licto, Chimborazo. In 1884, he led a rebellion against diezmos and in 1895 he joined Eloy Alfaro's liberal revolution. In reward for his support of the revolution, Alfaro named him to the rank of general.

Ulcuango, Neptalí (1921–). An Indigenous leader and educator who founded an Indian school on the Pesillo hacienda in 1945. He was the secretary for the teniente político in Olmedo under the Velasco Ibarra administration in 1948 and again in 1952–1954.

Vega, Agustín. A leader of the Tigua cooperative in Cotopaxi in the 1940s, and a founder of the FEI.

Velasco Ibarra, José María (1893–1979). A perennial populist president who managed to complete only the third of five terms in office (1934–1935, 1944–1947, 1952–1956, 1960–1961, 1968–1972).

Bibliography

ARCHIVES

Archivo General del Ministerio de Gobierno, Quito

Archivo Histórico del Banco Central del Ecuador, Fondo Bonifaz (AH / BC), Quito

Archivo Nacional de Historia (ANH), Quito

Archivo Nacional de Medicina del Museo Nacional de Medicina "Dr. Eduardo Estrella,"
Fondo Junta Central de Asistencia Pública (JCAP), Quito

Archivo Palacio Legislativo (APL), Quito

Biblioteca Ecuatoriana Aurelio Espinosa Pólit (BEAEP), Cotocollao

Centro Documentación Abya-Yala (Abya-Yala), Quito

Dirección Nacional de Desarrollo Campesino (DNDC), Ministerio de Agricultura, Quito

National Archives Records Administration (NARA), College Park, Maryland

Private Collection of Leonardo J. Muñoz, Quito

Private Collection of Mercedes Prieto, Quito

Private Collection of Galo Ramón, Quito

South and Meso American Indian Rights Resource Library (SAIIC), Oakland, California

PERIODICALS

América Indígena (Instituto Indigenista Interamericano, Mexico)

Boletín Indigenista (Instituto Indigenista Interamericano, Mexico)

Foreign Relations of the United States (Washington, U.S. Government Printing Office)

Hispanic American Report (Hispanic American Studies, Stanford University, 1948–1964)

BIBLIOGRAPHY

Lucha Campesina (FENOC, Federación Nacional de Organizaciones Campesinas, Quito)

Nacionalidades Indias (CONAIE, Confederación de Nacionalidades Indígenas del Ecuador, Quito)

Punto de Vista (CEDIS, Centro de Estudios y Difusión Social, Quito)

Registro Oficial (Quito)

SAIIC Newsletter (SAIIC, South and Meso American Indian Information Center, Oakland, California)

NEWSPAPERS

La Antorcha (Quito)

Campamento (Quito)

El Comercio (Quito)

Diario del Ecuador (Quito)

El Día (Quito)

Frente Obrero (Quito)

Germinal (Quito, Guayaquil)

La Hoz (Quito)

New York Times (New York)

Ñucanchic Allpa (Quito)

Mañana (Quito)

El Mercurio (Cuenca)

El Pueblo (Guayaquil, Quito)

Surcos (Federación de Estudiantes Universitarios del Ecuador, Quito)

El Tiempo (Quito)

La Tierra (Quito)

El Universo (Guayaquil)

La Vanguardia (Quito)

Weekly People (New York)

INTERVIEWS

Lino Alba, interviewed by Andrés Guerrero on September 9, 1976.

Tránsito Amaguaña, interviewed by Mercedes Prieto on November 26, 1977.

Tránsito Amaguaña, interviewed by Andrés Guerrero on September 17, 1976.

Dolores Cacuango, interviewed by María Luisa Gómez de la Torre, 1968, 1974.

Luis Catucuamba, interviewed by Mercedes Prieto on August 6, 1977.

María Luisa Gómez de la Torre, interviewed by Mercedes Prieto on October 11, 1976.

Virgilio Lechón, interviewed by Mercedes Prieto on March 4, 1978.

Virgilio Lechón and María Clotilde Tarabata, interviewed by Andrés Guerrero on September 8, 1976.

Nela Martínez, interviewed by Marc Becker on April 27, 1996, Quito.

Ricardo Paredes, interviewed by Mercedes Prieto on April 13 and 20, 1977, and July 7 and 14, 1977.

Neptalí Ulcuango, interviewed by Mercedes Prieto on July 7 and 8, 1977.

Juan José Perugachi, Secretario de la Tenencia Política de Olmedo, interviewed by Mercedes Prieto on October 27, 1976.

Juez Político de Cayambe, interviewed by Mercedes Prieto on October 19, 1976.

BOOKS AND ARTICLES

Agencia Latinoamericana de Información (ALAI). "La CONAIE: Un paso a la autodeterminación." *Agencia Latinoamericana de Información* 2nd ser., 9, no. 88 (February 1987): 9–11.

Aguilar Vazquez, A. *Informe a la nación, 1941.* Quito: Imprenta del Ministerio de Gobierno, 1941.

Aguirre, Manuel Agustín. *Informe al XX Congreso del Partido Socialista Ecuatoriano.* Quito: La Tierra, January 28, 1954.

———. *Teoría y acción socialistas: Un informe del secretario general del partido, al XXI congreso socialista.* Quito: La Tierra, 1955.

Albó, Xavier. "Andean People in the Twentieth Century." In *The Cambridge History of the Native Peoples of the Americas,* ed. Frank Saloman and Stuart B. Schwartz, 765–871. Cambridge: Cambridge University Press, 1999.

———. "Bases étnicas y sociales para la participación Aymara." In *Bolivia, la fuerza histórica del campesinado con una cronología de Bolivia, América Latina y el Imperio Español, 1492–1983,* ed. Fernando Calderón G. and Jorge Dandler, 401–42. Ginebra, Switzerland: Instituto de Investigaciones de las Naciones Unidas para el Desarrollo Social, 1986.

———. "El retorno del Indio." *Revista Andina* 9, no. 2 (December 1991): 299–345.

Albornoz, M. A. *Informe del Ministerio de Gobierno y Previsión Social a la nación, 1930–1931.* Quito: Imprenta Nacional, 1931.

Albornoz Peralta, Osvaldo. *El caudillo indígena Alejo Saes.* Cuenca: Instituto de Investigaciones Sociales, 1988.

———. *Dolores Cacuango y las luchas indígenas de Cayambe.* Guayaquil: Editorial Claridad S.A., 1975.

———. *Ecuador: Luces y sombras del liberalismo.* Quito: El Duende, 1989.

——. *Historia del movimiento obrero ecuatoriano: Breve sintesis.* Quito: Editorial Letra Nueva, 1983.

——. "Jesús Gualavisí y las luchas indígenas en el Ecuador." In *Los comunistas en la historia nacional,* ed. Domingo Paredes, 155–88. Guayaquil: Editorial Claridad, S.A., 1987.

——. *Las luchas indígenas en el Ecuador.* Guayaquil: Editorial Claridad S.A., 1971.

Alexander, Robert J. *Organized Labor in Latin America.* New York: Free Press, 1965.

——. "Sobre algunos aspectos del problema indígena." *Cuadernos de la Realidad Ecuatoriana,* 1 (October 1984): 45–77.

Allen, Catherine J. *The Hold Life Has: Coca and Cultural Identity in an Andean Community.* Washington, D.C.: Smithsonian Institution Press, 1988.

Almeida, Ileana. "Consideraciones sobre la nacionalidad Kechwa." In *Lengua y cultura en el Ecuador,* ed. Ileana Almeida et al., 11–48. Otavalo: Instituto Otavaleño de Antropología, 1979.

——. "La cuestión indígena como cuestión nacional." *Antropología, Cuadernos de Investigación* 2 (January 1984): 18–26.

Almeida, José. "El levantamiento indígena como momento constitutivo nacional." In *Sismo etnico en el Ecuador: Varias perspectivas,* ed. José Almeida et al., 7–28. Quito: CEDIME–Ediciones Abya-Yala, 1993.

Almeida, José et al. *Sismo étnico en el Ecuador: Varias perspectivas.* Quito: CEDIME– Ediciones Abya-Yala, 1993.

Almeida, José, and Mercedes Prieto. "Modalidades organizativas." *Cuadernos de Nueva* 7 (June 1983): 35–38.

Andolina, Robert. "The Sovereign and Its Shadow: Constituent Assembly and Indigenous Movement in Ecuador." *Journal of Latin American Studies* 35, no. 4 (November 2003): 721–50.

Andrango, Alberto. "Como indígenas tenemos nuestros planteamientos políticos." *Ecuador Debate* 12 (December 1986): 247–58.

——. "Contra la discriminación y la pobreza." *Cuadernos de Nueva* 7 (June 1983): 50–52.

Andrews, George Reid. *Afro-Latin America, 1800–2000.* New York: Oxford University Press, 2004.

Ayala Mora, Enrique. *El Partido Socialista Ecuatoriano en la historia.* Quito: Ediciones La Tierra, 1988.

——, ed. *Nueva Historia del Ecuador.* Quito: Corporación Editora Nacional, 1983–1995.

Aymara, Joaquín. *¿Cuál es la vía revolucionaria en el Ecuador?* Quito: Editorial Raúl Cedeño, 1966[?].

Baquero de la Calle, José Antonio. *Informe a la nación, 1960–1961.* Quito: Editorial "Fray Jodoco Ricke," 1961.

Barrionuevo Silva, Ney. *Constituyente de los pueblos: Salida histórica*. Quito: Casa de la Cultura Ecuatoriana "Benjamín Carrión," 1997.

Barsky, Osvaldo. *La reforma agraria ecuatoriana*, 2nd ed. Quito: Corporación Editora Nacional, 1988.

Barth, Fredrick, ed. *Ethnic Groups and Boundaries: The Social Organization of Cultural Difference*. Boston: Little, Brown, 1969.

Basile, David G., and Humberto Paredes. *Algunos factores económicos y geográficos que afectan a la población rural del noreste de la provincia de Pichincha, Ecuador*. Quito: Instituto de Investigaciones Económicas de la Facultad de Ciencias Económicas de la Universidad Central, 1953.

Baud, Michiel. "The *Huelga de los Indígenas* in Cuenca, Ecuador (1920–1921)." In *Indigenous Revolts in Chiapas and the Andean Highlands*, ed. Kevin Gosner and Arij Ouweneel, 217–39. Amsterdam: CEDLA, 1996.

———. "*Libertad de Servidumbre*: Indigenista Ideology and Social Mobilization in Late Nineteenth Century Ecuador." In *Nation Building in Nineteenth Century Latin America: Dilemmas and Conflicts*, ed. Hans-Joachim König and Marianne Wiesebron, 233–53. Leiden, The Netherlands: Research School CNWS, School of Asian, African, and Amerindian Studies, 1998.

Bauer, Arnold J. "Rural Workers in Spanish America: Problems of Peonage and Oppression." *Hispanic American Historical Review* 59, no. 1 (February 1979): 34–63.

Beck, Scott H., and Kenneth J. Mijeski. "Barricades and Ballots: Ecuador's Indians and the Pachakutik Political Movement." *Ecuadorian Studies / Estudios Ecuatorianos* 1 (September 2001). http://www.ecuatorianistas.org/journal/1/beck/beck.htm.

Becker, Marc. "Coaliciones interétnicas en los años treinta: Movimientos indígenas en Cayambe." *Revista Yachaykuna* 2 (December 2001): 76–92.

———. "Comunas and Indigenous Protest in Cayambe, Ecuador." *The Americas* 55, no. 4 (April 1999): 531–59.

———. "Ecuador: Opposition to Wider Trade Pact Grows." *NACLA: Report on the Americas* 36, no. 3 (November / December 2002): 1.

———. "La historia del movimiento indígena escrita a través de las páginas de *Ñucanchic Allpa*." In *Estudios ecuatorianos: Un aporte a la discusión*, ed. Ximena Sosa-Buchholz and William F. Waters, 133–53. Quito: FLACSO, Abya-Yala, 2006.

———. "Indigenous Communists and Urban Intellectuals in Cayambe, Ecuador (1926–1944)." *International Review of Social History*, Supplement 12, no. 49 (2004): 41–64.

———. "Indigenous Struggles for Land Rights in Twentieth-Century Ecuador." *Agricultural History* 81, no. 2 (Spring 2007): 159–81.

———. "Mariátegui, the Comintern, and the Indigenous Question in Latin America." *Science and Society* 70, no. 4 (October 2006): 450–79.

———. "Peasant Identity, Worker Identity: Multiple Modes of Rural Consciousness in Highland Ecuador." *Estudios Interdisciplinarios de América Latina y el Caribe* 15, no. 1 (January–June 2004): 115–39.

———. "Race, Gender, and Protest in Ecuador." In *Work, Protest, and Identity in Twentieth-Century Latin America,* ed. Vincent C. Peloso, 125–42. Wilmington, Del.: Scholarly Resources, 2003.

———. "State Building and Ethnic Discourse in Ecuador's 1944–1945 Asamblea Constitu-yente." In *Highland Indians and the State in Modern Ecuador,* ed. A. Kim Clark and Marc Becker, 105–19. Pittsburgh: University of Pittsburgh Press, 2007.

Belote, Linda Smith, and Jim Belote. "Drain from the Bottom: Individual Ethnic Identity Change in Southern Ecuador." *Social Forces* 63, no. 1 (September 1984): 24–50.

Black, Chad T. *The Making of an Indigenous Movement: Culture, Ethnicity, and Post-Marxist Social Praxis in Ecuador.* Albuquerque, N.M.: University of New Mexico, Latin American Institute, 1999.

———. "The Making of an Indigenous Movement: Meaning and Materiality in Ecuador." M.A. thesis, University of New Mexico, 1999.

Blanco, Hugo. *Land or Death: The Peasant Struggle in Peru.* New York: Pathfinder Press, 1972.

Bonifaz Andrade, Diego. *Guachalá: Historia de una hacienda de Cayambe.* Quito: Ediciones Abya-Yala, 1995.

Bonifaz, Emilio. *Los indígenas de altura del Ecuador,* 3rd ed. Quito: Publitécnica, 1979.

———. "Origen y evolución de una hacienda histórica: Guachalá." *Boletín de la Academia Nacional de Historia* (BANH) 53, no. 115 (January-June 1970): 115–22.

———. "Origen y evolución de una hacienda histórica: 'Guachalá' II." *Boletín de la Academia Nacional de Historia* (BANH) 53, no. 116 (July-December 1970): 338–50.

———. *Sobre la pobreza del campesino del callejón interandino.* Quito: Instituto Ecuatoriano de Antropología y Geografía, 1965.

Bonilla, Adrián. *En busca del pueblo perdido: Diferenciación y discurso de la izquierda marxista en los sesenta.* Quito: FLACSO-Editorial Abya-Yala, 1991.

Borja y Borja, Ramiro. *Las constituciones del Ecuador.* Madrid: Ediciones Cultura Hispanica, 1951.

Botero, Luis Fernando. *Indios, tierra y cultura.* Quito: Ediciones Abya-Yala, 1992.

———. *Movilización indígena, etnicidad y proceso de simbolización en Ecuador: El caso del líder indígena Lázaro Condo.* Quito: Ediciones Abya-Yala, 2001.

Boughton, Bob. "The Communist Party of Australia's Involvement in the Struggle for Aboriginal and Torres Strait Islander People's Rights 1920–1970." In *Labour and Community: Historical Essays,* ed. Raymond Markey, 263–94. Wollongong, Australia: University of Wollongong Press, 2001.

Brinton, Crane. *The Anatomy of Revolution*, rev. ed. New York: Vintage Books, 1965.

Brysk, Alison. "Acting Globally: Indian Rights and International Politics in Latin America." In *Indigenous Peoples and Democracy in Latin America*, ed. Donna Lee Van Cott, 29–51. New York: St. Martin's Press, 1994.

——. *From Tribal Village to Global Village: Indian Rights and International Relations in Latin America*. Stanford, Calif.: Stanford University Press, 2000.

Buechler, Steven M. "New Social Movement Theories." *Sociological Quarterly* 36, no. 3 (summer 1995): 441–64.

Buitrón, Aníbal. "Situación económica y social del indio Otavaleño." *América Indígena* 7, no. 1 (January 1947): 45–62.

Buitrón, Aníbal, and Bárbara Salisbury Buitrón. *Condiciones de vida y trabajo del campesino de la provincia de Pichincha*. Quito: Instituto Nacional de Previsión, Dept. de Propaganda, 1947.

Bulnes, Martha. *Me levanto y digo, testimonio de tres mujeres quichua*. Quito: Editorial El Conejo, 1990.

Burns, E. Bradford. *The Poverty of Progress: Latin America in the Nineteenth Century*. Berkeley: University of California Press, 1980.

Burns, James MacGregor, and Stewart Burns. *A People's Charter: The Pursuit of Rights in America*. New York: Knopf, 1991.

Bustamante, Marco A., and Victor Manuel Madrid. *Monografía de la provincia de Pichincha*. Quito: n.p., 1952.

de la Cadena, Marisol. *Indigenous Mestizos: The Politics of Race and Culture in Cuzco, 1919–1991*. Durham, N.C.: Duke University Press, 2000.

Calla Ortega, Ricardo. "Hallu hayllisa huti: Identificación étnica y procesos políticos en Bolivia." In *Democracia, etnicidad y violencia política en los países andinos*, ed. Alberto Adrianzén et al., 57–81. Lima: Instituto Frances de Estudios Andinos; Instituto de Estudios Peruanos, 1993.

"El campesinado indígena y el estado." *Movimiento* 1 (July 1980): 8.

Carr, Barry. *Marxism and Communism in Twentieth-Century Mexico*. Lincoln: University of Nebraska Press, 1992.

Castillo-Cárdenas, Gonzalo. *Liberation Theology from Below: The Life and Thought of Manuel Quintín Lame*. Maryknoll, N.Y.: Orbis Books, 1987.

Castrillón Arboleda, Diego. *El indio Quintín Lame*. Bogota: Tercer Mundo, 1973.

Centro de Educación Popular (CEDEP). *Las luchas campesinas, 1950–1983: Movilización campesina e historia de la FENOC*, 2nd ed. Quito: CEDOC / CEDEP, 1985.

——. *Lorenza Abimañay: Llactacunapac quishpiripica huarmipish canmi (La mujer en la lucha del pueblo)*. Quito: CEDEP, 1983.

——. *Una historia de rebeldía: La lucha campesina en el Ecuador*. Quito: CEDEP, 1984.

———. *Viva la huelga! Las luchas populares, 1971–1981.* Quito: CEDEP, 1981.

Centro de Estudios y Difusión Social (CEDIS). *Historia de las luchas populares.* Quito: CEDIS, 1985.

Centro de Estudios y Difusion Social (CEDIS) and Centro Ecuatoriana de Organizaciones Clasistas (CEDOC). *XIV Congreso Nacional CEDOC.* Quito: CEDIS / CEDOC, 1982.

Cevallos S., Arturo. "Sublevaciones y conflictos indígenas en Chimborazo, 1920–1930." In *Estructuras agrarias y movimientos sociales en los Andes ecuatorianos (1830–1930),* ed. Instituto de Investigaciones Económicas (IIE), 264–370. Quito: IIE-PUCE-CONUEP, 1990.

Chiriboga, Manuel. "El levantamiento indígena ecuatoriano de 2001: Una interpelación." *Íconos* 10 (April 2001): 28–33.

———. "Los programas de desarrollo económico y social y la población indígena." In *Política estatal y población indígena,* ed. Oficina Nacional de Asuntos Indígenas Ministerio de Bienestar Social, 123–30. Quito: Abya-Yala, 1984.

———. "La reforma agraria en el Ecuador y América Latina." *Nariz del Diablo* 11 (August 1988): 30–36.

———. "Transformaciones Agrarias, Nuevos Movimientos Sociales, Nuevas Organizaciones." *Revista Paraguaya de Sociología* 25, no. 71 (January-April 1988): 119–34.

Chiriboga, Manuel, and Fredy Rivera. "Elecciones de Enero de 1988 y participación indígena." *Ecuador Debate* 17 (March 1989): 181–221.

Cifuentes Navarro, Germán. "Rubén Rodríguez." In *Personajes ilustres del Cantón Cayambe, 1867–1980,* 27–29. Cayambe: Ilustre Municipio de Cayambe, 1993.

Clark, A. Kim. "Indians, the State and Law: Public Works and the Struggle to Control Labor in Liberal Ecuador." *Journal of Historical Sociology* 7, no. 1 (1994): 49–72.

———. "Race, 'Culture,' and Mestizaje: The Statistical Construction of the Ecuadorian Nation, 1930–1950." *Journal of Historical Sociology* 11, no. 2 (June 1998): 185–211.

———. *The Redemptive Work: Railway and Nation in Ecuador, 1895–1930.* Wilmington, Del.: SR Books, 1998.

Cliche, Paul. *Anthropologie des communautés andines équatoriennes: Entre diable et patron.* Paris: Éditions L'Harmattan, 1995.

Colloredo-Mansfeld, Rudi. " 'Dirty Indians,' Radical *Indígenas,* and the Political Economy of Social Difference in Modern Ecuador." *Bulletin of Latin American Research* 17, no. 2 (May 1998): 185–205.

Colvin, Jean G. *Arte de Tigua, una reflexión de la cultura indígena en Ecuador.* Quito: Abya-Yala, 2004.

Comité Central del Partido Comunista del Ecuador (PCE). *Exposición a la Corte Suprema.* Pasto, Colombia: Imp. Nariño, 1937.

———. *Por un gobierno democrático al servicio del pueblo; contra la reacción, los golpes de estado y el continuismo; programa electoral del Partido Comunista del Ecuador.* Quito: Ediciones "El Pueblo," 1956.

Comité Interamericano de Desarrollo Agrícola (CIDA). *Tenencia de la tierra y desarrollo socio-económico del sector agrícola: Ecuador.* Washington, D.C.: Unión Panamericana, 1965.

Communist International. *The Revolutionary Movement in the Colonies: Thesis on the Revolutionary Movement in the Colonies and Semi-Colonies, Adopted by the Sixth World Congress of the Communist International, 1928.* New York: Workers Library, 1929.

Confederación de Nacionalidades Indígenas del Ecuador (CONAIE). "500 años de resistencia india." *Casa de las Américas* 29, no. 174 (May-June 1989): 115–18.

———. "Anteproyecto de ley de nacionalidades indígenas del Ecuador, 1988." In *Documentos Indios: Declaraciones y pronunciamientos,* ed. José Juncosa, 202–12. Quito: Ediciones Abya-Yala, 1991.

———. "Declaration of Quito," *Ecuador, July 1990.* Quito: CONAIE, 1990. http://www.nativeweb.org/papers/statements/quincentennial/quito.php.

———. *Las nacionalidades indígenas en el Ecuador: Nuestro proceso organizativo,* 2nd ed. Quito: Ediciones Tincui–Abya-Yala, 1989.

———. *Proyecto político de la CONAIE.* Quito: CONAIE, 1994.

Confederación de Trabajadores del Ecuador (CTE). "Estatutos de la Confederación de Trabajadores del Ecuador (C.T.E.)." In *28 de mayo y fundación de la C.T.E.,* ed. Osvaldo Albornoz et al., 194–211. Quito: Corporación Editora Nacional, 1984.

Coordinadora Agraria Nacional (CAN). *Proyecto de ley agraria integral.* Quito: Confederación de Nacionalidades Indígenas del Ecuador (CONAIE), 1994.

Cordero Crespo, Gonzalo. *Informe a la nación, 1959.* Quito: Editorial "Fray Jodoco Ricke," 1959.

Cornejo Menacho, Diego, ed. *INDIOS: Una reflexión sobre el levantamiento indígena de 1990.* Quito: ILDIS, 1992.

Cornell, Stephen. *The Return of the Native: American Indian Political Resurgence.* New York: Oxford University Press, 1988.

Cornell University, Andean Indian Community Research and Development Project, and Instituto Ecuatoriano de Reforma Agraria y Colonización. *Indians in Misery: A Preliminary Report on the Colta Lake Zone, Chimborazo, Ecuador: A Report Prepared for and in Collaboration with the Ecuadorian Institute of Agrarian Reform and Colonization.* Ithaca, N.Y: Andean Indian Community Research and Development Project, Dept. of Anthropology, Cornell University, 1965.

Coronel Valencia, Valeria. "Hacia un 'control moral del capitalismo': Pensamiento social y experimentos de la Acción Social Católica en Quito." In *Estudios ecuatorianos: Un aporte a la discusión*, ed. Ximena Sosa-Buchholz and William F. Waters, 57–78. Quito: FLACSO, Abya-Yala, 2006.

Coronel Valencia, Valeria, and Mireya Salgado Gómez. *Galo Plaza Lasso: Un liberal del siglo XX, democracia, desarrollo y cambio cultural en el Ecuador.* Quito: Museo de la Ciudad, 2006.

Costales Samaniego, Alfredo. *Fernando Daquilema, ultimo guaminga,* 2nd ed. Quito: Instituto Ecuatoriano de Antropología y Geografía, 1963.

Crespi, Muriel. "Changing Power Relations: The Rise of Peasant Unions on Traditional Ecuadorian Haciendas." *Anthropological Quarterly* 44, no. 4 (October 1971): 223–40.

——. "Mujeres campesinas como líderes sindicales: La falta de propiedad como calificación para puestos políticos." *Estudios Andinos* 5, no. 1 (1976): 151–71.

——. "The Patrons and Peons of Pesillo: A Traditional Hacienda System in Highland Ecuador." University of Illinois, Urbana-Champaign, Department of Anthropology, 1968.

——. "St. John the Baptist: The Ritual Looking Glass of Hacienda Indian Ethnic and Power Relations." In *Cultural Transformations and Ethnicity in Modern Ecuador,* ed. Norman E. Whitten Jr., 477–505. Urbana: University of Illinois Press, 1981.

Crespo Ordoñez, Nicolas, and Ministro de Previsión Social y Trabajo. *Informe a la nación, 1960.* Quito: Editorial "Espejo" S.A., 1960.

Crespo Toral, Jorge. *El comunismo en el Ecuador.* Quito: n.p., 1958.

Cueva, Agustín. *The Process of Political Domination in Ecuador.* New Brunswick, N.J.: Transaction Books, 1982.

Dandler, Jorge, and Juan Torrico. "From the National Indigenous Congress to the Ayopaya Rebellion: Bolivia, 1945–1947." In *Resistance, Rebellion, and Consciousness in the Andean World, 18th to 20th Centuries,* ed. Steve J. Stern, 334–78. Madison: University of Wisconsin Press, 1987.

Dávalos, Pablo. "Ecuador: Las transformaciones políticas del movimiento indígena ecuatoriano." *Observatorio Social de América Latina* 1, no. 1 (June 2000): 25–29.

——. "Movimiento indígena ecuatoriano: La construcción de un actor político." *Ciencias Sociales* 2nd ser., no. 20 (June 2001): 111–38.

Degregori, Carlos Iván. "Ethnicity and Democratic Governability in Latin America: Reflections from Two Central Andean Countries." In *Fault Lines of Democracy in Post-Transition Latin America,* ed. Felipe Agüero and Jeffrey Stark, 203–34. Boulder, Colo.: Lynne Rienner Publishers, 1998.

Deler, Jean-Paul. *Ecuador: Del espacio al estado nacional.* Quito: Banco Central del Ecuador, 1987.

Delgado-P., Guillermo. "Ethnic Politics and the Popular Movement: Reconstructing a Social Justice Agenda." In *Latin America Faces the Twenty-First Century,* ed. Susanne Jonas and Edward J. McCaughan, 77–88. Boulder, Colo.: Westview Press, 1994.

Dirección General de Obras Públicas. *Informe de la Dirección General de Obras Públicas, 1926–1930.* Quito: Talleres Tipográficos Nacionales, 1930.

División de Estadística y Censos. *Primer censo agropecuario nacional: Resumen de los principales datos preliminares, 1954.* Quito: República del Ecuador, 1955.

Donoso Armas, Manuel et al. *El 15 de noviembre de 1922 y la fundación del socialismo: Relatados por sus protagonistas,* 2 vols. Quito: Corporación Editora Nacional-INFOC, 1982.

Dore, Elizabeth. *Myths of Modernity: Peonage and Patriarchy in Nicaragua.* Durham, N.C.: Duke University Press, 2006.

Douglass, Frederick. *Frederick Douglass: Selected Speeches and Writings,* Chicago: Lawrence Hill Books, 1999.

Drake, Paul W. *The Money Doctor in the Andes: The Kemmerer Missions, 1923–1933.* Durham, N.C.: Duke University Press, 1989.

Draper, Elizabeth Bobsy. "Minga in Ecuador." *Z Magazine* (December 1990): 33–38.

Du Bois, W. E. B. *The Souls of Black Folk: Authoritative Text, Contexts, Criticism.* New York: Norton, 1999.

Dubly, Alain, and Alicia Granda. *Desalojos y despojos: Los conflictos agrarios en Ecuador, 1983–1990.* Quito: El Conejo, 1991.

Durango, C. Augusto. *Informe del Ministro de Previsión Social, 1939.* Quito: Imprenta del Ministerio de Educación, 1939.

Ecuarunari. *Historia de la nacionalidad y los pueblos quichuas del Ecuador.* Quito: Ecuarunari, 1998.

——. "El movimiento campesino indígena." In *Población indígena y desarrollo amazonico,* ed. Ministerio de Bienestar Social, 43–50. Quito: Ediciones Abya-Yala, 1984.

Ecuarunari and FENOC. *Luchando por nuestros derechos: Organizaciónes campesinas de América Latina.* Quito: Agencia Latinoamericana de Información (ALAI), 1984.

Ecuarunari, FENOC, and ALAI, eds. *Nuestra voz, nuestra cultura: Memoria del Taller Andino de Intercambio de Experiencias en Educación y Comunicación de Organizaciones Campesinos Indígenas (Quito, 7–11 octubre 1987).* Quito: Ecuarunari / FENOC / ALAI, 1989.

Edelman, Marc. *Peasants Against Globalization: Rural Social Movements in Costa Rica.* Stanford, Calif.: Stanford University Press, 1999.

Endara, César. "La fundación del partido: Una experiencia testimonial." In *Los comunistas en la historia nacional,* ed. Domingo Paredes, 39–57. Guayaquil: Editorial Claridad, 1987.

Erickson, Edwin E. et al. *Area Handbook for Ecuador.* Washington, D.C.: U.S. Government Printing Office, 1966.

Escobar, Manuel. "La FEI . . . el indio de poncho colorado." *Cuadernos de Nueva* 7 (June 1983): 48–49.

Federación de Centros Shuar. *Federación de Centros Shuar: Solución original a un problema actual.* Sucúa: La Federación, 1976.

Federación Ecuatoriana de Indios (FEI). *Estatutos de la Federación Ecuatoriana de Indios.* Guayaquil: Editorial Claridad, 1945.

——. *Por una F.E.I. poderosa y combativa.* Quito: Confederación de Trabajadores del Ecuador, 1989.

——. *Segundo congreso de indios ecuatorianos . . . del 8 al 10 febrero de 1946.* Quito: Editorial Casa de la Cultura Ecuatoriana, 1946.

——. *VII Congreso Federación Ecuatoriana de Indios FEI; Documents, Quito 27–28 de julio de 1989.* Quito: Federación Ecuatoriana de Indios, 1989.

——. *VIII Congreso Ordinario: Documento Central.* Riobamba: Federación Ecuatoriana de Indios, 1995.

Federación Nacional de Organizaciones Campesinas (Ecuador) (FENOC). "Consejo Nacional de la FENOC." *Boletín Ecuador* 11 (August 1979): 13–21.

——. "FENOC: Situación de los indígenas en el Ecuador." In *Campesinado e indigenismo en America Latina,* ed. Enrique Valencia, 258 66. Lima: Ediciones CELATS, 1978.

——. *La FENOC y la movilización campesina: Las luchas campesinas entre 1970 y 1978.* Quito: CEDIS, FENOC, 1980.

——. "Manifiesto campesino." *La FENOC Informe* 5 (April 1979): 8.

——. "Organizaciones: FENOC: Programa agrario y plataforma de lucha." *Acción: Boletín informativo agrario* 2nd ser., no. 10 (October 1987): 46–52.

——. "La situación de los campesinos en el país." In *Pensamiento agrario ecuatoriano,* ed. Carlos Marchán Romero, 373–87. Quito: Banco Central del Ecuador; Corporacion Editora Nacional, 1986.

Federación Pichincha Riccharimui. *500 años de resistencia indígena y popular.* Quito: Secretaría de Educación Alfabetización y Cultura Pichincha Riccharimui, May 1990.

——. "Hacia el XII Congreso de la Federación Pichincha Riccharimui!" *Rumiñahui* 6 (December 1995): 1.

——. *Historia de la organización indígena en Pichincha: Federación Indígena Pichincha Runacunapac Riccharimui.* Quito: Ediciones Abya-Yala, 1993.

Feierman, Steven. *Peasant Intellectuals: Anthropology and History in Tanzania.* Madison: University of Wisconsin Press, 1990.

Fiallo, Celso, and Galo Ramón. *La lucha de las comunidades indígenas del cantón Pujilí y su encuentro con el pensamiento comunista.* Quito: Documento CAAP, 1980.

Field, Les. "Ecuador's Pan-Indian Uprising." *Report on the Americas* 25, no. 3 (December 1991): 39–44.

——. "The Land Issue in the Ecuadorian Highlands." *Cultural Survival Quarterly* 14, no. 4 (winter 1990): 17–20.

Fitch, J. Samuel. "Post-Transition Coups: Ecuador 2000. An Essay in Honor of Martin Needler." *Journal of Political and Military Sociology* 33, no. 1 (summer 2005): 39–58.

Foerster, Rolf, and Sonia Montecino Aguirre. *Organizaciones, lideres y contiendas mapuches, 1900–1970* [Santiago, Chile]: Ediciones CEM, 1988.

Foweraker, Joe. "Popular Movements and Political Change in Mexico." In *Popular Movements and Political Change in Mexico,* ed. Joe Foweraker and Ann L Craig, 3–20. Boulder, Colo.: Lynne Rienner Publishers, 1990.

Foweraker, Joe, and Todd Landman. *Citizenship Rights and Social Movements: A Comparative and Statistical Analysis.* Oxford: Oxford University Press, 1997.

Franck, Harry A. *Vagabonding down the Andes: Being the Narrative of a Journey, Chiefly Afoot, from Panama to Buenos Aires.* New York: Century Co., 1917.

Freile-Granizo, Juan. "Leyes Indigenistas: Compilación." *Sarance* 19 (1994): 1–242.

Frente Amplio de la Izquierda de Ecuador (FADI). *Documentos del proceso de constitución del Frente Amplio de la Izquierda de Ecuador (FADI) y primera declaración pública.* Montreal, Quebec: Agence latino-americaine d'information, 1978.

Galarza Zavala, Jaime. *Los campesinos de Loja y Zamora.* Quito: Universidad Central del Ecuador, 1973.

——. *El yugo feudal: Visión del campo ecuatoriano,* 7th ed. Cuenca: n.p., 1992.

——. "La vida misma: A propósito del artículo de R. Santana." *Cuadernos de la Realidad Ecuatoriana* 1 (October 1984): 89–98.

Gallegos Lara, Joaquín. *Biografía del pueblo indio.* Quito: Casa de la Cultura Ecuatoriana, 1952.

Gangotena, Francisco. "El 'coronel' Ambrosio Laso." *Cuadernos de Nueva* 7 (June 1983): 21–22.

——. "Peasant Social Articulation and Surplus Transference: An Ecuadorean Case." Ph.D. diss., University of Florida, 1981.

——. "The Socio-Economic System of an Ecuadorean Indian Community." M.A. thesis, University of Florida, 1974.

Garaycoa, Xavier, and Luis Emilio Veintimilla. "Defending Democracy and Fighting for the Working People's Rights." *World Marxist Review* 29, no. 5 (May 1986): 93–99.

García, María Elena, and José Antonio Lucero. "Un País Sin Indígenas? Re-thinking Indigenous Politics in Peru." In *The Struggle for Indigenous Rights in Latin America,* ed. Nancy Grey Postero and Leon Zamosc, 158–88. Brighton, U.K.: Sussex Academic Press, 2004.

García, Fernando. "¿Un levantamiento indígena más? A propósito de los sucesos de febrero de 2001." *Íconos* 10 (April 2001): 34–38.

Garfield, Seth. *Indigenous Struggle at the Heart of Brazil: State Policy, Frontier Expansion, and the Xavante Indians, 1937–1988.* Durham, N.C.: Duke University Press, 2001.

Gerassi, John. *The Great Fear in Latin America,* rev. ed. New York: Collier Books, 1965.

Gerlach, Allen. *Indians, Oil, and Politics: A Recent History of Ecuador.* Wilmington, Del.: SR Books, 2003.

Gibson, Charles. *The Aztecs under Spanish Rule: A History of the Indians of the Valley of Mexico, 1519–1810.* Stanford, Calif.: Stanford University Press, 1964.

Glave, Luis Miguel. "The 'Republic of Indians' in Revolt (c. 1680–1790)." In *The Cambridge History of the Native Peoples of the Americas,* vol. 3, pt. 2, ed. Frank Saloman and Stuart B. Schwartz, 502–57. Cambridge: Cambridge University Press, 1999.

Gotkowitz, Laura. " 'Under the Dominion of the Indian': Rural Mobilization, the Law, and Revolutionary Nationalism in Bolivia in the 1940s." In *Political Cultures in the Andes, 1750–1950,* ed. Nils Jacobsen and Cristóbal Aljovín de Losada, 137–58. Durham, N.C.: Duke University Press, 2005.

Gould, Jeffrey L., and Aldo Lauri-Santiago. " 'They Call Us Thieves and Steal Our Wage': Toward a Reinterpretation of the Salvadoran Rural Mobilization, 1929–1931." *Hispanic American Historical Review* 84, no. 2 (May 2004): 191–237.

Gow, Rosalind. "Yawar Mayu: Revolution in the Southern Andes, 1860–1980." Ph.D. diss., University of Wisconsin, Madison, 1981.

Gualle, Estuardo. "FEI." In *Forjando la unidad: El movimiento popular en Ecuador,* ed. Agencia Latinoamericana de Información (ALAI), 42–43. Quito: Communicare, 1985.

Guaña, Pablo, Pedro Camino, and Quimbia Ulco. *Inti Raymi Cayambi: La fiesta sagrada del sol en la mitad del mundo; la fiesta de San Pedro en Cayambe.* Cayambe: CICAY-Museo Cayambe, 1992.

Guardino, Peter F. *Peasants, Politics, and the Formation of Mexico's National State: Guerrero, 1800–1857.* Stanford, Calif.: Stanford University Press, 1996.

Guerrero, Andrés. "The Construction of a Ventriloquist's Image: Liberal Discourse and the 'Miserable Indian Race' in Late-Nineteenth-Century Ecuador." *Journal of Latin American Studies* 29, no. 3 (October 1997): 555–90.

——. *De la economía a las mentalidades (Cambio social y conflicto agrario en el Ecuador).* Quito: Editorial El Conejo, 1991.

——. "La desintegración de la administración étnica en el Ecuador." In *Sismo etnico en el Ecuador: Varias perspectivas,* ed. José Almeida et al., 91–112. Quito: CEDIME–Ediciones Abya-Yala, 1993.

——. *Haciendas, capital y lucha de clases andina: Disolución de la hacienda serrana y lucha política en los años 1960–64,* 2nd ed. Quito: Editorial El Conejo, 1984.

——. "Poblaciones indígenas, ciudadanía y representación." *Nueva Sociedad* 150 (July–August 1997): 98–105.

——. *La semántica de la dominación: El concertaje de indios.* Quito: Ediciones Libri Mundi, 1991.

Guerrero Arias, Patricio. *El saber del mundo de los condores: Identidad e insurgencia de la cultura andina.* Quito: Ediciones Abya-Yala, 1993.

Guerrero Cazar, Fernando, and Pablo Ospina Peralta. *El poder de la comunidad: Ajuste estructural y movimiento indígena en los Andes ecuatorianos.* Buenos Aires: CLACSO, 2003.

Guevara, Darío C. *Puerta de El Dorado: Monografía del Cantón Pelileo.* Quito: Editora Moderna, 1945.

Gutiérrez, Gustavo. *Theology of Liberation.* New York: Orbis Books, 1973.

Hall, Stuart. "Subjects in History: Making Diasporic Identities." In *The House That Race Built,* ed. Wahneema H. Lubiano, 289–99. New York: Vintage Books, 1997.

Harvey, Neil. *The Chiapas Rebellion: The Struggle for Land and Democracy.* Durham, N.C.: Duke University Press, 1998.

Hassaurek, Friedrich. *Four Years among the Ecuadorians.* Carbondale: Southern Illinois University Press, 1967.

Haywood, Harry. *Black Bolshevik: Autobiography of an Afro-American Communist.* Chicago: Liberator Press, 1978.

Healy, Kevin. "Allies and Opposition Groups to the 1990 Indigenous Political Mobilizations in Ecuador and Bolivia." Paper presented at the Seventeenth International Congress of the Latin American Studies Association, September 24–27, 1992, Los Angeles, California, 1992.

Hellman, Judith Adler. "The Riddle of New Social Movements: Who They Are and What They Do." In *Capital, Power, and Inequality in Latin America,* ed. Sandor Halebsky and Richard L. Harris, 165–83. Boulder, Colo.: Westview Press, 1995.

Hertzberg, Hazel W. *The Search for an American Indian Identity: Modern Pan-Indian Movements.* Syracuse: Syracuse University Press, 1971.

hooks, bell. *Teaching to Transgress: Education as the Practice of Freedom.* New York: Routledge, 1994.

Howard, James H. "Pan-Indian Culture of Oklahoma." *Scientific Monthly* 81, no. 5 (November 1955): 215–20.

Ibarra, Alicia. *Los indígenas y el estado en el Ecuador: La práctica neoindigenista,* 2nd ed. Quito: Ediciones Abya-Yala, 1992.

———. "Los indios del Ecuador y su demanda frente al Estado." *Boletín de Antropología Americana* 26 (December 1992): 69–85.

Ibarra, Hernán. "Cambios agrarios y conflictos étnicos en la sierra central (1820–1930)." In *Estructuras agrarias y movimientos sociales en los Andes ecuatorianos (1830–1930),* ed. Instituto de Investigaciones Económicas (IIE), 143–263. Quito: IIE-PUCE-CONUEP, 1990.

———. "Intelectuales indígenas, neoindigenismo, e indianismo en el Ecuador." *Ecuador Debate* 48 (December 1999): 71–94.

———. *"Nos encontramos amenazados por todita la indiada": El levantamiento de Daquilema (Chimborazo 1871).* Quito: Centro de Estudios y Difusión Social (CEDIS), 1993.

Icaza, Jorge. *Huasipungo.* Quito: Imprenta Nacional, 1934.

———. *Huasipungo*. Carbondale: Southern Illinois University Press, 1964.

Imbaquingo, Manuel. "Ecuarunari." In *Forjando la unidad: El movimiento popular en Ecuador*, ed. Agencia Latinoamericana de Información (ALAI), 44–46. Quito: Communicare, 1985.

Instituto de Investigaciones Económicas (IIE). *Estructuras agrarias y movimientos sociales en los Andes ecuatorianos (1830–1930)*. Quito: IIE-PUCE-CONUEP, 1990.

Instituto Ecuatoriano de Reforma Agraria y Colonización (IERAC). *Historia de un arrimado*. Ecuador: Instituto Ecuatoriano de Reforma Agraria y Colonización, n.d.

———. *Historia de un Huasipunguero*. [Quito]: Mision Andina, n.d.

Instituto Nacional de Desarrollo Agrario (INDA). "Reglamento organico y funcional del Instituto Nacional de Desarrollo Agrario." In *Ley de desarrollo agrario y reglamentos*, 141–87. Quito: Editorial Jurídica del Ecuador, 1995.

Jacobsen, Nils. *Mirages of Transition: The Peruvian Altiplano, 1780–1930*. Berkeley: University of California Press, 1993.

James, C. L. R. *The Black Jacobins: Toussaint L'Ouverture and the San Domingo Revolution*, 2nd ed. New York: Vintage Books, 1963.

Jaramillo Alvarado, Pío. *El indio ecuatoriano: Contribución al estudio de la sociología indoamericana*, 2 vols., 6th ed. Quito: Corporación Editora Nacional, 1983 [1922].

Jarrín Cuvi, Andrés Mateo. "Protestantism, the Indigenous, and Political Participation in Ecuador." M.A. thesis, University of California, San Diego, 2004.

Jenkins, Keith. *Re-thinking History*. New York: Routledge, 2003.

Joseph, Gilbert M., and Daniel Nugent, eds. *Everyday Forms of State Formation: Revolution and the Negotiation of Rule in Modern Mexico*. Durham, N.C.: Duke University Press, 1994.

Junta Central de Asistencia Pública (JCAP). *Informe de la Dirección de la Junta Central de Asistencia Pública (1930)*. Quito: Imprenta Nacional, 1931.

———. *Informe presentado por el Director de la Junta Central de Asistencia Pública de Quito al Ministerio del Ramo*. Quito: Talleres Graficos Nacional, 1948.

Junta Nacional de Planificación y Coordinación Económica. *Solicitud de crédito no. 1–63 que el Gobierno del Ecuador presenta al Banco Interamericano de Desarrollo para al recolonización de las haciendas: San Vicente de Pusir, Pesillo y Aychapicho*. Quito: Junta Nacional de Planificación y Coordinación Económica, 1963.

Karakras, Ampam. "CONACNIE." In *Forjando la unidad: El movimiento popular en Ecuador*, ed. Agencia Latinoamericana de Información (ALAI), 47–48. Quito: Communicare, 1985.

———. "Las nacionalidades indias y el estado ecuatoriano." *Antropología, Cuadernos de Investigación* 3 (November 1984): 105–12.

Klehr, Harvey, John Earl Haynes, and Fridrikh Igorevich Firsov. *The Secret World of American Communism.* New Haven, Conn.: Yale University Press, 1995.

Knight, Alan. "Mexican Peonage: What Was It and Why Was It?" *Journal of Latin American Studies* 18, no. 1 (February 1986): 41–74.

Kofas, Jon V. "The IMF, the World Bank, and U.S. Foreign Policy in Ecuador, 1956–1966." *Latin American Perspectives* 28, no. 5 (September 2001): 50–83.

Korovkin, Tanya. "Indigenous Movements in the Central Andes: Community, Class, and Ethnic Politics." *Latin American and Caribbean Ethnic Studies* 1, no. 2 (September 2006): 143–63.

Kulikoff, Allan. *The Agrarian Origins of American Capitalism.* Charlottesville: University Press of Virginia, 1992.

Kuznesof, Elizabeth Anne. "Ethnic and Gender Influences on 'Spanish' Creole Society in Colonial Spanish America." *Colonial Latin American Review* 4, no. 1 (1995): 153–76.

Kyle, David. *Transnational Peasants: Migrations, Networks, and Ethnicity in Andean Ecuador.* Baltimore: Johns Hopkins University Press, 2000.

Landsberger, Henry A. "The Role of Peasant Movements and Revolts in Development." In *Latin American Peasant Movements,* ed. Henry A. Landsberger, 1–61. Ithaca, N.Y.: Cornell University Press, 1969.

Langer, Erick D. "Andean Rituals of Revolt: The Chayanta Rebellion of 1927." *Ethnohistory* 37, no. 3 (summer 1990): 227–53.

———. *Economic Change and Rural Resistance in Southern Bolivia, 1880–1930.* Stanford, Calif.: Stanford University Press, 1989.

Larson, Brooke. "Andean Communities, Political Cultures, and Markets: The Changing Contours of a Field." In *Ethnicity, Markets, and Migration in the Andes: At the Crossroads of History and Anthropology,* ed. Brooke Larson, Olivia Harris, and Enrique Tandeter, 5–53. Durham, N.C.: Duke University Press, 1995.

———. *Trials of Nation Making: Liberalism, Race, and Ethnicity in the Andes, 1810–1910.* Cambridge: Cambridge University Press, 2004.

Lear, John. "The Lady Pack Mule Rebels." *Saturday Evening Post* 217, no. 26 (December 23, 1944): 17, 63–64.

LeGrand, Catherine. *Frontier Expansion and Peasant Protest in Colombia, 1850–1936.* Albuquerque: University of New Mexico Press, 1986.

León Trujillo, Jorge. *De campesinos a ciudadanos diferentes: El levantamiento indígena.* Quito: CEDIME–Ediciones Abya-Yala, 1994.

———. "Las organizaciones indígenas: Igualdad y diferencia, la afirmación de los conquistados." In *INDIOS: Una reflexión sobre el levantamiento indígena de 1990,* ed. Diego Cornejo Menacho, 373–417. Quito: ILDIS, 1992.

———. "Versiones de los protagonistas: Los hechos históricos y el valor de los testimonios disidentes." In *Sismo etnico en el Ecuador:Varias perspectivas,* ed. José Almeida et al., 113–43. Quito: CEDIME–Ediciones Abya-Yala, 1993.

Lind, Amy. *Gendered Paradoxes: Women's Movements, State Restructuring, and Global Development in Ecuador.* University Park: Pennsylvania State University Press, 2005.

Lindqvist, Sven. *The Shadow: Latin America Faces the Seventies.* Harmondsworth, U.K.: Penguin, 1972.

Linke, Lilo. "Ecuador's Politics: President Velasco's Fourth Exit." *The World Today* 18, no. 2 (February 1962): 57–69.

López Cando, Flavio, Angel Martínez Espinoza, and Héctor Castillo Castillo. *Pilahuín: El páramo y los indios.* Quito: Corporación de Organizaciones Campesinos de Pilahuin (COCAP), 2002.

Löwy, Michael, ed. *Marxism in Latin America from 1909 to the Present: An Anthology.* Atlantic Highlands, N.J.: Humanities Press, 1992.

Lucas, Kintto. *We Will Not Dance on Our Grandparents' Tombs: Indigenous Uprisings in Ecuador.* London: Catholic Institute for International Relations (CIIR), 2000.

Lucero, Jose Antonio. "Arts of Unification: Political Representation and Indigenous Movements in Bolivia and Ecuador." Ph.D. diss., Princeton University, 2002.

———. "Crisis and Contention in Ecuador." *Journal of Democracy* 12, no. 2 (April 2001): 59–73.

———. "Locating the 'Indian Problem': Community, Nationality, and Contradiction in Ecuadorian Indigenous Politics." *Latin American Perspectives* 30, no. 1 (January 2003): 23–48.

Lurie, Nancy Oestreich. "The Contemporary American Indian Scene." In *North American Indians in Historical Perspective,* ed. Eleanor Burke Leacock and Nancy Oestreich Lurie, 418–40. New York: Random House, 1971.

Luxemburg, Rosa. "The Junius Pamphlet: The Crisis in the German Social Democracy." In *Rosa Luxemburg Speaks,* ed. Mary-Alice Waters. New York: Pathfinder Press, 1970.

Lyons, Barry J. *Remembering the Hacienda: Religion, Authority, and Social Change in Highland Ecuador.* Austin: University of Texas Press, 2006.

Macas, Luis. *El levantamiento indígena visto por sus protagonistas.* Quito: Instituto Científico de Culturas Indígenas (ICCI), 1991.

———. "La ley agraria y el proceso de movilización por la vida." In *Derechos de los pueblos indígenas: Situación jurídica y políticas de estado,* ed. Ramón Torres Galarza, 29–37. Quito: CONAIE / CEPLAES / Abya-Yala, 1995.

———. "Los Saraguros: 'Unidad con los grupos marginados.' " *Cuadernos de Nueva* 7 (June 1983): 53–56.

Maiguashca, Segundo. *El indio, cerebro y corazón de América: Incorporación del indio a la cultura nacional.* Quito: Ed. Fray Jodoco Ricke, 1949.

Maldonado, Efendy. *El Cantón Cayambe*. Cayambe: Abya-Yala, 1987.

Maldonado, Luis. "CONAIE: Educación, cultura y ciencia." In *Nuestra voz, nuestra cultura: Memoria del Taller Andino de Intercambio de Experiencias en Educación y Comunicación de Organizaciones Campesinos Indígenas (Quito, 7–11 octubre 1987)*, ed. Ecuarunari, FENOC, and ALAI, 92–93. Quito: Ecuarunari / FENOC / ALAI, 1989.

——. "Indígenas y elecciones 1992." In *Sismo etnico en el Ecuador: Varias perspectivas*, ed. José Almeida et al., 305–10. Quito: CEDIME–Ediciones Abya-Yala, 1993.

Mallon, Florencia E. *Peasant and Nation: The Making of Postcolonial Mexico and Peru*. Berkeley: University of California Press, 1995.

Malo, Enrique, and Ministro de Previsión Social. *Memoria mayo 1939—marzo 1940*. Quito: Talleres Gráficos de Educación, 1940.

Marchán Romero, Carlos, ed. *Pensamiento agrario ecuatoriano*. Quito: Banco Central del Ecuador; Corporacion Editora Nacional, 1986.

Marcos, Subcomandante Insurgente. *Our Word Is Our Weapon: Selected Writings*. New York: Seven Stories Press, 2001.

Mariátegui, José Carlos. "The Anti-Imperialist Point of View." In *Marxism in Latin America from 1909 to the Present: An Anthology*, ed. Michael Löwy, 39–44. Atlantic Highlands, N.J.: Humanities Press, 1992.

——. "The Indigenous Question in Latin America." In *The Heroic and Creative Meaning of Socialism: Selected Essays of José Carlos Mariátegui*, ed. Michael Pearlman, 94–109. Atlantic Highlands, N.J.: Humanities Press, 1996.

——. *Seven Interpretive Essays on Peruvian Reality*. Austin: University of Texas Press, 1971.

Martin, Pamela. *The Globalization of Contentious Politics: The Amazonian Indigenous Rights Movement*. New York: Routledge, 2003.

Martínez J., Patricio. *Guayaquil, Noviembre de 1922: Política oligárquica e insurrección popular*, 2nd ed. Quito: Centro de Estudios y Difusión Social, 1989.

Martínez, Nela. "Dolores Cacuango: Capítulo de una biografía." *Nuestra Palabra* 1 (January 1963): 18–23.

——. *Yo siempre he sido Nela Martínez Espinosa: Una autobiografía hablada*. Quito: CONAMU-UNIFEM, 2006.

Martínez, Nicolás. "La condición actual de la raza indígena en la provincia de Tungurahua." In *Indianistas, indianófilos, indigenistas; Entre el enigma y la fascinación: una antología de textos sobre el 'problema' indígena*, ed. Jorge Trujillo, 207–43. Quito: ILDIS, 1993.

Martz, John D. "Marxism in Ecuador." *Inter-American Economic Affairs* 33, no. 1 (summer 1979): 3–28.

Marx, Karl. *The Eighteenth Brumaire of Louis Bonaparte, with Explanatory Notes*. New York: International Publishers, 1963.

Mattiace, Shannan L. *To See with Two Eyes: Peasant Activism and Indian Autonomy in Chiapas, Mexico*. Albuquerque: University of New Mexico Press, 2003.

Maugé, René. "Las tareas actuales de nuestro movimiento." In *Los comunistas en la historia nacional*, ed. Domingo Paredes, 219–55. Guayaquil: Editorial Claridad, S.A., 1987.

Maxwell, William J. *New Negro, Old Left: African-American Writing and Communism between the Wars*. New York: Columbia University Press, 1999.

Maynard, Eileen. "Indian-Mestizo Relations." In *The Indians of Colta: Essays on the Colta Lake Zone, Chimborazo (Ecuador)*, ed. Eileen Maynard, 1–36. Ithaca, N.Y.: Dept. of Anthropology, Cornell University, 1966.

McClintock, Anne. *Imperial Leather: Race, Gender, and Sexuality in the Colonial Contest*. New York: Routledge, 1995.

Meisch, Lynn A. *Andean Entrepreneurs: Otavalo Merchants and Musicians in the Global Arena*. Austin: University of Texas Press, 2003.

——. "We Will Not Dance on the Tomb of Our Grandparents: 500 Years of Resistance in Ecuador." *Latin American Anthropology Review* 4, no. 2 (winter 1992): 55–74.

Mériguet Cousségal, Raymond. *Antinazismo en Ecuador, años 1941–1944: Autobiografía del Movimiento Antinazi de Ecuador (MPAE-MAE)*. Quito: R. Meriguet Coussegal, 1988.

Merlo Vasquez, Jorge H. *Informe a la nación, 1958*. Quito: Talleres Gráficos Nacionales, 1958.

Milk, Richard Lee. "Growth and Development of Ecuador's Worker Organizations, 1895–1944." Indiana University, 1977.

——. *Movimiento obrero ecuatoriano el desafío de la integración*. Quito: Ediciones Abya-Yala, 1997.

Miller, Francesca. "The Suffrage Movement in Latin America." In *Confronting Change, Challenging Tradition: Women in Latin American History*, ed. Gertrude Matyoka Yeager, 157–76. Wilmington, Del.: Scholarly Resources, 1994.

Ministerio de Bienestar Social. *Política estatal y población indígena*. Quito: Ediciones Abya-Yala, 1984.

Ministerio de Previsión Social y Trabajo. *Código del Trabajo: Leyes anexas, convenios y recomendaciones internacionales*. Quito: Talleres Gráficos Nacionales, 1954.

Monroy, Joel L. *El Convento de la Merced de Quito (de 1616–1700)*. Quito: Editorial Labor, 1932.

Moore, Barrington Jr. *Social Origins of Dictatorship and Democracy: Lord and Peasant in the Making of the Modern World*. Boston: Beacon, 1966.

Moreno Yánez, Segundo E. *Alzamientos indígenas en la Audiencia de Quito, 1534–1803*, 2nd ed. Quito: Ediciones Abya-Yala, 1989.

——. *Sublevaciones indígenas en la Audiencia de Quito: Desde comienzos del siglo XVIII hasta finales de la Colonia*, 3rd ed. Quito: Ediciones de la Universidad Católica, 1985.

Moreno Yánez, Segundo E., and José Figueroa. *El levantamiento indígena del inti raymi de 1990*. Quito: Ediciones Abya-Yala, 1992.

Moscoso, Martha. "'Cabecillas' y 'huelgistas' en los levantamientos de inicios del siglo XX." In *Poder y violencia en los Andes*, ed. Mirko Lauer and Henrique Urbano, 225–35. Cusco: Centro de Estudios Regionales Andinos Bartolomé de Las Casas, 1991.

——. "Estado, comunidad y levantamientos indígenas en las provincias del Azuay y Cañar, 1830–1930." In *Estructuras agrarias y movimientos sociales en los Andes ecuatorianos (1830–1930)*, ed. Instituto de Investigaciones Económicas (IIE), 1–69. Quito: IIE-PUCE-CONUEP, 1990.

——. "Mujer indígena y sociedad republicana: Relaciones étnicas y de género en el Ecuador, siglo XIX." In *Mujeres de los Andes: Condiciones de vida y salud*, ed. A.C. Defossez, Dedier Fassin, and M. Viveros, 223–43. Colombia: Instituto Frances de Estudios Andinos, 1992.

Mullo, Mario. "El movimiento indígena en la provincia de Pichincha." In *Historia de la organización indígena en Pichincha*, ed. Federación Pichincha Riccharimui, 31–38. Quito: Ediciones Abya-Yala, 1993.

Municipio de Cayambe. *Personajes ilustres del Canton Cayambe, 1867–1980*. Cayambe: Ilustre Municipio de Cayambe, 1993.

Muñoz, Leonardo J. *Testimonio de lucha: Memorias sobre la historia del socialismo en el Ecuador*. Quito: Corporación Editora Nacional, 1988.

Muñoz Vicuña, Elías. *Masas, luchas, solidaridad*. Guayaquil: Universidad de Guayaquil, 1985.

Muñoz Vicuña, Elías, and Leonardo Vicuña Izquierdo. *Historia del movimiento obrero del Ecuador (resúmen)*. Guayaquil: Dept. de Publicaciones de la Facultad de Ciencias Economicas, 1978.

Muratorio, Blanca. "Protestantism and Capitalism Revisited, in the Rural Highlands of Ecuador." *Journal of Peasant Studies* 8, no. 1 (October 1980): 37–60.

——. "Protestantism, Ethnicity, and Class in Chimborazo." In *Cultural Transformations and Ethnicity in Modern Ecuador*, ed. Norman E. Whitten Jr., 506–34. Urbana: University of Illinois Press, 1981.

——. "Los tinterillos o abogados callejeros: El papel de los intermediarios judiciales en una communidad boliviana." In *Procesos de articulación social*, ed. Sidney M. Greenfield et al., 112–35. Buenos Aires: Amorrortu, 1977.

Nagel, Joane. *American Indian Ethnic Renewal: Red Power and the Resurgence of Identity and Culture*. New York: Oxford University Press, 1996.

Navarro, Marysa, Virginia Sánchez Korrol, and Kecia Ali. *Women in Latin America and the Caribbean: Restoring Women to History*. Bloomington: Indiana University Press, 1999.

North American Congress on Latin America (NACLA). "Gaining Ground: The Indigenous Movement in Latin America." *NACLA Report on the Americas* 29, no. 5 (March / April 1996): 14.

O'Connor, Erin. "Dueling Patriarchies: Gender, Indians, and State Formation in the Ecuadorian Sierra, 1860–1925." Ph.D., diss., Boston College, 1997.

——. *Gender, Indian, Nation: The Contradictions of Making Ecuador, 1830–1925*. Tucson: University of Arizona Press, 2007.

——. "Helpless Children or Undeserving Patriarchs? Gender Ideologies, the State, and Indian Men in Late Nineteenth-Century Ecuador." In *Highland Indians and the State in Modern Ecuador*, ed. A. Kim Clark and Marc Becker, 56–71. Pittsburgh: University of Pittsburgh Press, 2007.

——. "Indians and National Salvation: Placing Ecuador's Indigenous Coup of January 2000 in Historical Perspective." In *Contemporary Indigenous Movements in Latin America*, ed. Erick D. Langer and Elena Muñoz, 65–80. Wilmington, Del.: Scholarly Resources, 2003.

——. "Widows Rights Questioned: Indians, the State, and Fluctuating Gender Ideas in Central Highland Ecuador, 1870–1900." *The Americas* 59, no. 1 (July 2002): 87–106.

Oberem, Udo. "Contribución a la historia del trabajador rural de américa latina: 'Conciertos' y 'huasipungueros' en Ecuador." In *Contribución a la etnohistoria ecuatoriana*, ed. Segundo Moreno and Udo Oberem, 299–342. Otavalo: Instituto Otavaleño de Antropologia, 1981.

Ojeda, Ramón. "Efectos del ferrocarril en la agricultura y la ganadería." In *Pensamiento agrario ecuatoriano*, ed. Carlos Marchán Romero, 647–56. Quito: Banco Central del Ecuador; Corporacion Editora Nacional, 1986.

Olesen, Thomas. *International Zapatismo: The Construction of Solidarity in the Age of Globalization*. London: Zed, 2005.

Ortiz Villacís, Marcelo. *La ideología burguesa en el Ecuador: Interpretación socio-política del hecho histórico en el período 1924–1970*. N.p., 1977.

Ossio, Juan M. "Cosmologies." *International Social Science Journal* 49, no. 4 (December 1997): 549–62.

Pacari, Nina. "Taking on the Neoliberal Agenda." *NACLA Report on the Americas* 29, no. 5 (March / April 1996): 23–32.

Paige, Jeffery M. *Coffee and Power: Revolution and the Rise of Democracy in Central America*. Cambridge, Mass: Harvard University Press, 1997.

Pallares, Amalia. "From Peasant Struggles to Indian Resistance: Political Identity In Highland Ecuador, 1964–1992." Ph.D. diss., University of Texas, Austin, 1997.

———. *From Peasant Struggles to Indian Resistance: The Ecuadorian Andes in the Late Twentieth Century*. Norman: University of Oklahoma Press, 2002.

Paredes, Domingo, ed. *Los comunistas en la historia nacional*. Guayaquil: Editorial Claridad, S.A., 1987.

Paredes, Ricardo. *Homenaje a la Unión de Repúblicas Soviéticas Socialistas en el 25 aniversario de la revolución*. Quito: Editorial Pichincha, 1942.

———. "El movimiento obrero en el Ecuador." *La Internacional Sindical Roja* 1 (August 1928): 76–81.

———. *La política internacional y la posición del Partido Comunista del Ecuador*. Quito: Publicaciones del Partido Comunista del Ecuador, June 15, 1946.

———. "VI World Congress, Reply to Bukharin on Draft Programme." *International Press Correspondence* 8, no. 66 (September 25, 1928): 1176–78.

Parkman, Patricia. *Nonviolent Insurrection in El Salvador: The Fall of Maximiliano Hernández Martínez*. Tucson: University of Arizona Press, 1988.

Partido Comunista del Ecuador (PCE). *Abajo las maniobras dictatoriales de Velasco Ibarra!* Quito: Imp. Gómez, 1935.

———. *Democrácia, independencia y paz para el pueblo del Ecuador: Lineamientos programáticos del Partido Comunista del Ecuador. Aprobados por su VI Congreso*. Quito: Editorial El Pueblo, May 1957.

———. *Documentos IX Congreso Partido Comunista del Ecuador*. Guayaquil: Ediciones Claridad, 1973.

———. *Manifiesto del Partido Comunista del Ecuador sobre las elecciones de 1960*. Quito: Ediciones El Pueblo, 1960.

———. *Por la paz por la democracia y el progreso*. Quito: Partido Comunista del Ecuador, 1949.

———. *Por la reconstitución histórica de la izquierda, hacia una nueva sociedad: Documento central de debate político del XII Congreso Nacional del Partido Comunista del Ecuador*. Quito: Partido Comunista del Ecuador, 1993.

———. *Programa y estatutos*. Guayaquil: Editorial Claridad, 1968.

———. *Proyecto de programa inmediato del Partido Comunista del Ecuador*. Quito: Ediciones El Pueblo, 1956.

———. "Saludo del Comité Central del P.C.E. al camarada Pedro A. Saad, Secretario General del Partido, en su sexagésimo aniversario." *Bandera Roja* 7 (June 1969): 17–29.

———. *Unidos para la democracia y el progreso: Posición del Partido Comunista del Ecuador en el momento actual*. Quito: Partido Comunista del Ecuador, May 7, 1945.

Partido Socialista Ecuatoriano (PSE). *Estatutos, declaración de principios del Partido Socialista Ecuatoriano*. Quito: Editorial de "El Correo," 1936.

———. *Estatutos, declaración de principios y programa minimo del Partido Socialista Ecuatoriano*. Quito: Editorial Editora Moderna, 1939.

——. *Estatutos, programas ideológicos de acción inmediata del Partido Socialista Ecuatoriano.* Ambato: Cap. A. M. Garcés, 1933.

——. *Labores de la Asamblea Nacional Socialista y Manifiesto del Consejo Central del Partido (16–23-Mayo), Quito, 1926.* Guayaquil: Imp. "El Tiempo," 1926.

——. *La primera Conferencia del Consejo Central Ampliado del Partido Socialista Ecuatoriano, sección de la III Internacional Comunista.* Quito: Imprenta del Partido Socialista Ecuatoriano, 1929.

Los partidos comunistas de América del Sur y del Caribe y el movimiento sindical revolucionario. Barcelona: Publicaciones "Edeya," 1933.

Paz y Miño Cepeda, Juan J. *Revolución Juliana: Nación, ejército y bancocracia.* Quito: Ediciones Abya-Yala, 2000.

Paz y Miño, Luis T. *Monografía de la provincia de Pichincha.* Quito: Tipografía y Encuadernación Salesianas, 1922.

Peloso, Vincent C. *Peasants on Plantations: Subaltern Strategies of Labor and Resistance in the Pisco Valley, Peru.* Durham, N.C.: Duke University Press, 1999.

de la Pena, Guillermo. "Etnicidad, ciudadanía y cambio agrario: Apuntes comparativos sobre tres países latinoamericanos." In *La construcción de la nación y la representación ciudadana, en México, Guatemala, Perú, Ecuador y Bolivia,* ed. Claudia Dary and Guillermo de la Pena, 27–86. Guatemala: FLACSO, 1998.

Peñaherrera de Costales, Piedad, and Alfredo Costales Samaniego. *Historia social del Ecuador.* Quito: Editorial Casa de la Cultura Ecuatoriana, 1964.

Perreault, Thomas J. "Development Identities: Indigenous Mobilization, Rural Livelihoods and Resource Access in Ecuadorian Amazonia." *Ecumene* 8, no. 4 (October 2001): 381–413.

——. "Shifting Ground: Agrarian Change, Political Mobilization and Identity Construction among Quichua of the Alto Napo, Ecuadorian Amazonia." Ph.D. diss, University of Colorado, 2000.

Perruchon, Marie. *I Am Tsunki: Gender and Shamanism among the Shuar of Western Amazonia.* Uppsala, Sweden: Uppsala University, 2003.

Pineo, Ronn F. *Social and Economic Reform in Ecuador: Life and Work in Guayaquil.* Gainesville: University Press of Florida, 1996.

Plaza Lasso, Galo. *Problems of Democracy in Latin America.* Chapel Hill: University of North Carolina Press, 1955.

Poeschel-Renz, Ursula. *"No quisimos soltar el agua": Formas de resistencia indígena y continuidad étnica en una comunidad ecuatoriana, 1960–1965.* Quito: Ediciones Abya-Yala, 2001.

Ponce Enríquez, Camilo. *Informe a la nación, 1954.* Quito: Talleres Gráficos Nacionales, 1954.

Postero, Nancy Grey, and Leon Zamosc. "Indigenous Movements and the Indian Question in Latin America." In *The Struggle for Indigenous Rights in Latin America,* ed. Nancy Grey Postero and Leon Zamosc, 1–31. Brighton, U.K.: Sussex Academic Press, 2004.

Prieto, Mercedes. "A Liberalism of Fear: Imagining Indigenous Subjects in Postcolonial Ecuador, 1895–1950." Ph.D. diss., University of Florida, 2003.

———. "Condicionamientos de la movilización campesina: El caso de las haciendas Olmedo-Ecuador (1926–1948)." Tesis de Antropología, PUCE, 1978.

———. "Haciendas estatales: Un caso de ofensiva campesina, 1926–1948." In *Ecuador: Cambios en el agro serraño,* ed. Miguel Murmis et al., 101–30. Quito: Facultad Latinoamericana de Ciencias Sociales (FLACSO)–Centro de Planificación y Estudios Sociales (CEPLAES), 1980.

Páez Cordero, Alexei. *Los orígenes de la izquierda ecuatoriana.* Quito: Fundación de Investigaciones Andino Amazónica (FIAAM); Ediciones Abya-Yala, 2001.

Pérez Guerrero, Alfredo. "La télesis social y la raza india." *Revista de la Sociedad de Estudios Jurídicos* 4, no. 28–32 (January–May 1922): 137–62.

Quijano, Aníbal. *Problema agrario y movimientos campesinos.* Lima: Mosca Azul Editores, 1979.

Quintero, Rafael. "La cuestión de la tierra . . . única posibilidad de sobrevivencia de una cultura." *Cuadernos de Nueva* 7 (June 1983): 120–21.

Quintero, Rafael, and Erika Silva. *Ecuador: Una nación en ciernes,* 3 vols., ed. Colección Estudios No. 1. Quito: FLACSO / Abya-Yala, 1991.

Radcliffe, Sarah A., and Sallie Westwood. *Remaking the Nation: Identity and Politics in Latin America.* London: Routledge, 1996.

Ramón, Galo. *Actores de una década ganada: Tribus, comunidades y campesinos en la modernidad.* Quito: COMUNIDEC, 1992.

———. "Cayambe: El problema regional y la participación política." *Ecuador Debate* 3 (August 1983): 161–74.

———. "La comunidad indígena ecuatoriana: Planteos políticos." In *Comunidad andina: Alternativas políticas de desarrollo,* 65–85. Quito: CAAP, 1981.

———. "La comunidad indígena ecuatoriana: Planteos políticos." *Nariz del Diablo* 1, no. 3 (July–August 1980): 25–31.

———."Estado plurinacional: Una propuesta innovadora atrapada en viejos conceptos." In *Pueblos indios, estado y derecho,* ed. Enrique Ayala Mora et al., 9–24. Quito: Corporación Editora Nacional, 1993.

———. "Política e interculturalidad indígena." In *La escuela india: ¿Integración o afirmación etnica? (La educación indígena vista por sus propios actores),* ed. Victor Hugo Torres, 213–18. Quito: COMUNIDEC, 1992.

———. *El regreso de los runas: La potencialidad del proyecto indio en el Ecuador contemporánea.* Quito: COMUNIDEC–Fundación Interamericana, 1993.

———. *La resistencia andina: Cayambe, 1500–1800*. Quito: Centro Andino de Acción Popular, 1987.

Ramos, Alcida Rita. "Cutting through State and Class: Sources and Strategies of Self-Representation in Latin America." In *Indigenous Movements, Self-Representation, and the State in Latin America*, ed. Kay B. Warren and Jean E. Jackson, 251–79. Austin: University of Texas Press, 2003.

Redclift, Michael. *Agrarian Reform and Peasant Organization in the Ecuadorian Coast*. London: Athlone Press, 1978.

Restrepo Jaramillo, Marco Antonio. *El rey de la leña*. Buenos Aires: Tall. Graf. Capricornio, 1958.

Rivera, Salomón. "El caso del Portento: Una cooperativa indígena." In *Estudios de la realidad campesina: Cooperacion y cambio; informes y materiales de campo recogidos en Venezuela, Ecuador y Colombia*, ed. Ramon Pugh, 59–111. Ginebra: Instituto de Investigaciones de la Naciones Unidas para el Desarrollo Social, UNRISD, 1970.

Rivera Cusicanqui, Silvia. *Oppressed but Not Defeated: Peasant Struggles among the Aymara and the Qhechwa in Bolivia, 1900–1980*. Geneva: United Nations Research Institute for Social Development, 1987.

Robalino Dávila, Luis. *El 9 de julio de 1925*. Quito: Editorial La Unión, 1973.

Rodas Chaves, Germán. *La izquierda ecuatoriana en el siglo XX (Aproximación histórica)*. Quito: Ediciones Abya-Yala, 2000.

Rodas Morales, Raquel. *Crónica de un sueño: Las escuelas indígenas de Dolores Cacuango: Una experiencia de educación bilingüe en Cayambe*, 2nd ed. Quito: Proyecto de Educación Bilingüe Intercultural, MEC-GTZ, 1998.

———. *Dolores Cacuango: Gran líder del pueblo indio*. Quito: Banco Central del Ecuador, 2006.

———. *Nosotras que del amor hicimos. . . .* Quito: Raquel Rodas, 1992.

———. *Tránsito Amaguaña: su testimonio*. Quito: CEDIME, 1987.

Rodríguez, Lilya. "Acción por el Movimiento de Mujeres." In *Homenaje a Nela Martínez Espinosa*, 15–26. Quito: Acción por el Movimiento de Mujeres, 1990.

Rodríguez, Linda Alexander. *The Search for Public Policy: Regional Politics and Government Finances in Ecuador, 1830–1940*. Berkeley: University of California Press, 1985.

Rodríguez Rojas, Silvia M. "Datos biograficos del Señor Rubén Rodríguez Mera: Resumen de su vida pública y personalidad." *Revista Centenario* (1983): 8–12.

Romo-Leroux, Ketty. *Movimiento de mujeres en el Ecuador*. Guayaquil: Editorial de la Universidad de Guayaquil, 1997.

Ron Proaño, Francisco. "Las movilizaciones campesinas en Ecuador: 1968–1977, El caso del movimiento Ecuarunari." Tesis de Antropología, CLACSO-PUCE, 1978.

Roper, J. Montgomery, Thomas Perreault, and Patrick C. Wilson. "Introduction." *Latin American Perspectives* 30, no. 1 (January 2003): 5–22.

Roseberry, William. "Beyond the Agrarian Question in Latin America." In *Confronting Historical Paradigms: Peasants, Labor, and the Capitalist World System in Africa and Latin America,* ed. Frederick Cooper et al., 318–68. Madison: University of Wisconsin Press, 1993.

Rosenthal, Anton. "The Arrival of the Electric Streetcar and the Conflict over Progress in Early Twentieth-Century Montevideo." *Journal of Latin American Studies* 27, no. 2 (May 1995): 319–41.

———. "Controlling the Line: Worker Strategies and Transport Capital on the Railroads of Ecuador, Zambia and Zimbabwe, 1916–1950." Ph.D. diss., University of Minnesota, 1990.

———. "Streetcar Workers and the Transformation of Montevideo: The General Strike of May 1911." *The Americas* 51, no. 4 (April 1995): 471–94.

Rubin, Jeffrey W. *Decentering the Regime: Ethnicity, Radicalism, and Democracy in Juchitán, Mexico.* Durham, N.C.: Duke University Press, 1997.

Rubio Orbe, Alfredo, ed. *Legislación indigenista del Ecuador.* Mexico City: Instituto Indigenista Interamericano, 1954.

Ruiz Hernández, Margarito, and Aracely Burguete Cal y Mayor. "Indigenous People without Political Parties: the Dilemma of Indigenous Representation in Latin America." In *Challenging Politics: Indigenous Peoples' Experiences with Political Parties and Elections,* ed. Kathrin Wessendorf, 20–63. Copenhagen, Denmark: IWGIA, 2001.

Saad, Pedro. *La nueva ley de reforma agraria del Ecuador.* Guayaquil: Ediciones Claridad, 1973.

———. *Obras escogidas.* Guayaquil: Editorial Claridad, 1977.

———. *La realidad agropecuaria del Ecuador,* 3rd ed. Guayaquil: Editorial Claridad, 1975.

———. *La reforma agraria democratica,* 2nd ed. Guayaquil: Editorial Claridad, 1987.

———. "Sobre la alianza obrero campesina." *Bandera Roja* 1, no. 3 (May-December 1961): 28–56.

Sáenz, Moisés. *Sobre el indio ecuatoriano y su incorporación al medio nacional.* Mexico City: Publicaciones de la Secretaría de Educación Pública, 1933.

Saint-Geours, Yves. "La sierra centro y norte (1830–1925)." In *Historia y región en el Ecuador, 1830–1930,* ed. Juan Maiguashca, 143–88. Quito: Corporación Editora Nacional, 1994.

Salamea, Lucía. "La transformación de la hacienda y los cambios en la condición campesina." In *Ecuador: Cambios en el agro serrano,* ed. Miguel Murmis et al., 249–300. Quito: Facultad Latinoamericana de Ciencias Sociales (FLACSO)–Centro de Planificación y Estudios Sociales (CEPLAES), 1980.

———. "Transformación de la hacienda y los cambios en la condición campesina." Master en Sociología Rural, PUCE / CLACSO, 1978.

Salazar, Ernesto. "The Federación Shuar and the Colonization Frontier." In *Cultural*

Transformations and Ethnicity in Modern Ecuador, ed. Norman E. Whitten Jr., 589–613. Urbana: University of Illinois Press, 1981.

Salots Galarza, Napoleón, ed. *La rebelión del arcoiris: Testimonios y análisis.* Quito: Fundación José Peralta, 2000.

Sánchez Parga, José. "Entre Marx y Rumiñahui: Para una crítica de la razón etnica." *Nariz del Diablo* 2nd., no. 12 (1989): 81–83.

——. "Etnia, estado y la 'forma' clase." *Ecuador Debate* 12 (December 1986): 25–77.

——. *Etnia, poder y diferencia en los andes septentrionales.* Quito: Ediciones Abya-Yala, 1990.

——. *Presente y futuro de los pueblos indígenas: Análisis y propuestas.* Quito: Ediciones Abya-Yala, 1992.

Santana, Roberto. "Actores y escenarios étnicos en Ecuador: El levantamiento de 1990." *Caravelle* 59 (1992): 161–88.

——. *Campesinado indígena y el desafío de la modernidad.* Quito: Centro Andino de Acción Popular, 1983.

——. "El caso de Ecuarunari." *Nariz del Diablo* 2, no. 7 (1981): 30–38.

——. *¿Ciudadanos en la etnicidad? Los indios en la política o la política de los indios.* Quito: Ediciones Abya-Yala, 1995.

Sattar, Aleezé. "An Unresolved Inheritance: Postcolonial State Formation and Indigenous Communities in Chimborazo, Ecuador, 1820–1875." Ph.D. diss., New School University, 2001.

Saunders, J. V. D. "Man-Land Relations in Ecuador." *Rural Sociology* 26, no. 1 (March 1961): 57–69.

Sawyer, Suzana. "The 1992 Indian Mobilization in Lowland Ecuador." *Latin American Perspectives* 24, no. 3 (May 1997): 65–82.

——. *Crude Chronicles: Indigenous Politics, Multinational Oil, and Neoliberalism in Ecuador.* Durham, N.C.: Duke University Press, 2004.

Schodt, David. *Ecuador: An Andean Enigma.* Boulder, Colo.: Westview Press, 1987.

Schroder, Barbara. "Ethnic Identity and Non-Capitalist Relations of Production in Chimborazo, Ecuador." In *Perspectives in U.S. Marxist Anthropology,* ed. David Hakken and Hanna Lessinger, 123–39. Boulder, Colo.: Westview Press, 1987.

Schryer, Frans J. *Ethnicity and Class Conflict in Rural Mexico.* Princeton, N.J.: Princeton University Press, 1990.

Scott, James C. *Weapons of the Weak: Everyday Forms of Peasant Resistance.* New Haven, Conn.: Yale University Press, 1985.

Scott, Joan W. "Gender: A Useful Category of Historical Analysis." *American Historical Review* 91, no. 5 (December 1986): 1053–75.

Segundo Congreso Obrero. "Programa, reglamento y proyectos." In *Pensamiento popular ecuatoriano,* ed. Jaime Durán Barba, 197–235. Quito: Banco Central del Ecuador, 1981.

Selverston-Scher, Melina. *Ethnopolitics in Ecuador: Indigenous Rights and the Strengthening of Democracy.* Coral Gables, Fla: North-South Center Press, 2001.

——. "The Politics of Culture: Indigenous Peoples and the State in Ecuador." In *Indigenous Peoples and Democracy in Latin America,* ed. Donna Lee Van Cott, 131–52. New York: St. Martin's Press, 1994.

Silverblatt, Irene. *Moon, Sun, and Witches: Gender Ideologies and Class in Inca and Colonial Peru.* Princeton, N.J.: Princeton University Press, 1987.

Simbaña, Floresmilo. "Lecciones de marzo y julio." *Boletín ICCI Rimay* 1, no. 7 (October 1999): http://icci.nativeweb.org/boletin/oct99/simbana.html.

Smith, Carol A. "Conclusion: History and Revolution in Guatemala." In *Guatemalan Indians and the State: 1540 to 1988,* ed. Carol A. Smith, 258–85. Austin: University of Texas Press, 1990.

Smith, Gavin A. *Livelihood and Resistance: Peasants and the Politics of Land in Peru.* Berkeley: University of California Press, 1989.

Solórzano Freire, José. *Nuestra gente: Relatos del Cayambe antiguo.* Quito: Pasquel Producciones Periodisticas, 2004.

St. Geours, Ives. "Economía y sociedad: La sierra centro-norte (1830–1875)." In *Nueva Historia del Ecuador. Volumen 7: Epoca republicana I,* ed. Enrique Ayala Mora, 37–101. Quito: Corporación Editora Nacional, 1983.

Staar, Richard F. et al., eds. *Yearbook on International Communist Affairs.* Stanford, Calif.: Hoover Institution Press, 1966–1991.

Stark, Louisa. "El rol de la mujer en los levantamientos campesinos de las altas llanuras del Ecuador." In *Antropolgia política en el Ecuador: Perspectivas desde las culturas indígenas,* ed. Jeffrey Ehrenreich, 35–56. Quito: Ediciones Abya-Yala, 1991.

Striffler, Steve. "Communists Communists Everywhere! Forgetting the Past and Living with History in Ecuador." In *Culture, Economy, Power: Anthropology as Critique, Anthropology as Praxis,* ed. Winnie Lem and Belinda Leach, 107–20. Albany: State University of New York Press, 2002.

——. *In The Shadows of State and Capital: The United Fruit Company, Popular Struggle, and Agrarian Restructuring in Ecuador, 1900–1995.* Durham, N.C.: Duke University Press, 2002.

Stutzman, Ronald. "*El Mestizaje:* An All-Inclusive Ideology of Exclusion." In *Cultural Transformations and Ethnicity in Modern Ecuador,* ed. Norman E. Whitten Jr., 45–94. Urbana: University of Illinois, 1981.

Suárez, Pablo Arturo. *Contribución al estudio de las realidades entre las clases obreras y campesinas.* Quito: Imprenta de la Universidad Central, 1935.

Sylva Charvet, Paola. *Gamonalismo y lucha campesino.* Quito: Ediciones Abya-Yala, 1986.

Talbot, Steve. "Free Alcatraz: The Culture of Native American Liberation." *Journal of Ethnic Studies* 6, no. 3 (fall 1978): 83–96.

Tatamuez, Mesías. "FENOC." In *Forjando la unidad: El movimiento popular en Ecuador*, ed. Agencia Latinoamericana de Información (ALAI), 39–41. Quito: Communicare, 1985.

Taylor, William B. *Drinking, Homicide, and Rebellion in Colonial Mexican Villages.* Stanford, Calif.: Stanford University Press, 1979.

Thiesenhusen, William C. "Land Reform in Latin America: Some Current Literature." *Latin American Research Review* 18, no. 2 (1982): 199–211.

Thomas, Robert K. "Pan-Indianism." In *The American Indian Today*, ed. Stuart Levine and Nancy Oestreich Lurie, 77–85. Deland, Fla.: Everett / Edwards, 1968.

Tibán, Lourdes, Raúl Llaquiche, and Eloy Alfaro, ed. *Historia y proceso organizativo.* Latacunga: Movimiento Indígena y Campesino de Cotopaxi, 2003.

Tillería, Ylonka. "Andrés Guerrero redefine el Estado-Nación: La identidad nacional cuestionada." *Tintají* 58 (December 2004): 10–11.

Torre, Carlos de la. "Populism and Democracy: Political Discourses and Cultures in Contemporary Ecuador." *Latin American Perspectives* 24, no. 3 (May 1997): 12–24.

Torre, Patricia de la. *Patrones y conciertos: Una hacienda serrana, 1905–1929.* Quito: Corporación Editora Nacional; Ediciones Abya-Yala, 1989.

Treakle, Kay. "Ecuador: Structural Adjustment and Indigenous and Environmentalist Resistance." In *The Struggle for Accountability: The World Bank,* NGOs, and Grassroots Movements, ed. L. David Brown and Jonathan A. Fox, 219–64. Cambridge, Mass: MIT Press, 1998.

Tribunal Supremo Electoral (TSE). *Elecciones y democracia en el Ecuador. Volumen 3, Legislación electoral ecuatoriana.* Quito: Tribunal Supremo Electoral; Corporacion Editora Nacional, 1990.

Trujillo, Jorge. *La hacienda serrana, 1900–1930.* Quito: Instituto de Estudios Ecuatorianos; Ediciones Abya-Yala, 1986.

Uggen, John. "Peasant Mobilization in Ecuador: A Case Study in Guayas Province." Ph.D. diss, University of Miami, 1975.

Ulcuango, Neptalí. "Antecedentes a la organización indígena en la provincia." In *Historia de la organización indígena en Pichincha*, ed. Federación Pichincha Riccharimui, 5–9. Quito: Ediciones Abya-Yala, 1993.

Ulianova, Olga. "El levantamiento campesino de Lonquimay y la Internacional Comunista." *Estudios Públicos* 89 (Summer 2003): 173–233.

Van Cott, Donna Lee. "From Exclusion to Inclusion: Bolivia's 2002 Elections." *Journal of Latin American Studies* 35, no. 4 (November 2003): 751–75.

——. *From Movements to Parties in Latin America: The Evolution of Ethnic Politics.* Cambridge: Cambridge University Press, 2005.

——. "Indigenous Peoples and Democracy." In *Indigenous Peoples and Democracy in Latin America*, ed. Donna Lee Van Cott, 1–27. New York: St. Martin's Press, 1994.

Van Young, Eric. "Mexican Rural History since Chevalier: The Historiography of the Colonial Hacienda." *Latin American Research Review* 18, no. 3 (1983): 5–61.

Vasconcelos, José. *The Cosmic Race / La raza cósmica*. Baltimore: Johns Hopkins University Press, 1997.

Vega Ugalde, Silvia. *La Gloriosa: De la revolución del 28 de mayo de 1944 a la contrarrevolución velasquista*. Quito: Editorial El Conejo, 1987.

Veilleux, Peter G. "Ecuador: 500 Kilometers of Resistance; Amazon Indians March on Quito." *IWGIA Newsletter* 3 (July / August / September 1992): 36–38.

Vela Monsalve, Carlos. *Las tácticas del comunismo*. Quito: Editorial Don Bosco, 1961.

Velasco, Fernando. *Reforma agraria y movimiento campesino indígena de la sierra*, 2nd ed. Quito: Editorial El Conejo, 1983.

Villavicencio Rivadeneira, Gladys. *Relaciones interétnicas en Otavalo-Ecuador. ¿Una nacionalidad india en formación?* Mexico City: Instituto Indigenista Interamericano, 1973.

Viteri, Alfredo. "Los pueblos de la Amazonía se unen." *Cuadernos de Nueva* 7 (June 1983): 44–47.

Wade, Peter. *Race and Ethnicity in Latin America*. London: Pluto Press, 1997.

Walsh, Catherine. "The Ecuadorian Political Irruption: Uprisings, Coups, Rebellions, and Democracy." *Nepantla: Views from South* 2, no. 1 (spring 2001): 173–204.

Warren, Jonathan. "Socialist Saudades: Lula's Victory, Indigenous Movements, and the Latin American Left." In *The Struggle for Indigenous Rights in Latin America*, ed. Nancy Grey Postero and Leon Zamosc, 217–31. Brighton, U.K.: Sussex Academic Press, 2004.

Warren, Kay B. *Indigenous Movements and Their Critics: Pan-Maya Activism in Guatemala*. Princeton, N.J.: Princeton University Press, 1998.

Wasserstrom, Robert. "Indian Uprisings under Spanish Colonialism: Southern Mexico in 1712." In *Power and Protest in the Countryside: Studies of Rural Unrest in Asia, Europe, and Latin America*, ed. Robert P. Weller and Scott E. Guggenheim, 42–56. Durham, N.C: Duke University Press, 1982.

Weismantel, Mary. *Cholas and Pishtacos: Stories of Race and Sex in the Andes*. Chicago: University of Chicago Press, 2001.

——. *Food, Gender, and Poverty in the Ecuadorian Andes*. Philadelphia: University of Pennsylvania Press, 1988.

Whitten, Norman E., Jr. *Sacha Runa: Ethnicity and Adaptation of Ecuadorian Jungle Quichua*. Urbana: University of Illinois Press, 1976.

——., ed. *Millennial Ecuador: Critical essays on cultural transformations and social dynamics*. Iowa City: University of Iowa Press, 2003.

Whitten, Norman E., Jr., Dorothea Scott Whitten, and Alfonso Chango. "Return of the Yumbo: The Indigenous Caminata from Amazonia to Andean Quito." *American Ethnologist* 24, no. 2 (1997): 355–91.

Williams, Derek. "Popular Liberalism and Indian Servitude: The Making and Unmaking of Ecuador's Antilandlord State, 1845–1868." *Hispanic American Historical Review* 83, no. 4 (November 2003): 697–733.

Willingham, Eileen. "Creating the Kingdom of Quito: Patria, History, Language and Utopia in Juan de Velasco's *Historia del Reino de Quito* (1789)." Ph.D. diss., University of Wisconsin–Madison, 2001.

Wilson, Patrick Charles. "Indigenous Federations, NGOs, and the State: Development and the Politics of Culture in Ecuador's Amazon." Ph.D. diss., University of Pittsburgh, 2002.

Wogan, Peter. *Magical Writing in Salasaca: Literacy and Power in Highland Ecuador.* Boulder, Colo: Westview Press, 2004.

Yánez del Pozo, José. *Yo declaro con franqueza (Cashnami causashcanchic); memoria oral de Pesillo, Cayambe,* 2nd ed. Quito: Ediciones Abya-Yala, 1988.

Yashar, Deborah J. *Contesting Citizenship in Latin America: The Rise of Indigenous Movements and the Postliberal Challenge.* Cambridge: Cambridge University Press, 2005.

Young, Crawford. *The Politics of Cultural Pluralism.* Madison: University of Wisconsin Press, 1976.

Zamosc, Leon. "Agrarian Protest and the Indian Movement in the Ecuadorian Highlands." *Latin American Research Review* 29, no. 3 (1994): 37–68.

——. "The Indian Movement in Ecuador: From Politics of Influence to Politics of Power." In *The Struggle for Indigenous Rights in Latin America,* ed. Nancy Grey Postero and Leon Zamosc, 131–57. Brighton, U.K.: Sussex Academic Press, 2004.

——. *Peasant Struggles and Agrarian Reform: The Ecuadorian Sierra and the Colombian Atlantic Coast in Comparative Perspective.* Meadville, Pa.: Allegheny College, 1990.

Zinn, Howard. *You Can't Be Neutral on a Moving Train: A Personal History of Our Times.* Boston: Beacon Press, 1994.

Index

MARC BECKER is associate professor of history at Truman State University in Kirksville, Missouri. He is the author of *Mariátegui and Latin American Marxist Theory* (1993) and editor (with Kim A. Clark) of *Highland Indians and the State in Modern Ecuador* (2007).

Library of Congress Cataloging-in-Publication Data

Becker, Marc.
Indians and leftists in the making of Ecuador's
modern indigenous movements / Marc Becker.
p. cm.   Includes bibliographical references and index.
ISBN 978-0-8223-4256-4 (cloth : alk. paper)
ISBN 978-0-8223-4279-3 (pbk. : alk. paper)
1. Indians of South America—Ecuador—Cayambe—Politics and government.
2. Indians of South America—Ecuador—Cayambe—Social conditions.
3. Social movements—Ecuador—Cayambe. 4. Communism—Ecuador—Cayambe.
5. Cayambe (Ecuador)—Politics and government.
6. Cayambe (Ecuador)—Social conditions. I. Title.
F3721.1.C29B43 2008   305.898'086613—dc22
2008011049

DATE DUE